# European Union Political Economy

# European Union Political Economy

## Theory and Policy

Konstantinos Hazakis

LEXINGTON BOOKS
*Lanham • Boulder • New York • London*

Published by Lexington Books
An imprint of The Rowman & Littlefield Publishing Group, Inc.
4501 Forbes Boulevard, Suite 200, Lanham, Maryland 20706
www.rowman.com

Unit A, Whitacre Mews, 26-34 Stannary Street, London SE11 4AB



British Library Cataloguing in Publication Information Available

**Library of Congress Cataloging-in-Publication Data Available**

LCCN 2018947263 | ISBN 9781498560054 (cloth: alk. paper) |
ISBN 9781498560061 (electronic)

∞™ The paper used in this publication meets the minimum requirements of American National Standard for Information Sciences—Permanence of Paper for Printed Library Materials, ANSI/NISO Z39.48-1992.

Printed in the United States of America

# Contents

# Acknowledgments

This book would not have been realized without the support of many people. I would like to express my great appreciation to the editors and reviewers for their constructive recommendations and useful critiques on this research work. I am also grateful to colleagues and students in Democritus University of Thrace who provided a stimulating intellectual environment during endless but fruitful discussions and debates on European economy issues. Finally, I wish to thank my family and my parents for the encouragement and enthusiastic support throughout my research.

# List of Abbreviations

| | |
|---|---|
| ABSPP | Asset-backed securities purchase programme |
| ACP | African, Caribbean and Pacific countries |
| AGS | Annual growth survey |
| AMR | Alert mechanism report |
| ANCS | Areas of natural constraint scheme |
| APs | Adjustment programmes |
| APP | Asset purchase programme |
| ASEAN | Association of Southeast Asian nations |
| BEPG | Broad economic policy guidelines |
| BIT | Bilateral investment treaty |
| BPS | Basic Payment Scheme |
| Brexit | British exit (from European Union) |
| CAB | Cyclically adjusted general government budget position |
| CAP | Common agricultural policy |
| CBPP | Covered bond purchase programme |
| CCP | Common commercial policy (of European Union) |
| CEPR | Center for Economic Policy Research |
| CETA | Comprehensive Economic and Trade Agreement |
| CFSP | Common foreign and security policy |
| COGECA | General Confederation of Agricultural Cooperatives in the EU |
| CMO | Common Market Organisation |
| COPA | Committee of Professional Agricultural Prganizations |
| CoR | Committee of the Regions |
| CSDP | Common security and defense policy |
| CSF | Community support framework |
| CSPP | Corporate sector purchase programme |
| CUs | Customs Union |

| | |
|---|---|
| DCFTA | Deep and Comprehensive Free Trade Area |
| DP | Decoupled direct payments |
| DG | Directorate General |
| EAFRD | European Agricultural Fund for Rural Development |
| EAGGF | European Agricultural Guidance and Guarantee Fund |
| EBA | Everything but Arms |
| EC | European Commission |
| ECA | European Court of Auditors |
| ECB | European Central Bank |
| ECCL | Enhanced conditions credit line |
| ECJ | European Court of Justice |
| ECU | European Currency Unit |
| ECOFIN | Council of Economics and Finance Ministers of European union |
| ECSC | European Coal and Steel Community |
| EDC | European Defense Community |
| EDF | European Development Fund |
| EDP | Excessive deficit procedure |
| EDPS | European Data Protection Supervisor |
| EEAS | European External Action Service |
| EEC | European Economic Community |
| EEG | European economic governance |
| EESC | European Economic and Social Committee |
| EFC | Economic and Financial Committee |
| EFSF | European financial stability facility |
| EGAF | European Globalization Adjustment Fund |
| EIB | European Investment Bank |
| ELA | Emergency liquidity assistance |
| EMFF | European Maritime and Fisheries Fund |
| EMI | European Monetary Institute |
| EMS | European monetary system |
| EMU | Economic and monetary union |
| ENI | European Neighborhood Instrument |
| ENP | European Neighborhood Policy |
| EPAs | Economic Partnership Agreements |
| EP | European Parliament |
| EPC | Economic and Policy Committee |
| EPPs | Economic partnership programmes |
| ERM | Exchange rate mechanism |
| ERP | European Recovery Program |
| ERDF | European Regional Development Fund |
| ESCB | European System of Central Banks |
| ESF | European Social Fund |

| | |
|---|---|
| ESI | European Structural and Investment funds |
| ESM | European stability mechanism |
| ESS | European Statistical System |
| ETC | European Territorial Cooperation |
| EU | European Union |
| EURATOM | European Atomic Energy Community |
| EWG | Euro Working Group |
| FCT | Fiscal compact treaty |
| FDI | Foreign Direct Investment |
| FFA | Financing assistance facility agreement |
| FTAs | Free trade areas |
| GATT | General Agreement on Tariffs and Trade |
| GBER | General Block Exemption Regulation |
| GDP | Gross domestic product |
| GGDS | Government to Government dispute settlement |
| GLF | Greek loan facility |
| GNP | Gross national product |
| GPS | Greening Payment Scheme |
| GREXIT | Greek exit (from euro area) |
| GSP | General System of Preferences |
| IAs | Investment agreements |
| IAEA | International atomic energy agency |
| ICS | Investment court system |
| IDR | In-depth review |
| IMF | International monetary fund |
| IS-LM | Investment-saving and liquidity preference-money supply intersection |
| LDC | Least developed countries |
| LFAs | Less-Favored Areas |
| LI | liberal intergovernmentalism |
| MFF | Multi-annual financial framework |
| MFN | Most-favored nation clause |
| MIP | Macroeconomic imbalance procedure |
| MOU | Memorandum of understanding |
| MROs | Main refinancing operations |
| MTOs | Medium-term objectives |
| NAFTA | North American Free Trade Agreement |
| NATO | North Atlantic treaty organization |
| NRPs | National reform programmes |
| NTBs | Nontariff barriers |
| NUTS | Nomenclature of territorial units for statistics |
| OCAs | Optimum currency areas |

| | |
|---|---|
| OEEC | Organization for European economic cooperation |
| OECD | Organization for economic cooperation and development |
| OLAF | European Anti-Fraud Office |
| PCCL | Precautionary conditioned credit line |
| POs | Producer organisations |
| PSC | Political and security committee |
| PSI | Private sector involvement haircut (of bonds) |
| PSPP | Public sector purchase programme |
| PTAs | Preferential trade areas |
| R and D | Research and development |
| RCI | Regional competitiveness index |
| RDP's | Regional rural development programs |
| RQMV | Reverse qualified majority |
| RPS | Redistributive Payment Scheme |
| RULC | Real unit labor cost |
| SAPS | Single area payment scheme |
| SCPS | Stability and convergence programmes |
| SEA | Single European Act |
| SEM | Single European market |
| SFS | Small farmers' scheme |
| SGP | Stability and growth pact |
| SMEs | Small and medium-sized enterprises |
| SMP | Single market programme |
| SMSF | Secondary market support facility |
| SOCs | State-owned companies |
| SPS | Single Payment Scheme |
| TBTs | Technical barriers to trade |
| TEU | Treaty of European Union |
| TFEU | Treaty on the function of European Union |
| TLTROs | Targeted longer-term refinancing operations, or |
| TSCG | Treaty on Stability, Coordination and Governance |
| TTIP | Transatlantic trade and investment partnership |
| UAA | Utilized agricultural area |
| USA | United States of America |
| USSR | Union of Soviet Socialist Republics |
| VAT | Value added tax |
| VCSS | Voluntary coupled support scheme |
| WEU | Western European Union |
| WB | World bank |
| WTO | World Trade Organization |
| YFS | Young Farmers' Scheme |

## *Chapter 1*

# Introduction

The European project faces a severe and prolonged operational, institutional, and legitimacy crisis. In the economic field, rates of economic development are anemic, regional inequalities remain, unemployment rates are high, social cohesion is downgraded, and private/sovereign debt crisis in euro area continues to raise systemic risk and policy uncertainty.

At policy level there is no consensus on widening/deepening of European integration, no collective perception on the pillars of a European social welfare state. Moreover, fierce disagreements persist over the policy priorities of European integration and how to finance them. Finally, many vital issues of "high politics" such as common foreign policy challenges, security threats from terrorist groups, uncontrollable inflows of refugees are not addressed in a reliable and long-term way.

Although, successes and failures have always been present in European integration process since late 1950s (and too often have been windows of policy opportunity to advance integration) the aforementioned interaction of all European integration challenges shake EU institutional edifice and could lead if not properly and adequately addressed to European disintegration.

Is the solution to the European integration problems an EU dismantling? The answer is negative for many reasons. First, EU succeeded in preserving peace, stability, and liberal democracy in EU containing state antagonisms for more than 60 years. Consensual and voluntary institutionalized integration deliver win-win interstate cooperation in contradiction with bloody and military imposed hegemonic integration plans in European history. Without European integration framework, small and fragile European states would have been vulnerable to great power politics and antagonism and extremely sensitive to the unprecedented repercussions of economic globalization. Further, Franco-German rapprochement is based on European integration.

Second, EU succeeded in creating a strong and reliable internal market; uniting previous existing fragmented markets; forwarding free circulation of people, capital, services, and goods; and enforcing economies of scale and scope in EU. Based on this "acquis communautaire," EU states enforce their collective bargaining in the international economic system and in international negotiations in all issue areas of global politics.

Third, EU project restored in the aftermath of the disastrous and traumatic Second World War the confidence of European citizens in the values and durability of European civilization and it acted as an anchor of democracy and model welfare for third states. Despite its shortcomings and weaknesses the European integration was perceived as an innovative institutional design for integration.

Fourth, European integration proved to be an efficient framework for facilitating a smooth transition of former communist and fascist regimes to liberal democracies putting in parallel an end to cold war divisions.

But even if someone ignores or rejects the abovementioned positive effects of European integration there remains the question of the reliable alternative scheme to EU. Are protectionism and beggar-thy-neighbor policies a reliable alternative?

Euroskepticism raises serious doubts over the validity of European integration policies and some of its supporters even become euro negativists demanding the complete demolition of European integration process. They underline the asymmetry between market integration policies and social protection policies and accuse EU institutions as a self-reinforcing policy framework which promotes elitism and has minimal contribution for EU citizens. They argue that EU lacks transparency and democratic accountability leading to the demerit of national decision-making and of national identities.

On the other hand, it becomes evident that European institutions cannot hold their supremacy in integration due to institutional and policy inertia. Will European integration advancement be realized through the provisions of current EU treaties, through a (non-treaty) ad hoc intergovernmental agreement or through a profound and multilevel consensual reform? Which issue areas and institutions should be prioritized in such a systemic reform?

The book analyses the rationale, the causes, and the implications of EU integration in key issue areas from a political economy view. In this way, it seeks to uncover the different motivations and the multiple interactions of heterogeneous actors in European integration such as firms, national governments, technocrats, political parties, interest groups. In each chapter of the book there is a critical insight of the variables and procedures that shape integration so as to allow the reader to assess in an academic way the limits and shortcomings of European integration in the key issue areas as well as the linkages between European integration theory and policies. More specifically, such an approach helps European integration understanding in four ways.

First, it highlights the distribution of benefits/costs of EU policy as well as the mechanisms through which the hierarchies and preferences of the key actors involved in the decision-making are shaped. It underlines the trade-offs between economies of scale and scope in a regional economic union and the costs of common intergovernmental policies in heterogeneous national populations. Although economies of scale and scope in the provision of public goods internalize negative externalities and provide security against crises/ shocks, they involve preferences and hierarchies which are not neutral neither without political and economic cost.

Who should bear the burden of policies and necessary reforms in EU? Should it be the wealthier citizens in all member states of EU or all the EU taxpayers? Policy internalization differs according to the embeddedness of EU policies in national economies and according to the characteristics and structures of national institutional/political settings.

Second, a political economy approach underlines the multiple interactions of economics and politics in European integration theory and policy. Is it possible to perceive the main targets of ECB monetary policy without understanding the perceived trade-off between inflation and unemployment or between inflation and macroeconomic stability? Is it possible to understand the EU treaties dynamics without a reference to the domestic political contradictions on European integration priorities? Economics are at the core of European integration but ideas and politics shape the policy framework to promote EU integration.

Third, political economy uncovers the limits and problems of overlapping jurisdictions and responsibilities in EU policy and decision-making. Despite the long practice of subsidiarity principle and of different intergovernmental cooperation methods there are still complex problems in EU decision-making which are not purely economic or political.

Fourth, input and output legitimacy of EU policies and institutions cannot be realized without an analysis which focuses on the intersection of economics and politics. Equally important, any integration effort proves to be both risky and inefficient if it is not based on a strong democratic consensus of EU citizens (input) and if it cannot deliver fundamental public goods and welfare in a distinct direct and improved way (output). Efficiency and democratic legitimacy are both crucial for the European integration project.

Relevant to this necessity is the ability of EU mechanisms to provide effective learning, adaptation, and convergence mechanisms so as to accommodate the multiple repercussions of EU policies and priorities on the daily life of EU citizens. As such mechanisms are complex, one should underline that it takes time, resources, and effective leadership to deliver long-standing results. This also means that a European integration process, which is based on short-term tactics to reach compromises and to avoid national political costs, ignores the three aforementioned mechanisms and will lead European integration to an impasse.

Indeed, EU integration is a bicycle which should continuously be in motion as former president of EC Jacques Delors mentioned. Thus, there is a need for political leadership to apply long-term EU policies which sustain legitimacy and improve EU participation and inclusiveness of all actors. The role of personalities has been crucial in the past decades for the survival of European integration process. Decisive political figures such as Konrad Adenauer, Helmut Kohl, Jacques Delors, Francois Mitterrand, Valéry Giscard D'Estaing, Helmut Schmidt, Maurice Faure, Jean Monnet, Robert Schuman, bypassed bureaucratic inertia, gained popular support for their European agenda, and succeeded to keep European vision alive. The current tragedy is that European leaders have a common understanding of the causes and failures of European integration but they also have strong disagreements over the necessary European integration reform.

The book unfolds in four parts and thirteen chapters as follows. Chapter 2 provides a critical insight into the theories of European integration while chapter 3 offers an in-depth analysis of the history of European integration. Chapter 4 focuses on the EU institutions and decision-making. In part two of the book, chapter 5 explores the institutional framework and challenges of the EMU. Chapter 6 analyzes the main pillars and rationale of the OCAs and chapter 7 explains the mechanisms and content of the economic adjustment in Eurozone.

In part three of the book, chapter 8 assesses the functioning of the CAP and chapter 9 explores the economics of the European single market. Chapter 10 analyzes the traits and implications of the regional policy of EU and chapter 11 discusses the European external trade policy. Finally, in part four, chapter 12 examines the latest repercussions and challenges of the Brexit and chapter 13 concludes.

I hope that the book contributes to the extensive debate on European integration and will provide useful thoughts for a clear understanding of the European integration challenges in the coming years.

# *Chapter 2*

# The Theories of European Integration

European Integration is distinguishable from other political/economic integration processes elsewhere in the globe. The complexity is clearly reflected in a variety of interpretations by political economists (Sadeh and Verdun, 2009). As Bulmer (1997, 8) eloquently mentions, "The sui generis assumptions of some political integration theory and the lack of interdisciplinary dialogue have risked confining European integration to an intellectual ghetto within the social sciences."

However, this does not mean that theories on European integration could not provide critical insights and methodological/policy implications for integration theory. Scholars and journalists have emphasized different strategies, motivations, and interactions among the multiple actors involved in the European integration process ranging from domestic interest groups and transnational firms to supranational institutions.

The chapter adopts a traditional categorization in political economy literature and underlines four fundamental approaches to European integration namely, functionalist approach, intergovernmentalism, institutionalism, and cognitive approach. Although it is difficult to introduce readers to the diversity and richness of European integration, it is vital to sketch the fundamental pillars of theoretical approaches as all European actions and policies are grounded on particular sets of hypotheses and assumptions.

## A FUNCTIONALIST APPROACH OF THE EUROPEAN ECONOMIC INTEGRATION

Functionalism conceives European integration as a response to functional targets of countries. A key political document is the declaration of R. Schumann (May 9, 1950) which proposed a Franco-German production of coal and steel under a common high authority with the framework of an organization open to the participation of the other countries in Europe. Inspired by Jean Monnet ideas, the document targeted the avoidance of conflictual national interests through strong European interdependencies.

While adherents of the approach (Niemann and Schmitter, 2009; Tranholm-Mikkelsen, 1991) do not refuse the fundamental role played by states in promoting national interests, they suggest that liberalization of investment, trade, and labor flows across west Europe has the potential to alter interstate rivalry that is blamed for two disastrous world wars. According to functionalism the national governments concede a wider scope of authority to regional organizations waiting for the derived increased returns from integration process. International and domestic agents engage in regional integration in order to ameliorate efficiency in several policy issue areas through interstate cooperation. Thus, elites and interest groups do play a crucial role in promoting functional ties among states (i.e., Jean Monnet in the 1950s and Jacques Delors in the 1980s).

Moving policy responsibilities to supranational institutions sets in motion mechanisms for integration. Positive effects include enhanced efficiency in policy implementation, convergence of national preferences, and convergence of norms and demands. As problems are faced through common action in several policy issue areas, irreversibility of integration becomes evident in the meaning that national agents find it costly and dangerous to reverse the process.

EMU is a clear example because it entails significant sunk costs for Eurozone states and firms. The integration of capital-financial markets and the evolving productive-trade-labor interdependencies increase not only positive spillover effects but also mutual vulnerability rendering enhancement of EEG feasible and necessary. Citizens also shift gradually their loyalty and expectations to supranational structures being satisfied by positive spillover effects of integration in economic and social issue areas.

The major tenets of the approach are summarized as follows:

a. Decisions are taken by rational national agents who have the capacity to learn from cooperative decision-making processes in regional level (Haas, 1958, 291). Actors modify their preferences through cooperation procedure and develop collective identities in several issue areas. As Lindberg and Scheingold (1970, 119) eloquently mention "participants in the policy making process, from interest groups to bureaucrats and statesman, begin to develop new perspectives, loyalties and identifications as a result of their mutual interactions." Within this framework conflicts are perceived as a challenge to combine different national preferences and to redefine collective obligations in order to reach agreements.

b. Decision-making is incremental and all decisions are influenced by past experience as well as by unexpected exogenous variables. Impeding crises and bargaining deadlines exert strong pressure on state capacity to comply by mutually agreed collective targets. For example, in May 2010, the GLF proved to be an ad hoc financial mechanism to deal with Greek debt problems in the absence of EU firewall mechanisms. The GLF finally led to the creation of EFSF and to ESM.
c. Agreements are reached through compromises and are based on win-win positive sum bargaining games.
d. Functions or issue areas are the central pillar of the integration process and cooperation frequently starts with those issues that are less controversial and easiest to deal with.
e. Solution to problems of one issue area does have a positive and strong impact in other policy issue areas and lead to demands for their inclusion in cooperative integration.
f. Finally, integration is a dynamic and complicated process and its results are transient.

The fundamental trait of the functionalist theory is the process of spillover. The sectoral (functional) spillover refers to the expansion of integrative activities (Lindberg, 1963, 10) from one sector to another. Lindberg (1963, 10) further mentions that "spillover refers to a situation in which a given action, related to a specific goal, creates a situation in which the original goal can be assured only by taking further actions, which in turn creates a further condition and a need for more action, and so forth." Interdependence of policy issue areas is strong and "actors discover that they cannot do A . . . without also doing B and perhaps C" (Lindberg and Scheingold, 1970, 117). Actors should perceive sectoral rationale as necessary in order to promote it and to incorporate it in political decision-making. Collective intentionality in key issue areas increases and national elites demand stronger rules based on key common traits of the European integration political discourse. A well-known example is the spillover effects from the initial ECSC in 1951 to CAP and to common trade policy.

The political spillover also involves politicization of sectoral activity and political stimulus to European integration. According to Haas (1958, 16) "Political integration is the process whereby political actors in several distinct national settings are persuaded to shift their loyalties, expectations and political activities toward a new center, whose institutions possess or demand jurisdiction over the preexisting national states." Interest groups and political elites in involved states learn by incremental integration process that major problems are addressed more efficiently through cooperation and supranational institutions and finally convey their expectations to supranational structures in regional level. A well-known example is the spillover effects from initial coordination of monetary and exchange rate policies in 1970s to European and monetary union and the euro launch after 1999.

Padoa-Schioppa underlined that (2004, 4) "the road toward the single currency looks like a chain reaction in which each step resolved a preexisting contradiction and generated a new one that in turn required a further step forward. The steps were the start of the EMS (1979), the relaunching of the single market (1985), the decision to accelerate the liberalization of capital movements (1986), the launching of the project of monetary union (1988), the agreement of Maastricht (1992) and the final adoption of euro (1998)."

Indeed, the single economic act played a fundamental role in Maastricht treaty provisions since abolition of capital controls between states created strong pressure for further action in monetary issue areas. The two types of spillover increase their interaction and their common policy initiatives and lead to deep integration in European continent. Which are the shortcomings of the functionalist approach?

The optimistic expectations of the functionalist theory have been partly fulfilled and evidence demonstrates that there is no automatic functional integration. Further, as a normative integration approach, functionalism downgrades the hurdles that eventually do have a strong impact on the incremental process of integration toward political union. Although European Community achieved an important geographical and thematic integration expansion, population's heterogeneous preferences and cultural traits did not fully converge and thus collective European identity is still not a reality. Another weakness of the approach is the emphasis on the autonomy/power of supranational European structures compared to national governments of member states.

As Gilbert (2012, 3) noted in fundamental policy issue areas, supranational institutions "could not work for a week in the absence of the will to cooperate of the member states, especially the largest ones—Germany and France—above all." The SGP is a notorious example, as soon after 2003 France and Germany used their power to avoid institutional sanctions against their own noncompliance to pact norms and rules. Equally important, functionalism did not shed light on the disagreements between different interest groups within each member state and thus the dimension of balancing internal conflicts was not significantly examined.

Overall, functionalist approach is useful in analyzing the long-term dynamics of European economic integration through the key role of spill-over mechanisms as well as of transnational actors (mainly EC and ECJ) to European economic and political policymaking. Functionalism has similarities with neoliberal institutionalism (NI) stressing under which terms the state and supranational institutional agents accept to convey their loyalties to supranational structures. Efficiency and policy effectiveness do influence such decisions of sovereignty transfer in both major approaches of European integration.

## INTERGOVERNMENTALISM AND THE STUDY OF EUROPEAN INTEGRATION

LI (Bickerton et al., 2015; Puetter, 2014) is based on a liberal approach of state preferences and a liberal approach of international interdependence. It argues that European integration process could be perceived if one analyzes the power positions and national interests of involved European countries.

As Moravcsik (1998, 18) eloquently notes LI understands "European integration . . . as a series of rational choices made by national leaders." He further underlines (1998, 4) that "a tripartite explanation of integration-economic interests, relative power, credible commitments—accounts for the form, substance and timing of major steps towards European integration." Thus, LI applies two theoretical types, namely a theory of national preferences formation and a theory of interstate bargaining.

Moravcsik (1993, 518) pinpoints the fundamental differences between LI and neo-functionalist approach as follows: "Where neo-functionalism emphasizes domestic technocratic consensus, liberal intergovernmentalism looks to domestic coalitional struggles. Where neo-functionalism emphasizes opportunities to upgrade the common interest, liberal intergovernmentalism stresses the role of relative power. Where neo-functionalism emphasizes the active role of supranational officials in shaping bargaining outcomes, liberal intergovernmentalism stresses instead passive institutions and the autonomy of national leaders. Ironically, the ECs democratic deficit may be a fundamental source of its success."

More specifically, the preferences of states on European integration process are issue specific, are not the outcome of learning process, result from domestic processes, and target increasing welfare benefits at domestic level. Within this conceptual framework national agents promote integration process if they believe that coordinated action brings more benefits to a state than autonomous or ad hoc policy strategy. This presupposes common conception of global interdependence among involved agents and rational attitudes to overcome organizational hurdles during coordination. Apparently, cause-effect relations are evident during all phases of negotiation process.

As Moravcsik (1993, 509) mentions the "stream of future substantive decisions expected to follow from alternative institutional designs" is a solid base for member states' cost-benefits analysis and leads them to accept qualified majority voting or to delegate to supranational institutions. He further suggests that all involved countries take into account the gains from cooperation, the level of uncertainty regarding the details of specific delegated or pooled decision as well as the level of political risk for individual governments or interest groups with intense preferences.

Domestic politics do play a crucial role as a filter between national economic decision-making and European integration structures. The following nature and intensity of the domestic debate on integration issues depend on the effects of integration and the way domestic social groups' preferences are aggregated through political institutions (Moravcsik, 1993, 481). Thus, preferences have different content in different time periods.

As Walsh (2001, 76) underlined, "Preferences regarding European monetary institutions did not converge during the 1990s. The French and Italians continued to propose the centralization of economic policy authority in political bodies, giving greater attention to employment and the coordination of countercyclical fiscal policies, whereas German preferences leaned in the opposite direction toward buttressing the independence of ECB and limiting fiscal policy flexibility. German negotiators succeeded in pushing through the SGP's requirements for the management of the single currency over the opposition of most other states, although they did concede that states could temporarily run excessive deficits under restricted circumstances and that the Ecofin would have a modest degree of political leeway in interpreting national fiscal policies."

## IS INTERGOVERNMENTALISM RELEVANT TO EUROPEAN INTEGRATION PROCESS?

European debt crisis (2010–2016) provided incentives to national euro area decision-making systems for enforced interdependence under the condition that euro area states perceived cooperation as an opportunity for enhanced benefits from integration. Moreover, common state interests concern the survival of euro area and avoidance of internal Eurozone conflict but also create the background for banking and fiscal integration in order to avoid future macroeconomic asymmetries. However, the question should include a clear and long-term answer to the question of how risks/costs will be distributed and how adjustment will be realized.

This brings us to the second analytical level of LI (the interstate bargaining) which is fierce if stakes are high for involved states in euro area. The result of interstate talks depends on the content of bargaining and specifically on the cost of disintegration for all involved member states. Intergovernmental bargaining is preferred if euro area solvent states also perceive that SGP rules are strengthened, crisis management is effective, structural reforms are implemented at national level, euro currency is enforced in the long-term, and positive spillovers occur for their national economic interests in the medium/long-term. At the end, substantive agreements are the outcome of national preferences constellation and bargaining power. Obviously, solvent states of euro area rescue highly indebted euro area states but shape the conditions of the rescue package and hold preponderance in European agenda setting.

Another example is the coal and steel community realized from the beginning of European integration. According to Milward (1984) the coal and steel community was proposed by France to constrain German control over its industry taking into consideration USA target in 1949 to establish a German state relatively free of allied supervision. On the other hand, Germany embraced Schuman project because through European Community of coal and steel it could attain the removal of ceilings on permissible levels of production in industry.

Finally, LI argues that institutional design mirrors the institutional preferences of euro area states with superior bargaining power. Moravcsik mentions (1993, 507), "In the integovernmentalist view, the unique institutional structure of the EC is acceptable to national governments only insofar as it strengthens rather than weakens their control over domestic affairs." Consequently, the type and content of Eurozone problems determine the institutional features of European mechanism. All institutional outflows target enhancement of euro credibility and stabilization of euro area macroeconomics.

Which is the role of European institutions in European integration history? LI suggests that European governance structures are created in order to strengthen member states in three ways. First, they reduce transaction costs and thus enforce the efficiency of interstate bargaining taking into account the distributional outcomes. As Moravcsik stresses (1993, 507) institutions are "deliberate instruments to improve the efficiency of bargaining between states." Second, they enforce legitimacy of collective policies since they increase the autonomy of politicians vis-à-vis the strong interests of domestic groups. Finally, institutions reduce information asymmetries in interstate bargaining and create linkages across policy issue areas in European integration. Thus, the principals (member states) delegate specific responsibilities to agents (European regimes) taking into account that the advantages of collective action outweigh risks to national ad hoc policy moves. Which are the major weaknesses of LI theory?

First, LI does not take into consideration the endogeneity of the integration process in the meaning that integration is influenced by the effects of earlier integration decisions (Pierson, 1996). In this way, it endangers missing the fundamental role of long-term targets and principles that have influenced the content of integration process. For example, it is difficult to analyze the initial incentives of forming European Community of coal and steel isolating national economic interests from the target to prevent beggar-thy-neighbor competitive policies and interstate political rivalries in continental Europe.

Second, the LI approach does not properly face all the issues linked with principal-agent delegation process. EC draws many times its own agenda in specific policy areas based on its expertise and its long-term knowledge. In the same manner, the European Court evolves through decisions in an influential actor for European integration (Eichener, 1993).

Third, as Cowles mentions (2003, 105) LI does not consider that multiple nongovernmental organizations such as environmental groups, transnational enterprises, and consumer groups can participate simultaneously in domestic and in international politics. Non-state agents do participate with different intensity in the formation of policy proposals during and after the delegation of authority in specific issue areas and as a result lobbying in Brussels becomes crucial in interstate bargaining and in agenda setting in several issue areas.

Finally, as Wind (1997, 28) stresses, in LI approach "important institutional elements such as the evolution and the change of norms, ideas and historically produced codes of conduct-discursive as well as behavioral, are completely expelled from analysis."

Summing up, LI approach is useful in analyzing the dynamics of treaty negotiation and interest bargaining as well as in studying the formation of state preferences in European integration process. In contrast to supranationalism, LI does not concede to supranational institutions a fundamental role in shaping negotiation results and in contrast to constructivist approach it does not attribute a similar role to normative constrains in interstate bargaining. Institutional design is not the outcome of federalist thinking, European legitimacy, or collective democratic norms and values but reflects national preferences.

## CONSTRUCTIVISM AND EUROPEAN INTEGRATION

Constructivism questions the capacity of both LI and functionalist approaches to identify the mechanisms which form preferences, interests, and policies in European integration (Checkel, 2001; Lewis, 2005). A central tenet of the theory is that preferences are not static but plastic in the face of ideas

(Christiansen, 2001) and incorporate experience about how EU evolves and how European integration proceeds. Governance is "both a process and a state whereby public and private actors engage in the intentional regulation of societal relationships and conflicts" (Kohler-Koch, Rittberger, 2006, 28).

Keck and Sikkink (1998, 30) argue that there are three major types of transnational agents taking into consideration their motives, namely those with essentially instrumental goals such as banks and multinational forms, those motivated by shared causal ideas such as epistemic groups, and those motivated by shared principled ideas and values such as international advocacy networks.

The first key point of the approach is that intersubjective understandings determine the content of national and societal interests. Ongoing interaction changes intersubjective understandings and transnational communication and leads to idea diffusion to all involved agents. Indeed, idea diffusion facilitates cooperation, influences interstate bargaining, and renders decision-making on European integration rapid and consensual. Thus, intersubjective meanings are vital and are transformed or sustained through daily interaction.

As McNamara (2006) indicates for EEG "It was not functional, material conditions that directly caused the shift in many European policy makers views about monetary policy in the context of the exogenous backdrop of rising capital mobility . . . while the international economic environment creates sets of challenges for policy makers, it does not directly instruct them as to the correct answers. The meaning of those economic challenges, their interpretation and analysis will all be mediated by the cultural and ideational setting that policy actors exist within a particular point in time and place on the globe . . . monetary policy consensus redefined state interests in cooperation, underpinned stability in the EMS and induced political leaders to accept the domestic policy adjustments needed to stay within the system."

Thus, ideas as "beliefs about cause-effect relationships which derive authority from the shared consensus of recognized elites" (Goldstein and Keohane, 1993, 10) do influence preferences and economic prioritization.

Diffusion of preponderant ideas and economic paradigms (Haas, 1992) eases interstate bargaining and makes decision-making consensual. Haas (1990, 23–24) underlines that as politicians "go through the learning process it is likely that they will arrive at a common understanding." Thus, norms are not imposed through authority structures but through learning and socialization processes which persuade actors based on common frameworks of understanding (Saurugger, 894). For example, euro area member states follow expansionary austerity strategy because they have internalized the monetarist strategy.

Experience in EMU further underlines that adjustment strategy for reduction of economic asymmetries is based on a strong European consensus at the heuristic level (how the fundamental problems of adjustment are framed in euro area states); at the ontological level (what are the key hypotheses about the structure of an economy in adjustment); at the methodological level (what methods are implemented to put forward and to test economic APs effectiveness); and at the policy level (how to match adjustment austerity measures with economic strategies looking for efficiency and welfare). Indeed, if someone pays closer attention to the logic underpinning national economic APs in euro area, it becomes clear that the core of macroeconomic strategy during 2010–2016 remains the tetralogy "fiscal stabilisation—low inflation—primary surplus—structural reforms."

The second pillar of the approach is that domestic politics do play a role in the socialization of common ideas and in the formation of European collective identity. The latter is influenced by domestic factors deeply entrenched in social, political, and institutional discourses. Hooghe, for example (2005), argues that European socialization in EC is the outcome of national socialization and thus as Horpf (2002, 1) put it "Domestic society . . . must be brought back into any constructivist account of world politics." The links between structures and national agents are crucial central and the two analytical pillars are not separate but are co-constituted. As a result, agents are influenced by the social norms of institutional structures and identity is part and parcel of the whole process.

Finally, constructivists focus on the importance of experts and expertise in order to diffuse economic paradigms—ideas and so as to realize socialization and learning. Experts' communities have privileged access to vital information which perpetuates group structures and gives meaning to the dependence of national political agents on experts.

As Heipertz and Verdun (2005, 1000) underline "Experts . . . process this information through the incorporation of certain paradigms and ideas. Paradigms contain fundamental principles which are upheld over a longer period of time and form the world view of the experts. The paradigm makes up a certain way to see the economic world: it is a mentally constructed model of reality (i.e. the stability paradigm in euro area). The term idea is used to describe the variety of ways in which one can translate the paradigm into practice."

The stability paradigm, for example (Artis and Winkler, 1999), sets specific principles for economic growth (i.e., price stability) which are realized by an independent ECB irrespective of electoral cycles.

Which are the major weaknesses of the constructivist paradigm? First, as Walsh stresses (2001, 77), domestic political arrangements are more durable in the face of policy failure than much of constructivism suggests and thus there is a need to focus on how ideas diffusion interacts with domestic institutions and political coalitions in order to understand its dynamics. Second, constructivists often attribute enhanced role to social structures and norms to the detriment of the agents who help create and change them in the first place (Checkel, 1998, 234). Finally, initial constructivist approaches over emphasized norms and principles of public agents and elites, underestimating the importance of private and non-state actors.

Overall, constructivist approach analyzes European economic integration through identity formation and ideas communication action, taking the role of discourses seriously.

## THE INSTITUTIONALIST LOGIC BEHIND THE EUROPEAN INTEGRATION

Within the last 20 years several institutional theories have been proposed for European integration (Dowding, 2000; Aspinwall and Schneider, 2001; Jupille and Caporaso, 1999). Most studies examined not only legislative and executive EU politics including several aspects of EU decision-making and member state voting power but also the impact of politics on EU governments and EU integration evolution (Hodson, 2009). The focus of empirical research is on intra-institutional dynamics (i.e., the EU Council consensual decision-making) but also on inter-institutional relations among ECB, EU Parliament, European Council, and EC. Thus, EU institutions are analyzed either as independent variables that explain how policy outcomes at several policy issue areas are realized (Nugent, 2006) or as dependent variables created by member states to perform specific roles/functions within European integration framework.

Institutionalists try to explain why states surrender their sovereignty to European supranational institutions. Regimes, sets of rules, norms and specific organizational frameworks offer to states positive spillovers that they would be unable to safeguard on their own.

As Keohane mentions (1984, 97), "Far from being threats to governments, they permit governments to attain objectives that would otherwise be unattainable. They do so in part by facilitating intergovernmental agreements. Regimes facilitate agreements by raising the anticipated costs of violating others property rights, by altering transaction costs through the clustering of issues and by providing reliable information to members. Regimes are relatively efficient institutions compared with the alternative of having a myriad of unrelated agreements, since their principles, rules and institutions create linkages among issues that give actors incentives to reach mutually beneficial agreements." Which are the major tenets of the approach?

Institutionalists suggest that European states create supranational institutions to realize joint gains through cooperation and to avoid negative spillovers, externalities, and asymmetries of noncooperative options. European institutions promote cooperative behavior by increasing information about other states' goals, behavior, and expectations which render the process to detect noncompliance and defection easily. Moreover, European institutions increase decision-making trust which makes states willing to promote further cooperation and to achieve medium and long-term cooperative gains.

Pollack (1997) argues that member states deliver authority to supranational institutions concerning four functions namely to monitor member states compliance to rules, to solve problems of contracting, to serve as independent regulator, and to set the agenda for the principals. For example, SGP provides transparent and clear rules of the game against which to evaluate compliance with the target of price stability eliminating beggar-thy-neighbor policies and national currencies competition within euro area. Institutions deliver a monetary straight jacket but at the same time they realize gains in the form of stable exchange rates that reduce the risks to trade and investment, support euro area factors of production circulation, and reduce vulnerability to US dollar fluctuations. This does not mean that national preferences of euro area states are downgraded since any agreement or institutionalization of principles presupposes convergence of national preferences.

Second, institutional theory underlines the embeddedness of agents' action within the networks of EU institutions. Complexity of policy areas increases embeddedness and renders daily interaction of European experts, conditio sine qua non for effective European decision-making. Acquis communautaire (the sum of existing EU practice and legislation) influences integration needs and leads incremental revision of policymaking in several integration issue areas. This does not lead to "lock-in" of member states' preferences but certainly does mean limitation of "degrees of freedom" in decision-making thus limitation of national capacity for policy maneuvering. The rules of the game have been constructed through such intensive, long-term, and complex interstate negotiations that it is impossible to bypass them without undermining the essence of EU institutional and integration dynamics.

Further, member states' expectations and preference may diverge in several policy issue areas but their common denominator is not to place insurmountable question marks on European institutional structures and principles. This long-term embeddedness generates sunk costs, creates commitments, makes systemic reversal unlikely to occur, and increases exit cost for all member states. EU decision-making systematically designs strategies to minimize transaction costs in the negotiation and implementation process of EU policies. Member states act not always as strategic utility maximizers but according to the logic of appropriateness, enfolding the ordering and content of national preferences within a given institutional environment.

This means that even in crises institutional inertia prevails, taking into consideration that states are not only afraid of sub-efficient EU institutional performance but, even more, they are afraid of policy uncertainty linked with less controllable and untested institutional reforms. As Rawls (1999, 98–99) argues all polities come across the fundamental question of whether in extreme circumstances there are limits on what they can do. Path dependence is also evident since early decisions provide incentives for national agents to perpetuate behavioral patterns and policy choices from the past.

Third, EU institutions create arrangements in issue areas that allow reasonably efficient decision-making and effective compliance despite the involvement of states with divergent preferences. This means that European institutions have the ability to influence agenda setting, frame policy problems, and accommodate often conflicting national targets. Crucially important in this procedure is the internalization of EU institutional norms and principles in national fiscal and macroeconomic frameworks. EU collective action dilemmas do not end up in collective suboptimal solutions because national preferences and national expectations converge, avoiding unilateral maximization of states utilities and calculations.

Usually, institutional methodology is based on three fundamental levels of analysis (Hazakis, 2015). At the first level, there are basic concepts, norms, routines, and values of European integration which are the most enduring and resistant to policy change. Concepts are extremely important for institutional analysis as they exert the greatest influence at all policy levels, defining the cognitive conditions that lead to compliance or to noncompliance with EEG framework.

For example, as far as it concerns economic adjustment of euro area states after 2010, it is argued that concepts, norms, and values reflect and shape the preferences of states and influence how economic assistance is distributed in euro area states, how economic conditionality is structured, and what kind of economic action-remedy is taken.

Obviously, the question of how to institutionalize "expansionary austerity" (Scott, 2014) principles/norms at the domestic level retains the essence of economic APs action. As a consequence, the priority at the first analytical level is to assess the simplicity of programmes' rules, their durability, their effectiveness, their concordance, their raison d'être, and how the latter is embedded in the complex institutional environment of EEG. The "institutionalization" of principles exerts influence to the operating rules/norms of national macroeconomic decision-making systems, delinking national development issues from short/medium-term adjustment strategy, and as a consequence the priority of fiscal stabilization overrules all other targets of adjustment. Economic APs require countries to adhere to fiscal stabilization irrespective of national macroeconomic cycle dynamics and adjustment is de facto identified with stabilization.

Although article 9 of the TFEU underlines that in applying its policies and activities the EU takes into account the sustainable level of employment, the guarantee of adequate social protection, the fight against social exclusion, and a high level of education, training, and protection of human health, economic APs give exclusive priority to fiscal consolidation. Despite the fact that article 7 (para 7, subpar 2) of regulation 472/2013/EU states that at the initiative of the parliament any macroeconomic AP should take into account "the need to ensure sufficient means for fundamental policies, such as education and healthcare" social inclusion policies are downgraded.

The second level of analysis concerns institutional arrangements and includes complex institutional networks and institutional hierarchies, influencing national economic agent motives and risk/profits/burden sharing in European policy implementation. In other words, despite areas of discord among its members, EEG imposes fundamental traits of a strong institutional network in procedures.

Any assistance provided within Eurozone is conditional and provisional. Conditionality is not an emergency and exceptional instrument but becomes (regulation 472/2013/EU) the cornerstone of economic APs. Through conditionality clause, EEG is not only engaged in programmes' design and surveillance but also in the micromanagement of fundamental domestic public policies (governance-related conditionality). Article 136 (para 3, TFEU) underlines that "the granting of any required financial assistance under the mechanism will be made subject to strict conditionality." Eurozone states that accept assistance are required "to prepare in agreement with the commission acting in liaison with the ECB and where appropriate with the IMF a macroeconomic AP" (regulation 472/2013/EU, article 7, para 1, subpar 1). In this way, reforms and installments are linked tightly and financial support is contingent upon full compliance of member states to budgetary, structural, and macroeconomic targets of memoranda.

The third level of analysis concerns not institutions per se but the systemic dimension of European governance structure. The sustainability of EU policies rests not only on getting EU organizations and national economic decision-making systems working more efficiently on an individual basis but to do so in an interconnected fashion. The third level of analysis also concerns the hierarchy of European policy issue areas and the multiple linkages among them.

While each of the issue areas discussed has some autonomy, an institutional logic leads all issue areas into a common cognitive configuration. This occurs because all issue areas are highly embedded in European institutional framework and as a consequence their logics are symbolically grounded on same values (first level analysis), organizationally structured around already existed European institutions (second level analysis), technically constrained by the same SGP rules (second level analysis), materially specified according to power sharing among core euro zone states, and politically legitimized according to well-established national economic decision-making and EEG procedures.

Overall, institutionalists analyze both the resilience and adaptability of EEG and examine how European institutions constrain national states preferences and how they form European collective intentionality in several issue areas. Crucially important in this process is the bargaining power of state and supranational actors, the functional and organizational interdependencies between policy issue areas, the available learning/adaptation processes for involved agents, and the switching costs of alternative policy options for agents. Which are the main points of criticism for institutionalism?

First, the assumption that supranational institutions behave always as unitary actors is questionable and thus neglects the dynamics of internal workings of EU agents such as EC and euro group. EU agency autonomy depends on the internal dynamics of EU institutions decision-making and how EU targeting is balanced with the scope and limits of member states (principals) activities. Further, member states do not surrender national autonomy once and for all but do intervene to defend national preferences and interests at crucial phases of European integration. This was the case at Maastricht, Amsterdam, and Nice treaties and this also occurred during the GREXIT bargaining in from May to July 2015.

Second, learning and adaptation processes in states' behavior are much more complicated than firms' adjustment and are more vulnerable to unpredicted events. Member states learning from crises (i.e., European debt crisis) may lead not to compliance by the rules or to initiatives for integration deepening but to noncompliance and unilateral actions.

Moreover, studies on the recognition of the public and private interaction in EU policymaking argue (Cowles, 2003, 106–107) that non-state agent together with institutions do have an impact on the calculus of principles to delegate authority and do participate in the shaping of policy proposals prior to, during and after the completion of authority delegation. Equally important, non-state agents do provide under specific circumstances legitimacy to supranational institutions decision-making and policy initiatives.

## CONCLUSIONS: REFLECTING ON EUROPEAN INTEGRATION THEORIES

The developments in European integration theory are not separate from European integration policy and pragmatism. European integration resembles to a pendulum shifting from the national to supranational and vice versa with no consensus on how and why European integration evolves or should be evolved. Different methodological approaches lead to different questions. Some authors ask why a sui generis integration process is taking place in Europe while others focus on how this integration occurs through dense political—economic—institutional interactions. Others try to explain how European integration unfolds, how it proceeds, and which is the role and value of involved agents. Some scholars analyze questions of democratic reform and legitimacy of European institutions while others study the dynamics of interstate bargaining and the role of epistemic communities.

From the abovementioned analysis it seems that the fundamental challenge is the synthesis of existing integration theories in order to explain different perspectives of EU reality.

As Puchala (1999) argues, "European integration is clearly more than one thing and much of the theoretical confusion generated in attempts to explain it has stemmed from theorists' insistence that it has been a single, complex phenomenon. Particularly useful for now would be a more modest attempt to define and delimit what institutionalism and intergovernmentalism as well as other approaches respectively do explain about the half century long transformation of intra-European international relations and what they respectively do not explain."

What is often missing in European integration analysis is a holistic framework of how risks, benefits, and burdens of European integration are distributed and how they can be accommodated in European institutional/economic/cognitive structures avoiding the ghost of multispeed or variable integration geometry. Against Euroskepticism one should always remember that if properly addressed, European integration crises could be sources of European progress and institutional breakthroughs and not expressions of political failure.

## BIBLIOGRAPHY

Artis, M. J and Winkler, B. 1999. "The stability pact: Trading off flexibility for credibility?" In *Fiscal aspects of European Monetary Integration,* eds. Hallett A. Hughes, M. M. Hutchison and S. E. H. Jensen. New York: Cambridge University Press.

Aspinwall, M and Schneider, G., eds. 2001. *The rules of integration: Institutionalist approaches to the study of Europe*. New York: Manchester University Press.

Bickerton, Christopher., Hodson, Dermot., and Puetter, Uwe. 2015. "The new intergovernmentalism: European integration in the post Maastricht era". *Journal of Common Market Studies*, 53(4): 703–722.

Bulmer, S. 1997. "New institutionalism, the single market and EU governance". *Arena working papers*. 97/25, Oslo: Arena.
Checkel, Jeffrey T. 1998. "The constructivist turn in international relations theory". *World Politics,* 50(2): 324–348.
Checkel, Jeffrey T. 2001. "Why comply? Social learning and European identity change". *International Organization*, 55(3): 553–588.
Christiansen, Thomas., Knud, Eric Joergensen., and Antje Wiener, eds. 2001. *The social construction of Europe.* London: Sage Publications.
Cowles, Maria G. 2003. "Non-state actors and false dichotomies: Reviewing IR/IPE approaches to European integration". *Journal of European Public Policy*, 10(1): 102–120.
Dowding, Keith. 2000. "Institutionalist research on the European Union: A critical review". *European Union Politics*, 1(1): 125–144.
Eichener, V. 1993. "Social dumping or innovative regulation?" *EUI working papers.* 92/28, Florence: European University Institute.
Gilbert, Mark. 2012. *European integration. A concise history*. Lanham: Rowman and Littlefield.
Goldstein, J and Keohane, R. O. 1993. "Ideas and foreign policy: An analytical framework". In *Ideas and foreign policy*, eds. J. Goldstein and R. Keohane, 3–30. Ithaca: Cornell University Press.
Haas, E. 1958. *The uniting of Europe: Political, social and economic forces, 1950-1957.* London: Stevens.
Haas, E. 1990. *When knowledge is power.* Berkeley and Los Angeles: University of California Press.
Haas, E. 1992. "Introduction: Epistemic communities and international policy coordination". *International Organization*, 46: 1–35.
Hazakis, Konstantinos. 2015. "Designing an effective framework for economic adjustment programs in euro area: An Institutionalist perspective" paper presented at the International Conference on public policy, Milan, July 2015.
Heipertz, Martin and Verdun, Amy. 2005. "The stability and growth pact-theorizing a case in European integration". *Journal of Common Market Studies*, 43(5): 985–1008.
Hodson, D. 2009. "Reforming EU economic governance: A view from (and on) the principal-agent approach". *Comparative European politics*, 7(4): 455–475.
Hooghe, Liesbet. 2005. "Several roads lead to international norms but few via international socialization: A case study of the European commission". *International Organization*, 59(4): 861–898.
Horpf, Ted. 2002. *Social construction of international politics: Identities and foreign policies, Moscow, 1955 and 1999*. Ithaca, NY: Cornell University Press.
Jupille, J and Caporaso, J. A. 1999. "Institutionalism and the European union: Beyond international relations and comparative politics". *Annual Review of Political Science*, 2: 429–444.
Keck, M. E and Sikking, K. 1998. *Activists beyond borders: Advocacy networks in international politics*. Ithaca: Cornell University Press.
Keohane, R. 1984. *After hegemony: Cooperation and discord in the world political economy.* Princeton: Princeton University Press.

Kohler –Koch, B and Rittberger, B. 2006. "The governance in turn in EU studies". *Journal of Common Market Studies*, 44(1): 27–49.

Lewis, Jeffrey. 2005. "The Janus face of Brussels: Socialization and everyday decision making in the European Union". *International Organization,* 59(4): 937–972.

Lindberg, L. 1963. *The political dynamics of European integration.* Stanford, CA: Stanford University Press.

Lindberg, L and Scheingold, S. 1970. *Europe's would be polity.* Englewood Cliffs, NJ: Prentice Hall.

McNamara, Kathleen R. 2006. "Economic governance, ideas and EMU: What currency does policy consensus have today?" *Journal of Common Market Studies,* 44(4): 803–821.

Milward, Alan R. 1984. *The reconstruction of Western Europe, 1945-1951.* New York: Methuen.

Moravcsik, A. 1993. "Preferences and power in the European community: A liberal intergovernmentalist approach". *Journal of Common Market Studies*, 31(4), December: 473–524.

Moravcsik, A. 1998. *The choice for Europe. Social purpose and state power from Messina to Maastricht.* Ithaca, NY: Cornell University Press.

Niemann, A and Schmitter, P. 2009. "Neofunctionalism". In *European integration theory,* eds. A. Wiener and T. Diez, 45–66. Oxford: Oxford University Press.

Nugent, N. 2006. *The government and politics of the European Union.* Palgrave: Macmillan.

Padoa-Schioppa, Tommaso. 2004. *The euro and its central bank. Getting united after the union.* Cambridge, MA: MIT Press.

Pierson, P. 1996. "The path to European integration: A historical institutionalist perspective". *Comparative Political Studies*, 29(2): 123–163.

Pollack, M. 1997. "Delegation, agency and agenda setting in the European community". *International Organization*, 51(1): 99–135.

Puchala, Donald J. 1999. "Institutionalism, intergovernmentalism and European integration: A review article". *Journal of Common Market Studies*, 37(2), June: 317–331.

Puetter, Uwe. 2014. *The European council and the council: New intergovernmentalism and institutional change*. Oxford: Oxford University Press.

Rawls, J. 1999. *The law of peoples*. Cambridge, MA: Harvard University Press.

Sadeh, Tel and Verdun, Amy. 2009. "Explaining Europe's monetary union: A survey of literature". *International Studies Review*, 11: 277–301.

Saurugger, S. 2013. "Constructivism and public policy approaches in the EU: From ideas to power games". *Journal of European Public Policy*, 20(6): 888–906.

Scott, G. 2014. "Structural adjustment comes to Europe: Lessons for the Eurozone from the conditionality debates". *Global Social Policy*, 14(1): 51–71.

Tranholm-Mikkelsen, J. 1991. "Neo-functionalism: Obstinate or obsolete?" *Millenium,* 20(1): 1–22.

Walsh, James. 2001. "National preferences and international institutions: Evidence from European Monetary Integration". *International Studies Quarterly,* 45: 59–80.
Wind, Marlene. 1997. Rediscovering institutions: A reflectivist critique of rational institutionalism. In *Reflective approaches to European governance,* eds. Eric Jorgensen Knud, 15–35. Houndsmills: Macmillan Press.

## FURTHER DISCUSSION

1. Is European integration the outcome of national preferences convergence or is it the result of intergovernmental strategic interaction?
2. Can the major approaches of European integration explain the creation of the SGP and its major shortcomings until 2010?
3. Did European institutional structures succeed in mediating national interests of member states to the benefit of the common interest of EU as a whole?
4. To what extent do previous institutional choices of EU decision-making determine the path of EU response to crises?
5. Had idea diffusion a greater influence on the development and dynamics of EMU than domestic politics of EU member states?
6. To what extent neo-functionalism is relevant for explaining the management of European debt crisis?
7. To what extent is constructivism relevant in explaining the drive toward a complete fiscal and banking union in Europe?

# *Chapter 3*

# The Historical Evolution of European Union

## SETTING THE SCENE FOR EUROPEAN INTEGRATION: THE BEGINNINGS OF COOPERATION

European Union is a sui generis international entity which influences heavily not only the economic behavior of its citizens but also the content and principles of the global economic system. The story of European integration is worth telling not only because of its dynamics but also because of its impact on international economic and political order. Deepening and enlargement are the two dimensions which characterize European integration progress and too often become the reasons of fierce intra-European disagreements and political conflicts. Having begun as one of competing European projects, the EEC quickly overruled all other regional integration schemes and became the center of European integration process. Thus, understanding the evolution and history of EU is essential to understand the process of European integration. European integration is not a new idea but its roots go back to the days of Charlemagne, who became Holy Roman emperor in 800. Many years later in the fourteenth century, Pierre Dubois, who supported the idea of a European confederation, proposed the principles of a united Christendom. The cognitive pillars of European integration were placed soon after First World War (Gillingham, 2003; Molle, 2006). France due to demographic and economic growth lagging relative to Germany faced a security concern. The problem was further aggravated by the heavy reparation obligations posed on Germany which not only did not contain geopolitical ambitions of Germany but favored the rise of German revisionism.

However, the real spinning of the European integration process is traced in the immediate aftermath of the disastrous Second World War (Gilbert, 2012; Poidevin, 1986). In 1945, the necessity of restoration and restructuring of the economy was evident in west Europe. Under the pressure of adverse economic and political conditions, ruined European countries realized their common interests and needs and agreed to constrain their sovereignty rights in specific issue areas of economy giving birth to supranational organizations. Indeed, national governments surrendered sovereignty in selected policy areas so as to enhance their international status, to spin their economic welfare, and to secure the highly fragile internal national political systems. Thus, rebalancing national economic interests was an urgent priority if European states targeted the avoidance of future conflicts and beggar-thy-neighbour policies.

Undeniably, one should not dismiss the idealism of the key political figures of European integration. Personalities such as Robert Schuman, German chancellor Konrad Adenauer, and Italian Prime Minister Alcide de Gasperi were inspired by a vision for European unity and were eager to put into action all necessary political initiatives. Without their decisive influence building the consensus regarding Europeans' political values would not have been feasible.

## A BRIEF HISTORY OF EUROPEAN INTEGRATION (1918–1950)

The European idea gathered steam soon after 1918. Richard Coudenhove Calergi, an Austro-Hungarian aristocrat, fully inspired by pan-American vision, founded the Pan-European Movement in 1923 having in mind an association of European countries. In his book Pan-Europa (1923), Coudenhove-Kalergi proposed a federal union of European countries based on France and Germany and on the pillars of the fundamental democratic ideas and values.

Aristide Briand, Prime Minister of France, who held an honorary presidency of the Pan-European Movement in 1927, formed the details of the proposal for European integration. According to his plan, states should be united, but their sovereignty should not be touched. Briand collaborated with German minister Gustav Stresemann, to provide a solid basis for a Franco-German rapprochement, denouncing France's punitive behavior toward Germany after 1918. He further collaborated with Britain's foreign minister in realizing the Locarno Treaty (October 1925), guaranteeing the borders of Western European countries.

The momentum was such that Briand and Gustav Stresemann had a summit meeting in the small village of Thoiry, in September 1926, and succeeded to agree on a number of key issues on German reparations. The effort was culminated on September 5, 1929, when Briand and Stresemann supported

European integration based on the establishment of a EU within the League of Nations and even suggested the possibility of a common currency. However, Stresemann's death in October 1929 ended Franco-German ambitious rapprochement.

Although Briand issued a memorandum in May 1930 proposing an association of European countries (Briand, 1930), subordinate to the League of Nations, to achieve coordination of economic policies and political union, it became apparent that the project for European integration did not have a chance to succeed in a European environment of emerging interstate tensions, trade wars, protectionist markets, and enforced economic nationalism.

Almost a decade later, in July 1941, Altiero Spinelli and other political figures, detained on the island of Ventotene, issued a Manifesto for a Free and United Europe; in 1943 they founded the European Federalist Movement. The European integration effort had been further strengthened in 1946 when Winston Churchill proposed the creation of "the United States of Europe" (for an overview of key documents on European idea, see Lipgens, 1985; 1986; 1988).

From 1947 onward initiatives for integration came one after another at an unprecedented pace. In 1947 the economic commission for Europe was established as the regional European institutional organization of United Nations in European continent targeted at economic reconstruction of devastated European states. In 1948 the Brussels treaty organization was established by France, the Netherlands, Belgium, UK, and Luxembourg as an effort to secure the participating states relative to future threats and a year later the necessity of the collective defense of free Western European states led to the NATO Treaty (signed by 12 states in Washington in April 1949).

The statute of the Council of Europe was signed in London (May 5, 1949), by ten countries, namely, Belgium, Denmark, France, Ireland, Italy, Luxembourg, Norway, the Netherlands, the UK, and Sweden. The Council had its permanent seat in Strasbourg and sought to attain unity among its member states, to forward economic and social progress, and to preserve the democratic ideals and principles that are their common heritage. However, the first representatives of the new parliamentary assembly were appointed by their governments. Equally important, the assembly discussed several times plans for a united Europe and proposed plans for a federal political authority but it did not manage to gain the approval of a majority of its members or even the support of the committee of ministers. The assembly of the organization did not have any legislative power and was served as a consultative body reaffirming British volition on intergovernmentalism and national sovereignty in high politics issues. Further, the committee of ministers which was established as the executive institutional tool of the council of Europe had decision-making power but only through unanimity.

The Council of Europe achieved the intensification of cooperation in cultural, social, and scientific issues forwarding conventions regarding university cooperation, the protection of artistic and archaeological heritage, and the harmonization of social security systems. Especially, in the field of human rights it achieved in November 1950 to put in place the European Convention for the protection of human rights and fundamental freedoms, which is considered a key tool for the protection of human rights. The Convention also outlined individuals' civil and political rights and established an EC of human rights to deal with appeals, submitted by the contracting countries or by persons that are then referred to the European Court of human rights. The European Court of human rights also ensured that the administrations and courts of its member countries respect fundamental rights.

Evidently, the establishment of the Council of Europe in 1949 and the European Court of human rights as well as the signing of the European Convention on human rights contributed to the integration, especially from the perspective of public life in general and also of the primary value system of Western Europe in contrast with Eastern European existing socialism regimes.

Moreover, the Council of Europe targeted the enforcement of parliamentary democracy and human rights in west Europe and acted as a cognitive framework for the promotion of European values.

US government was not indifferent to the evolving European integration process. In the light of rising prices and shortages in agricultural products in west Europe in 1947–1948 it became evident that US encouragement of European integration was necessary. Already in March 1947, the Truman Doctrine expressed US volition to support free peoples who are resisting attempted subjugation by armed minorities, or by outside pressure and more specifically it had the purpose to address potential threat-aggression by existing socialism countries (Staab, 2008). As a result in 1948 the US government proposed a reconstruction plan named the ERP, later known as the Marshall Plan. More specifically, the US Secretary of State, G. Marshall during a speech at Harvard University in June 1947, promised significant economic aid to Europe proclaiming a policy against hunger, poverty, despair, and chaos. The American volition in rebuilding Europe would have been realized without the distinction east-west but the negative stance of the Soviet Union limited the implementation of the aid mainly in west Europe.

Undeniably, European integration advanced further in 1948 with the creation (with thirteen members) of OEEC, renamed as OECD in 1961. As Staab (2008, 7) mentioned the OEEC served as the forum for Western European states to promote supranational integration and economic cooperation through an institutionalized framework. The role of the new organization was crucial not only in dividing US aid in its members but also in limiting intra-European trade obstacles and in significantly ameliorating intra-European system of payments through the European payments system (the latter was established in 1950 to facilitate economic cooperation in postwar Europe).

Taking into account that intra-European trade was on the rise, Boltho and Eichengreen (2008, 14) underlined that the European payments system (EPU) was essential to put into action a phasing out of exchange controls and discriminatory trade obstacles that had been applied during the war years and the second half of the 1940s. It is also extremely important to note that in a period of immediate reconstruction necessity the OEEC permitted more than 60% of private intra-European trade flows to freed putting the pillars for GDP rising and export improvements in 1950s.

However, the integration process inspired by Jean Monnet (the architect of Franco-German rapprochement) reached a milestone with the Schuman declaration of May 9, 1950, named after France's minister for foreign affairs Robert Schuman. The declaration was a way "to make it plain that any war between France and Germany becomes not merely unthinkable, but materially impossible" and underlined the need that "Franco-German production of coal and steel as a whole be placed under a common high authority, within the framework of an organization open to the participation of the other countries of Europe." The focus on the key issue area of coal and steel production was perceived as "a first step in the federation of Europe."

## THE REASONS FOR EUROPEAN INTEGRATION

The key motive of the European unification idea from the years of Immanuel Kant is perseverance of peace among European sovereign states and regulation of the state of anarchy in European interstate relations. The enormous number of casualties and the extent of economic destruction in the two world wars rose serious concerns over the ability of European nations to achieve long-term peace without effective supranational institutions.

Indeed, the image of Europe in 1945 was disappointing. Roads and rail networks were destroyed and key infrastructure facilities such as water, heating, and electricity were in need of immediate restoration. In Western Europe alone more than eight million people were killed while the Soviet Union had more than twenty million deaths. René Streiff mentioned in his article "*Le plan Monnet et l'économie française en 1950*" (1950), that France's economy was in disarray with a finance system shattered, severely damaged transportation lines, and underperforming agricultural and manufacturing sectors.

David Henderson underlined in his article "German Economic Miracle" (2008) that in 1945 almost 20% of all houses had been destroyed while Martin Bull and James Newell also argued in their book *Italian politics:*

*Adjustment under duress* (2005, 20) that after 1945 Italy faced low levels of growth and industrialization, high levels of unemployment, significant wealth inequalities, and a lack of fundamental raw materials. In 1951, 43.9% of employees in Italy were employed in the agriculture sector, underlying the country's anemic economic conditions.

Karen Alter and David Steinberg also argued in "The Theory and reality of the European Coal and Steel Community" (2007) that a lack of steel spread fears to most west European politicians. Finally, East-West bloc confrontation and the cold war geopolitical terms after 1945 raised serious doubts over the ability to preserve a lasting peace in Europe.

Soon after the end of the Second World War it was widely accepted that punishing the losers of war, as occurred with the Treaty of Versailles at the end of the First World War, was a non-viable and ineffective solution which could enforce extreme right and extreme left forces. Indeed, the Treaty of Versailles, signed on June 28, 1919, was based on heavy financial compensations and was proved highly fragile. It is important to notice that John Maynard Keynes denounced the financial provisions of the Versailles Treaty of 1919 treaty in his book, *The Economic consequences of the peace*, published in 1920 insisting that reparations became a drain on the German economy and enforced German militarism. Evidently, the League of Nations did not restructure European interstate relations and did not succeed to establish a permanent and stable framework of peace and conflict resolution.

Thus, instead of isolation, the new idea was full integration of defeated states in the European system so as to attain conciliation and reparation, which would have made the idea of another confrontation unfavorable. Accordingly, the German question was conceived as a fundamental feature of the preservation of peace. Contrary to past strategies of military encirclement which enforced aggressive militarism, the new strategy was to build commonly regulated issue areas of an economy with positive spillovers for all participating states. The new political game was not a zero sum game to the detriment of the losers but a positive sum (win-win) game where all participating states gained although at a different pace. Accordingly, the "German problem" would have been overcome through the consolidation of democracy in the West German Federal Republic (the former western zones of occupation), guaranteeing that the Germans fully adhered to the ideals of embedded liberalism and the principles of the newly created Bretton Wood's institutions. Equally important, French's and German's irreconcilable national economic interests were regulated by putting in place a supranational organization to manage the two countries' coal and steel resources. In this way, a recovery of German economy did not put French recovery in danger and Franco-German rapprochement could be realized through the Coal and Steel Community.

As Desmond Dinan's argued (2014) a community would have permitted French government to have full access to coal in the Ruhr region and to restructure its economy. He also noted that a supranational organization in coal and steel could have made easier French-German economic and political relations as France would be able to keep access to the coal it needed from Germany so as to preserve its steel industry.

Dinan (2014) further underlined that a weak West Germany also meant a weak Western European economy putting US allies in a difficult position relative to Soviet Bloc. The US influence on French government to integrate the West German economy was also based on the conviction that European economic growth could not be realized otherwise. As Staab (2008, 7) mentioned the complex regional environment raised security concerns and thus the USA had no option than to motivate west Europeans into collaborative action. Anemic economic conditions could have destabilized political systems in west Europe leading to rising influence of soviet-led communist parties.

Jean Monnet eloquently underlined in his *Memoirs* (1978, 293) that "if the victors and the vanquished agreed to exercise joint sovereignty over part of their joint resources . . . then a solid link would be forged between them, the way would be wide open for further collective action and a great example would be given to the other nations of Europe." Thus, judged by the historical facts, Schumann's proposal for the community in coal and steel proved to be a pragmatic approach for west European reconstruction.

The second important reason for the intensification of European integration was the fact that national markets in Europe were too small for rationalization of production and thus quick and sustainable productivity improvements could not be achieved putting west European competitiveness in a disadvantaged position vis-à-vis the USA and the Soviet Union. As Poelmans (2012, 6) emphasized German recovery was part and parcel of west European recovery since German industry was a locomotive of development and growth. Germany controlled the Ruhr region, and preserved technological knowledge but could not act alone to sustain its competitive advantage.

## THE EUROPEAN COAL AND STEEL COMMUNITY: A TURNING POINT IN THE HISTORY OF EUROPE

A fundamental leap toward European integration was taken with the establishment of ECSC. The Schumann declaration (May 9, 1950) led in April 18, 1951 to the establishment of ECSC among six countries, France, West Germany, Italy, the Netherlands, Belgium, and Luxembourg. As Philippe Mioche mentioned in his book *Les Cinquantes Années de l'Europe du Charbon et de l'Acier* (2004, 9) the six countries accounted together for 16% of the global production in coal, and 20% for the production of steel. The institutional model of ECSC (Moravcsik, 1998; Rector, 2009) was also served as a paradigm for the EDC and the EPC.

Which were the key motives for the establishment of ECSC? According to Milward (1984), France supported the coal and steel community to constrain German control of its own industry, and as Berger and Ritschl (1995) suggested, French access to German coal turned to be “the most important element of the Monnet plan for France’s reconstruction.”

On the other hand, Germany agreed to the Schuman plan (Eichengreen, 2006, 802) because by sharing management of coal and steel, it could achieve concessions, such as “the removal of ceilings on permissible levels of industrial production.” In any case the elimination of rivalry and competition between France and Germany seemed feasible for the first time after centuries (Poelmans, 2012). One should not also underestimate the US influence on west European states to adopt Schumann’s proposal, as the only way to integrate West German economy, without which European growth could not have taken place.

Which was the institutional framework of ECSC? French foreign minister Robert Schumann put in place a carefully designed proposal concerning the establishment of the European supranational organization. A high authority was created (which contrary to the experience of the council of Europe was given authority in specific issue areas of coal and steel and in many cases without prior consent of the Council of Ministers), while the assembly (representatives of each member state) and the Council of Ministers (of the six member states) had specific and carefully designed competences. The treaty further gave the right to the high authority (whose members were designated by the member states and acted as an independent decision-taking body), under the supervision of the Council of Ministers, the capability to negotiate and establish diplomatic relations with foreign governments in the issue areas of coal and steel.

The targets of the treaty were clearly stated in the preamble. The treaty called for a substitution of old interstate rivalries and an increase in the standard of living in each member state. Moreover, the treaty also applied a framework of principles (Stirk et al., 1999) that enforced competition of the market among others the obligation for transparency with respect to prices, policies to avoid illegal subsidization of industry, a ban of cartels, transparency of labor practices, and an equalization of transport rates for all steel companies regardless of nationality (Jovanovic, 2005a; 2005b).

Dinan (2014) suggested, the ECSC encouraged and required the close cooperation of governments, manufacturers, and interests groups across borders with each other and the supranational institutions of the ECSC, most notably the high authority. These increased interactions created pressure for national governments to transfer responsibility for related policy areas to other and newly created institutions and to expand the range of European governance and its capabilities. The organization took an effort to provide solution to the Saar region problem but also permitted West Germany to make important steps in its reintegration in European and the international community. As a result of the ECSC, companies of the six member states started to internationalize their activities and new steel firms were established because of a fall in energy costs.

Conclusively, the treaty acted as a laboratory for integration testing and put in place a sui generis regional economic organization to realize sectoral integration in controlled economic conditions and interstate cooperative principles. The federalists also felt that a great victory was realized since the organization had important responsibilities and did not follow the disappointing effort of the Council of Europe where no powers were delivered to an independent commission and the rule of unanimity blocked important integration initiatives.

## THE EUROPEAN ECONOMIC COMMUNITY: A MILESTONE IN EUROPEAN ECONOMIC INTEGRATION

The rejection by the French national assembly of the EDC treaty on August 30, 1954, together with the demise of the initiative to put in place a EPC, ended the efforts for political and military union in west Europe.

However, the idea of integration was not abandoned and the meeting of the ministers of foreign affairs of the members of the ECSC in the Italian city of Messina, Sicily, in June 1–3, 1955 contributed to this end. An intergovernmental committee chaired by Belgian foreign minister Paul-Henri Spaak had been formed and held several meetings (the first one in July 1955) until it finally presented its report in April 1956. The members of the committee were preoccupied with the key issue of the common market, and with the perspective of integration in other fields such as energy sources, nuclear energy, and transport. Indeed, intensive negotiations took place in Noordwijk, near Hague, on September 6, 1955, and then in the Brussels on February 11–12, 1956. Spaak preference was for a CU favoring parallelly the institutional flexibility of the new organization.

The negotiators favored the establishment of four institutions: a Council of Ministers, a body resembling the high authority, a parliamentary Assembly, and a Court of Justice. By contrast, Robert Schuman favored a federalist view of European integration and sought above all to promote reconciliation between France and Germany.

From May 29 to 30 1956, the Ministers for Foreign Affairs of the six states of the ECSC took part in a conference on the island of San Giorgio Maggiore in Venice to reach agreement on the Spaac report and to establish a common market and a treaty putting in place EURATOM. A little later on June 26, 1956 (Brussels) the representatives of the six states dealt thoroughly with the common market and EURATOM and a drafting group was put in place with the duty to reach an agreement on the principles and rules of the treaties.

The two treaties were decided on March 25, 1957 (Rome) and came into force on January 1, 1958. The key political figures signed the treaty among others, Paul-Henri Spaak (Minister of Foreign Affairs of Belgium), Konrad Adenauer (Federal Chancellor of Germany), Christian Pineau (Minister of Foreign Affairs of France), Antonio Segni (President of the Council of Ministers of Italy), Joseph Bech (Prime Minister of Luxemburg), and Joseph Luns (Minister of Foreign Affairs of the Netherlands).

The treaty was structured into six parts. Part one referred to the principles, the aims, and the scope of Community (articles 1 and 2). Part two was dedicated to the bases of the Community and included four titles, (title one dedicated to the general subject of "Free movement of goods," title two was dedicated to agriculture [articles 38–47], title three was dedicated to free movement of persons, services and capital [articles 48–73], and title four was dedicated to transport [articles 74–84]).

Part three dealt with the policies of the Community (common, economic, and social) and covered competition, dumping practices, state subsidies, commercial policy, and legislative convergence. Part four was fully dedicated to the subject of the special relationship of the overseas countries and territories, while part five dealt in detail with the functioning of the institutions, with a title dedicated to revenues and budget. Finally, part six summed up with general provisions.

More specifically, article 1 of part one was dedicated to principles, and named the organization that was born: the EEC. Article 2 stated that the aim of the Community was the foundation of a common market targeting to the progressive approximation of the economic policies of member countries, to the promotion throughout the Community of a harmonious development of economic activities, to the achievement of a continuous and balanced expansion, to an increased stability, and to an accelerated rising of the standard of living and closer relations between its member countries.

The activities of the Community (article 3) included the elimination of customs duties; the establishment of a common customs tariff and a common commercial policy; the abolition of the obstacles to the free movement of persons, services, and capital, a CAP, a common transport policy, a system ensuring competition; the coordination of the economic policies, the approximation of local laws for the functioning of the common market, a ESF; a EIB; and the association of overseas countries and territories with the Community.

Article 4 (para 1) established the four fundamental institutions, namely, an Assembly, a Council, a Commission, and a Court of Justice. According to article 8 the common market would have been "progressively established in the course of a transitional period of twelve years," divided into three stages of four years each.

Part two referred to the "Bases of the Community." Title I was dedicated to the free movement of goods, underlining in article 9 (para 1) that the Community "shall be based upon a CU covering the exchange of all goods and comprising both the prohibition, as between member states, of customs duties on importation and exportation and all charges with equivalent effect and the adoption of a common customs tariff in their relations with third countries."

Chapter 1 of title I ("free movement of goods") of the treaty (CU) dealt with the elimination of customs duties in stages while section 2 of title one of the treaty was dedicated to the establishment of the common customs tariff. Extremely important was the provision of article 18 which outlined that the EC countries were committed to "contribute to the development of international commerce and the reduction of barriers to trade by entering into reciprocal and mutually advantageous arrangements directed to the reduction of customs duties below the general level which they could claim as a result of the establishment of a customs union between themselves."

Title II of part two of the treaty was dedicated to agricultural issues. Article 38 (1) underlined that the common market "shall extend to agriculture and trade in agricultural products" through the establishment of a CAP. Article 39 (1) developed in detail the targets of CAP, namely, to increase agricultural productivity by developing technical progress, to ensure a fair standard of living for the agricultural population, to stabilize markets, to guarantee regular supplies, and to ensure reasonable prices in supplies to consumers. Article 40 (1) outlined the CAP would have been developed during a specific transitional period, while article 41 highlighted the necessity for the provision of "an effective co-ordination of efforts undertaken in the spheres of occupational training, research and the popularization of rural economy."

Title III (part two) of the treaty outlined the provisions for free movement of persons, services, and capital. Chapter 1 was titled "the workers" and included "the right, subject to limitations justified by reasons of public order, public safety and public health," to accept offers of employment, to move about freely for this purpose within the territory of member countries, to stay in any member state in order to carry on an employment in conformity with the legislative and administrative provisions governing the employment of the workers of that country, and to live on terms which were the subject of regulations laid down by the Commission in the territory of a member state after having been employed there.

According to the provisions of article 49 the tools to achieve this target were close collaboration between national labor administrations: abolishment of administrative procedures and practices that were an obstacle to the freeing of the movement of workers, abolishment of conditions imposed on workers of other member countries conditions for the free choice of employment different from these imposed on workers of the state concerned, and application of appropriate machinery for connecting offers of employment and requests for employment. Article 50 favored the exchange of young workers while article 51 outlined the adoption of measures of protection to migrant workers.

Chapter two of title 3 dealt with the right of establishment. More specifically, article 52 stated that "restrictions on the freedom of establishment of nationals of a member state in the territory of another member state shall be progressively abolished" and underlined that "freedom of establishment shall include the right to engage in and carry on non-wage-earning activities, and also to set up and manage enterprises and, in particular, companies."

Article 54 outlined that "wage-earning workers of one member state employed in the territory of another member state may remain in that territory for the purpose of undertaking a non-wage-earning activity there," and granted the right to individuals of one EEC state "to acquire and exploit real property situated in the territory of another member state." Article 57(1) referred to the "mutual recognition of diplomas, certificates and other qualifications" while article 58 noted that companies constituted in accordance with the law of an EEC state would have been "assimilated to natural persons being nationals of member states."

Chapter 3 of the same title of the treaty dealt with services. More specifically, article 59 stated that "restrictions on the free supply of services within the community shall be progressively abolished" while article 60 outlined the services supplied for remuneration activities of an industrial character, activities of a commercial character, artisan activities, and activities of the liberal professions.

Chapter 4 referred to capital and mandated from the beginning (article 67 para 1) that the EEC countries "progressively abolish as between themselves restrictions on the movement of capital belonging to persons resident in member states and also any discriminatory treatment based on the nationality or place of residence of the parties or on the place in which such capital is invested."

Title IV (part 2) of the treaty tackled the issue area of transport and prohibited (article 81 para 1) as

> incompatible with the common market any agreements between undertakings, decisions by associations of undertakings and any concerted practices which may affect trade between the member states and which have as their object or effect of prevention, restriction or distortion of competition within the common market, and in particular: (a) the direct or indirect fixing of purchase or selling prices (b) the limitation or control of production, markets, technical development or investment (c) market-sharing or the sharing of sources of supply (d) the application to parties to transactions of unequal terms in respect of equivalent supplies, thereby placing them at a competitive disadvantage or (e) the subjecting of the conclusion of a contract to the acceptance by a party of additional supplies which, either by their nature or according to commercial usage, have no connection with the subject of such contract.

In part 3 of the treaty the community policies were thoroughly analyzed. The importance of fair competition within the economic community was evident from the provisions of the treaty which mandated in article 86 the impossibility "to take improper advantage of a dominant position within the common market or within a substantial part of it," and highlighted that the practice was "incompatible with the common market." Examples of such practices were the direct or indirect imposition of any inequitable purchase or selling prices or of any other inequitable trading conditions and were the limitation of production.

Section 2 of title 1 (part 3 of the treaty) dealt with dumping practices while section 3 tackled the sensitive subject of aid granted by EEC countries underlining that practices "incompatible with the common market" are aid of a social character granted to individual consumers, provided that such aid are granted without any discrimination based on the origin of the products concerned.

Moreover, aid was permitted when it intended to remedy damage caused by natural calamities or other extraordinary events or when granted to the economy of certain regions of the Federal Republic of Germany affected by the division of Germany, to the extent that such aid are necessary "in order to compensate for the economic disadvantages caused by such division."

The treaty permitted aid intended to promote the economic development of regions where the standard of living was abnormally low or where there existed serious underemployment, aid intended to promote the execution of important projects of common European interest or to remedy a serious disturbance of the economy of an EEC state, and aid intended to facilitate the development of certain activities or of certain economic regions.

The commercial policy was detailed in chapter 3. Article 110 underlined that "by establishing a customs union between themselves the member states intend to contribute, in conformity with the common interest, to the harmonious development of world trade, the progressive abolition of restrictions on international exchanges and the lowering of customs barriers," while article 111 mandated member states to coordinate their commercial relations with other states so as to attain the terms necessary to the implementation of a common policy in external trade. If member states "abolish or reduce quantitative restrictions in regard to third countries, they shall inform the Commission before hand and shall accord identical treatment to the other member states."

Title III of the treaty (part 3) tackled social policy and chapter 1 (title 3, part 3) dealt with social provisions. More specifically, article 117 underlined that member states agreed

> "upon the necessity to promote improvement of the living and working conditions of labor so as to permit the equalization of such conditions in an upward direction" and "consider that such a development will result not only from the functioning of the common market which will favor the harmonization of social systems, but also from the procedures provided for under this Treaty and from the approximation of legislative and administrative provisions."

According to article 118 the Commission promoted close collaboration between member states in the social field, particularly relating to employment, labor legislation and working conditions, occupational and continuation training, social security, protection against occupational accidents and diseases, industrial hygiene, the law as to trade unions, and collective bargaining.

Finally, part four of the treaty dealt with the special relationship of the overseas countries and territories while part five dealt in detail with the functioning of the institutions, with a title dedicated to revenues and budget. Part six of the treaty summed up with general provisions.

Conclusively, as Dinan (2014) argued, the treaty was a political compromise due to differences in targeting of the countries involved. West German government argued in favor of tariff reductions to increase trade and open markets within west Europe, highlighting the importance of positive relations with France and embedding the new Federal Republic within European institutions. On the other hand, strong protectionist ideas were present in France despite Jean Monnet and other prominent politicians influence.

In any case, the establishment of the EEC and EURATOM was a milestone in European integration process that although involved initially only six states, it put the institutional and cognitive pillars to the deepening of European integration. Despite the fact that until the merger treaty of 1965 the three EC entities had its own institutions, namely, a council (of ministers), a commission (high authority for ECSC) a EP (or assembly), and a Court of Justice there was in place a common march of the three parallel circles toward common European targets.

## THE EURATOM

The EURATOM treaty was a plan that began at the Messina Conference in June 1955 to ensure the security of atomic energy supply and to put in place a relevant and suitable monitoring system. Following the organizational design of the ECSC, EURATOM was also an effort to keep integration momentum after the failure of the EDC in 1954. Apparently, attaining energy independence individually was not possible and thus west European nations had to find a common ground on key issues such as research and production as well as safety standards in the field of atomic energy. Among the specific tasks of EURATOM were (article 2) to promote research and ensure the dissemination of technical information, to establish uniform safety standards, to protect the health of workers and of the general public and ensure that they are applied, to facilitate investment and ensure the establishment of the basic installations necessary for the development of nuclear energy in the EU, and to ensure that all users in the EU receive a regular and equitable supply of ores and nuclear fuels.

As the preamble of EURATOM underlined, "Nuclear energy represents an essential resource for the development and invigoration of industry and will permit the advancement of the cause of peace." Accordingly, European countries should "create the conditions necessary for the development of a powerful nuclear industry which will provide extensive energy resources, lead to the modernization of technical processes and contribute, through its many other applications, to the prosperity of their peoples."

Moreover, there was a need to put in place "conditions of safety necessary to eliminate hazards to the life and health of the public" and "to cooperate with international organizations concerned with the peaceful development of atomic energy."

The treaty had 234 articles developed under six titles. The first title was linked to the seven tasks of the Community while the second title was dedicated to the provisions to encourage progress in the field of nuclear energy. The third title set out the institutions of the Community. The fourth, the fifth, and the sixth sections were dedicated to financial and to general provisions as well as to details of the initial period of functioning.

The institutional framework of the EURATOM Treaty followed that of the EEC Treaty (Council, Commission, and EP) also having an Economic and Social Committee as an advisory pillar. The treaty established an agency with a right of option on ores, source materials, and an exclusive right to conclude contracts relating to the supply of ores, source materials, and special fissile materials coming from inside the Community or from outside.

The EURATOM supply agency had legal personality and financial autonomy and was under the supervision of the Commission. The latter ensured that source materials were not diverted from the intended uses and guaranteed that the provisions relating to supply are complied with. Equally important, the Commission had the right to send inspectors who had access at all times to all places and data and to all persons who, by reason of their occupation, dealt with materials, equipment, or installations subject to the safeguards. Lastly, the EURATOM rules were applied in conjunction with those of IAEA.

## THE FIRST ENLARGEMENT: DENMARK, IRELAND, UK (JANUARY 1, 1973)

A key issue of the first enlargement was UK accession in European Community which faced serious obstacles since France's president Charles de Gaulle had reservations (Staab, 2008) and blocked UK membership in the 1960s. UK government also insisted during pre-accession period negotiations to defend its specific relation with the Commonwealth states and to hold its specific economic-political-security ties with USA.

However, in the 1970s things changed drastically. On the one hand, France dropped its objections realizing the need to counterbalance future emerging economic supremacy of Germany (President Charles de Gaulle resignation also opened the way for completion of UK accession negotiations) and on the other hand British trade patterns with overseas Commonwealth states had changed. As far as it concerns the latter while the Commonwealth states accounted in 1954 for 48% of UK imports and absorbed 49% of its exports; by 1972, UK economy was importing 19% of its goods from the Commonwealth states. Accordingly, UK government realized the need for a more flexible negotiating framework. On July 7, 1971, the UK government published a White Paper titled "The United Kingdom and the European Communities," which reviewed the benefits of British accession to the EEC.

However, two issues still acted as a bottleneck to accession namely UK's financial contribution to EEC and the terms of participation in the CAP. As far as it concerns financial contribution, France insisted that UK should pay its entire contribution (one-fifth of the entire budget) as soon as it became member of the EEC but was also prepared behind the negotiation curtain, to offer a longer transitional period in order to reach an agreement. Finally, the French president Georges Pompidou met, from May 20 to 21, 1971, the British Prime Minister Edward Heath and agreed to overcome the problems to accession and especially that of the contribution to the financing of the EEC budget that would gradually be raised until it reached 19% of the total community budget.

In January 1973, the UK together with Ireland and Denmark joined EEC. The Accession Treaty (January 22, 1972) provided for a transitional period of five years (as for Ireland and Denmark), with the UK contribution to rise from 8.6% of EEC resources in 1973 to 18.9% in 1977 (in 1974, Harold Wilson's Government opposed the principle of a juste retour of each country's contribution).

Some years later, UK prime minister Margaret Thatcher demanded (1979) a reduction of the UK contribution. Indeed, from 1979 to 1980, the UK contributed 20% of EEC revenue but took back only 12% of its expenditure. Although she succeeded for the years 1980 and 1981, to reduce by two-thirds of UK's net contribution (the difference between what it paid and what it received), she demanded an even better financial balance. After three more years of fierce negotiations a compromise was attained in Fontainebleau European Council (June 25–26, 1984) which granted UK an annual compensation, which totaled two-thirds of the difference between its VAT payments and its revenue from the EEC budget.

Ireland's application for accession was linked to the UK application and consequently had been abandoned twice, in 1963 and 1967, following the French negative stance to UK application for accession. Especially, Irish agricultural producers looked toward the European market and the benefits accrued by participation in the CAP. Thus, it was not surprising that in the referendum (May 10, 1972) for ratification of the treaty of accession 81% of the Irish citizens vote in favor of accession in the communities.

Denmark, Finland, Norway, and Sweden followed a different negotiation route and started negotiations in April 1968 so as to set in place (by January 1974), a customs and economic union to be known as Nordek. Nordek would have facilitated Nordic states access to EEC and could have acted as an alternative integration option through the implementation of a system of Nordic preference in trade issues. The submitted report on the draft treaty was published on July 17, 1969 and suggested the establishment of a CU from January 1, 1972. There was also a prediction for the creation of a Nordic investment bank as well as for the establishment of a Nordic common agricultural market. However, national interests prevailed over collective bargaining and Finland was the first country to differentiate its position from the proposed union, signing a protocol with the USSR on July 20, 1970. Although Denmark insisted to continue the process without Finland, Sweden and Norway abandoned the effort putting in question the effectiveness of the initiative.

Denmark hoped to benefit from its membership of the EEC but the Danish referendum which took place on October 2, 1972 did not ratify the expected result for a positive attitude from voters.

Norway followed a different negotiation strategy looking for the protection of highly sensitive issues in the primary sector. Indeed, during the period of negotiations for entry, Norwegian agriculture (and especially fishing) turned out to be the most sensitive issue to be resolved. Fishing was considered an essential economic sector for Norway (which has more than 2000 km of coastline). Norwegian fishermen, whose trawlers were inferior to the French ships, were not prepared to agree free access to their extremely rich territorial waters instantly taking into account that overfishing had caused a reduction in marine resources. Further, Norwegian agriculture, which was mainly mountainous and was not competitive, was largely subsidized by the central and local authorities. However, this direct financial aid was contrary to the principles of the CAP.

Under those circumstances the referendum of September 26, 1972 led to a "no" vote by 53.5%. The negative referendum result led to rejection of Norwegian membership of the EEC and to the resignation of the government, but was followed by a free trade agreement between Norway and the European Communities in May 1973, by which the customs duty on a range of industrial products was progressively lifted.

## THE SECOND ENLARGEMENT: THE ACCESSION OF GREECE (JANUARY 1, 1981)

The EEC's second round of enlargement had an entirely different dynamic from the first enlargement. Greece became member of EEC (January 1981) not purely on economic criteria (to modernize and internationalize its production structures) but also on political reasons (to consolidate the democracy which emerged from a dictatorial regime).

Since July 9, 1961, Greece had the status of associate member of the European Community and set out the establishment of a CU at the end of a 22-year transitional period. The free movement of persons, services, and capital was designed to take place at the end of a 12-year period while article 72 of the association agreement provided the ability for accession in EEC. However, the military coup of April 21, 1967 suspended the provisions of the Agreement until the restoration of parliamentary democracy in 1974. Greece submitted its official application to EEC on June 12, 1975 and the EC (January 29, 1976) proposed that EEC should apply a pre-accession period so as to permit Greek government to smoothly adopt the community acquis.

However, the Greek economy had significant economic structural differences relative to the nine states of EEC and Greek agricultural products (olive oil, wine, and fruit and vegetables) competed with agricultural products in Italy and France. Accordingly, the Commission proposed a transitional period from seven to eight years. The prescribed negotiation impasse was dissolved due to the support of the president of the French Republic Valéry Giscard d'Estaing as well as the German foreign minister Hans-Dietrich Genscher who supported the immediate promotion of Greek membership.

Accession negotiations started on July 27, 1976 and finished on May 23, 1979 followed by the signing of the Treaty of Accession on May 28, 1979 in Athens. Greece became the 10th member country of the European Community on January 1, 1981 under favorable terms since it was a beneficiary rather than a net contributor to the European Community budget. During 1980s it also achieved a rise in Community aid so as to modernize the structures of its economy through specific funds of European regional policy and the CAP.

## THE THIRD ENLARGEMENT: THE ACCESSION OF SPAIN AND PORTUGAL (JANUARY 1, 1986)

The EEC's third round of enlargement had also an entirely different dynamic from the first enlargement. Portugal and Spain became members of EEC (January 1986) not purely on economic criteria (to modernize and internationalize the production structures) but also on political reasons (to consolidate the democracies which emerged from dictatorial regimes in the mid-1970s).

Since 1973 Portugal enjoyed a free trade agreement with EEC including industrial and agricultural products but submitted its application for accession on March 28, 1977. The EC approved the application on May 19, 1978 and accession negotiations started on October 17, 1978. The signing of the Accession Treaty between Portugal and the EEC took place in Lisbon on June 12, 1985 and Portugal became officially member from January 1, 1986.

Spain enjoyed a preferential tariff agreement from October 1970 but submitted its application for accession to the European Community on July 28, 1977. The EC approved the application on November 29, 1978, negotiations started on February 5, 1979 and the signing of Spain's Treaty of accession to the EEC took place on June 12, 1985 in Madrid.

## THE SINGLE ECONOMIC ACT: PRELUDE FOR DEEPER ECONOMIC INTEGRATION

Although liberalization of industrial goods was completed on July 1, 1968, the CAP established a unified market for agricultural products with guaranteed prices and intra-community trade had been promoted through the reduction of quotas, major obstacles remained to free movement of factors of production. Differences in national legislations (i.e., issues of safety and quality standards and NTBs to trade) remained despite the fact that on February 20, 1979 (in the Cassis de Dijon case) the Court of Justice ruled that "any product lawfully produced and marketed in one member state must, in principle, be admitted to the market of any other member state." Moreover, there were exemptions to common rules of competition for public undertakings, significant differences in direct and indirect taxation, and national controls over financial markets were rigid. Equally important, fundamental obstacles on free circulation of labor within the community distorted the terms to efficiently provide services (i.e., banks, insurance).

Undeniably, there existed a window of opportunity for the new presidency of Jacques Delors. Lord Cockfield, the Commissioner for the internal market, issued a programme for the completion of the internal market, arguing in favor of abolition of physical, technical, and fiscal frontiers on the basis of a 7-year schedule and proposed 310 directives and regulations to be adopted by the Council of Ministers. The programme known as the White Paper was submitted to the Council on June 14, 1985 and was approved by the European Council in Milan (June 28–29). In September 1985, the Commission presented a complete chapter on the "Internal Market: An Area without Internal Frontiers" and in October, it presented a text on the institutional provisions that would be required for the completion of a single market. The SEA became operative on July 1, 1987 with the target to promote the four freedoms, namely, free circulation of goods, services, labor, and capital.

Indeed, the SEA enabled for all individuals the freedom of movement and of establishment within community. Customs formalities on goods were eliminated on January 1, 1993 and progress was also made in the mutual recognition of professional qualifications. Intra-community trading was enforced by the mutual recognition of product manufacturing rules under the condition that they were compatible with health and safety requirements adopted by the European Council. In the services sector, banks had freedom of establishment and insurance firms enjoyed freedom to provide services while liberalization in the maritime transport, air transport, and road transport was applied gradually. The telecommunications market was fully liberalized on January 1, 1998.

As far as it concerned monopolistic public services and subsidized national undertakings, the universal service principle was adopted, which permitted the liberalization of public services to be limited in certain cases. Further, competition policy was applied to prevent firms from holding or abusing dominant positions, by controlling mergers and by closely monitoring state aid. The SEA also enforced the resources on economic and social cohesion issues so as to face economic disparities within and between regions of European Community.

## THE TREATY ON EU

On December 15, 1990, two intergovernmental conferences took place in Rome examining the potential of EMU and the prospect for political union. Strong differences existed regarding the extension of European Community responsibilities to issue areas of national sovereignty (i.e., foreign policy, defense) and the resulting new balance between the Council of Ministers, EC, and EP. Two months after the intergovernmental negotiations the treaty on EU was signed in Maastricht on February 7, 1992 (in force from November 1, 1993) with the target of "an ever closer union among the peoples of Europe."

Indeed, the treaty put in place strengthened important principles and rules for European integration. It enforced the principle of subsidiarity, whereby the European Community may take action only when the targets of the union cannot be achieved by a member state. Of course, the principle may be implemented only to issue areas where competences are shared with the member countries and not to issues where the European Community has exclusive competence.

European citizenship was also a key reform granting new rights to European citizens and strengthening European identity, including the right to vote and to stand as a candidate in European and municipal elections in the country in which one resides and not only in his or her state of origin, the right to submit a complaint to the Ombudsman, and the right of recourse in a third state to diplomatic representation of another member state, if the country of origin does not have representation there.

Although the fundamental policies remained intact (common agricultural policy, customs union, transport policy, and competition policy) there were major innovations in other issue areas. The structural funds were reformed and as a result a cohesion fund to help the countries where per capita GNP was lower than 90% of the European average (Spain, Greece, Ireland, and Portugal) came in force from April 1, 1993. Equally important, the environment policy was strengthened by European Council's moving to qualified majority voting. Further, the TEU enforced the single market initiative including new chapters on education and culture, public health, consumer protection, and the development of trans-European networks.

In the issue area of social policy, the TEU took over the chapter from the Treaty of Rome, (reformed by the SEA) and enforced closer cooperation between the member countries in social issues. Despite the fact that already from December 9, 1989 the Charter of fundamental social rights was adopted by eleven member countries (the UK preferred the "opt out" clause ) with the target to enforce European competence and to promote social rights within internal market, the adoption of protocol no. 14 annexed to the treaty (which set out an agreement among the eleven on social policy, with minimum requirements adopted by means of directives) deprived the full potential of the European initiative (social policy was also included in the Treaty of Amsterdam on June 18, 1997).

As far as it concerned decision-making, qualified majority voting in the Council of Ministers was extended to several community policies (education, health, vocational training, consumer protection, and social policy), but its scope was reduced when the simple adoption of recommendations was involved. Unanimity was maintained vis-à-vis constitutional provisions (i.e., revision of the treaty, admission of new countries, own resources of the Community budget) and other key policies of the union (i.e., economic and social cohesion, tax, framework programme of research, industry, culture, the environment).

Democratic legitimacy was also increased, since the EP had the right of scrutiny on the appointment by the governments of the EC President and of the approval of the College of Commissioners. Moreover, it had the right to approve or reject decisions reached by the European Council in many issue areas, such as the establishment of the cohesion fund, the amendment of some provisions of the statute of the ESCB, or the adoption of a uniform procedure in all member states for the election of members of the EP.

## THE FOURTH ENLARGEMENT: AUSTRIA, FINLAND, AND SWEDEN (JANUARY 1, 1995)

In the years from 1989 to 1992, four European states applied officially for accession in European Community, namely, Austria on July 14, 1989, Sweden on July 1, 1991, Finland on March 18, 1992, and Norway on November 24, 1992. Based on the political agreement by the twelve member states leaders at the Edinburgh European Council (held on December 11 and 12, 1992), negotiations started in Brussels on February 1, 1993 with Austria, Finland, and Sweden and on April 5 with Norway.

There were many issues to be solved in sensitive issue areas of the economy during negotiations such as agriculture, regional aid, contributions to the European Community budget, and the fishing quotas. The Nordic states had a guaranteed price level higher than that offered by the EU and had far higher farm prices than those in the EU. Norway rejected the common fisheries policy, granted no permission to European vessels access to its territorial waters, and refused to suspend whale hunting. Austria asked for the continuation of subsidizing to its mountain farming, the restriction of heavy goods transit by road in the alpine regions and the protection of the property of its own nationals from purchase of land by foreign nationals in the regions popular with tourists. As far as it concerned budget contributions Sweden, like the other applicants, asked its contribution to all the European Community costs to be progressive.

The negotiations concluded in March 1994 and the applicant states were asked to accept the acquis communautaire as well as the provisions of the EU Treaty. The applicant states held referendums on whether to accede to the EU. Austria approved the ratification on June 12 by 66.6%, Finland also approved on October 16 with 56.9%, and Sweden on November 13 with 52.2%. However, Norway voters (which denied accession in 1972) denied again accession with 52.2% of the vote on November 28. The institutions of EU were adjusted for the new member states and each of three newcomers would have one European Commissioner while in the EP, Sweden would have 22 MEPs, Austria 21 and Finland 16.

## THE PROVISIONS OF THE TREATY OF AMSTERDAM

Many contentious issues were resolved at the Amsterdam European Council on June 16 and 17, 1997 and the treaty of Amsterdam was finally signed by the ministers on October 2. After the usual ratifications, the treaty entered into force on May 1, 1999. However, the interstate rivalries and the institutional tensions were obvious in the annex of the treaty as well as in the 13 protocols and the 51 declarations attached to the treaty.

The treaty of Amsterdam enforced the principles of freedom, democracy, and rule of law within EU with the decision to establish a union-wide area of freedom, security, and justice and made more effective the policies on the environment, health, and consumer protection. It also set out a chapter on employment. However, unanimity was retained for policies relating to social security and employer-employee issues.

Equally important, the CFSP remained intergovernmental with minor reforms such as the introduction of a High Representative for the CFSP to help the application of the six-monthly Council presidencies, and a policy planning and early warning unit was created.

Significant reforms took place relative to democratization of decision-making promoting legislative co-decision of the EP with the Council in new fields. However, in the Council of Ministers, majority voting in the first pillar of the EU, already extended by the Maastricht treaty, was not enforced and a blocking minority could be realized more easily.

More specifically, the provisions of the treaty of Amsterdam left untouched the issues of the efficiency of the decision-making process in a union that had enlarged from 12 to 15 member countries and would be further enlarged. The two fundamental issues were the number of European Commissioners and the weighting of votes of member states. The smaller states desired to have their own Commissioner and the larger EU countries insisted on the re-weighting of votes in the European Council based on the demographic importance of each EU country. The compromise was achieved in the protocol annexed to the treaty of Amsterdam which outlined that with any further enlargement "the Commission shall comprise one national of each of the member states, provided that, by that date, the weighting of the votes in the Council has been modified (. . .) in a manner acceptable to all member states."

The treaty also enlarged the limits of integration and provided for "closer cooperation" on the first and third pillars of the union (but not the CFSP), although the terms were such that practically it was difficult to achieve.

## THE SCHENGEN AREA

Soon after the systemic political and economic change in east and central European states from 1989 to 1990, it became evident that EU needed a common policy toward the rising influx of asylum seekers and refugees in west Europe. On June 14, 1985 the five countries (the Benelux countries, where the free movement of persons already existed plus France and Germany) formed the Schengen Group, named after the village in Luxembourg where the borders of the Grand Duchy, France, and Germany, met and signed an agreement on the gradual abolition of checks at their common borders. The other states of the EU joined the agreement in different periods (Italy on November 27, 1990; Spain and Portugal on June 25, 1991; Greece on November 6, 1992; Austria on April 28, 1995; Sweden, Finland, and Denmark on November 19, 1996). Despite the fact that Norway and Iceland were not members of EU they acceded to the Schengen Area as associate members on December 19, 1996.

More specifically, the Schengen Agreement abolished controls in the borders between the involved states and strengthened surveillance of external borders. It applied both short-term measures (i.e., simplifying internal border checks) and long-term measures (i.e., police cooperation and the harmonization of visa policies). A convention applying the Schengen Agreement was signed on June 19, 1990 so as to set out the specific procedures for issuing uniform visas, to harmonize procedures regarding the right of asylum, to establish a Schengen information system, and to take measures against drug trafficking.

The Schengen acquis and the safeguarding of internal security became the primary objective of the EU since the treaty of Amsterdam in October 1997. Indeed, the key elements of the third community pillar (except criminal law) were transferred to the first pillar, and an "area of freedom, security and justice" was established, irrespective of the institutional structure to which it belonged (first or third pillar). A protocol annexed to the treaty of Amsterdam permitted UK and Ireland to keep their border controls and to opt out of the new EU policies forming part of the first pillar of the union (i.e., on visas, immigration and other issues relevant to the free movement of persons).

Two years after the Amsterdam treaty, the Tampere (Finland) European Council took place on October 15 and 16, 1999 and considered again internal security as one of the key issues of EU, giving to the EC the capability to design legislative proposals and to review progress by compiling a scoreboard every six months. The Tampere European Council had the role to develop a common European policy on asylum and immigration and to apply a European area of justice, by guaranteeing mutual recognition of civil and criminal legislation and easier access to justice for European people, by strengthening fight against crime through Europol, by establishing Eurojust (an organization responsible for coordinating investigations into organized crime), and by harmonizing the criminal law of the member states.

## THE PROCESS OF FIFTH ENLARGEMENT: MAY 2004 (CYPRUS, THE CZECH REPUBLIC, ESTONIA, HUNGARY, LATVIA, LITHUANIA, MALTA, POLAND, THE SLOVAK REPUBLIC, SLOVENIA)

The Copenhagen European Council of June 21 and 22, 1993 set the criteria for accession to the EU for states of Central and Eastern Europe in order to be able to accede. Excessive fears that the accession would have provoked influx of immigrants or that the structural funds needed for regional convergence would have been huge were accommodated by carefully designed accession policy from the part of EC.

Indeed, the fifth enlargement was a critical quantitative and qualitative challenge since many issues had been raised including how the new member countries would be represented in the European institutions (number of votes in the Council, number of Commissioners, members of the EP, and representatives on the consultative committees). A clear indication of the intergovernmental tension was the declaration by three states (Belgium, France, and Italy), annexed to the Treaty of Amsterdam (signed on October 2, 1997) that "reinforcement [of the institutions] is an indispensable condition for the conclusion of the first accession negotiations."

Two years after the Amsterdam treaty, the Cologne European Council (June 3–4, 1999) suggested that an intergovernmental conference would take place in 2000 so as to solve the fundamental issues, namely, the size and composition of the EC and the weighting of votes in the Council (the Feira European Council from June 19 to 20, 2000 added the issue of closer forms of cooperation, which was set out by the Amsterdam treaty under restrictive conditions).

Thus, the most serious challenge remained the effective operation of institutions with the 25 member states. To understand the seriousness of the problem, the EC of the fifteen (20 members) would have to reach 30 members with the inclusion of 10 Commissioners from the acceding states. The EP, elected in June 2004, approved Barroso Commission, which undertook office on November 1, 2004 and the College of Commissioners was composed of 25 members, one for each member state. The right to vote in the Council of Ministers was given on May 1, 2004. Equally important, the weighting of votes in the Council of the EU since January 1, 2007 was as follows: France, Germany, Italy, and UK (29 votes each); Spain, Poland (27 votes each); Romania (14 votes); the Netherlands (13 votes); Belgium, Czech Republic, Greece, Hungary, Portugal (12 votes each); Austria, Bulgaria, Sweden (10 votes each); Denmark, Finland, Ireland, Lithuania, Slovakia (7 votes each); Cyprus, Estonia, Latvia, Luxembourg, Slovenia (4 votes each); Malta (3 votes).

The number of votes for the achievement of a qualified majority was 255 out of 345.

## THE NICE TREATY: AN EFFORT TO KEEP INTEGRATION MOMENTUM

European Council met in Nice on December 7, 8, and 9, 2000 (French Presidency) to set out the amendments to be made to the TEU. The Council approved the report on CSDP, adopted the agreement on the statute for a European company (for companies operating in more than one member country), adopted the European social agenda to enforce and modernize social issues, and dealt with priority objectives to enforce employment and social protection over a five-year period. It further strengthened measures relating to maritime safety and it set up a European food safety authority, with an advisory role. It also enforced freedom, security, and justice through the mutual recognition of judicial decisions and the introduction of Eurojust (a body to forward cooperation in criminal justice) and put in place an action plan for mobility in order to develop mobility within Europe for students, researchers, and teachers.

In order to accommodate the rise in the number of cases being brought before the Court of Justice and the Court of First Instance of the European Communities, the treaty also introduced reforms to the structure and functioning of the judiciary which strengthened its capacity, particularly through the provision for specialist judicial chambers to hear appeals on certain subjects at first instance.

The Nice Council facilitated and made more flexible the "enhanced cooperation" procedure (established by the Treaty of Amsterdam to enable some member countries to proceed faster in European integration areas) and widened the scope of enhanced cooperation to include the CFSP of the union. Three states (UK, Ireland, and Sweden) succeeded to limit the cooperation arguing that it had to be constrained to the application of common actions or positions agreed unanimously by the Council and could not take place in issues with military or defense implications.

According to the provisions of the treaty, the European Council took the right to appoint the Commission President by qualified majority (and not by unanimity), and nominated the members of the EC, who then had to be approved by the EP. Concerning the representation of states in commission, the treaty ruled that the big five states would have only one Commissioner each as of January 1, 2005 and upon accession each of the new member countries would be entitled to appoint one Commissioner. There was no significant progress on extending qualified majority voting in the Council, even though this had been an urgent issue to prevent the unanimity principle from leading to institutional paralysis after enlargement.

With regard to qualified majority voting, the most important factor was the weighting of votes in the Council of Ministers and how they were allocated among the member states. The Treaty of Nice made decision-making more difficult by imposing three conditions, namely, weighted majority of votes, numerical majority of the member countries, and majority of the union's population.

The Treaty of Nice was finally signed on February 26, 2001. As far as it concerned ratification process, in Ireland, (the first country to vote, on June 7, 2001), the "no" campaign won by a 54% majority. Despite the negative result, the leaders of the EU noted that any renegotiation of the Treaty of Nice was ruled out and that the timetable for the accession of new member states would remain intact. However, in a second referendum, held on October 19, the Irish voters were convinced for the necessity of the treaty and voted "yes" by 62.9% of the votes. The other ratifications were spread over a long period and the Treaty of Nice entered into force on February 1, 2003.

## THE SIXTH ENLARGEMENT (ROMANIA AND BULGARIA)

Romania and Bulgaria signed, on February 1 and March 8, 1993 respectively the association agreements that established the framework for their accession into the EU. The agreements entered into force on February 1, 1995 and included all necessary details for the gradual establishment of a free trade area, the application of political dialogue, approximation of legislation, and issues of economic, financial, and cultural cooperation.

Despite the volition of the two states for quick accession, they fall behind in the reforms needed to attain the Copenhagen criteria and they were experiencing fundamental hurdles in transposing the Community acquis into national law. This led the EC to issue, in July 1997, a negative opinion on the accession applications of the two states despite their progress in the fulfillment of the economic criteria. As a result, Bulgaria and Romania were not within the group of states with which accession negotiations were to begin in 1998.

Finally, the Helsinki European Council of December 10 and 11, 1999 accepted the EC's new opinion to open the accession negotiations and began in February 2000, bilateral intergovernmental conferences. The accession negotiations with the two countries were concluded in 2004 and on February 22, 2005, the EC issued a positive opinion on the applications for accession to the EU. On April 25, 2004, the Council of the EU accepted Bulgaria and Romania applications for accession and the representatives of the two states signed the Treaty of Accession to the EU in Luxembourg. Two years later, the EC's final Monitoring Report on the state of preparedness for accession in Bulgaria and Romania was positive and following Council approval on October 17, 2006, the accession of the two countries took place on January 1, 2007.

## THE EUROPEAN CONVENTION (FEBRUARY 2002–JULY 2003)

A draft declaration was presented at the Laeken European Council (December 14 and 15, 2001) but the tensions between the larger EU members states remained. The European Council concluded on the need of a convention with the responsibility to prepare an intergovernmental conference where the ultimate decisions would have been taken. A declaration settled the composition of the Convention. The latter would have as Chairman Valéry Giscard d'Estaing, former president of the French Republic, was helped by two

Vice-Chairmen, namely, Giuliano Amato—former president of the Italian Council, and Jean-Luc Dehaene—former Belgian prime minister.

Giscard d'Estaing organized wisefully the work of the convention so as to attain maximum transparency and to facilitate consensus building. Initially, there was a listening period which gave the opportunity to the members of the convention to express their opinions on many issue areas and subjects such as the content of subsidiarity, the provisions of the Charter of fundamental rights, the legal personality of the union, economic governance, EU external action, EU defense, simplification of procedures, security, and justice. Finally, the phase of proposing and finalizing a draft text was realized between January and July of 2003.

On institutional issues France, Spain, and UK favored a permanent European Council President and a European foreign affairs chief while Germany desired an enhanced role for the president of the Commission. The Benelux states had a preference for a Commission President elected by the EP, while the EP favored an enforcement of its powers and competences. Small- and medium-sized states of EU and all the candidate states desired equality between member states, maintenance of the inclusion of a representative in the Commission of all the countries in the union, and perseverance of the rotating presidency of the Council.

Giscard published his own institutional proposals on April 22, 2002 and looked after for a balance between the big countries of the union, which had the largest populations and were the biggest contributors to the budget of the union, and the other countries, which were more numerous (but had smaller populations) and were net beneficiaries of Community funds.

Giscard d'Estaing submitted the final draft to the European Council meeting in Thessaloniki on June 20, 2003 but it took over a year and several meetings before the European Constitution was adopted by the Brussels European Council (June 17 and 18, 2004) despite tensions among member states. The treaty establishing a constitution for Europe was signed in Rome on October 29, 2004 by the representatives of the twenty-five member states with the ambition to simplify institutional working and to maximize the positive spillovers of the principles and competences of EU functioning.

The treaty included a preamble, four parts (448 articles) and 36 protocols. Two annexes were attached to the treaty together with 41 declarations adopted by the intergovernmental conference. More specifically, the treaty was structured as follows: (a) Preamble; (b) Part I—Constitution (Definition and objectives of the Union); (c) Part II—The Charter of fundamental rights of the union; (d) Part III—The policies and functioning of the union; (e) Part IV—General and final provisions; (f) Protocols and annexes; (g) Final act.

## THE TREATY OF LISBON

The treaty for a constitution for Europe (signed in Rome on October 29, 2004) did not enter into force due to negative referendums in France and the Netherlands and despite the fact that it had been ratified by eleven EU countries. The only solution to the crisis seemed to be a new reform and a far less ambitious treaty and it led to the Treaty of Lisbon, approved on December 13, 2007, (in force since December 1, 2009) which amended the TEU and the Treaty establishing the European Community. The new treaty was titled the TFEU.

The new treaty merged the three pillars (the Community and two areas of intergovernmental cooperation), gave legal personality to the EU (which replaced the communities), put in place fundamental institutional reforms, and made the Charter of fundamental rights legally binding. It also enforced the legislative and budgetary powers of the EP, it extended qualified majority voting in the Council, and it created the post of High Representative of the Union for Foreign Affairs and Security Policy and strengthened the role of national parliaments.

On June 12, 2008, Ireland, rejected by referendum, the treaty, and the solution recommended by the June 2008 European Council, was to continue the ratification process that had been started. By that stage, the parliaments of the 19 member states had already approved the treaty and a renegotiation of the text was inconceivable. After obtaining further guarantees from the European Council, Ireland held a second referendum on October 2, 2009 obtaining a positive vote. The ratification of the treaty from the national parliaments of the other member states permitted the Treaty of Lisbon to enter into force on December 1, 2009.

## THE ACCESSION OF CROATIA IN EU (JULY 1, 2013)

Croatia signed the stabilization and association agreement on October 29, 2001 (the agreement entered into force on February 1, 2005). It officially applied for membership in the EU on February 21, 2003 in Athens conference but it was only after the positive opinion by the EC (COM, 2004, 257 final) that the European Council granted Croatia the status of candidate country for membership in EU. Negotiations started on October 3, and it was on June 30, 2011 that EU closed the accession negotiations with Croatia and gave green light for the signature of the Accession Treaty on December 9, 2011. Croatia's accession to the EU was supported by 66.27% of Croatian citizen at the referendum of January 22, 2012 and after ratification of Accession Treaty from the Croatian Parliament, Croatia became a member of EU on July 1, 2013.

The Act on Cooperation between the Parliament and the Government of the Republic of Croatia in European Affairs outlined that the Parliament controlled the government's work within the EU institutions, participated in the cooperation between national parliaments, cooperated with the EP, and reviewed all EU reports and documents.

## WHICH THEORETICAL FRAMEWORK EXPLAINS THE DYNAMICS OF EUROPEAN INTEGRATION?

A variety of interpretations by political scientists and political economists has been proposed so as to analyze the theoretical framework behind the successes and failures of European integration (for further analysis, see Eichengreen, 2006; Sadeh and Verdun, 2009). Key questions often arised. Which are the trade-offs and the costs-benefits when heterogeneous populations are integrated under a common authority? Is economic, institutional, and political unification feasible when various population groups have different cultures, identities, and preferences for public policies and institutions? (Alesina and Spolaore, 1997; 2003). Does gradual integration, which is successful in issue areas with low costs, deliver the same positive results in issue areas with much higher heterogeneity costs?

There are different views on how European integration progress had been advanced (Burgess, 2000; Staab, 2008) but the two most influential are functionalism and intergovernmentalism.

Intergovernmentalists favor European integration through the cooperation of national governments while supranational functionalists favor supranational institutions building and issue areas cooperation. The latter fully inspired by Jean Monnet's perception to delegate functions to supranational institutions in technical and economic issue areas expect the spontaneous spillover of integration in other issue areas over time.

According to intergovernmentalists, European integration not only did not undermine the nation state, as federalists argued, but it strengthened it under adverse economic and political conditions in west Europe after 1945. They further suggested that the development of the EC was part of the postwar reconstruction of the European nation state and consequently the process required the delimitation of specific areas of national sovereignty in favor of the supranational.

Milward asked himself in his book, *The Reconstruction of Western Europe*, why the nation states in west Europe surrendered sovereignty to a supranational entity at the same time that they were becoming more powerful and had no reason to do it. How could European nation states be strengthening and weakening within this integration process? He underlined that "there is no . . . antithesis between the nation state and supranationality" and that "the evolution of the Community since 1945 has been an integral part of the reassertion of the nation state as an organizational concept."

According to his analysis, the ECSC facilitated a diplomatic reconciliation between France and Germany, without which stability in west Europe would have been an illusion and he noted that the European payments union facilitated trade flows, without which Western Europe could not have prospered.

As time passed priorities of involving in the integration process states diverged. The reunified Germany's priority was enlargement of the union to include east and central Europe states enforcing its position in Europe. The tensions in the Franco-German relations were evident in 1998 (President Chirac's disagreed about the Presidency of the ECB with Chancellor Kohl) and in 1999 (President Chirac's disagreed with Gerhard Schröder over European spending on agriculture) and culminated in Vittel summit (on 10 November 2000) when the two countries openly disagreed about the weighting of votes in European Council and about the number of European Commissioners.

Moravcsik (1993, 1998) suggested that national governments have established European institutions so as to pursue their own economic interests. Based on his theoretical framework of LI, Moravcsik argued (1993) that from the Treaty of Rome to the Maastricht Treaty, "The EC has developed through a series of celebrated intergovernmental bargains, each of which set the agenda for an intervening period of consolidation" (1993, 473); thus "the EC can be analysed as a successful intergovernmental regime designed to manage economic interdependence through negotiated policy coordination."

> Refinements and extensions of existing theories of foreign economic policy, intergovernmental negotiation and international regimes, provide a plausible and generalisable explanation of its evolution. Such theories rest on the assumption that state behavior reflects the rational actions of governments constrained at home by domestic societal pressures and abroad by their strategic environment. An understanding of the preferences and power of its member states is a logical starting point for analysis. Although the EC is a unique institution, it does not require a sui generis theory." (1993, 474)

Accordingly, (Moravcsik, 2012) the euro mirrors the interests of powerful national producers underlining the link from domestic economic interests to national policies toward European integration process (see also Frieden, 1998, 2002).

Moravcsik further insisted that integration takes place in three stages. Initially, states formulate preferences expressed by domestic groups, in the framework of international constraints. Second, they reach agreements in international negotiations, where bargaining power is heavily influenced by differential preference intensity. Finally, they establish sovereignty institutions for the fulfillment of the agreements so as to limit transaction costs and to control domestic agendas. Preferences and power do play a key role on the content of newly formed supranational institutions.

Two episodes in the European integration theory seem to approve the intergovernmental thesis. The first one is when De Gaulle in 1960s had blocked the transition to the new decision-making system in EEC because of a negative attitude toward federalism and because it was in favor of French national interests. Efforts to bridge the gap and to enforce Franco-German (Élysée Treaty of January 22, 1963) proved unsuccessful and the "empty chair" crisis in 1965 took place bringing the European Community's institutions near to a standstill.

Indeed, the "empty chair crisis" was a shock for the embryonic EEC institutional building as French politicians did not participate in the European Council and its committee substructure causing a standstill in European operation. The main reason for the crisis was the proposal of the EC to provide resources for the CAP between the end of the initial financial regulation in 1965 and the expiration of the transitional period in 1970. The way the commission proposed the budgetary system broke the golden rule of unanimity and ignored indirectly the French position and thus annoyed President De Gaulle. The crisis was initially aggravated despite French-German meetings and led France to announce on June 30, 1965 that it recalled its permanent representative as well as that French officials would no more take part in European Council or its committees. De Gaulle insisted until the Luxembourg compromise (January 1966), whereby it was agreed that although European Council could take decisions by qualified majority vote, de facto a state could prevent a vote being taken by claiming that "when very important issues are at stake discussions must be continued until unanimous agreement is reached." The Council gave green light to temporary funding for the CAP in 1966 and the EC plans to revise budgetary process collapsed. Although national interests of strong states prevailed over community's common interests, the worst did not take place and this meant after six months of institutional paralysis that European integration edifice survived.

The second episode took place because of the Margaret Thatcher's intergovernmentalist thesis that European Community should not enter high politics but should stay on issue areas like the abolition of obstacles to trade and investment. The former issues should be solved on an intergovernmental basis and thus based on the primacy of national interests she underlined the unfairness of UK's contribution in European Community budget. After fierce negotiations and temporary measures the issue was finally solved at the Fontainebleau meeting during the French presidency (the agreement did reduce UK's contribution by ten billion pounds in the period 1984–1990). Demands for budgetary reform helped the EEC to put its finances in order in the early 1980s and to control CAP expenditures while her support in favor of deregulation and economies of scale provided a powerful impetus for the SMP later in the decade.

Thatcher also disagreed with her counterparts on the issues of cohesion policy and monetary union, which were considered economically unsound and politically undesirable. Of course, one should not avoid noting that other countries too (Denmark and Sweden) were skeptical of integration processes to sharing national sovereignty in key issue areas of high politics so as to attain monetary and economic targets.

The rejection of the EDC from France and the success of the ECSC enforced political realism in the mind of Jean Monnet (Duchêne, 1994). It became evident that issue area integration in low politics issues such as coal and steel could be achieved while integration in high politics issue areas such as defense and policy coordination would face too strong opposition. The treaty of Paris, which went on to establish the ECSC, proved to be a turning point, not only for Franco-German affairs, which often dominated and dictated the events of the continent over the last several centuries, but for European affairs as a whole.

Functionalists argue that European integration process is influenced heavily by national elites and sectoral interest groups that transcend national boundaries highlighting the role of key figures like Jean Monnet in the 1950s and Jacques Delors in the 1980s. The approach underlines the results of transferring functions like the regulation of coal and steel production to the ECSC or the monetary policy to the ECB which after a certain period leads to further integration in other issue areas of the economy, not only economic but also political (Haas, 1964, 1975; Pierson, 1996; Sandholtz and Stone Sweet, 1998).

The functionalists also suggest that learning process is vital in integration enforcement as political figures and interest groups see the advantages of integrating a few issue areas and will desire more. Learning also alters the preferences of people since falling obstacles to communication and interaction and convergence of values and norms lead to the desire for more integration.

In his book, *The Uniting of Europe* (1958), Ernst B. Haas (1958, 11) argues that integration should be conceived "not as a condition but as a process, the conceptualization relies on the perception of interests and values by the actors participating in the process." National economic interests will gradually coincide and expand into several issue areas through spill over process.

As Schumann also notes in his declaration, "Europe will not be made all at once, or according to a single plan. It will be built through concrete achievements." Thus, incompleteness in one issue area of the economy forms the basis for further integration in another issue area. Moreover, technocrats lead the integration process since politicians and voters are much less informed and consequently could not perceive the content and complexity of integration (Pierson, 1996; Eichengreen, 2006). Crises are also understood through different analytical lens since they create windows of opportunity for intensification of European integration contrary to intergovernmentalism which examines them as influential factors to rebalance national interests.

Although functionalism was considered a useful approach to the perception of European integration in the 1950s and early 1960s (Haas, 1975), the "empty chair crisis" put his main arguments in doubt. As already mentioned French president Charles de Gaulle boycotted the institutions of European Community and denied more supranational integration. The solution was an "intergovernmentalist" (the Luxembourg compromise in 1966), in which de facto veto power was delivered to every state of the European Community on issues of important national interest. Another issue area of low integration performance is that of CFSP where national governments are unwilling to share sovereignty.

However, functionalists regained ground in the 1980s and 1990s when Jacques Delors became head of the EC and when charismatic leaders as the German chancellor Helmut Kohl and the French president Francois Mitterrand permitted deeper economic and monetary integration. Jacques Delors promoted single market fully aware of its positive and long-term "spillovers" (the fact that action in one issue area necessitates involvement in related issue areas) on the establishment of an operational common market with free circulation of production factors.

In 1992 the TEU at Maastricht put stronger foundations for European institutional structures and forwarded EMU, setting the framework for the euro.

As Padoa-Schioppa (2004, 14), one of the architects of the EMU and member of the Delors Committee, eloquently underlined that

> the road toward the single currency looks like a chain reaction in which each step resolved a preexisting contradiction and generated a new one that in turn required a further step forward. The steps were the start of the EMS [European monetary system] (1979), the re-launching of the single market (1985), the decision to accelerate the liberalization of capital movements (1986), the launching of the project of monetary union (1988), the agreement of Maastricht (1992), and the final adoption of the euro (1998).

Although EMU lagged in fundamental traits of an OCA (absence of a lender of last resort, no banking union, no fiscal union) it was believed that the incompleteness could set in motion processes for deeper integration in due course. As countries of euroarea become economically more homogeneous after the launch of euro, preferences and economic behavior endogenously converge, emphasizing macroeconomic stability. Centralized European authority in key issue areas efficiently provides public goods (such as monetary stability) with lower transaction cost and without the danger of free riding.

Overall, successful integration is more likely to succeed in issue areas such as commercial integration, where heterogeneity obstacles are low but when heterogeneity costs increase integration becomes politically prohibitive, operational inefficiencies are intensified and interstate crises erupt. Thinking that incomplete and inefficient arrangements are better than no agreements, functionalists do not feel pessimists when state disputes over integration put obstacles to European Community issues.

Functionalists suggest that as manufacturers and interest groups cooperated in Coal and Steel Community with each other and interacted with the Community's institutions, (mainly the high authority), spillovers press participating states to transfer responsibility for other issue areas and expand European governance. According to their theory, it is not only ECSC but also EEC in 1958 (which put in place a common market for goods and realized the free movement of all factors of production) which is a success integration story for their method.

Lastly, they underline the role of institutions in European integration and especially the role of the ECJ. It is beyond dispute that the Court of European Community did play an influential role in European integration through fundamental decisions when the participating states in European integration process and the supranational institutions disagree in key issues of economic regulations (Pierson, 1996; Stone Sweet, 2000). The court insisted that European Community norms influence member countries (Weiler, 1991; Krasner, 1999) and that European Community individuals could make reference to European law before member countries and European courts (i.e., the 1963 case of Van Gend en Loos v Nederlandse Administratie der Belastingen, case 26/62, which favored a Dutch importer of German chemical products that had objected to a tariff charged by the Dutch authorities in violation of article 12 of the Treaty of Rome, which forbids member states from raising customs duties between themselves or introducing new ones).

## CONCLUSIONS

The history of European integration reflects the tension between national governments of member states as well as between supranational institutions of EU and national governments. Nevertheless, intergovernmentalism and federalism are not irreconcilable. Although European integration is based on compromises of national interests and is guided by political and bureaucratic elites prioritizing national economic targets, one should not underestimate the role of European institutions in the depending on European integration. Moreover, as Joseph Weiler (1999, 239) argued, integration cannot be understood without an axiological dimension, a commitment to "the promise of Europe" that mobilized its political leaders.

The evolution of European Community was admiral. Although the initial agreement did fall short of Jean Monnet's and Robert Schuman's ambitions, the integration process attained major milestones. The free circulation of people, goods, and services within EU reduced national economic antagonism. Small states of the union gained negotiation strength through collective EU institutions. The most important success however is that Europe is after 72 years an area of peace, mutual respect, and democracy. EU also contributed to European stability by helping to consolidate democracy in regimes in Southern and Eastern Europe.

The evolution of the European integration provides key lessons and useful points for reflection. At first, establishing and functioning effectively a supranational organization is not a one-off act but is a dynamic and complex one which goes through progressive stages of integration. Too often national political leaders follow short-term electoral motives and adopt protectionist attitudes which are at the detriment not only of interstate relations but also of the long-term welfare of their citizens. However, having in mind that they will not be in power when the problems erupt the politicians prefer myopic political gains and not long-term benefits from integration.

Second, and highly relevant to the aforementioned point, the EU institutions lack flexibility to address challenges of the political and economic environment; when they finally act the people perceive their policies as "too little-too late." Thus, although the EU provides a useful framework for cooperation for its countries to reach concerted actions to several issue areas it does not have a centralized and effective operating system of immediate actions when needed in key economic and political problems. This reality enforces Euroskepticism and downgrades the high importance of EU work.

On the other hand, EU is also in front of great challenges. The European social model has not gone too far. The CAP did not bear the competitiveness improvements it was designed to deliver. Growth of EU is anemic and euroarea faces structural and design problems. Structural funds did not eliminate regional inequalities and productive distortions. Even more important Brexit was realized having brought a strong hit in the heart of European integration process.

Regardless of the future of EU and euroarea, European integration is thus far an important process that has benefited European nations. It is too early to reach a jury on whether European economic and political integration is enduring or it will fall over due to insisting interstate rivalries, political populism, and unexpected international economic problems. Even if the latter comes true, nothing can reduce the impact of European integration process in the last seven decades and nothing can limit the value of European institutions.

Is there a prospect of political union in EU after two or three decades? The jury remains out but the contradiction holds firm between a consensus on common European destiny in economic, political, and technological issues and an equally tremendous Euroskepticism that European identity and solidarity are ideals not suitable for current problems in the European continent.

## BIBLIOGRAPHY

Alesina, Alberto and Enrico, Spolaore. 1997. "On the number and size of nations". *Quarterly Journal of Economics*, 112(4): 1027–1056.

Alesina, Alberto and Enrico, Spolaore. 2003. *The size of nations.* Cambridge, MA: MIT Press.

Alesina, Alberto and Perotti, Roberto. 2004. "The European Union: A politically incorrect view". *Journal of Economic Perspectives,* 18(4): 27–48.

Berger, Ritschl. 1995. "Germany and the political economy of the marshall plan: 1947–1952, a revisionist view". In *Europe's Postwar Recovery*, ed. Eichengreen Barry, 199–245. Cambridge: Cambridge University Press.

Boltho, Andrea and Eichengreen, Barry. 2008. "The economic impact of european integration". Discussion paper no 6820, *Center for economic policy research*, May, London.

Brian, Aristide. 1930. "Memorandum on the organization of a regime of European federal union". *International Cocilliation,* Special bulletin, June 17th may.

Burgess, Michael. 1995. *The british tradition of federalism.* London: Leicester University Press.

Burgess, Michael. 2000. *Federalism and European Union: The building of Europe, 1950–2000.* London: Routledge.

Bull, Martin and Newell, James. 2005. *Italian politics: Adjustment under duress.* London: Polity.

Coudenhove-Kalergi, R. N. 1923. *Pan-Europa, Vienna: Pan-Europa-Verlag*, translated as Pan-Europa. New York: A. A. Knopf, 1926.

Delzell, Charles F. 1960. "The European federalist movement in Italy: First phase, 1918–1947". *Journal of Modern History,* 32(3), September: 244–245.

Desmond, Dinan. 2014. "The historiography of European integration". In *Origins and evolution of the European Union*, second edition, ed. Dinan Desmond, 345–375. Oxford: Oxford University Press.

Duchêne, François. 1994. *Jean Monnet: The first statesman of iInterdependence.* New York: Norton.

Eichengreen, Barry. 2006. "European integration". In *Oxford handbook of political economy*, eds. Barry R. Weingast and Donald A. Wittman, 799–813. Oxford: Oxford University Press.

Eichengreen, Barry. 2012. "European Monetary Integration with benefit of hindsight". *Journal of Common Market Studies*, 50(1): 123–136.

Frieden, Jeffry A. 1998. "The Euro: Who wins? who loses?". *Foreign Policy*, 112: 24–40.

Frieden, Jeffry A. 2002. "Real sources of European currency policy: Sectoral interests and European Monetary Integration". *International Organization,* 56(4): 831–860.

Garrett, Geoffrey. 1993. "The politics of Maastricht". *Economics and Politics,* 5(2): 105–123.

Garton, Ash Timothy. 1993. *In Europe's name: Germany and the divided continent.* New York: Random House.

Gilbert, Mark. 2012. *European integration: A concise history.* Lanham: Rowman & Littlefield.

Haas, Ernst B. 1958. *The uniting of Europe: Political, social, and economic forces, 1950–1957.* Stanford, CA: Stanford University Press.

Haas, Ernst B. 1964. *Beyond the nation-state: Functionalism and international organization.* Stanford CA: Stanford University Press.

Haas, Ernst B. 1975. *The obsolence of regional integration theory.* Institute of International Studies, University of California.

Hallstein, Walter. 1962. *United Europe: Challenge and opportunity.* Cambridge, MA: Harvard University Press.

Henderson, David R. 2008. "German Economic Miracle", *The Concise Encyclopedia of Economics,* Library of Economics and Liberty, http://www.econlib.org/library/Enc/GermanEconomicMiracle.html, accessed 10th June 2017.

Jovanović, Miroslav. 2005a. *European coal and steel, The economics of European integration limits and prospects.* Cheltenham, UK: Edward Elgar.

Jovanović, Miroslav. 2005b. *European economic integration: Limits and prospects.* London: Routledge.

Karen, Alter and Steinberg, David. 2007. *The theory and reality of ECSC.* Working paper no. 07-001, January, Buffett center for international and comparative studies working paper series, USA.

Keynes, John Maynard. 1920. *The economic consequences of the Peace.* New York: Harcourt, Brace, and Howe.

Krasner, Stephen D. 1999. *Sovereignty: Organized hypocrisy.* Princeton: Princeton University Press.

Marsh, David. 2011. *The Euro: The battle for the new global currency.* New Haven: Yale University Press.

Milward, Alan. 1984. *The reconstruction of western Europe, 1945–1951.* Berkeley: University of California Press.

Milward, Alan. 1992. *The European rescue of the nation state.* Berkeley: University of California Press.

Mioche, Philippe. 2004. *Les cinquantes annees de carbon et de l'acier.* Luxembourg: Commission Europeenne.

Monnet, Jean. 1978. *Memoirs*. Garden city, NY: Doubleday & Company Inc.
Moravcsik, A. 1993. "Preferences and power in the European community: A liberal intergovernmentalist approach". *Journal of Common Market Studies,* 4: 473–524.
Moravcsik, Andrew. 1998. *The choice for Europe, social purpose and state power from Messina to Maastricht.* Ithaca: Cornell University Press.
Padoa-Schioppa, Tommaso. 2004. *The Euro and its central bank. Getting united after the Union.* Cambridge, MA: MIT Press.
Pierson, Paul. 1996. "The path to European integration: A historical institutionalist analysis". *Comparative Political Studies,* 29: 123–163.
Poelmans, Eline. 2012. "Changes in the structure of coal and steel industries under the ECSC (1952–1967): Was West Germany kept "Small"?". *Essays in Economic & Business History, The journal of the Economic and Business Historical Society,* 30, Bucknell University Press: 5–29.
Poidevin, Raymond. 1986. *Origins of European integration, March 1948–May 1950.* Brusseles: Bruylant.
Rector, David. 2009. *Federations: The political dynamics of cooperation.* Ithaca: Cornell University Press.
Sadeh, Tel and Verdun, Amy. 2009. "Explaining Europe's monetary union: A survey of the Literature". *International Studies Review,* 11: 277–301.
Seidel, Katja. 2010. *The process of politics in Europe: The rise of European elites and supranational institutions.* London: Tauris Academic.
Sontag, Raymond J. 1971. *A broken world: 1919–1939.* New York: Harper and Row.
Staab, Andreas. 2008. *The European Union explained: Institutions, actors, global impact.* Bloomington: Indiana.
Steiner, Zara. 2007. *The Lights that failed: European international history, 1919–1933.* Oxford: Oxford University Press.
Stone, Sweet Alec. 2000. *Governing with judges: Constitutional politics in Europe.* Oxford: Oxford University Press.
Streiff, René. 1950. "Le plan Monnet et l'économie française en 1950". *L'information Géographique,* 14(5): 169–182.
Strirk, M.R and Weigall, David. 1999. *The origins and development of European integration: A reader and commentary.* London and New York: Pinter.
Weiler, Jospeh H. 1991. "The transformation of Europe". *Yale Law Journal,* 100: 2403–2483.

## FURTHER READING

Craig, Parsons. 2003. *A certain idea of Europe.* Ithaca: Cornell University Press.
Deak, Francis. 1931. "Can Europe unite?" *Political Science Quarterly,* 46(3), September: 424–433.
Dyson, Kenneth and Featherstone, Kevin. 1999. *The road to Maastricht. Negotiating economic and monetary union.* Oxford: Oxford University Press.
Gillingham, John. 2003. *European integration, 1950–2003: Superstate or new market economy?* Cambridge: Cambridge University Press.

Gillingham, John. 2005. *Coal, steel, and the rebirth of Europe, 1945–1955*. Cambridge: Cambridge University Press.
Heater, Derek. 1992. *The idea of European unity*. New York: St. Martin's Press.
Herzog, Peter E. 1966. "The Procedure before the court of justice of the European communities". *Washington Law Review*, 438: 438–488.
Lipgens, Walter. 1985. *Documents on the history of European integration*, vol. 1. Baden-Baden: Nomos Verlag.
Lipgens, Walter. 1986. *Documents on the history of European integration,* vol. 2. Baden-Baden: Nomos Verlag.
Lipgens, Walter and Loth, W. 1988. *Documents on the history of European integration,* vol. 3. Berlin: De Gruytes.
Mayne, Richard. 1962. *The community of Europe: Past, present, and future.* New York: Norton.
Mitrany, David. 1965. "The prospect of integration: Federal or functional", *Journal of Common Market Studies,* 4(2): 119–150.
Molle, Willem. 1996. *The economics of integration: Theory, practice, policy,* Fifth edition. Aldershot: Ashgate Limited.
Sandholtz, Wayne and Sweet, Alec Stone. 1998. *European integration and supranational governance.* Oxford: Oxford University Press.
Weber, Eugen. 1976. *Peasants into Frenchmen: The modernization of rural France, 1870–1914*. Stanford: Stanford University Press.

## FURTHER QUESTIONS

1. How important was the impact of different ideological perceptions of integration on the formation of the ECSC and EEC?
2. Why did the ECSC succeeded when the EDC and the EPC failed?
3. Do opt-outs put significant obstacles in European integration process?
4. Analyze the role of USA in enforcing European integration process in 1950s.
5. Which were the main reasons for the establishment of EEC? Which are the fundamental differences/similarities of EEC relative to other integration efforts after 1945 in Western Europe?
6. Did Cold War political and security terms influence the content and speed of European integration in west Europe?
7. Why the six states established ECSC, EEC, and EURATOM?

# *Chapter 4*

# The Institutional Framework of the European Union

## THE PILLARS OF EU LAW

EU is not the result of a military conflict but was created from political will and is based from the beginning on legal rules, acts, and specific institutional procedures. Walter Hallstein, (first president of the EC in the period 1958–1967) noted in a speech (March 1962) that "the European Economic Community is a community of law [Rechtsgemeinschaft] . . . because it serves to realize the idea of law" (in 1986 the European Court of Justice used the words of Hallstein in the case of Les Verts v Parliament, C-294/83).

The rule of law includes key principles such as the obligation of officials to act within the framework of EU law following specific procedures for the legal amendments, and the obligation of EU institutions to apply laws which are general (applicable to all physical or legal entities in a similar situation) and are publicly available. However, in critical moments for the integration project, the EU faced its problems not only by the conviction that rules should be followed but also by the use of EU laws and institutions so as to enhance and deepen integration, what has been known as integration through law.

The provisions of EU treaties set the targets of the EU, the procedures for EU institutions, the content of the decision-making system, and the links between member countries and the EU. Significant roles in the creation, implementation, interpretation, and enforcement of EU law are played by the European Commission, the Parliament, and the Council. The ECJ interprets EU laws and controls their compatibility to the treaties while the implementation of EU law on a daily basis involves the role of national courts.

## THE KEY INSTITUTIONS OF EU

Before analyzing the prospects of EU integration process one should conceive the basic terms for integration dynamics (Leuffen et al., 2014; Schimmelfennig et al., 2014). The commonly used term of differentiated integration refers to "a model of integration strategies that tries to reconcile heterogeneity within the European Union and allows different groupings of member states to pursue an array of public policies with different procedural and institutional arrangements" (Stubb, 1996). This type of differentiation usually occurs when there is a high degree of political/economic interdependence as well as strong asymmetric politicization (Leuffen et al., 2014).

An equally important term is that of external differentiation where EU rules are implemented uniformly in all member states and selected third countries while internal differentiation refers to the situation where rules are not implemented uniformly to all EU countries because some of them do not adhere to a specific issue area of European integration (Leuffen et al., 2014).

Differentiation can be applied temporarily by some states during a transition period (multispeed Europe and à la carte Europe) or it can be applied permanently (the variable geometry or the concentric circles Europe). Examples of differentiation include the single market, EMU, the area of freedom, security and justice, the CFSP, and the CSDP.

In all issue areas of European integration the key challenge is how to reconcile federalists and inter-governmentalists, deepening (of political integration) and widening (enlargement of EU) in European integration without undermining state interests or the initial federal vision. Europhiles view differentiation as a Trojan horse to dilute the vision of a federal European state while Euroskeptics view homogenization of rules and supranational governance as Trojan horse to dilute the national sovereignty established in Europe almost 400 years ago. Euroskeptics prefer a Europe à la carte where flexibility in joining policy issue areas is not temporary but enforces national sovereignty and realizes national priorities and capabilities (usually through opt out clauses).

Schengen, for example, was initially based on an intergovernmental agreement among five member states but it was later incorporated into the EU treaties and now has 22 full participants including four non-EU states. Europhobes do not examine the questions of flexibility and convergence since they ab initio conceive all types of integration as hostile to national and people interests. Brexit rationale was based on this fear that EU will erase UK sovereignty.

Moderate federalists accept the compromise of targeted differentiation in specific policy issue areas under the condition that it is temporary, it does not undermine the final integration target, and it does not obstruct the avant-garde group of states from deepening in integration. For example, enhanced cooperation (in which a minimum of nine countries can apply advanced integration among themselves but within the EU framework) is considered a useful example of instrumental differentiation, complies with the EU treaties, as it respects the competences—rights of those countries which do not participate in it and is open to all states, subject to compliance with specific terms of participation (article 20 TEU; articles 326–334 TFEU).

It is no coincidence that at the European Council meeting on June 27, 2014, the EU's heads of state or government endorsed the commitment to an "ever closer Union," based on the TEU which "allows for different paths of integration for different countries, allowing those that want to deepen integration to move ahead, while respecting the wish of those who do not want to deepen any further" (European Council, Conclusions, Brussels, June 27, 2014).

Another example of a differentiated integration or a two-speed Europe is the EMU where the membership of the Eurozone has gradually increased from 11 to 19 member states. More specifically, TFEU notes in chapter four the provisions specific to the member states whose currency is the euro, and article 136 underlines the need for measures that strengthen coordination and surveillance of member states' budgetary discipline.

The complex institutional and legal framework of EU reflects the aforementioned debates and tries to accommodate the vertical relations of power between the states and the EU, the horizontal relations of power between EU institutions and the relations between EU and its citizens.

More specifically, the process of decision-making at EU involves the EP, (which is the representative body of EU's citizens and is elected by them), the European Council (the heads of state or government of the EU member countries), the Council (which represents the governments of the EU member states), and the EC (it represents the interests of the EU). Usually, the EC takes the legislative initiative, the EP and Council adopt them, and the member countries and the Commission apply them.

## THE EUROPEAN COUNCIL

The European Council is taking place at least four times a year and is comprised of the prime ministers and presidents along with its president and the president of the EC. However, additional meetings may take place to face key issues at the highest level usually in the issue areas of foreign policy or economics (this is why the High Representative of the Union for Foreign Affairs and Security Policy may also participate in the work of the European Council).

Representing the highest level of political cooperation between the member countries, the European Council usually reaches decisions on the direction and priorities of the EU by consensus which is mirrored in the conclusions of the meetings. There are cases of course where qualified majority applies (i.e., the election of its president, the appointment of the EC, the appointment of the High Representative of the Union for Foreign Affairs and Security Policy). Thus, the European Council has a key political role but it does not have the ability to adopt laws.

The coordination of the European Council work is taking place by its president (elected by the European Council for a once-renewable term of two and half years) who has the responsibility to convene and chair the meetings as well as the competence to represent the EU to the outside world.

## THE EURO SUMMIT

The heads of state or government of the countries who adopted the euro hold meetings at least twice a year, together with the president of the EC outside of the European Council. Established by TSCG the euro summit examines all issues related to the governance of the Eurozone.

The president of the euro summit is appointed by the heads of state or government of Eurozone countries, and its term has the same duration as that of the president of the European Council. However, the president of the EP may also be invited to participate in the euro summit meetings as well as the president of the ECB.

## THE COUNCIL

The Council is a vital EU decision-maker comprised of the ministers of EU countries who discuss, reach an agreement, and amend/adopt laws on several EU issues areas. The Council meetings are attended by one minister from each of the EU's countries according to the subjects of the Council agenda (the "configuration" of the Council). The presidency of the Council (which rotates between the countries of EU every six months) is responsible to organize and chair the different Council meetings except the Foreign Affairs Council which is chaired by the High Representative of the Union for Foreign Affairs and Security Policy.

In order to achieve continuity in the process, the 6-monthly presidencies work in groups of three and decide on a joint programme of Council work over 18 months. More specifically, the Council is responsible to pass European laws and to legislate jointly with the EP through the ordinary legislative procedure, also known as co-decision, to coordinate the EU countries' policies, to enforce the EU's CFSP, to conclude international agreements between the EU and other countries/international organizations and to decide jointly with the EP on EU budget.

Decisions are taken by vote and usually demand a qualified majority or even a unanimous vote (i.e., taxation issues). The most interesting and complex part of the process is the decision-making according to which all decisions taken by the Council have support across EU but in the same time small minorities cannot stop decisions from being taken. Thus, in case where a proposal is to be decided by qualified majority, a double majority of both EU countries and population is required (in 2017, the votes in favor must be at least 55% of the EU countries, that is, 16 of the 28 countries and EU countries must represent 65% of the EU's population). To stop a decision there must be at least four EU states voting against, representing more than 35% of the population.

The work of ministers in the different Council configurations is helped by numerous working parties and committees comprised of experts from all EU countries. Upon the submission of a legislative proposal by the Commission, the Council and the EP examine thoroughly all its content (the "reading"). In many cases there are three readings before the Council and the Parliament give approval or reject a proposal.

During the first reading, the Council's final opinion cannot be reached until the EU Parliament gives its own first reading opinion. In order to maximize transparency and legitimacy and to guarantee the technical scrutiny of the proposal, the latter passes at each reading through three levels at the Council namely working party level, permanent representatives committee (Coreper is composed of the EU national governments' permanent representatives to the EU who represent national interests at EU level and meet weekly), and Council configuration.

More specifically, the way Coreper handles the legislative proposal is linked to the level of agreement reached at working party level. If there is a clear volition for agreement without discussion, issues appear on part one of the Coreper agenda. However, issues appear in part two of the Coreper agenda if agreement has not been achieved in the working party. It is not odd in Coreper practice that proposals appear on the agenda of Coreper many times to address differences that the working party has not settled.

If Coreper reaches agreement on a proposal, the item becomes an "A" item on the Council agenda (agreement will occur without discussion and objections). On the other hand, the "B" items of the Council agenda refer to issues not decided by Council meetings, not agreed in Coreper or at working party level, or issues that are politically sensitive to be settled at a lower level.

Following the consent procedure the Council adopts legislative proposals after having the consent of the EP as the latter has the authority to accept or reject a proposal by an absolute majority vote (although it cannot amend it).

Equally important, the Council has no authority to overrule the Parliament's opinion. As a legislative procedure, consent is used when new legislation on combating discrimination is being adopted but it is also required as a non-legislative procedure, when the Council adopts certain international agreements negotiated by the EU, when there is a serious breach of fundamental rights (article 7 of the TEU), for the accession of new countries in EU and for arrangements for withdrawal from the EU.

## THE EUROPEAN COMMISSION

The commission proposes laws, policies, and programmes and applies the decisions of the EP and the Council. Further, it represents the EU to the world except in issues of foreign and security policy.

The term "Commission" refers to the institution itself (and the personnel) but also to the members of the Commission appointed by the EU countries and the Parliament (known as Commissioners). The Commission analyzes and justifies its policies in EP and replies to written and oral questions posed by members of EP. It is important to notice that it remains politically answerable to the EP, which under certain terms can dismiss it by adopting a motion of censure.

A new Commission is appointed every five years (and within six months of the elections to the EP), and the Commission President is elected by the EP. Soon after the presidential election, the members of the commission are chosen in close cooperation with EU states. The Parliament interviews all proposed members and gives its opinion on the entire "College."

The work of the Commission is complex and its president is helped by vice-presidents. Indeed, the EC has many responsibilities which are crucial for the effective management of EU institutional structure and for the accomplishment of the provisions of EU treaties.

First, it has the "right of legislative initiative" and presents proposals to the Parliament and the Council. In order to be aware of the EU problems it is in continuous discussion with the interest groups, with national parliaments and governments and with two advisory bodies, namely, the EESC (the employers' and trade union representatives) and the CoR (the representatives of local and regional authorities). Following the subsidiarity principle (dealing with things at the lowest possible level), the Commission takes action only if it considers that a problem cannot be solved more efficiently by national, regional, or local action.

Second, the EC applies EU policies and the EU budget. This is taking place under the supervision of the ECA. The role of latter is crucial since EP grants to the Commission the responsibility to apply the budget only if it agrees with the Court of Auditors' annual report. The directorates of the EC draft the Commission's legislative proposals and the College at its weekly meeting decides on their adoption. The proposals are also controlled by the legal service as well as by the relevant Commission department.

When an agreement is reached, the College adopts the legislative proposal which is sent to the Council and the EP for their consideration. However, in the case of disagreements among the Commissioners, the president may ask them to vote on it and only if the majority has a positive stance, the proposal will be adopted.

Third, the commission is considered the "guardian of the treaties" and it enforces European law (jointly with the Court of Justice). When EU law is violated the commission takes specific steps to stop the infringement. Initially, it sends to the government of an EU state an official letter analyzing why the Commission considers that an EU law is violated, and sets a deadline for sending the Commission a detailed reply. If no corrective action is taken or the action fails to correct the issues in question, the Commission refers the problem to the Court of Justice, which takes binding decisions for the state and can impose penalties.

Finally, the commission represents the EU around the world. One of the vice-presidents of the commission acts as the High Representative of the Union for Foreign Affairs and Security Policy and collaborates with the Council. Further, in the issues areas of trade policy and humanitarian aid it represents all 28 member countries.

## THE EUROPEAN PARLIAMENT

The Parliament represents the EU citizens and its members are directly elected by EU citizens in elections which are held every five years (the Parliament had in 2017, 751 MEPs from the 28 member states). The president of the parliament is elected for a 2½-year term and represents the institution to the world assisted by 14 vice-presidents. Together with the president of the Council, he signs all legislative acts once they are adopted.

Although the official seat of the EP is in Strasbourg (France), the work of the institution is taking place in Strasbourg (the meetings of the whole Parliament, known as "plenary sessions" which occur 12 times per year), Brussels (Belgium), and Luxembourg. The plenary sessions are attended by all members of the parliament and examine proposed legislation. Which are the key competences of the parliament?

First, together with the Council, it has the authority to legislate through the "ordinary legislative procedure" (or co-decision procedure). Moreover, it should give the green light for all international agreements in issue areas covered by the ordinary legislative procedure in order to be applied. Equally important, its approval is "conditio sine qua non" for significant decisions in several issue areas such as social security and harmonization of direct/indirect taxation. Normally, the Parliament takes decisions by a majority of votes cast when at least one-third of the members of EP are present for a vote. However, there are specific decisions which demand that a majority of the entire members votes positively (i.e., when the Parliament elects the Commission President or votes in the second reading of an ordinary legislative procedure).

Second, the parliament supervises all the institutional edifice of EU, has the authority to approve or reject the nomination of the president of the Commission and Commissioners, and has the power to censure the Commission as a whole leading it to resignation. Not only it holds auditions of all the members and the president of the commission to be appointed but it monitors the reports sent to it by the Commission asking for necessary clarifications. The same holds true for the work of the Council through written and oral questions. Equally important, at the opening of each EU summit, the president of the Parliament presents the Parliament's concerns on many issues listed on the European Council's agenda.

Third, the parliament holds a strong authority on EU spending and can adopt or reject the budget in its entirety. Moreover, through its committee on budgetary control it controls how the budget is spent.

## THE COURT OF JUSTICE

The General Court is composed of 28 judges appointed for a 6-year period by EU states. Its president is elected for 3 years by the 28 judges. The Court sits in chambers of 3 or 5 judges to hold hearings (in more than two-thirds of the cases) while a chamber of 13 or 28 judges meets when the case is highly complex or extremely important.

The Court of Justice of the EU (the Court) ensures that EU legislation is interpreted and applied in the same way in each member state and is identical for all parties and in all circumstances. To this end, the Court interprets EU law at the request of national courts, controls the legality of the actions of the EU institutions, and ensures that EU countries comply with their obligations. The Court of Justice is composed of 28 Judges, one from each member state, so that all the EU national legal systems are represented. Nine advocates general give reasoned opinions on the cases brought before the Court.

The Court has also the authority to settle legal disputes between EU countries, EU institutions, businesses, and individuals. To facilitate its work, since there are many cases, it is divided into two main bodies: the Court of Justice, which examines requests for preliminary rulings from national courts and specific actions for annulment and appeals, and the General Court, which provides rulings on all actions for annulment brought by citizens and firms and actions brought by EU countries. The civil service tribunal (a specialized tribunal) adjudicates in disputes between the EU and its civil servants.

In the infringement proceedings, the Commission, or (in some rare cases) an EU country, can initiate the process if it believes that a certain EU country is failing to fulfill its obligations under EU law. The allegations are investigated and if the court decides that a state is at fault, immediate action by the latter should be taken to restore the things right so as to avoid the imposition of fines.

In the proceedings for annulment an EU state, the Council, the Commission, or the Parliament considers that a particular EU law is illegal and asks the Court to annul it.

Finally, in the proceedings for failure to act, the treaty requires the European Parliament, the Council, and the Commission to decide under certain terms.

After the submission of a case to the registry at the Court, a judge and an advocate general are assigned. In the first stage of examination all the parties involved give written statements and the judge assigned summarizes them in a report which is forwarded for discussion at the Court's general meeting. During the second phase, the public hearing takes place, and after a process involving a draft ruling opinion the judges deliver their judgment by a majority.

Under the provisions of article 263 of the TFEU physical persons may appeal to the court against an EU institution for acts of direct and individual concern to them; may bring actions for annulment to cancel the implementation of a regulation, directive, or decision adopted by an institution, body, office, or agency of the EU; and may bring actions for failure to act against an EU institution failure to act.

Preliminary ruling is binding and takes place if a national court is in any doubt about the interpretation or validity of an EU law.

## THE EUROPEAN COURT OF AUDITORS

Created in 1977, the ECA is an independent external audit institution which controls the sound management of EU finances and expenditure and the correct application of EU budget. It is comprised of 28 members (one from each EU country and divided into chambers) who are appointed by the Council, after consultation with the EP, for 6 years (on their turn they elect the president of the Court of Auditors for 3 years).

In order to accomplish its mission it realizes audits of EU income or expenditure at the institutions managing the funds and the beneficiaries of the funds, publishing in detail its findings in annual reports. It also delivers to the EP and the Council the annual report on the application of the EU budget for the previous financial year. Further, when requested by other EU institutions, the court gives advice on new or revised EU regulations with financial impact.

The ECA has been very effective in many cases uncovering fraud in close cooperation with OLAF.

## THE EUROPEAN ECONOMIC AND SOCIAL COMMITTEE

The EESC (comprised of 353 members from 28 EU member states in 2017) has an advisory role in the EU edifice and serves as a framework for consultation and consensus between representatives from different professional and community associations. More specifically, the committee provides advice to the EP, the Council, and the EC, in many issue areas foreseen by the EU treaties and provides opinions on demand by EU lawmakers.

The members of the committee are appointed by the Council for five years, work independently, and are organized into employers, workers, and various interests. They held nine meetings a year in plenary sessions and opinions are approved by simple majority voting. The specific sections of the committee are the section for EMU and economic and social cohesion; the section for the single market, production, and consumption; the section for agriculture, rural development, and the environment; the section for external relations; the section for employment, social affairs, and citizenship; the section for transport, energy, infrastructure, and the information society; and the consultative commission on industrial change.

## THE COMMITTEE OF THE REGIONS

The CoR has an advisory role and is comprised of representatives of EU's regional and local authorities. Its consultation is obligatory on several issue areas such as regional policy, environment, education, and transport and on all EU legislative proposals that have an impact on local and regional authorities (i.e., civil protection). The decisions are taken during the plenary sessions by a majority vote and opinions of the committee are based on them.

The CoR members are elected politicians at municipalities or regions and are appointed by the Council after EU governments nomination for a period of five years (the president of the CoR is elected by its members, for two and half years).

The strategy and the opinions of the committee is decided during the plenary sessions (five times a year) while issues are analyzed in the six specialist commissions, namely, the Commission for territorial cohesion policy; the Commission for economic and social policy; the Commission for sustainable development; the Commission for education, youth, culture, and research; the Commission for environment, the climate change, and energy; the Commission for citizenship, governance, institutional and external affairs; and the Commission for natural resources.

## THE EUROPEAN OMBUDSMAN

The European Ombudsman is an independent institution which is elected for five years by the EP and examines the complaints from EU citizens, firms, and institutions on failed and inadequate administration by institutions of EU (i.e., discrimination, abuse of power, application of incorrect procedures). However, the Ombudsman can only examine complaints against EU institutions and bodies and not complaints against national or local government authorities.

In many cases it is suffice just to inform the institution concerned about a complaint so as to give solution to a problem. When the problem is not resolved the Ombudsman gives recommendations to find a solution and if this effort also fails he makes a special report to the EP.

## THE EUROPEAN DATA PROTECTION SUPERVISOR

The EDPS protects data and information on EU citizens and residents held by European institutions and ensures that EU institutions comply with best practice. Each EU institution has a data protection officer who ensures that certain obligations are respected. The EDPS also supervises the EU administration's processing of personal data and provides advice on policies and acts that influence privacy not only to EU institutions but also to similar institutions in EU countries.

## THE EUROPEAN INVESTMENT BANK

The EIB is owned by EU countries and provides capital and expertise for investments that support the EU targets (i.e., in the issue areas of innovation and skills, climate policies, trans-European networks for transport, energy, and IT). The money required is raised through the issuance of bonds on global markets. As EIB holds an AAA rating for her bonds, it has enough capital to finance not only loans to small and medium-sized firms but also loans (above 25 million euros) to governments and large firms.

The decisions of the bank and its general lending strategy are taken by the board of governors consisted of the ministers from all EU countries. The board of directors (chaired by the president of the bank) is responsible for the approval of lending and borrowing operations. Finally, the management committee is the bank's executive body responsible for the daily operations.

## THE DECENTRALIZED AGENCIES

The decentralized agencies have their own legal personality and are dispersed in different cities of EU (i.e., the European Banking Authority, the European Insurance and Occupational Pensions Authority, the European Securities and Markets Regulator, the Europol). There are also the EURATOM agencies and bodies which operate according to the provisions of EURATOM treaty to coordinate research on the peaceful use of nuclear energy and to guarantee the sufficiency and security terms of atomic energy.

## THE COMMON FOREIGN AND SECURITY POLICY

The CFSP is applied by the European Council and the Council working together. The main targets are to promote democratic values, the rule of law, the human rights, and freedom and the principles of equality and solidarity through partnerships with other states and organizations around the world.

More specifically, the European Council, chaired by the president, sets the CFSP taking into account the EU defense interests. The Foreign Affairs Council (chaired by the High Representative of the Union for Foreign Affairs and Security Policy) defines the ways to apply the European Council guidelines based on national and EU resources.

The EEAS acts as a foreign ministry and diplomatic service for the EU and uses thousands of experts transferred from the Council, the EU countries, and the EC. The latter is responsible for trade and funding for non-EU countries (i.e., humanitarian aid or development aid) and represents the EU in all areas of EU competence outside foreign and security policy. The EU delegations around the world are part of the EEAS and join their forces with the national embassies of EU countries. In most of the cases, decisions are taken unanimously.

Within CFSP the common security and defense issues gain momentum. Although up to the present the effort is focused on crisis management operations and humanitarian and peace-making/peace-keeping missions, there are efforts to coordinate action with NATO and to use more the common EU military resources.

The PSC analyzes the geopolitical terms and defines the EU's actions during a crisis situation abroad, the EU military committee (the chiefs of defense from all EU states) sets EU military action, while the EU military staff (the military experts who work at a permanent military headquarters in Brussels) provides crucial help to the EUMC.

## THE SOURCES AND PRINCIPLES OF EU LAW

Three are the main sources of EU law namely primary law, secondary law, and supplementary law.

Primary law stems from the TEU and the TFEU which defines competences between the EU and the member countries and clarifies the responsibilities of EU institutions. Primary law also includes the protocols annexed to the EU treaties as well as the treaties on countries' accession to the EU.

Secondary law includes unilateral acts, conventions, and agreements. Unilateral acts comprise regulations, directives, decisions, opinions, and recommendations (article 288 of the TFEU) and non-typical acts such as recommendations and communications as well as white and green papers. Conventions and agreements refer to international agreements, signed by the EU and a state/organization, agreements between EU countries and agreements between the EU institutions.

Regulations are binding and directly apply in all the EU countries as soon as they enter into force and thus it is not necessary to be transposed into national law. Further, they supersede national laws which are not compatible with their substantive provisions.

The directive is also a binding law for the implementation of a specific target but there is a need to be transposed into national law to become applicable and thus it is up to EU countries to decide the methods for implementation. This means that citizens are bound by the legal act only after the adoption of the transposing act has been adopted (in some cases the Court of Justice of the EU based on the principles of effectiveness, the prevention of treaty violations and legal protection has ruled that specific provisions of a directive may, exceptionally, have direct results). However, transposition must occur within the period laid down in the directive.

A decision is binding in its entirety and is addressed to countries of EU, groups of people, or individuals. However, an individual may invoke the rights conferred by a decision addressed to an EU state only if that country has adopted a transposing act.

Recommendations and opinions are not binding and do not give rights or apply obligations on those to whom they are addressed, but act as useful guides to the interpretation and content of EU law.

In addition to the abovementioned sources, there are supplementary sources which comprise Court of Justice case-law, international law, and general principles of law.

A principle of EU law is the "direct effect" meaning that subject to certain terms, individuals can invoke an EU law or EU provision before a national or European Court. Direct effect (used for the first time by the Court of Justice of the EU in a judgment on February 5, 1963 namely the case *NV Algemene Transporten Expeditie Onderneming van Gend en Loos v. Nederlandse Administratie der Belastingen*, case 26/62) can be applied to directives, provisions of EU treaties, regulations, and decisions.

Vertical direct effect refers to the link between EU law and domestic law, and the member country's obligation to ensure its laws are compatible with EU legislation (i.e., in *Foster v. British Gas* case, 18/89). Horizontal direct effect means that individuals can invoke the direct effect of EU treaties provisions which confer individual rights, so as to raise claims against other individuals before national courts. Finally, the indirect effect of EU law obliges national courts to interpret national law consistently with directives.

The supremacy of EU law is also a key principle and means that Community law with direct effect takes precedence over national laws (i.e., *Flaminio Costa v. ENEL*, case 6/64). Even in the case of directives where article 288 TFEU states that "a directive shall be binding, as to the result to be achieved, upon each member state to which it is addressed, but shall leave to the national authorities the choice of form and methods," the CJEU succeeded through its rulings to extend the direct effect principle.

## THE LEGISLATIVE PROCESS AND THE TYPES OF EU DECISION

EU competences are divided, according to TFEU, into exclusive competences (article 3), shared competences (article 4), and supporting competences (article 6). However, when there is no power to achieve one of the targets set out in the treaties, the institutions may implement the provisions of article 352 TFEU, and take the so-called appropriate measures.

The hierarchy of secondary legislation is laid down in articles 289, 290, and 291 of TFEU between legislative acts, delegated acts, and implementing acts. Legislative acts are adopted through the ordinary or a special legislative procedure while delegated acts are non-legislative acts of general application which supplement or amend specific non-vital elements of a legislative act (the Parliament and the Council delegate the necessary power to the Commission and define the content and duration of the delegation of power in the legislative act).

Implementing acts are adopted by the EC (and by the Council in specific cases and in areas of CFSP) where uniform terms for applying legally binding acts are necessary.

All the EU legislative initiatives are EU treaty based and comply with specific procedures. The EU treaty determines the process of decision-making and sets the rules of voting when unanimity is required, and when a qualified majority is sufficient for the Council to adopt legislation. A key distinction is made between the ordinary legislative procedure (co-decision) and the special legislative procedures, which concerns specific cases where EU Parliament has a consultative role. The usual EU decision-making process is known as ordinary legislative procedure (co-decision) in the meaning that the Parliament and the Council share legislative power and thus EP has to give green light to EU legislation together with the Council.

Initially, the Commission promotes a specific proposal, the Commission gathers different opinions from governments, firms, and civil society and the Commission proposal is presented to the Council and the Parliament. The submitted proposal is discussed by the Council and the Parliament, and in the inability to reach an agreement at the second reading the proposal is forwarded to a conciliation committee which is composed by representatives of Council and Parliament. If agreement is attained the text is sent for a third reading to the European Parliament and the Council and it becomes law.

Usually, the Parliament votes by simple majority and the Council by qualified majority and at least half of EU countries, representing about two-thirds of the EU population, must vote positively in favor.

In the special legislative process the procedure differs substantially. The EC has the right of legislative initiative, the Council is, in practice, the legislator, and the EP is required to give its consent to a legislative proposal.

During the first stage of special legislative process (consultation procedure) the Council takes the consultation of the EP on a proposal made from the Commission usually in issue areas, such as competition and internal market exemptions. During the consent process, the EP can either accept or reject the proposal, but cannot suggest any amendments. Further, there are important advisory bodies that must be consulted when proposed laws involve issues of their interest such as the EESC and the CoR or the ECB (proposals on economic or financial issues).

One should also note that European citizens can also take the initiative of a legislative proposal on a particular issue (under the condition that there are

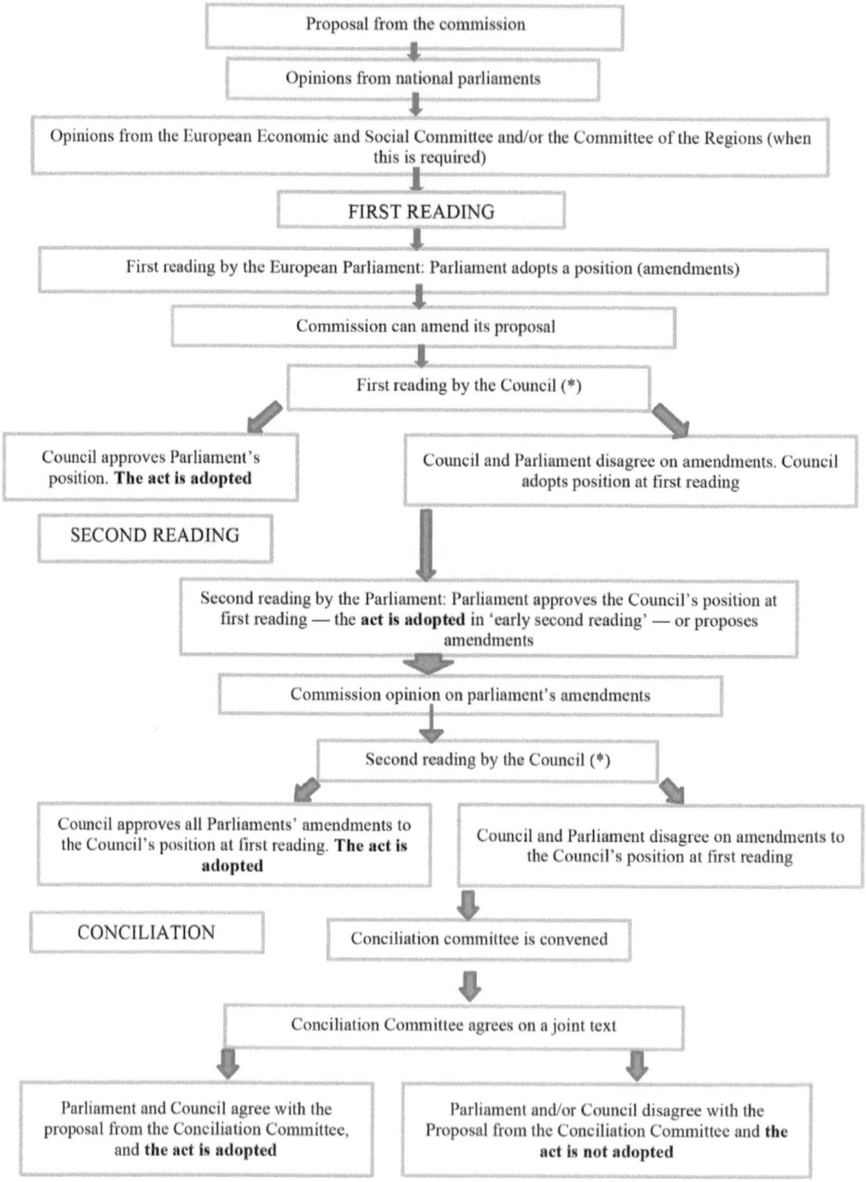


**Figure 4.1 The ordinary legislative procedure in European Union.** *European Union website, 2017.*

at least one million EU citizens from at least one quarter of the EU countries) and EP is obliged to discuss them.

When the EC forward proposals it evaluates the economic, social, and environmental impact that they may have through the impact assessments.

The parliaments of EU states express their reservations if they feel that it would be better to deal with an issue at national rather than EU level and all physical/legal persons can participate in the consultation process.

After 2009 (Lisbon Treaty provisions), there is an effective clarification of the competences of national parliaments within the EU. More specifically, national parliaments control the implementation of this principle (subsidiarity means that, except in the areas where it has exclusive powers, the EU only acts where action will be more effective at EU level than at national level) in EU decision-making. Thus, an EU national parliament gives a reasoned opinion if the draft proposal fails to comply with the principle of subsidiarity and the EC is obliged to reconsider its proposal and to decide whether to maintain, adjust, or withdraw it.

Further, there are issue areas where EU possesses exclusive competence; thus decisions are taken at EU level by the member countries meeting in the Council and the EP. In other issue areas, decision-making is shared between the EU and the countries (i.e., protection of consumers, internal market, transport, agriculture, and environment). Thus, if a law is adopted at EU level, then it has priority but if it not passed at EU level, then the countries may pass it at national level. Equally important, if an issue area is not included in a treaty, the EC cannot propose a law.

## THE ENHANCED COOPERATION

Under this process some EU countries have the ability to cooperate more closely in issue areas that are not the exclusive competence of the EU and agreement cannot be reached involving all the other EU countries. The enhanced cooperation gives the opportunity to at least nine member countries to use the EU institutions to attain closer cooperation under the condition that the cooperation promotes the targets of the EU. The process is open to all other EU countries if they wish to join (i.e., the cooperation for a unitary patenting system).

## CONCLUSIONS: IS THERE A NEED FOR INSTITUTIONAL REFORMS?

What will be the form and status of Europe in 20 years from now? It is undeniable that EU is already a union of multiple speeds and thus integration is characterized by flexibility and differentiation (Alesina and Grilli, 1993; Blockmans et al., 2017; Bresso and Brok, 2017). However, challenges demand new policy tools and reforms seem necessary.

Many questions are raised. Can reforms be applied within the EU's framework or there is a need for treaty changes? Are current institutional arrangements effective for EU multilevel governance? Is there a need to forward integration based on a core of EU states? Which are the policy priorities in this "integration deepening" strategy? Institutional flexibility is the vehicle to political union or the tool to guarantee the intergovernmental dominance in European decision-making?

Evidently, there is no consensus on the speed of integration and on the policy of integration in many issue areas rendering difficult a long-term vision on EU (Pirozzi and Tortola, 2017; Rubio, 2017; Schimmelfennig and Winzen, 2014; Vai et al., 2017).

The most recent effort to analyze the challenges for the EU edifice and to put in place relevant policies for forwarding European integration project is undertaken by the EC in the "White paper on the future of Europe" (2017).

The report suggests five possible scenarios for the EU analyzing their main strategies and repercussions.

In scenario one the EU strategy is reform-oriented which means that the EU-27 focuses "on jobs, growth and investment by strengthening the single market and by stepping up investment in digital, transport and energy infrastructure" (White Paper on the future of Europe 2017, 16). The EU effort includes euro enforcement and effectiveness because the single currency is considered crucial for economic growth and for confrontation of asymmetric shocks diffusion while emphasis is also given to financial supervision rules, to the sustainability of public finances, and to enforcement of capital markets.

Defense cooperation is strengthened in issue areas such as research, industry, joint procurement, military capabilities and foreign policy targets, efficient management of external borders, better organization of the European Border and coast guard and international involvement in climate, financial stability, and sustainable development issues. Apparently, the scenario leads to deepening of European integration and to institutional reforms; thus collective intentionality within EU takes primacy over national sovereignty.

In the second scenario titled "Nothing but the single market" the focus is on single market and thus no collective action is going to take place in migration, security, or defense by 2025 (White Paper on the future of Europe 2017, 18). Bilateral cooperation and not supranational organization is the main tool within this scenario to face the challenges in migration and foreign policy areas (which means among others the intensification of controls at national borders), to reach international trade agreements, to reduce regulatory burden, and thus differences are expected to increase in issue areas such as consumer, social and environmental standards, taxation, and public subsidies. Euro is not abandoned but there are no institutional reforms to enforce fiscal cooperation or effectiveness of the pillars of an OCA (i.e., mobility of workers or access to regulated professions) putting at risk the currency integrity. In this scenario intergovernmentalism is the main framework of cooperation and the vision is not a federal Europe but a Europe of sovereign states with a strong internal market.

In scenario three titled "Those who want more do more" the EU adopts the enhanced cooperation method and willing states promote integration in specific issue areas such as defense (i.e., strong common research and industrial base, joint procurement, integrated capabilities, and enhanced military readiness for joint missions abroad), internal security, taxation, or social issues (White Paper on the future of Europe 2017, 20).

Integration deepening is taking place in the Schengen Area, there is enforcement of cooperation between police forces and intelligence services in the fight against organized crime- and terrorism-related activities, creating a common justice area in civil matters. Greater harmonization of tax rules and rates reduces compliance costs and limits tax evasion while agreed social standards provide certainty for business and contribute to improved conditions for workers. Industrial cooperation is enforced in cutting-edge technologies, products, and services and relations with third countries, including trade, remain within the competence of EU acting on behalf of all EU countries. This scenario is a moderate federalist one but its evolution surely depends not only on the member states political volition but also on the speed and intensity of external political, economic, and security challenges.

In scenario four "Doing less more efficiently" there is a trade-off between specific issue areas targets due to the fact that the priorities of integration absorb all forces in certain policies (White Paper on the future of Europe 2017, 22). It is a "refocus strategy" to the perceived core competencies of the EU with all the derived consequences concerning EU resources. The target is that EU-27 acts much quicker and more decisively in specific priority areas in competition policy or banking supervision and enhances cooperation in fields such as innovation, trade, security, migration, the management of borders and defense.

New rules are put in place for the single market and large-scale investment is realized in new EU-wide projects (i.e., high-tech clusters and regional energy hubs). Cooperation between police and judicial authorities is facilitated by a common European counterterrorism agency, joint defense capacities are established, and the European border and coast guard fully take over the management of external borders. The necessary crowding out effect of the limited EU resources is realized to the detriment of policies in the issue areas of regional development, public health, and social protection not directly related to the functioning of the single market. State aid control is further delegated to national authorities. Finally, euro area is consolidated and all efforts in the EMU concern the stability of the common currency. This scenario is a realist one since it tries to attain specific targets which deliver positive results for all member states without undermining single market forces.

In scenario five "Doing much more together" the EU adopts integration initiatives collectively and in many issue areas (White Paper on the future of Europe 2017, 24). Taking into account that the complex challenges demand collective and not national actions, the member states decide to share more power, resources, and decision-making; thus cooperation between all countries proceeds in all domains.

In the same manner, the euro area is enforced and international representation of EU is strengthened in trade and economic issues giving to EP a key role especially on international trade agreements. Moreover, European defense union is created and migration policy is prioritized. Initiatives in the single market are crucial for its advancement in the field of energy, digital, and services and fully integration of capital markets. Strong coordination on fiscal, social, and taxation matters is taking place as well as European supervision of financial services. Finally, there is volition to raise EU financial support so as to respond to shocks at regional, sectoral, and national level. This scenario is a federal one targeting to closer union of the member states.

Irrespective of the scenario or mix of scenarios that is going to occur, integration in any form should also give an answer to the type and content of linkages between EU and the states in the EU's neighborhood. Moreover, there is a need to examine carefully the social and territorial repercussions of reforms and the need for real and not just nominal convergence of EU NUTS-2 regions.

Finally, there is a need to redraw the linkages of euro area, EU competencies, and institutional roles and how they will not evolve in different integration initiatives which create a danger for European integration scheme to fall apart. Evidently, the question of integration involves many challenges outside the EU member states capabilities and jurisdiction and integration dynamics demand flexibility and political will.

Thus, the key theme is not how to avoid differentiation but how to combine effectively the political, economic, institutional, and cultural priorities of differentiated integration, how to apply reforms that permit different national paths parallel to European ones without destroying the positive spillovers of the stronger union, and how to forward different perceptions of integration within an effective, legitimate and long-term European vision.

At the same time, the reforms should not construct a fortress Europe, an inner integration cycle of states with insiders and outsiders. The answers to the challenges include more and not less Europe and at the same time more effective and flexible and less bureaucratic Europe.

**Table 4.1 The Five Scenarios of the European Commission for European Integration Evolution by 2025**

| *Scenarios/Issue Areas* | *Scenario 1 Carrying on* | *Scenario 2 Nothing but the Single Market* | *Scenario 3 Those Who Want More* | *Scenario 4 Doing Less More Efficiently* | *Scenario 5 Doing Much More Together* |
|---|---|---|---|---|---|
| Single market and trade | Single market is strengthened, including in the energy and digital sectors; the EU-27 pursues progressive trade agreements | Single market for goods and capital strengthened; standards continue to differ; free movement of people and services not fully guaranteed | As in "Carrying on," single market is strengthened and the EU-27 pursues progressive trade agreements | Common standards set to a minimum but enforcement is strengthened in areas regulated at EU level; trade exclusively dealt with at EU level | Single market strengthened through harmonization of standards and stronger enforcement; trade exclusively dealt with at EU level |
| Economic and monetary union | Incremental progress on improving the functioning of the euro area | Cooperation in the euro area is limited | As in "Carrying on" except for a group of countries who deepen cooperation in areas such as taxation and social standards | Several steps are taken to consolidate the euro area and ensure its stability; the EU-27 does less in some parts of employment and social policy | Economic, financial, and fiscal Union is achieved as envisioned in the report of the Five Presidents of June 2015 |
| Schengen, migration and security | Cooperation in the management of external borders stepped up gradually; progress toward a common asylum system; improved coordination on security matters | No single migration or asylum policy; further coordination on security dealt with bilaterally; internal border controls are more systematic | As in "Carrying on" except for a group of countries who deepen cooperation on security and justice matters | Cooperation on border management, asylum policies, and counterterrorism matters are systematic | As in "Doing less more efficiently," cooperation on border management, asylum policies, and counterterrorism matters are systematic |

(*Continued*)

**Table 4.1 (*Continued*)**

| *Scenarios/Issue Areas* | *Scenario 1 Carrying on* | *Scenario 2 Nothing but the Single Market* | *Scenario 3 Those Who Want More* | *Scenario 4 Doing Less More Efficiently* | *Scenario 5 Doing Much More Together* |
|---|---|---|---|---|---|
| Foreign policy and defense | Progress is made on speaking with one voice on foreign affairs; closer defense cooperation | Some foreign policy issues are increasingly dealt with bilaterally; defense cooperation remains as it is today | As in "Carrying on" except for a group of countries who deepen cooperation on defense, focusing on military coordination and joint equipment | The EU speaks with one voice on all foreign policy issues; a European Defense Union is created | As in "Doing less more efficiently," the EU speaks with one voice on all foreign policy issues; a European Defense Union is created |
| EU budget | Partly modernized to reflect the reform agenda agreed at 27 | Refocused to finance essential functions needed for the single market | As in "Carrying on," additional budgets are made available by some member states for the areas where they decide to do more | Significantly redesigned to fit the new priorities agreed at the level of the EU-27 | Significantly modernized and increased, backed up by own resources; a euro area fiscal stabilization function is operational |
| Capacity to deliver | Positive agenda for action yields concrete results; decision-making remains complex to grasp; capacity to deliver does not always match expectations | Decision-making may be easier to understand but capacity to act collectively is limited; issues of common concern often need to be solved bilaterally | As in "Carrying on," a positive agenda for action at 27 yields results; some groups achieve more together in certain domains; decision-making becomes more complex | Significantly modernized and increased, backed up by own resources; a euro area fiscal stabilization function is operational | Decision-making is faster and enforcement is stronger across the board; questions of accountability arise for some who feel that the EU has taken too much power away from the member states |

*Source*: European Commission, White Paper on the Future of Europe, 2017.

## BIBLIOGRAPHY

Alesina, A and Grilli, V. 1993. "On the feasibility of a one-speed or multispeed European Monetary Union". *Economics and Politics*, 5(2): 145–165.

Blockmans, Steven and Russack, Sophia. 2017. Regroup and reform. Ideas for a more responsive and effective European Union, Report of a CEPS Task Force, Brussels, *Centre for European Policy Studies (CEPS),* February, https://www.ceps.eu/node/12248

Bresso, Mercedes and Brok, Elmar. 2017. Report on improving the functioning of the European Union building on the potential of the Lisbon Treaty (A8-0386/2016), *European Parliament Committee on Constitutional Affairs,* http://www.europarl.europa.eu/sides/getDoc.do?type=REPORT&reference=A8-2016-0386&language=EN

European Commission. 2017. White paper on the future of Europe. Reflections and scenarios for the EU27 by 2025 (COM/2017/2025), 1st March, *European Commission,* http://dx.doi.org/10.2775/32364

European Council. 2014. *Conclusions*, 26–27 June. http://data.consilium, europa.eu/doc/document/ST-79-2014-INIT/en/pdf

Leuffen, Dirk., Rittberger, Bertholdn., and Schimmelfennig, Frank. 2013. *Differentiated integration: Explaining variation in the European Union.* New York: Palgrave Macmillan.

Leuffen, Dirk., Rittberger, Berthold., and Schimmelfennig, Frank, 2014. The European Union as a system of differentiated integration, *Political Science series.* working paper no. 137.

Pirozzi, Nicoletta., and Tortola, Pier Domenico. 2017. "Negotiating the European Union's dilemmas: Proposals on governing Europe". In *Governing Europe. How to make the EU more efficient and democratic*, eds. Lorenzo Vai, Pier Domenico Tortola, and Nicoletta, Pirozzi. 225–243. Brussels: P.I.E. Peter Lang.

Rubio, Eulalia. 2017. "Federalizing the Euro zone: Towards a true European budget?" In *Governing Europe. How to make the EU more efficient and democratic,* eds. Lorenzo Vai, Pier Domenico Tortola, and Nicoletta Pirozzi. 169–190. Brussels: P.I.E. Peter Lang.

Schimmelfennig, Frank and Winzen, Thomas. 2014. "Instrumental and Constitutional Differentiation in the European Union". *Journal of Common Market Studies,* 52(2): 354–370.

Stubb, Alexander. 1996. "A categorization of differentiated integration". *Journal of Common Market Studies,* 34(2): 283–296.

Vai, Lorenzo., Tortola, Pier Domenico., and Pirozzi, Nicoletta, eds. 2017. *Governing Europe. How to make the EU more efficient and democratic.* Brussels: P.I.E Peter Lang.

Van, Rompuy, H., Barroso, J., Juncker, J., and Draghi, M. 2012. *Towards a genuine Economic and Monetary Union.* European Council, Brussels.

Véron, N. 2013. *A realistic bridge towards European banking union*. Brussels: Bruegel.

Von, Hagen, J. 2007. *"Achieving economic stabilization by sharing risk within countries"*. In *Intergovernmental Fiscal Transfers: principles and practice,* eds. R. Boadway and A. Shah, 107–132. Washington, D.C.: The World Bank.

## FURTHER READING

Anderson, S. and Sitter, N. 2006. "Differentiated integration: What is it, and how much can the EU accommodate?" *Journal of European Integration,* 28(4): 313–330.

Bastasin, C. 2014. *Saving Europe: Anatomy of a dream*, second edition. Washington, D.C.: Brooking Institution Press.

Bergvall, D., Charbit, C., Kraan, D. J., and Merk, O. 2006. "Intergovernmental transfers and decentralized public spending". *OECD Journal on Budgeting*, 5(4): 111–158.

Blöchliger, H and King, D. 2006. "Fiscal Autonomy of sub-central governments". *OECD working papers on Fiscal Federalism.* no. 2, Paris.

Centre for European Policy Studies. 2014. Shifting EU Institutional reform into high gear, *Report of the CEPS High Level Group*. Brussels: CEPS.

De Schoutheete, P and Micossi, S. 2013. "On political union in Europe: The changing landscape of decision-making and political accountability". *CEPS Policy Brief*, February, Brussels.

Dyson, K and Sepos, A., eds. 2010. *Which Europe? The politics of differentiated integration.* New York: Palgrave Macmillan.

European Parliament. 2012. New institutional solutions for multi-tier governance. *Directorate General for Internal Policies.* Constitutional Affairs. Brussels, 29 October.

Fossum, J. E and Menendez, A. J. 2011. *The Constitution gifts: A Constitutional theory for a democratic European Union.* Lanham, MD: Rowman and Littlefield.

Glencross, A. 2014. "The absence of political constitutionalism in the EU: Three models for enhancing constitutional agency". *Journal of European Public Policy,* 21(8): 1163–1180.

Hinarejos, A. 2013. "Fiscal federalism in the European Union: Evolution and future choices for EMU". *Common Market Law Review*, 50: 1621–1642.

Leuffen, D. 2013. "European Union as a blueprint? Nine hypotheses on differentiated integration in a comparative perspective", *WAI-ZEI paper*, no. 8, Bonn: University of Bonn.

Padoa-Schioppa, T. 1987. *Efficiency, stability and equity: A strategy for the evolution of the economic system of the European community*. Oxford: Oxford University Press.

Puetter, U. 2014. *The European council and the council: New intergovernmentalism and institutional change*. Oxford: Oxford University Press.

Somek, A. 2013. "What is a political union?" *German Law Journal,* 14(5): 561–580.

Spinelli Group and Bertelsmann Stigtung. 2013. *A fundamental law of the European Union.* Bielefeld: Verlag Bertelsmann Stiftung.

Tondl, G. 2000. "Fiscal federalism and the reality of the European Union budget". In *After the Euro – shaping institutions for governance in the wake of European Monetary Union,* ed. C. Crouch. Oxford: Oxford University Press.

Toth, A. G. 1992. "The Principle of subsidiarity in the Maastricht treaty". *Common Market Law Review,* 29: 1079–1105.

Wolff, G. B. 2012. "A budget for Europe's Monetary Union". *Bruegel Policy Contribution* 2012/22.

## QUESTIONS

1. Will EU operate better if decision-making becomes more decentralized? Choose an issue area of EU action and analyze the benefits and disadvantages of such an approach.
2. Is there a need for a different allocation of competences between EU countries and EU institutions?
3. Describe the origins of EP and how its role has evolved since the Lisbon Treaty.
4. Is there need for a strong EU constitution or current EU treaties are sufficient for deeper economic/political integration in Europe?
5. Which are the main institutional obstacles for a deeper political integration of EU states?
6. Will European integration be advanced by centralization or decentralization of policy competences?
7. With which integration theory described in chapter 2 of the book does enhanced cooperation fit?
8. Using the qualified majority voting weights, calculate all possible coalitions to a specific economic issue area at EU level.

## *Chapter 5*

# The Framework of Economic and Monetary Union

### HOW EMU CAME INTO EXISTENCE

The international currency instability in 1968–1969 had significant negative repercussions on major economic and policy issue areas of EEC. Under the guidance of P. Werner a high-level group issued a report on how EMU could be achieved by 1980 and thus how macroeconomic and institutional obstacles to closer union should be dealt.

The Werner group proposed a three-stage process to achieve EMU within 10 years and soon the EEC countries put in place the first stage of Werner project which was narrowing currency fluctuations. However, persisted unfavorable macroeconomic and financial conditions postponed the implementation of Werner report and only in 1979 the EMS was launched.

Undeniably, in the evolution of the monetary union project a key accomplishment of the EEC states was the creation of ECU, a weighted average of EMS currencies according to which exchange rates had been defined. An ERM was also put in place so as to keep national currencies within a narrow band and to set in motion a limited coordination of monetary policies between the member countries.

Equally important, the committee of governors of the central banks of the member countries of the EEC (in place since May 1964) had been enforced (especially through the Council Decision of March 12, 1990) with two targets, the coordination of the monetary policies of the member countries, and the achievement of price stability.

A major breakthrough for the monetary union was achieved with the Delors Report which proposed a three-stage project for EMU and the euro area (1990–1999).

On the basis of the Delors Report, the European Council decided in June 1989 to activate the first stage of EMU on July 1, 1990. The first stage (1990–1993) included the abolition of all obstacles to capital movements and restrictions under the condition that they constituted a threat to the operation of the EU. Moreover, public deficit financing through the central bank was prohibited and programmes of long-run convergence had been put in place. A narrow band in the exchange rates of all EEC countries was applied and measures against any modification of the composition of the ECU basket had been taken.

In the second stage of the project (1994–1996) convergence of economies was based on specific targets such as control of the public deficit and debt (the former to 3% of GDP and the latter to 60% of GDP), the operation of the EMI, and the national reforms to comply member states' central banks legislative framework to the principles of the EU.

The establishment of the EMI on January 1, 1994 signaled the second stage of EMU (the committee of governors was abolished) with three fundamental objectives, namely, to enforce cooperation of central banks, to strengthen monetary policy coordination, and to prepare the terms for the establishment of the ESCB, for the conduct of the single monetary policy and for the circulation of a single currency in the third phase. Finally, the third stage was scheduled to start on January 1, 1997 or January 1, 1999 at the latest.

A key moment for EMU was when EU state leaders decided during the European Council in the Dutch city of Maastricht in December 1991 to establish an EMU (the Maastricht treaty) underlining specific convergence criteria that each country would have to apply so as to take part in the euro area. As scheduled and already mentioned, the major targets of the treaty were to constrain government deficits (to 3% of GDP) and public debt levels (to 60% of GDP).

Four years later, the European Council agreed in December 1995 to name the ECU to be circulated at the beginning of stage three, the "euro," and confirmed the beginning of stage three of EMU on January 1, 1999 (the euro symbol (€) was inspired by the Greek letter epsilon (Є) and the two parallel lines running through the symbol imply stability).

The EMI provided in December 1996 the European Council with a specific report analyzing the principles and key traits of the new ERM (ERM II, adopted in June 1997). The operation of EMI reached to an end soon after the establishment of the ECB on June 1, 1998 and went into liquidation.

The Council of the EU unanimously decided in May 2, 1998 that 11 EU countries had fulfilled the terms necessary for the participation in the third stage of EMU and were ready for the adoption of the euro as a common currency on January 1, 1999 (Belgium, Germany, Spain, France, Ireland, Italy, Luxembourg, the Netherlands, Austria, Portugal, and Finland). Indeed, the euro was launched on January 1, 1999, monetary policy passed to the ECB (established on June 1, 1998) but euro coins and banknotes circulated on January 1, 2002 in 12 EU states (Austria, Belgium, Finland, France, Germany, Greece, Ireland, Italy, Luxembourg, the Netherlands, Portugal, and Spain).

Thus, on January 1, 1999 the irrevocable fixing of the exchange rates of the currencies of the 11 member countries took place and the conduct of a single monetary policy was entrusted to the ECB (Greece joined the monetary union on January 1, 2001, Slovenia on January 1, 2007, Cyprus and Malta joined the monetary union on January 2008, Slovakia joined the monetary union on January 1, 2009, Estonia on January 1, 2011, Latvia on January 1, 2014, and Lithuania on January 1, 2015). In 1998, the SGP preventive rules were applied and in 1999 the corrective rules entered into force.

The establishment of euro targeted less transaction costs, less foreign exchange risks and enhanced transparency in cross-border transactions. Moreover, it was anticipated that the euro would have made easier the comparison of prices of goods/services, it would have strengthened cross-border trade, and it would have diminished the risks of fluctuating exchange rates. Meanwhile, euro circulation enhanced monetary power of the euroarea states and provided economic stability.

However, the European sovereign debt crisis underlined the necessity for the redesign of the EU fiscal governance framework. The experience of the common currency demonstrated the ineffective compliance of the member states to the EU fiscal governance provisions and the inability of eurozone institutions to achieve in the long-term macroeconomic sustainability.

EEG was put under significant pressure during the years 2002–2005 and 2009–2013. In the first crisis, the EEG provisions failed to impose its provisions in France and Germany which had excessive deficits. Indeed, in February 2002, the Council of Ministers, contrary to the recommendation of the EC's recommendation, did not issue an early warning against Portugal and Germany; on November 25, 2003, it rejected the imposition of sanctions to both countries whose annual net borrowing was above 4% of GDP.

In the second crisis, the EEG did not prevent the evolution of a more complicate crisis which involved a banking crisis, a sovereign debt crisis, and a competitiveness crisis. In order to understand the peculiarities of the EEG structure one should thoroughly analyze the content and institutional pillars of EEG.

## HOW EMU OPERATES

The operation and management of EMU involve four main economic activities so as to ensure stability and growth: implementing an effective monetary policy for the euro area with the objective of price stability, coordinating economic, and fiscal policies in EU countries, ensuring the maximization of single market results and last but not least supervising and monitoring financial institutions.

The responsibility for economic policy is shared between member countries and the EU institutions. More specifically, the European Council puts into place the basic policy targets, the Council of the EU (the Council) is responsible for the coordination of economic policymaking and for the key decision whether a member country may adopt the euro, while the Eurogroup coordinates common interest policies of the eurozone countries.

The EC controls performance and compliance and the EP shares with the Council all necessary legislation for economic governance. The member countries determine their national budgets and policies on tax, pensions, labor, and capital market issues but have in mind that they should follow specific rules for deficit and debt. In any case, the Council keeps a close eye on member countries' fiscal and economic policies and has the right to address recommendations to a country (after specific proposal from the Commission) when imbalances persist and even has the right to sanction a eurozone country that does apply corrective measures to face excessive deficit and debt.

Which is the role of ECB? Monetary policy is the main competence of the ECB (which together with the national central banks of the eurozone states make up the Eurosystem) in the eurozone (19 countries) while fiscal, labor, and welfare policies are decided by the 28 member countries having in mind that decisions must always comply with EU rules.

Price stability is the fundamental target although ECB should take care as central supervisor of financial institutions and of the operation of banks in the eurozone. This competence is vital and demands single bank resolution and single deposit insurance. Besides, EU countries which are not members of eurozone coordinate their monetary policy with the ECB within the ESCB.

Are there specific conditions for entry to the euro area? The economic entry criteria (known as Maastricht or convergence criteria) were agreed by the EU countries in 1991 and are intended to ensure that a member country's economy is prepared for adoption of the euro and of the common monetary regime. There are also many obligations that a Eurozone candidate state must undertake concerning its central bank operations.

More specifically, the convergence criteria are a set of macroeconomic indicators which measure price stability, soundness of public finances, exchange rate stability, and long-term interest rates. Participation in the ERM (ERM II) for at least two years without strong deviations from the ERM II central rate is a key issue for state willing to join euroarea and is controlled by the general council of the ECB.

**Table 5.1 The Five Convergence Criteria of Maastricht Treaty**

| | | | | | |
|---|---|---|---|---|---|
| What is measured: | Price stability | Sound fiscal finances | Sustainable public finances | Durability of convergence | Stability of exchange rates |
| How it is measured: | Consumer price inflation rate | Government deficit as % of GDP | Government debt as % of GDP | Long-term interest rate | Deviation from a central rate |
| Convergence criteria: | Not more than 1.5 percentage points above the rate of the three best performing member states | Reference value: not more than 3% | Reference value: not more than 60% | Not more than two percentage points above the rate of the three best performing member states in terms of price stability | Participation in ERM II for at least two years without severe tensions |

*Source*: European Union website, 2017.

The exchange rate stability criterion is considered vital because it guarantees that a member country does not have problems of excessive currency fluctuations and gives a strong indication of the appropriate conversion rate that should be implemented when the country's currency will be irrevocably fixed.

The Commission and the ECB assess the progress made by the eurozone candidate states and reach specific conclusions on convergence reports.

## THE LEGAL FRAMEWORK OF EEG

The provisions of the SGP are based on articles 121 (ex-article 99 TEC, on multilateral surveillance) and 126 (ex-article 104 TEC concerning the EDP) of the TFEU. Protocol 12 of the treaty refers thoroughly to the EDP while article 136 of the TFEU analyzes the provisions to be adopted for the eurozone to strengthen coordination and surveillance of budgetary discipline, in accordance with the relevant procedures from articles 121 and 126. It is also the basis for the so-called six-pack and the two-pack regulations in the euro area.

More specifically, article 121 of TFEU obliges member states to consider their economic policies as a common concern issue and to coordinate them. It further puts into action a multilateral surveillance procedure based on the BEPG (adopted by the Council after discussion at European Council level) which analyze the framework against which countries' policies will be evaluated.

The secondary legislation of EEG includes regulation 1466/97 (which refers to the surveillance of budgetary positions and the surveillance and coordination of economic policies thus the preventive arm of SGP), regulation 1467/97 (which refers to the implementation of the EDP thus the corrective arm of the SGP), regulation 479/2009 (the application of the protocol on the EDP), regulation 1173/2011 (it concerns the enforcement of budgetary surveillance in the eurozone), regulation 1174/2011 (how to correct excessive macroeconomic imbalances in the eurozone), and regulation 1176/2011 (prevention and correction of macroeconomic imbalances).

Directive 2011/85/EU analyzes the requirements for budgetary frameworks of the member countries while regulation 473/2013 of the EP and of the Council of May 21, 2013 refers to the provisions for monitoring and assessing draft budgetary plans, ensuring the correction of excessive deficit of the eurozone countries. The regulation is crucial for the surveillance cycle of Eurozone states and enforces the monitoring terms for states under EDP. Finally, regulation 472/2013 of the EP and of the Council of May 21, 2013 analyzes the economic and budgetary surveillance of eurozone countries experiencing financial stability hurdles.

## EUROPEAN ECONOMIC GOVERNANCE: AN ANALYSIS OF THE KEY INSTITUTIONS

In EMU the competence of fiscal (tax and spending), labor, and welfare policies belongs to national governments. However, the accomplishment of its targets rests on the efficient operation of EEG institutions. Let's examine in detail the role of each major institutional actor in the eurozone architecture.

### The Eurogroup

The Eurogroup, consisting of the ministers of economy and finance of the euro area members, coordinates economic policies and targets growth and financial stability in the euro area. Its meetings are informal (so as to maximize organizational and policy flexibility as well as confidentiality to the agenda setting), are attended by the EC and the president of the ECB, and take place one day before ECOFIN meetings, usually once a month (the first meeting of finance ministers of the Eurozone states occurred on June 4, 1998 at the Château de Senningen in Luxembourg). However, whenever urgent issues come up (i.e., urgent decisions on the implementation of the Greek

AP after 2010), teleconferences or meetings take place. The work programme of the euro group is defined every six months and sets the agenda for the Eurogroup meetings.

The protocol no. 14 to the Lisbon treaty clarifies the competences of the euro group (into force from December 1, 2009). More specifically, and mainly according to the Luxembourg resolution (resolution of the Luxembourg European Council in December 1997), the euro group discusses the economic situation and outlook in the Eurozone, the budgetary policies of the Eurozone member countries, the macroeconomic terms in Eurozone, the structural reforms that have an impact on growth, issues related to financial stability in the Eurozone, preparations for international meetings, issues of euro area enlargement, and the conditions of financial assistance for Eurozone countries experiencing financial problems.

Discussion on economic situation includes exchanges of views (the Commissioner for economic and monetary affairs and the president of the ECB are present) among others on the price developments in the Eurozone, on competitiveness in member countries (based on Commission forecasts), on monetary policy, and on the euro exchange rate. As far as it concerns budgetary policy, discussions include budgetary policy coordination, the appropriateness of the fiscal strategy for the Eurozone as a whole and for member countries, and the implementation of the provisions of the SGP.

On structural reforms, the interest of the euro group ministers is to examine progress of issues of the Lisbon agenda, structural reforms that have an impact on macroeconomic and financial terms of the internal market, reforms to enforce potential growth and to face structural rigidities, and methods to facilitate the interactions between the economic policies of Eurozone countries. The agreements of the Eurogroup meeting are formally decided upon in the ECOFIN meeting by the Eurogroup members.

The president of the Eurogroup is elected for two and a half years by a simple majority of votes and his work is supported by the general secretariat of the Council. He prepares the agenda of the Eurogroup, he chairs the meetings, he circulates informal conclusions in writing, he informs ECOFIN ministers if requested in the suitable formation on the results of the Eurogroup meetings, he presents Eurogroup discussions to the public, and he represents the Eurogroup in international fora.

## The Euro Working Group

The EWG provides ministers with short discussion papers on vital policy issues and underlines policy implications and suggestions for the policy follow-up. It also writes short essays (known as "terms of reference" or "common understandings") which form the basis for Eurogroup communications.

The EWG is comprised of EFC members from the administration of the eurozone countries, and the members from the ECB and the EC.

## The ECB's Role in EMU

The ECB was set up in 1998 as an independent institution and applies a monetary policy that targets price stability and low inflation rates. The executive board of the ECB consists of the president, the vice-president, and four other members (appointed by the European Council). The executive board is responsible for implementing monetary policy, the bank's day-to-day operations, and preparing governing council meetings as well as exercising certain powers delegated to it by the governing council. The president of the ECB represents it at high-level EU and international conferences.

The governing council of the ECB comprises the 6 members of the ECB executive board and the governors of the national central banks of the 19 euro area members which form the Eurosystem. The governing council is the main decision-taking body of the ECB and meets twice a month. As a rule, at its first meeting each month, the governing council assesses economic and monetary developments and takes its monthly monetary policy decisions.

ECB's governing council takes monetary policy decisions every six weeks and follows monetary policy processes according to the EU treaties provisions. Its effectiveness was put under pressure after the sovereign debt crisis in 2010 and obliged it to implement nonstandard monetary policy measures so as to guarantee the target of price stability and to safeguard an appropriate monetary policy transmission mechanism.

A crucial role in the smooth operation of euroarea is played by the general council of the ESCB which comprises the governors of the 28 national central banks, together with the ECB president and vice-president.

The ECB determines the interest rates for lending to EU commercial banks and thus influences the supply and cost of money in Eurozone (if it issues many banknotes and coins, the consumer price inflation rate goes up). The governing council of the ECB determines the key interest rates, namely, the interest rate on the MROs which refers to the liquidity to the banking system, the rate on the deposit facility (banks use it to realize overnight deposits with the Eurosystem), and the rate on the marginal lending facility, (it concerns the overnight credit to banks from the Eurosystem).

ECB is also responsible for conducting foreign exchange operations, safeguarding the payment systems in support of the single market, and monitoring the production of euro banknotes by the Eurozone states.

As far as it concerns the operational dimension of the Eurosystem a variety of instruments (they differ in terms of target, regularity, and procedure) is used such as open market operations (they have a crucial role in steering interest rates, handling efficiently the liquidity in the Eurozone market and signaling the monetary policy), standing facilities, minimum reserve requirements for credit institutions, and nonstandard monetary policy measures.

More specifically, open market operations use five types of financial tools among which the most significant is the reverse transaction that is applied in the form of a repurchase agreement or of a collateralized loan. Further, the Eurosystem can also use outright transactions, debt certificates, foreign exchange swaps, and a collection of fixed-term deposits. The MROs occur in a decentralized way by the national central banks (on the basis of standard tenders) and refer to liquidity-providing reverse transactions conducted by the Eurosystem with a one week frequency and maturity, providing the majority of needed capital to the financial sector.

Longer-term refinancing operations have a significant maturity (three months or under specific terms a maturity of more than three months) and are also liquidity-providing reverse transactions. When maturities are more than three months (the TLTROs was the longest one), the objective is to provide counterparties with additional longer-term refinancing and to help the realization of other monetary policy objectives.

Fine-tuning operations (FTOs) take place on an ad hoc basis to handle the liquidity in the Eurozone market and to steer interest rates. The key objective is to face unexpected liquidity fluctuations (and their impact on interest rates) through reverse transactions although they can also be foreign exchange swaps or collection of fixed-term deposits. FTOs are applied by the Eurosystem through quick tenders or bilateral procedures.

In the case that the ECB wants to adjust the structural position of the Eurosystem relative to the financial sector, structural operations are applied by the Eurosystem through reverse transactions (standard tenders), outright transactions (bilateral procedures), and the issuance of debt certificates (standard tenders).

Standing facilities bound overnight market interest rates, provide overnight liquidity, and usually take place by the national central banks. In the marginal lending facility counterparties have access to overnight liquidity from the national central banks against eligible assets, and in the deposit facility counterparties make overnight deposits with the national central banks.

Minimum reserves are also a key element of the monetary policy in the Eurozone and each institution's reserve requirement is linked to its balance sheet. Compliance with the reserve requirement takes into account the institutions' average daily reserve holdings over a maintenance period of about one month and the required reserve holdings are remunerated at a level determined by the average interest rate over the maintenance period of the MROs.

The expanded APP of ECB concerns all programmes under which the securities of the private sector and public sector are purchased to face the risks of a too prolonged period of low inflation and includes the CBPP3, the ABSPP, the PSPP, and the CSPP.

As far as it concerns the latter, the Eurosystem started to buy CSPPs on June 8, 2016 in an effort to enforce the real economy and to provide further monetary policy accommodation. PSPPs programme started on March 9, 2015 and its securities include nominal- and inflation-linked central government bonds, bonds issued by recognized agencies, regional and local governments, international organizations, and multilateral development banks located in the euro area.

The ABSPPs programme was put in place on November 21, 2014 so as to provide capital injections in the real economy helping banking institutions to diversify funding sources and issue new securities. Lastly, CBPP3 started on October 20, 2014 facilitating credit provision to the real economy.

One should mention that the Eurosystem gives credit only against adequate collateral (marketable financial securities, such as bonds, or other of non-marketable assets or cash). The eligibility of assets (assets that are accepted as collateral by the Eurosystem) is evaluated by the national central banks according to the provisions of the euro system legal framework for monetary policy instruments.

Lastly, ECB plays a key role in the ELA process. In exceptional circumstances (temporary liquidity problems) Eurozone credit institutions can be recipients of central bank credit or any other assistance through ELA. The main prerequisite for banks demanding ELA is that they are solvent and the value of their assets is greater than the sum of their debt obligations. However, the risks and the responsibility for liquidity assistance lies with the national central banks and the ECB deserves the right to restrict at any time ELA operations, if it considers that these operations interfere with the targets of the Eurosystem. From 2010 onward, many banks in Ireland, Cyprus, Portugal, and Greece have been beneficiaries of ELA measures.

## The Macroeconomic Imbalances Procedure

The MIP (applied on December 13, 2011) is a process not only to prevent adverse macroeconomic imbalances in an EU economy becoming a threat to other EU states but also to discuss all EU macroeconomic problems with the EC and all other EU states. The aims of MIP framework is to preserve macroeconomic stability, to consider the potential risks associated with external macroeconomic shocks at an early stage, to highlight adjustment issues, and to take into account the impact of imbalances on eurozone as a whole.

MIP surveillance is wide in coverage (it includes different issue areas such as excessive debt and competitiveness losses) and does not follow automatic numerical rules. As already mentioned, the MIP surveillance is based on article 121 of the TFEU which analyzes the rationale for multilateral surveillance in the EU and is embedded in the EU economic governance cycle defined by the European semester.

The MIP is based on two pieces of legislation that were implemented as part of the "six-pack" reform of economic governance in 2011 namely regulation 1176/2011 on the prevention and correction of macroeconomic imbalances (it sets out the MIP procedure) and regulation 1174/2011 on enforcement measures to correct excessive macroeconomic imbalances (it specifies a sanction mechanism to enforce MIP recommendations for euro area states).

MIP is part of the "European semester" (which was introduced in 2010, was revised in 2015 with the aim to guarantee the effective surveillance of budgetary and economic policies, and was coordinated by the secretariat general of the Commission). The European semester begins each year with the AGS where the Commission evaluates the employment and macroeconomic trends in the EU and mentions the economic, budgetary, and reformative priorities for the following year.

The AMR (which is part of the macroeconomic imbalances procedure and of the European semester) provides key data for national macroeconomic imbalances which could create negative spillovers to EU countries or to the EMU. The AMR uses a set of selected indicators (the scoreboard) as well as other financial indicators to screen EU states for potential economic imbalances.

The analysis by the Commission is strongly based on a scoreboard of indicators (article 4 of regulation no. 1176/2011) which is used as a tool to facilitate early identification and to monitor imbalances (article 4 para 1) and comprises a small number of relevant, practical, simple, measurable, and available macroeconomic and macro-financial indicators for member countries (article 4 para 2).

Scoreboard indicators are evaluated against their respective thresholds which are specific for each indicator and common for all states (articles 3(1) and 4(4) of regulation no. 1176/2011) encompassing inter alia (article 4(3) of regulation no. 1176/2011) "indicators which are useful in the early identification of internal imbalances, including those that can arise from public and private indebtedness, financial and asset market developments, including housing, the evolution of private sector credit flow and the evolution of unemployment as well as external imbalances, including those that can arise from the evolution of current account and net investment positions of member states, real effective exchange rates, export market shares, changes in price and cost developments and non price competitiveness, taking into account the different components of productivity."

The values of the scoreboard variables are updated at least on an annual basis (article 4(8)); thus the appropriateness of the scoreboard, the composition of indicators, the thresholds set, and the methodology used are modified or adjusted where necessary and especially in the presence of heterogeneous economic conditions (article 4(4) of the regulation).

Indeed, the MIP scoreboard analyzes issues of external macroeconomic sustainability, trade performance and competitiveness, private sector indebtedness, government debt, financial sector-related risks, housing and mortgage markets, employment, and social developments.

More specifically, the scoreboard is comprised of 14 headline indicators concerning macroeconomic imbalances, competitiveness, and adjustment, complemented by 25 auxiliary indicators. The headline indicators consist of the following 14 indicators and indicative thresholds:

a. three-year backward moving average of the current account balance as percent of GDP, with thresholds of +6% and –4%
b. net international investment position as percent of GDP, with a threshold of –35%
c. five-year percentage change of export market shares measured in values, with a threshold of –6%
d. three-year percentage change in nominal unit labor cost, with thresholds of +9% for euro area countries and +12% for non-eurozone states.
e. three-year percentage change of the real effective exchange rates based on HICP/CPI deflators, relative to 41 other industrial countries, with thresholds of –/+5% for eurozone and –/+11% for non-eurozone states.
f. private sector debt in % of GDP with a threshold of 133%
g. private sector credit flow in % of GDP with a threshold of 14%
h. year-on-year changes in house prices relative to a Eurostat consumption deflator, with a threshold of 6%
i. general government sector debt in % of GDP with a threshold of 60%
j. three-year backward moving average of unemployment rate, with a threshold of 10%
k. yearly changes in total financial sector liabilities, with a threshold of 16.5%
l. three-year change in p.p. of the activity rate, with a threshold of –0.2%
m. three-year change in p.p. of the long-term unemployment rate, with a threshold of +0.5%
n. three-year change in p.p. of the youth unemployment rate, with a threshold of +2%

The conclusions derived from the two aforementioned reports are analyzed by EU governments and in-depth national review is taking place for the countries where an imbalance exists. After the AGS and the eurozone recommendations in the Council, the conclusions of the latter are sent to the European Council.

At the end of February, the Commission also presents, in the form of staff working documents, the country reports, for all countries evaluating their economic and social developments as well as economic and structural problems and reforms implementation. The reports further specify the existence of macroeconomic imbalances for those countries which need an IDR based on the reading of the AMR.

When a more detailed analysis is demanded by the results of the AMR, a country is subject to an analytical IDR, issued around February by the commission so as to underline all macroeconomic imbalances. The IDRs results are forwarded by the Commission to the EP, the Council, and the Eurogroup. All states that have imbalances are subject to Council recommendations within the European semester cycle.

The analysis in the IDRs is country-specific and takes into account many economic variables so as to identify macroeconomic imbalances and to evaluate their nature and severity of imbalances. On the basis of the analyses in the IDR, the Commission communicates the outcome to the EP, the Council, and the Eurogroup.

After the publication of the country reports and the European Council conclusions, member countries submit their SCPs no later than April 30 (to the Commission and the Council), indicating the national public finance plans. They also submit the NRPs which analyze the progress achieved over the past year.

Taking into account the country reports, the NRPs and the SCPs, the Commission proposes to the Council the country-specific recommendations and analyzes its opinion for relevant countries on their stability/convergence programme. Based on the Commission's proposals, the ECOFIN Council suggests the country-specific recommendations for each state.

Moreover, Eurozone states must present their national medium-term fiscal plans which include the information contained in the stability programmes and should comply with the provisions of the annual cycle surveillance. Since the entry into force of the two-pack in May 2013 (regulation (EU) 473/2013, article 4(1)), euroarea countries are obliged to publish their national medium-term fiscal plans at the same time as their stability programmes and may use the same document. Euroarea countries also submit the annual draft budgetary plans (by October 15 each year).

How institutions are involved in the European semester process? All main EU services have a role within the aforementioned highly complex process. DG ECFIN provides the analysis for the AMR and for many parts of the IDRs and coordinates several issues within the MIP surveillance.

Eurostat provides expertise and a common framework for the data used in the MIP helped by the ESS and the ESCB. The EPC provides a critical umbrella for the evaluation of findings of the AMR, IDRs, and country specific recommendations (November–June) and also provides technical feedback. The Lisbon methodology working group provides analysis in AMR and IDRs and reports to the EPC.

In any case, before their finalization, the recommendations of the EC for CSRs are discussed in Council committees (Economic and Financial Committee, Employment Committee, Economic and Policy Committee). The European semester also obliges the Commission to analytically inform the Council and the Parliament as well as the European social partner representatives.

A crucial role in EEG framework is played by the BEPG which are non-binding guidelines promoting coordination through annual cycles of economic policy discussions between European institutions, EU states, and EU institutions and are adopted by the EU Council on the basis of a Commission recommendation. The BEPG guidelines act as basis for CSRs, work hand in hand with the European semester, and determine the direction for EU states' NRPs.

In sum, the MIP evolves through a number of stages that can be described as follows:

a. Screening (articles 3 and 4 of regulation no. 1176/2011). The Commission selects countries which potentially face the risk of macroeconomic imbalances to be further investigated as a subsequent step-in IDRs. The conclusions on the selection of countries are communicated to the Parliament, the Council, and the Economic and Social Committee and are made public in the AMR. The Council discusses and assesses the AMR and the Eurogroup discusses the report as far as it relates to eurozone countries.
b. Identification and analysis of imbalances (articles 5 and 6(1) of regulation no. 1176/2011). The Commission realizes IDRs for the countries selected in the AMR and the conclusions are communicated to the Parliament, Council, and Eurogroup accordingly and are made public. The Council discusses the conclusions of IDRs.
c. Recommendations, monitoring, and enforcement (articles 6 to 12 of regulation no. 1176/2011 and regulation no. 1174/2011). The Council recommends policies for countries with imbalances upon a recommendation by the Commission.

## The Stability and Growth Pact

The SGP was adopted in June 1997 to safeguard the fiscal discipline in EMU. Crucial reforms in its content took place in 2005 and 2011 so as to strengthen budgetary discipline and to guarantee that government deficits are less than 3% of GDP and government debt is less than 60% of GDP.

More specifically, in 2005, a crucial amendment of SGP occurred in order to take into consideration national circumstances and to specify more the economic logic to the rules to be complied with (mainly surveillance and coordination—clarification of the EDP).

In 2011, the SGP was amended through the "six-pack" that was a set of laws to make EU's economic governance rules more comprehensive. The six-pack reform included: (i) four regulations on the prevention and correction of excessive fiscal and macroeconomic imbalances (no. 1175 and no. 1177 on budgetary deficits and regulations no. 1174 and no. 1776 on macroeconomic imbalances); (ii) one regulation on the effective enforcement of budgetary surveillance (no. 1173); and (iii) one directive on national fiscal frameworks (no. 85).

A milestone for the EEG was reached with the "Euro Plus pact on stronger economic policy coordination for competitiveness and convergence," agreed in 2011 by the heads of state and government of the euro area and Bulgaria, Denmark, Latvia, Lithuania, Poland, and Romania as an intergovernmental solution to foster reforms and coordination.

Unfortunately, from 2010 onward EEG's structural and policy problems have been multiplied. Realizing the complex aspects of European sovereign debt crisis, the euro area countries adopted in February 2012, the ESM, so as to provide emergency aid to Euro area countries. In December 2012, the four presidents' report titled "Towards a Genuine Economic and Monetary Union" acted as a framework for the completion of the EMU and set in motion the application and completion of an enhanced economic governance and of a banking union (adoption of a single supervisory mechanism and common rules on bank recovery/resolution, and on deposit guarantees).

The necessity for better surveillance in EEG led Eurozone states in January 2013 to an important breakthrough with the fiscal compact (part of the TSCG) which enforced the MTOs set by the SGP's preventive arm (the TSCG also introduced Euro summits which are held at least twice a year).

The two-pack reform (regulation 472/2013 and regulation 473/2013) further strengthened economic coordination between member countries and introduced new monitoring tools (which are into force since May 2013). The main traits of the fiscal compact were a balanced budget rule (with an automatic correction mechanism), a more organized framework of the EDP and a better reporting on public debt issuance issues.

Regrettably, the results of the abovementioned reforms were far below initial expectations; thus in 2015 the Commission suggested a new framework on how it will implement the SGP rules to enforce the linkages between structural reforms, investment, and fiscal responsibility in support of jobs and growth.

The five presidents' report titled "Completing Europe's economic and monetary union" was launched to deepen the EMU in three stages and to complete integration by 2025 at the latest. More specifically, it argued in favor of completion of four unions—an economic, financial, fiscal, and political.

During stage one "Deepening by Doing" (July 1, 2015–June 30, 2017) the target was to enforce competitiveness, to achieve structural convergence, to complete the financial union, and to strengthen democratic accountability through fiscal policies at national and eurozone level. During stage two "Completing EMU" (by 2025) the aim is to establish commonly agreed and legal binding benchmarks for convergence and to advance specific measures for the completion of EMU's economic and institutional edifice. In stage three (at the latest by 2025) a genuine EMU will provide stability and welfare for all citizens of the EU countries that use the euro.

In October 2015, the Commission adopted specific measures to start the application of the Five Presidents' Report among others—an ameliorated approach to the European semester, the implementation of national competitiveness boards, an advisory European fiscal board, specific procedures to complete the banking union (including a European deposit insurance guarantee scheme), and an improved unified representation of the euro area in global financial institutions.

Evidently, the SGP plays a crucial role in the whole process and its two pillars ("arms"), namely the preventive arm and the corrective arm, are analyzed in the following sections of this chapter.

## The Preventive Arm of SGP

According to EEG provisions, EU countries should pursue sound public finances so as to ensure economic growth and financial stability within the SGP. This obliges the countries to follow specific budgetary targets (MTOs) so as to attain the long-term sustainability of public finances.

MTOs concern the sustainability of debt levels and the attainment of fiscal rules and are updated every three years. The EU states should achieve their MTOs and adjust their structural budgetary positions at a rate of 0.5% of GDP per year as a benchmark (usually MTOs are updated every three years). However, the pace of adjustment takes into consideration the economic terms and the national business cycle swings.

More specifically, each year in April, all EU countries notify to the Commission the national medium-term budgetary measures either through stability programmes (eurozone countries) or through convergence programmes (non-eurozone countries). Both programmes are assessed by the EC and EU governments during the European semester taking into account if the

MTOs are set at an appropriate level, if the national adjustment plan is appropriate (based on the cyclical conditions and the sustainability risks), and if the economic hypotheses on which states base their programmes are plausible.

The SCPs include a thorough multi-annual macroeconomic scenario, information for the fundamental fiscal variables and quantification of the envisaged budgetary strategy, data on expenditure and revenue ratios (including one-off and other temporary measures), and projections of government expenditure and of government revenue so as to simplify state's compliance with the MTO requirements.

EU countries also propose the necessary structural reforms to enforce growth and employment in national reform programmes. Both programmes are thoroughly examined by the Commission which proposes specific national policy recommendations. The latter are discussed again with the EC and are integrated in national policies.

As far as it concerns eurozone countries the national draft budgetary plans are presented to the Commission and to other states of the eurozone, and if they have negative spillovers for the euroarea revised draft budgetary plans are submitted.

The economic information included in the SCPs refers to the year that just ended (year t-1), the current year (year t), and the following three years (year t+1 to year t+3). The MTOs are expressed in structural terms and thus they mirror the CAB, net of one-off, or other temporary measures.

Further, the MTOs should (according to the provisions of the regulations) provide a safety margin with respect to the 3% of GDP deficit limit, should ensure sustainability or rapid progress toward sustainability, and should allow room for budgetary maneuver, in particular taking into account the needs for public investment. The safety margin with respect to the 3% of GDP deficit limit takes into consideration output volatility and the budgetary sensitivity to output fluctuations and sets the minimum benchmark. Conclusively, if a state experienced greater output volatility and a larger budgetary sensitivity in the past years it should set a more demanding MTO so as to attain the 3% limit.

Concerning sustainability, the value of MTO takes into consideration implicit liabilities and debt, guaranteeing the convergence of debt levels toward realistic levels. If the evaluation points out that a significant deviation from the adjustment path to the MTO takes place, the Commission addresses a warning under article 121(4) TFEU to the country concerned and sets in motion the deviation procedure.

Based on a Commission recommendation, a Council recommendation is applied, highlighting the proper measures to overcome the deviation problems. In case that a state fails to take action within the prescribed deadline or no effective action is taking place, there is a strong possibility for imposition of sanctions for a Eurozone state.

Thus, the evaluation of compliance provides answers to three questions. Is the MTO set at an appropriate level? Taking into account the structural balance, do member states follow a proper adjustment strategy to attain MTOs? Finally, are national expenditure plans in line with the expenditure benchmark?

While regulation (EC) 1466/97 defined that Eurozone and ERM II states should have an annual improvement in their structural balance of 0.5% of GDP as a benchmark, for countries with debt in excess of 60% of GDP (or with risks of overall debt sustainability), a faster adjustment path should be planned (above 0.5% of GDP). However, the regulation provides an exception in article 5(1) of regulation (EC) 1466/97 mentioning that

> in the case of an unusual event outside the control of the member state concerned which has a major impact on the financial position of the general government or in periods of severe economic downturn for the euro area or the union as a whole, member states may be allowed temporarily to depart from the adjustment path towards the medium-term budgetary objective . . . provided that this does not endanger fiscal sustainability in the medium term.

Regulation (EC) 1466/97 also permits temporary deviation from the MTO ("structural reform clause") when a country applies key structural reforms and if those reforms have verifiable and positive budgetary effects in the long-term and under the condition that the budgetary position returns to the MTO within the programme horizon.

Thus, following the six-pack reform of the SGP, compliance with the provisions of the preventive arm is evaluated in two ways. The assessment of the structural balance (first pillar) is complemented by an evaluation of the growth rate of expenditure aggregate net of discretionary revenue measures, which constitutes the other pillar. Compliance with the preventive arm is assessed through an overall assessment which takes both elements into account.

Concerning the expenditure aggregate, it is comprised of overall government expenditure net of interest payments, spending on EU programmes paid for by EU funds, and cyclical elements of unemployment benefits. The rationale is to focus on government spending that is independent of cyclical terms.

Conclusively, states have in mind that public expenditure is in line with a medium-term rate of potential GDP growth unless above the target performance in growth leads to additional revenues.

## The Corrective Arm of SGP

The primary legal basis of the corrective arm of the SGP is article 126 TFEU and protocol no. 12 to the treaty, which specify that EU countries shall avoid excessive deficits and define budgetary and debt levels limits.

EEG considers consecutive deficits as inflationary and destabilizing and thus it insists on compliance to the rule of 3% of GDP. Further, high public sector debt levels are linked with high interest payments (as % of GDP), crowding out effects (to the detriment of private investments), and increased danger of default. This leads to the conviction that the rule of a debt below 60% of GDP is non-negotiable.

When a state is found through the Commission communication to have imbalances, excessive imbalances, or an excessive imbalance with corrective action, an EDP is being followed (the fourth category is the "no imbalances" case and thus no measures are needed). What is the meaning of imbalances in the process? Article 2(1) of regulation no. 1176/2011 refers to imbalances as "any trend giving rise to macroeconomic developments which are adversely affecting, or have the potential to adversely affect, the proper functioning of the economy of a member state or of the EMU, or of the Union as a whole" and to excessive imbalances as "severe imbalances, including imbalances that jeopardise or risk jeopardising the proper functioning of the economic and monetary union" (article 2(2)).

States with such problems apply country-specific recommendations and are subject to monitoring. However, IDRs can also be prepared when unexpected negative facts demand urgent analysis (IDRs have been incorporated since 2015 in the European semester's country reports).

In the case that EU countries run excessive budget deficits of more than 3% of GDP, or cannot reduce their excessive debts (above 60% of GDP) at a sufficient pace, the EDP is applied. Following EDP provisions, EU countries should reduce their excessive deficits or debts back to acceptable levels and in case of failure, they not only face fines that can reach 0.2% of their GDP but also regional subsidies from the EU's cohesion fund may also be withheld.

The EDP (art. 126) starts when a country breaches or is in risk of breaching the deficit threshold of 3% of GDP or has a government debt level above 60% of GDP, which is not being reduced at an adequate pace (i.e., the gap between a state's debt level and the 60% reference needs to be reduced by 1/20th annually).

When a state violates the deficit criterion, the Commission is obliged to prepare a report (article 126(3) TFEU) evaluating the case for application of an EDP process. The EFC prepares an opinion (article 126(4) TFEU), and if the Commission perceives that an excessive deficit exists it issues an opinion to the state concerned and delivers a proposal on the existence of an excessive deficit. It further prepares a recommendation to be adopted by the Council and sets time limits for compliance with the deficit and the debt provisions.

A sanction in the form of a noninterest-bearing deposit could also be recommended if a eurozone country has already lodged an interest-bearing deposit within the preventive arm framework or when there is noncompliance with the budgetary policy obligations in the SGP.

States in EDP have six months (or three months when there is a serious breach) to comply with recommendations and to control excessive deficit. The reporting permits the detection of a country at risk for not correcting its excessive deficit by the deadline set by the Council. If such a risk exists, the Commission may decide to issue a recommendation to the country to take further or different action.

In any case, the Commission and the Council evaluate the measures the country has taken and decide accordingly taking into account the existence of exceptional events outside state's control. If the latter holds true, they can extend the deadline for correction and they revise the recommendations. In the case of persistent noncompliance, the sanction for a eurozone state may be increased to include a variable component and may be imposed as long as the state does not take adequate action.

RQMV voting is used for the imposition of most fines and a qualified majority of member countries is necessary to reject a Commission proposal for a Council decision (introduced since the six-pack reform). RQMV process makes difficult the formation of a blocking majority because of the necessary high majority threshold.

The two-pack framework also obliges eurozone countries within the EDP to draft EPPs, analyzing the required structural reforms for the correction of the excessive deficit.

The EDP is closed when the excessive imbalances are corrected. According to article 11 of regulation no. 1176/2011 "the Council, on a recommendation by the Commission, shall abrogate recommendations issued under articles 7, 8, or 10 as soon as it considers that the member state concerned is no longer affected by excessive imbalances."

## THE ASSISTANCE MECHANISM FOR EURO AREA COUNTRIES IN FINANCIAL DISTRESS

When significant financial stability problems come up, EU states have the ability to request access to EU financial assistance mechanisms which provide loans linked to specific conditions and macroeconomic policies. The ESM (an intergovernmental institution based in Luxembourg) provides assistance to Eurozone states and has a lending capacity of 500 billion euros (2017). Euro zone states under ESM programmes, may also take advantage of the outright monetary transactions programme of the ECB.

ESM lending is realized through five tools namely loans (FFA), precautionary credit lines (precautionary conditioned credit line, PCCL, and enhanced conditions credit line, ECCL), primary market support facility (PMSF), secondary market support facility (SMSF), and (direct or indirect) financial institutions' recapitalization. Conditionality applies to all types of lending according to the ESM treaty.

FFAs are the main tool for states with debt rollover crises. The provision of a loan is subject to conditionality and application of APs, analyzed in the MOU, and negotiated by the EC—the ECB and the state concerned.

Precautionary facilities are credit lines to avoid crises. Their provision concerns only states with sound economic fundamentals and are not accompanied by conditionality. Of course, there are certain criteria to be applied prior and after the provision of facilities to a state which are continuously controlled. ECCLs concern states with economic weaknesses and problems to apply the criteria for PCCLs are conditional upon specific measures.

PMSFs provide the ability to ESM to engage in the purchase of sovereign bonds in primary market purchases and to provide a complementary tool to loans. SMSFs provide capital to states that already have an AP and apply specific conditionalities.

The last tool of ESM is crucial and concerns financial assistance to the requesting country or, assistance directly to the financial institution(s) under distress. Recapitalization is always linked to conditionality but it can be realized in a state without an AP.

When a non-euroarea member experiences balance of payments problems, EU provides assistance through conditional medium-term loans usually in cooperation with the IMF. Article 143 of the TFEU provides the ability to grant assistance to an EU state when balance of payments problems have serious threats to an economy. In such a case the state concerned submits a request to the Council and to the commission followed by a detailed strategy on the policies to address the balance of payments problems. The two institutions decide on the conditions, time period, and amount of the financial assistance, and set out in detail the borrowing terms and procedure in the MOU. The memorandum is then signed and assistance is provided in tranches after an assessment realization.

## A CRITICAL EVALUATION OF THE CURRENT EEG

The effectiveness of EEG is under question in the last decade. It is also evident that, even after the implementation of reforms (Buti and Carnot, 2013; De Grauwe, 2013; Buti and Carnot, 2012) such as the six-pack, the European semester (in force since 1/1/2011), and the Euro Plus pact (European Council on March 24–25, 2011), the following questions remain unanswered:

a. What will happen if a country is led to a disorderly default within the euro zone?
b. How can the EEG framework effectively provide fiscal assistance to a member state of the eurozone that is under default conditions for a long period of time, and simultaneously comply with the no bail out rule?
c. How can the EEG framework respond to the long-term liquidity and solvency crisis of a eurozone member state without an effective lender of last resort?
d. What can the EEG do when, contrary to macroeconomic theory, national automatic stabilizers are neither predictable nor effective and when fiscal multipliers further exacerbate the failures of macroeconomic adjustment?

The experience shows that many problems of eurozone structure are still present and prevent maximization of full positive spillovers form the monetary union. As Andrle et al. (2015) highlighted despite many reforms that occurred in the governance of fiscal policy in the EU compliance is rather low. Although progress has been made on the deficit criterion the performance of member states on the debt criterion is disappointing.

In 17 member countries, the debt-to-GDP ratio deteriorated between 2012 and 2016. Six states still have debt in excess of 100% of annual GDP (Belgium, Greece, Spain, Italy, Cyprus, and Portugal) and a further six are in the range from 80 to 100%(Ireland, France, Croatia, Austria, Slovenia, and UK). Automatic stabilizers do not face the macroeconomic asymmetries (Dolls et al., 2015; Fichtner and Haan, 2014; Dullien, 2014) and complex institutional procedures lead to a time lag between a cyclical downswing and euroarea action.

Apparently, the incomplete structure of the eurozone is reflected in the lack of strong and long-term adjustment mechanisms in the fields of capital and labor mobility as well as in the field of sovereign debt.

Moreover, experience until 2010 demonstrated that there was no systematic and effective monitoring of national economy statistics, in order to verify the type of financial information, the quality of data, the method of data collection, the proper classification of information, and the frequency of reporting (in spite of European regulations 3605/93, 475/2000, 351/2002, and 2103/2005, which provided for efficient supervision). Thus, contrary to the will to exercise preemptive control, the early warning mechanism of SGP did not function properly, simply because no system of checks and balances was in place; thus trust and reputation, two concepts that are essential for intergovernmental economic coordination and the orderly operation of regional economic regimes, had been undermined.

Despite the abovementioned problems in eurozone structure and operation, it seems that policymakers share normative and causal beliefs about means-ends of European economic integration and about the content/nature of monetary policy. EEG applies a series of standard policies (i.e., fiscal discipline irrespective of economic/business cycle and exchange rates targeting irrespective of competitive monetary policies of USA, Japan, Switzerland, and China) but also promotes specific cognitive routines (Eurosemester) and practices (Europact+) to accommodate these policies (Hazakis, 2013).

Accordingly, when poor macroeconomic performance in a eurozone state is observed the blame is put on the unwillingness of the state to comply with necessary reforms or as it is often written to the inability of a state "to do properly its homework." It is considered that eurozone states with significant deviation from EEG targets are either subjected to pressures of particular groups and populist demands or captured by perverse ruling political/economic elite. Vested interests and strong lobbies resist reforms so as to maintain access to rents (Annett et al., 2005). Based on this suggestion, the painful economic austerity package is presented as a necessary process in order to achieve sustainable growth in the long-term since it creates conditions for Schumpeterian creative destruction normalizing all products, labor, financial market imperfections. Structural reforms are presented as welfare and equity enhancing in the long run, as necessary tools to dismantle vested interests.

## But, Which are the Current Cognitive Pillars of EEG?

First, price stability is being given primacy (Maastricht treaty, article 105 and article 127, para 1, of the TFEU concerning the corresponding role of ESCB) over all other economic targets and thus low inflation rate is conditio sine qua non, for smooth euro zone operation. There could be no trade-off at any point of the economic cycle between inflation and unemployment or inflation and demand-led growth.

In order to guarantee a sterilized stability strategy irrespective of economic/business cycles, ECB is nominated as the key independent institution to exert monetary policy. The latter provides the anchor for inflation expectations and leads member of the eurozone area to plan their national budgets in line with SGP and from 2013 in line with FCT. Taking also into consideration the links between productivity growth, wage levels, and stability of prices, it is considered that real wage increases which are not above productivity growth trends maintain the key target of price stability. Apparently, fiscal, financial, and structural policies are subordinated to monetary policy priority in order to attain price stability (Hazakis, 2013).

However, many questions arise from the inflation superiority. What constitutes an acceptable level of inflation and who is responsible to define it, taking into consideration asymmetric spillovers and structural discrepancies in eurozone regions? Further, is inflation targeting per se sufficient or is it part and parcel of a monetary targeting based only on money supply techniques? Equally important, which are the repercussions of a monetary policy not just in structurally different regions but also in regions with different crisis traits? How could one sustain European living standards if internal devaluation strategy concerns only wages and pensions and not the prices of basic inelastic goods and services?

Unfortunately, European economic experience clearly demonstrates that price stability was pursued independently of economic cycle and national developmental needs and did not take into account the negative spillovers of fiscal contraction.

The second cognitive pillar of EEG is that budget stability in the form of primary fiscal surpluses accommodates European monetary policy and reduces public debt levels (Hazakis, 2013). Abiding by budgetary supervision (initially as part of the convergence criteria of EMU, later as part of SGP established with the treaty of Amsterdam, and now as part of FCT, macroeconomic balance procedure, and six-pack intergovernmental agreements) is necessary because budget deficits for one eurozone state create negative externalities to other eurozone states favoring free rider behavior to the detriment of stable monetary policy.

Negative spillovers also emerge from the incentive of states incurring budget deficits (Morris et al., 2006, 6–8) as all costs are born by the eurozone as a whole, aggravating further financial instability and interest levels of bonds. Equally important, it is argued that spending biases are strengthened by vested interests and bureaucrats who are willing to lock-in budget allocations (Niskanen, 1971) that are higher than efficient allocations. This also means that budget deficits aggravate intergenerational burdens since the current decision-making mechanism decides a non-efficient and exorbitant consumption-led deficit to the detriment of those who will pay it after 20 or 30 years (Cukierman and Meltzer, 1989). In adverse fiscal terms, central intervention may only make things worse by posing moral hazard issues, rewarding prolonged maintenance of unsound fiscal policies. This is exactly why FCT of the TSCG focuses both on fiscal procedures and on fiscal outcomes forwarding four major targets which are the following:

a. There is a balanced budget rule including an automatic correction mechanism to be applied in national law.
b. The EDP is strengthened.
c. There is a clear enforcement of the numerical benchmark for debt reduction for member states with government debt exceeding 60% of GDP.
d. There is an ex ante reporting on public debt issuance plans to the EC and the European Council which allows for a better coordination of debt

financing among member states, increasing the transparency of governments debt management strategy.

Finally, it is further underlined that fiscal policies are exerted with a view to limiting risks to price stability (i.e., articles 123–126 of the TFEU).

More precisely, the individual responsibility of the member states in the field of budgetary policy is explicitly underlined by the treaty's no bail out clause (article 103) which mentions that neither the community nor any member state shall be liable for the commitments of another member state.

The prohibition of monetary financing of public deficits by ECB (article 101) and of privileged access for public authorities to financial institutions (article 102) represents rigid and binding rules to the conduct of national fiscal policies (Schuknecht, 2004). Thus, it is easily understood that FCT and six-pack provisions oblige eurozone states to submit annual stability programmes and balances, outlining their budgetary plans in conformity with the MTO of budgetary positions close to balance or surplus. Evidently, sound public finances are not just another principle of economic policymaking in EU (article 4, par 3) but do have a specific content (Bergman et al., 2013).

However, a number of practical and ethical questions remain unanswered (Hazakis, 2013). From a legitimacy point of view, the FCT obliges people to accept budgetary rules that do not result directly from the national democratic deliberation. People should accept the rules as permanent either as precondition for financial aid or as a result of intergovernmental quid pro quo to save eurozone. The treaty on stability and convergence in the EMU also underlines that all contracting parties accept that their budgetary position of the general government shall be balanced or in surplus (article 3a) and that "the rule shall be deemed to be respected if the annual structural balance of the general government is at its country-specific medium-target objective as defined in the revised SGP with a lower limit of a structural deficit of 0.5% of the GDP at market prices. The contracting parties shall ensure rapid convergence towards their respective medium-term objective" (article 3b).

The preventive arm of the SGP further enforces member states to maintain or to adjust toward their respective MTOs while the corrective arm of the SGP ensures the correction of excessive deficits in case they still take place. Evidently, FCT becomes a self-enforceable compact through a repeated game of involved agents (governments of eurozone) which should behave cooperatively based on prescribed austerity rules since gains from following these rules always exceed gains from opportunistic behavior in net present value terms.

A front-loaded perception of stabilization of fiscal policy without adequate measures for growth measures acts at the detriment of political support at the domestic field.

Moreover, any eurozone state wishing to receive help from ESM is invited to ratify the treaty and to transpose the balanced budget rule into its legislation. As it is stated in article 136 (TFEU) "the granting of any required financial assistance under the mechanism will be made subject to strict conditionality." However, the problem of compliance is not solved in the long term through enforcement but through an alternative policy framework which once adopted (based on a strong cognitive consensus of involved states) it could provide credibility in EMU rules and principles.

As eurozone experience shows, automatic stabilizers can operate when eurozone economies are close to balance or when deficits are due to regular marginal ups and downs of economic/business cycles but not when there is a need to correct excessive structural deficits combined with high debt-to-GDP ratios and contraction in demand. Such a mixture of political economy conditions renders deficit adjustment without real convergence and welfare programmes not only unrealistic but also dangerous for long-term interstate cohesion in eurozone (Hazakis, 2013).

It is also clear that FCT and six-pack as the last version of SGP fiscal surveillance mechanism do not provide sufficient incentives for the correction of fiscal imbalances linked to productivity and growth but rather adopt a static target of fiscal discipline against long-term growth. But which is exactly (at the analytical level) the "qualities" of golden budget rule, that is, is there a direct positive relationship between budgetary contraction and national growth or even between budgetary contraction and vested interests proportion of national GDP?

Surveys on fiscal multipliers underline that in advanced economies stronger planned fiscal consolidations have been associated with lower growth than expected with the relation being particularly strong early in the crisis (Blanchard and Leigh, 2013). Equally important, it has been suggested that the position in the business cycle affects the impact of fiscal policy on output (Baum et al., 2012).

Further, from an ethical point of view which are the long-term costs of national economic adjustment and how they are distributed? Is there an agreement over the acceptable size of groups living in poverty due to automatic rules of balanced budgets? Is there a time frame for combating negative consequences of a general austerity programme on people of fragile eurozone societies?

It seems that the permanency of the "golden budgetary rule" imposes a means regardless of the target of well-being of eurozone people and regardless of economic conditions. Policymakers are in the same policy trap as in the 1990s when the launching of euro took place without a coherent and reliable fiscal policy although now the situation is the opposite. Fiscal rules are imposed irrespective not only of the necessities of business cycle but also of the fundamentals of the euro currency.

Conclusively, the problem is not only effective budgetary supervision but also budgetary solidarity, targeting equally national growth and national debt. Otherwise, budgetary supervision does not bring results as GDP is reduced, unemployment soars, and heavy tax burden diminishes tax revenues due to Laffer curve effect. A sharp negative demand shock does not solve debt-to-GDP problems but leads the country in further violations of the pacts. As fiscal adjustment involves automatic actions to do simultaneously dramatic spending cuts and reduction of personal disposable income through tremendous increases in direct/indirect taxation, it leads to inability of most households to pay their duties and it leads to further rise of national deficit and to further automatic measures under FCT logic. The derived outcome is smaller propensity to save, and lower national savings base putting already vulnerable (in capitalization) national banks in more problematic situation and thus asking for more liquidity from ECB and more recapitalization from ESM.

Accordingly, both ECB and ESM throw money with no impact on real economy or on development since there are no loans to product- or export-led enterprises but only capital for attaining capitalization targets. Equally important, a constant ratio of debt-to-GDP could be sustainable as long as GDP growth exceeds the real interest rate and thus it is an urgent priority to concentrate on stimulating economic growth through productivity upgrading than through lowering (without any effective benchmarking) governments deficits (Hazakis, 2013).

The third cognitive pillar of current EEG is that the debt ratio to GDP is a target which should be accomplished more through reduction of public expenditure and less through rise of GDP. ECB again is treated as a privileged creditor but it cannot grant debt cancellations which could jeopardize monetary/inflation targeting. The debtors within eurozone are committed to full implementation of conditionality in exchange for ad hoc and case-by-case rescheduling of national debt by the creditor eurozone countries and the new mechanism of ESM. Instead of finding solutions to financing the gap between national investment and national savings (I/S gap) debt reduction is based on an "irrespective of economic cycle and growth rates" logic which deprives national governments from any possibility to respond to the particular conditions of domestic economies in a flexible manner through a mixture of eurozone and national fiscal instruments.

The EEG guarantees national loans interest rate payments but does not accommodate long-term economic development. This clearly set the terms not for a transition from a suboptimal point of national economic production curve to an optimum point but it creates the conditions for further contraction. As EU experience underlines, contraction provoked by a structural and long-term high debt/GDP ratio in lagged economic regions did not automatically lead to a more efficient allocation of resources. The Greek paradigm clearly demonstrates that markets and prices refuse to adjust and thus social dichotomies and division between social groups become larger. Overall, there is a problem when deciding whether a deficit or debt-to-GDP ratio is excessive because noncompliance after initial stages of austerity measures maybe a result of contraction per se and not of excessive consumption-led domestic growth.

A related issue is that of national sovereign debt management within a monetary union and risk sharing of national sovereign debt. This could be realized through a mechanism of gradual debt mutualization by strengthening the financial capacity of the ESM and streamlining its governance. However, to be a credible insurer against liquidity crises, the ESM should be able to provide financing in sufficient quantity and there should be an agreement on the optimal timing and features of debt restructuring. The extension of joint guarantees to ESM operations by its shareholders could raise the lending capacity of the mechanism in a significant way. Besides its quantity, the timeliness and predictability of financing are keys to the effectiveness of ESM operations (Hazakis, 2013). Of course, no one denies that any assessment on the solvency of a sovereign debt involves several elements (deficit and debt dynamics, the maturity profile of liabilities, growth prospects, macroeconomic and demographic risks).

Fourth, eurozone cannot maximize performance without a sufficient central budget. Without an adequate EU budget with enough resources to realize an intervention when it is required by an adverse economic cycle the debt-to-GDP problem will jeopardize euroarea stability. Many authors suggest that the solution is enforcing a budgetary union and is based on the idea that monetary union without a strong budgetary mechanism is incomplete (i.e., MacDougall et al., 1977). As De Grauwe eloquently mentions, "A central budget is important as a redistributive device. It also matters as a stabilizing instrument. The absence of a central budget in the euro area implies that no budgetary policy aimed at stabilizing the business cycle in the union is available" (De Grauwe, 2006, 723).

De Grauwe (2014) eloquently mentioned that the problem in the euroarea is the asymmetry in output and growth between its members. Indeed, when a state is deprived of an independent monetary and commercial policy, the only methods to achieve adjustment is through internal devaluation or through a central public finance system with intestate transfers. More and more, it becomes clear that euro area was characterized until 2012 by a unique combination of centralized monetary policymaking and largely decentralized fiscal policymaking and that the feature of "a single monetary policy and many fiscal policies" was also a problem to the smooth functioning of EMU.

However, one should also ask what kind of eurozone fiscal policy do we really need and how a coordinated (or even centralized) policymaking could act in both preventive/corrective way to revive sustainable economic development in all regions of the euro area. There is now enough experience from eurozone crisis to suggest that regional and cyclical divergences within the EU will not be self-correcting but rather require development measures through an enhanced EU fiscal policy.

Critics argue that such a "federal budget" will promote opportunistic behavior on national macroeconomic policies and will weaken the incentives for reforms. To avoid such a policy, analysts favored the national fiscal councils introduced by the fiscal compact (Pisani-Ferry et al., 2013). Within this logical framework, an enhanced EU budget should not be considered a redistributive money mechanism for consumption growth but a compensation mechanism to allow growth for lagged regions and permitting real and not only nominal convergence.

Lastly, EEG cannot deliver long-term growth and productivity gains in all regions of EU. Many textbooks on European economic integration underline that a single market in which goods, services, capital, and labor circulate freely is a conditio sine qua non for integration. Without necessary instruments to tackle the roots of the structural/economic problems (Pasterniak, 2007), namely, rigidities in goods/services and labor markets, EEG cannot ensure in the long-term competitiveness, sustainable employment levels and high growth rates in euro area. Thus, it is suggested that economic structures robustness should be further strengthened against adverse economic shocks and fluctuations (Issing, 2002, 354).

A number of labor market questions should also be answered. If labor market flexibility and reform of employment procedures are so important steps to efficient operation of eurozone as an OCA why labor market targeting is not included as a target or even as an incentive in revised SGP? Since all member states are committed to the common goal of a high level of employment (article 2 of the treaty) why this goal is not given an equal foot in key economic policy decisions?

European law clearly favors employment targeting as a major pillar of European integration. Article 125 of the treaty calls for a coordinated strategy for employment and article 128 provides the basis for employment guidelines. Moreover, the Luxembourg process obliges member states to consider employment as a matter of common concern and the "Annual employment guidelines" set out recommendations and priority areas of action. Since 1998, the Cardiff process aims to advance reforms through monitoring analysis while the Lisbon strategy for growth and jobs underlines the necessity of sustainable employment rates. Despite all these decisions, employment is considered de facto as a tool at the disposal of the price stability meta-rule. Instead of providing incentives to member states to achieve convergence in labor market, analytical and policy priority is given on specific monetary issue areas.

So, is there a need for a new ethical framework of EEG? Ethics of EEG should face not choices within undisputable constraints but choice among constraints of alternative policies. In the same manner, choice among alternatives positions of efficiency-equity cannot be only technical but incorporate an ethical dimension. Obviously, trade-offs between equity and efficiency should be accommodated within European economic integration large picture and should not be based on short-term dogmatic principles. Accordingly, the emphasis is not on prevailing rules beyond willful change but on new rules under which eurozone states act, making European economic integration game, a better one. SGP arrangements are beneficial under the condition that efficient euroarea economic coordination occurs and gains accrue to all members states from joint action. Thus, the first ethical principle of an alternative ethical arrangement is fairness of the new EEG contract for all involved eurozone states.

Of course, a new ethical approach of EEG does not ignore the omnipresence of opportunities for gaining at the expense of others, nor does it ignore the temptation for self-interested egoistic actors to take advantage of such opportunities. However, the central argument is that a new EEG focusing on mutually beneficial coordination is a much more sustained source of gains and that accordingly there are prudential reasons for Eurozone states to seek to improve further the SGP game by full and long-term commission to meta-rules that encourage and facilitate cooperation while discouraging exploitative strategies. The new "give and take" is fair enough because it provides not simply strong punishment rules but also strong incentives to all as well as equal opportunities to drawing the new meta-rules of EEG from all Eurozone states.

So, the principal role of EEG ethics is not ad hoc improvement of specific macroeconomic outcomes but improvement of the processes from which outcomes result where improvements mean that national and collective (Eurozone) intentionality is the outcome of a strong consensus. By allowing trust between Eurozone states a new policy framework provides strong institutional/financial/structural incentives and long-term stability.

Further, one should not ignore that an important ethical dimension in EMU is that of well-being which usually represents a utilitarian principle. It revives a debate similar to that caused by the reunification and the inequality of economic development between the German Länder. It also raises the issue of European solidarity and the use of public funds in this context.

Moreover, it highlights the issue of living together that is the basis of any political community at federal level.

Again, the principal EEG role is to improve the nature of the processes from which allocation outcomes result, where improvement means to better enable eurozone states involved to advance developmental purposes collectively and nationally. Well-being is strengthened through developmental aid and not through unquestionable capital transactions for consumption-led growth and thus it is rent-seeking free.

One should always bear in mind that improving EEG framework so as to enhance the prospects of mutually beneficial transactions and joint economic activities is not only a technical matter within the OCA theory but it is also a key ethical principle for a fair economic integration. Prudential economic governance without welfare acts against any public intervention for social security and social cohesion provisions.

Hence, it is suggested that EEG will be efficient the stronger the consensus on its morals/ norms/practices and the higher its effectiveness on development/monetary/prosperity targets.

## CONCLUSIONS AND POLICY IMPLICATIONS FOR EEG

It seems that EEG has run out of steam suffering from persistent economic stagnation. The cost of going backward is almost prohibitive and the pressures to change make it impossible to stay still. The monetary advantages are less than what were promised, are inequitably distributed, and are inefficiently administered. Practice and results demonstrate that we have not chosen the option with the highest collective utility or with the minimum collective opportunity cost. Conclusively, Eurozone cannot go ahead through short-term compromise trade-offs but it is obliged to reorganize long-term policies to allow maximization of potential output in all its regions. Unavoidably, the assignment functions and the internal competences should be redesigned.

Despite the successive reforms in EEG, many questions remain open and concern the ability of euroarea to face new crises effectively and timely. There is still much uncertainty about the viability of the EMU and of the EU integration project.

On the one hand, the optimists argue that the "endogeneity of optimum currency area" effect (meaning that Eurozone will become an OCA after the start of the monetary integration even if it wasn't before) can lead to EEG effectiveness. This presupposes the intensification of trade flows, rigorous financial integration, effective labor mobility, and common handling of the asymmetric shocks.

On the other hand, more interventionists argue that asymmetries in euroarea expressed through current account imbalances, misplaced private investment, and demand central fiscal coordination and intervention. Applying a prolonged adjustment on debtors by internal devaluation seems unlikely to succeed politically and economically.

Other authors suggest that the solution to European economic integration impasse is not just a different policy mix but a resizing of euroarea which includes only the core countries or an "avant-garde" group of European states, (i.e., France, Germany, Italy, Belgium, the Netherlands, and Luxembourg) which have more symmetry in their economic structures and better synchronized economic cycles and thus perform the criteria of an OCA.

Differentiated integration (Alesina et al., 1993; Leuffen et al., 2013; Leuffen et al., 2014; Stubb, 1996) titled "two-speed" or "multispeed" Eurozone, "variable economic geometry" or "a la carte economic integration" underlines the need to forward integration in selected policy areas by some member countries and involving the remaining states at a later phase. The argument seems at a first glance pragmatic since the EMU itself, the fiscal compact, the ESM, the Schengen Area, the Bologna process are examples of a variable integration within the EU. The integration strategy is realized as a process within the treaties (the enhanced cooperation procedure) or even outside the treaties (the ESM and the Fiscal Compact).

However, one puts the question if the Eurozone institutions are sufficient to handle a massive exit of the non-core euroarea states from the common monetary union. Further, are we sure that the exit will strengthen the monetary fundamentals of the core states or euro will not lose its international stance? Will such an exit facilitate the convergence of the exit states or it will consolidate the structural and economic gaps within the EU creating new tensions between the EU members? Very easily, an exit scenario could be considered a step for the Eurozone's disintegration and could involve significant fiscal and economic costs for the states following exit.

No matter which policy camp one chooses all agree on the need for profound reforms in EEG. EEG should be based on the fulfillment of five criteria, namely, transparency, legitimacy, consistency, effectiveness, and flexibility. Legitimacy refers to the need that reforms should not only fully respect the existing legal framework of EU but also respect the ideological foundations of the EU in political terms meaning enhancement of participation and inclusiveness in all levels of decision-making. It also means enforcement of input legitimacy, (the role of the EP and European parties) and output legitimacy (linked with the effectiveness criterion) targeting sustainable welfare for European citizens. Flexibility means the possibility of granting temporary derogations for those states unable to follow all necessary adjustments for a strong fiscal union immediately.

Transparency means an enhanced role of the EP in Eurozone decision-making and enhanced involvement in the macroeconomic APs. Finally, effectiveness and consistency mean the ability of EEG to deliver sustainable growth and employment rates throughout Eurozone. This does not mean only national economic reforms but decisive EEG and national structural reforms so as to achieve real economic convergence tackling at the same time the challenges of social cohesion.

Of course, the key question to be answered is not only which institutional pillars of EEG should be enforced and how but also how can arrangements / processes of SGP be framed by rules so that eurozone states are enabled (to the largest possible extent) to pursue in mutually compatible ways national and collective (European) interests. Such an EEG framework presupposes a normative answer to the question "What is the ultimate purpose of a reformed EEG structure?" Thus, one needs critical and explicit reflection on the ends as well as on the means of EEG, on the what/why as well as on the how.

Apart from this, there is a need to uncover from an ethical point of view the causal linkages and asymmetries of power between EEG structures, institutions, and actors, underlining when and how national/collective/institutional intentionalities are in conflict. This clearly suggests that a relevant analysis should not focus on EEG institutions per se as isolated policy units but should focus on their interactions allowing a comprehension of their dynamics and effectiveness. Unavoidably, the focus is on the fundamental traits of SGP economic regime or put it in the Hayekian way on how the order of actions is influenced by the order of rules. It also concerns the practical question of how euro zone states could improve the SGP provisions within which they act by applying better the rules of European economic integration project (Hazakis, 2013).

Which are the key policy implications derived from previous economic analysis? One should underline the following (Hazakis, 2013):

a. Economic growth, social cohesion, and stability go hand in hand and thus bias in favor of price stability works to the detriment of development. Moreover, prudent fiscal rules have to be not only internally consistent but also consistent with other eurozone macroeconomic and developmental targets.
b. SGP is run by asymmetric incentives logic underlining sanctioning and downplaying incentives to behave according to commonly accepted ethical/numerical rules. Thus, there is a need to move from a sanction-oriented EEG framework toward an incentive-based approach that treats eurozone member states as partners.
c. Reformed ethics of EEG should target not only on fiscal/developmental targets but also on proper institutions to supervise both fiscal discipline

and bank exposure to non-reliable investments. This also calls for an EU agency to rate banking activity and capitalization adequacy.

d. There is a need for a new EMU regime strengthening "development and budgetary solidarity." In this way, Eurozone regions minimally advantaged by eurozone dynamics will tend to be compensated by strong developmental inflows targeting exclusively on restructuring of capital accumulation processes and on social safety nets during painful austerity period. It also follows that eurozone ethics is not just applying balanced budgets but it is providing each citizen in eurozone economies with the ability of equal access to Rawlsian basic goods such as education and health.

One way or another, there is a need for profound EEG reforms and thus priorities should evolve around specific targets such as enhancement of EEG capacity to address crises and macroeconomic shocks, real (and not only nominal) convergence of national economies, effectiveness of supranational governance, sustainable growth and employment. Regrettably, as long as EEG acts in a short sight way, the veil of uncertainty over the future of European economic integration will be robust.

## BIBLIOGRAPHY


Alesina, A and Grilli, V. 1993. "On the feasibility of a one-speed or multispeed European Monetary Union". *Economics and Politics*, 5(2): 145–165.

Andrle, M., Bluedorn, J., Eyraud, L., Kinda, T., Koeva-Brooks, P., Schwartz, G., and Weber, A. 2015. "Reforming fiscal governance in the European union", *IMF Staff Discussion Note* 15/09, Washington, D.C.: IMF Publications.

Annett, Anthony., Decressing, Jorg., and Deppler, Michael. 2005. "Reforming the stability and growth pact". *IMF Policy Discussion Paper*, February. PDP/05/2, Washington, D.C.: IMF.

Baum, Anja., Poplawski-Ribeiro, M., and Weber, Anke. 2012. "Fiscal multipliers and the state of the economy" *IMF Working Paper Series*. December. Washington, D.C.: IMF.

Bergman, M., Hutchison, M., and Svend, Hougaard Jensen. 2013. "Do sound public finances require fiscal rules or is market pressure enough?" *European Economy*, Economic papers 489. April. Brussels: European Commission.

Blanchard, Olivier and Leigh, Daniel. 2013. "Growth forecast errors and fiscal multipliers" *IMF Working Paper Series*. January. Washington, D.C.: IMF.

Buti, M and Carnot, N. 2012. "The euro debt crisis: Early lessons and reforms". *Journal of Common Market Studies,* 50(60): 899–911.

Buti, M and Carnot, N. 2013. "The debate on fiscal policy in Europe: Beyond the austerity myth". *ECFIN Economic Brief* no 20, March. Brusseles: European Commission.

Cukierman, A and Meltzer A. 1989. "A political theory of government debt and deficits in a neo-Ricardian framework". *American Economic Review,* 6: 353–398.

De Grauwe, Paul. 2006. "What have we learnt about monetary integration since the Maastricht Treaty?" *Journal of Common Market Studies,* 44(4): 711–730.

De Grauwe, P. 2011. "Governance of a fragile Eurozone". *CEPS Working Documents* WD 346. London: CEPS.

De Grauwe, Paul. 2013. "Design failures in the eurozone-can they be fixed?" *European Economy.* Economic paper 491. April. Brussels: European Commission.

De Grauwe, P. 2014. *Economics of Monetary Union,* tenth edition. Oxford: Oxford University Press.

Dolls, M., Fuest, C., Kock, J., Peichl, A., Wehrhöfer, N., and Wittneben, C. 2015. "Automatic stabilizers in the Eurozone: Analysis of their effectiveness at the member state and euro area level and in International comparison". Mannheim: *Centre for European Economic Research.*

Dullien, S. 2014. *A European unemployment benefit scheme: How to provide for more stability in the Euro zone.* Gütersloh: Bertelsmann Stiftung.

Dullien, S and Fichtner, F. 2013. "A common unemployment insurance system for the Euro Area". *DIW Economic Bulletin,* 1: 9–14.

European Central Bank. 2013. The importance and effectiveness of national fiscal frameworks in the EU, *Monthly Bulletin.* February: 73–88.

European Central Bank. 2015. "Real convergence in the euro area: Evidence, theory and policy implications". *ECB Economic Bulletin,* 5: 30–45.

European Commission. 2017. *White paper on the future of Europe. Reflections and scenarios for the EU27 by 2025* (COM/2017/2025), 1 March. http://dx.doi.org/10.2775/32364

European Council. 2014. Conclusions. 26–27 June. http://data.consilium, europa.eu/doc/document/ST-79-2014-INIT/en/pdf

Fichtner, F and Haan, P. 2014. "European unemployment insurance: Economic stability without major redistribution of household incomes". *DIW Economic Bulletin,* 10: 39–50.

Gruner, Hans. 2013. "The political economy of structural reform and fiscal consolidation revisited". *European Economy,* Economic papers 487. April. Brussels: European Commission.

Hazakis, K. 2013. "Reconsidering the ethics of the stability and growth pact: Key implications for European debt crisis". Paper presented at the Association for Heterodox Economics Annual Conference. London. 4–6 July.

Issing, Otmar. 2002. "On macroeconomic policy coordination in EMU". *Journal of Common Market Studies* 40 (2): 345–358.

Juncker, J. C., Tusk, D., Dijsselbloem, J., Draghi, M., and Schulz, M. 2015. *Completing Economic and Monetary Union.* Brussels: European Commission.

Lorenzo, Vai., Pier, Domenico Tortola., and Nicoletta Pirozzi, eds. 2017. *Governing Europe. How to make the EU more efficient and democratic.* Brussels: P.I.E Peter Lang.

Leuffen, Dirk., Rittberger, Berthold., and Schimmelfennig, Frank. 2013. *Differentiated integration: Explaining variation in the European Union.* New York: Palgrave Macmillan.

Leuffen, Dirk., Rittberger, Berthold., and Schimmelfennig, Frank. 2014. "The European Union as a system of differentiated integration". *Political Science Series.* Working paper no. 137.

MacDougall, D., Biehl, D., Brown, A., Forte, F., Fréville, Y., O'Donoghue, M., and Peeters, T. 1977. *Report of the study group on the role of public finance in European integration.* Brussels: Commission of the European Communities, downloaded, http://www.cvce.eu/content/publication/2012/5/31/c475e949-ed28-490b-81ae-a33ce9860d09/publishable_en.pdf

McNamara, K. R. 2015. "The forgotten problem of embeddedness: History lessons for the Euro". In *The Future of the Euro,* ed. M. Matthijs, 21–43. New York: Oxford University Press.

Morris, R., Ongena, H., and Schuknecht, L. 2006. "The reform and implementation of the stability and growth pact". *ECB Occasional Paper Series* 47. June. Frankfurt: ECB.

Niskanen, W. A. 1971. *Bureaucracy and representative government.* Chicago: Aldine-Atherton.

Pasterniak, Angelika. 2007. "The Lisbon strategy and the quality of public finances". *Intereconomics.* November-December: 322–336.

Pirozzi, Nicoletta and Pier, Domenico Tortola. 2017. "Negotiating the European Union's dilemmas: Proposals on governing Europe". In *How to make the EU more efficient and democratic*, eds. Lorenzo Vai, Pier Domenico Tortola, and Nicoletta Pirozzi, 225–243. Brussels: P.I.E. Peter Lang.

Pisani-Ferry, J., Vihriälä, E., and Wolff, G. 2013. "Options for a Euro-Area fiscal capacity". *Bruegel Policy Contribution*, 2013/01.

Rawls, J. 1971. *A theory of Justice*. Cambridge, MA: Harvard University Press.

Rubio, Eulalia. 2017. "Federalising the Eurozone: Towards a true European budget?" In *Governing Europe. How to make the EU more efficient and democratic,* eds. Lorenzo Vai, Pier Domenico Tortola, and Nicoletta Pirozzi, 169–190. Brussels: P.I.E. Peter Lang.

Schimmelfennig, Frank and Winzen, Thomas. 2014. "Instrumental and constitutional differentiation in the European Union". *Journal of Common Market Studies,* 52(2): 354–370.

Schuknecht, L. 2004. "EU fiscal rules: Issues and lessons from political economy". *ECB working paper series*, 421, December. Frankfurt: ECB.

Stubb, Alexander. 1996. "A categorization of differentiated integration". *Journal of Common Market Studies,* 34(2): 283–296.

Torres, F. 2013 "The EMUs legitimacy and the ECB as a strategic political player in the crisis context". *European Integration,* 35(3): 287–300.

United Nations Statistical Commission, and Economic Commission for Europe. 2010. "The Odyssey of Greek Public Finance Statistics". Conference European statisticians – UNECE work session on the Communication of Statistics. 30 June–2 July. Paris. Available at http://www.unece.org/fileadmin/DAM/stats/documents/ece/ces/ge.45/2010/wp.22.e.pdf

Van Rompuy, H., Barroso, J., Juncker, J., and Draghi, M. (2012). *Towards a genuine economic and monetary union*. European Council, Brussels.

Véron, N. 2013. *A realistic bridge towards European banking union.* Brussels: Bruegel.

Von Hagen, J. 2007. "Achieving economic stabilization by sharing risk within countries". In *Intergovernmental Fiscal Transfers: principles and practice,* eds. R. Boadway and A. Shah, 107–132. Washington, D.C.: The World Bank.

## FURTHER READING

Allard, C., Brooks, P., Bluedorn, J., Bornhorst, F., Christopherson, K., Ohnsorge, F., and Poghosyan, T. 2013. *Toward a fiscal union for the Euro area.* SDN/13/09, Washington, D.C.: International Monetary Fund.

Bayoumi, T and Masson, P. 1995. "Fiscal flows in the United States and Canada: Lessons for monetary union in Europe". *European Economic Review,* 39(2): 253–274.

Beblavý, M and Maselli, I. 2014a. An unemployment insurance scheme for the Euro area: A simulation exercise of two options. 98. Brussels: Centre for European Policy Studies.

Beblavý, M and Maselli, I. 2014b. Time for some shock (absorption): Reinsurance of national unemployment insurance should be a Commission priority. Brussels: Centre for European Policy Studies.

Beblavý, M., Gros, D., and Maselli, I. 2015. Reinsurance of national unemployment benefit schemes. 401. Brussels: Centre for European Policy Studies.

Begg, I. 2009. "Fiscal federalism, subsidiarity and the EU budget review". Swedish Institute for European Policy Studies, Report 1, Stockholm: SIEPS.

Beukers, T. 2013. "The Eurozone Crisis and the legitimacy of differentiated integration". In *The Euro crisis and the state of European democracy,* eds. B. De Witte, A. Héritier and A. Trechsel, 7–30. San Domenico di Fiesole: European University Institute, Robert Schuman Centre for Advanced Studies and European Union Democracy Observatory.

Boadway, R and Shah, A. 2009. *Fiscal federalism – Principles and practice of multi order governance.* Cambridge: Cambridge University Press.

Claeys, G., Darvas, Z., and Wolff, G. 2014. *Benefits and drawbacks of European unemployment insurance*, Brussels: Bruegel.

Commission of the European Communities. 1975. *"Economic and Monetary Union 1980. Report of the study group*". Brussels: Commission of the European Communities.

Committee for the study of Economic and Monetary Union. 1989. *Report on Economic and Monetary Union in the European Community.* Luxembourg: Commission of the European Communities.

Dafflon, B. 2006. "The Assignment of functions to decentralized Government: From theory to practice". In *Handbook of fiscal federalism,* ed. E. Ahmad, 271–306. Cheltenham: Edward Elgar.

De Grauwe, P. 2012. "In search of symmetry in the Eurozone", *CEPS Policy Brief* no. 268.

Enderlein, H., Bofinger, P., Boone, L., De Grauwe, P., Piris, J. C., Pisani-Ferry, J., Rodrigues, M. J., Sapir, A., and Vitorino, A. 2012. *Completing the Euro: A road map towards fiscal union in Europe,* Report of the Tommaso Padoa-Shioppa Group Brussels: Notre Europe.

Enderlein, H., Guttenberg, L., and Spiess, J. 2013. "Blueprint for cyclical shock insurance in the euro area". *Studies & Reports* No. 100. Paris: Jacques Delors Institute.

Essl, S and Stiglbauer, A. 2012. "Prevention and correction of macroeconomic imbalances: The excessive imbalance procedure". *Monetary Policy and the Economy,* Q4/11: 99–113.

European Commission. 2012. *A blueprint for a deep and genuine economic and monetary union: Launching a European debate* COM 777 final/2. Brussels: European Commission.

European Union. 2015. "*Completing Europe's Economic and Monetary Union",* The Five Presidents' report. 22 June. http://ec.europa.eu/priorities/economic-monetary-union/docs/5-presidents-report_en.pdf

Furceri, D and Zdzienicka, A. 2013. The euro area crisis: Need for a supranational fiscal risk sharing mechanism? *IMF working papers* 13(198). Washington, D.C.: IMF.

Gocaj, L and Meunier, S. 2013. "Time will tell: The EFSF, the ESM, and the euro crisis". *European Integration,* 35(3): 239–253.

Hinarejos, A. 2013. Fiscal Federalism in the European Union: Evolution and future choices for EMU'. *Common Market Law Review*, (50):1621–1642.

Ioannou, Demosthenes and Stracca, Livio. 2011. Have euro area and EU economic governance worked? Just the facts, ECB working paper series 1344. May. ECB Publications.

Moschella, M. 2014. "Monitoring macroeconomic imbalances: Is EU surveillance more effective than IMF surveillance?" *Journal of Common Market Studies*, 52(6): 1273–1289.

Reuter, W. H. 2015. "National numerical fiscal rules: Not complied with, but still effective?" *European Journal of Political Economy,* (39): 67–81.

Treaty on Stability, Coordination and Governance in the economic and monetary union. 2012. Brussels, available at http: //european-council.europa.eu/media/639235/st00tscg26_en12.pdf last accessed on: 21/8/2017

## FURTHER QUESTIONS

1. Discuss the logic behind the convergence criteria of the Maastricht treaty. Are they enough for future Eurozone membership?
2. Which are the results of euro area membership on national inflation, interest rates, and monetary policy?
3. Discuss the content of the last ECB communication on monetary policy relative to the ECB objectives/instruments/strategy.

4. How transparency and accountability of the euro system can be enforced?
5. What is the difference between cyclically adjusted budgets and actual budgets?
6. Analyze the no bail out clause and its impact on the countries with significant sovereign debt problems in euro area.
7. Is debt default incompatible with Eurozone membership?
8. Is there a need for a common euro area fiscal policy to maximize common monetary policy spillovers on euro area growth?

# *Chapter 6*

# The Optimum Currency Area Theory

Although 55 years have passed since the launching of OCA theoretical framework, there is no consensus on the operationalization of its criteria. Buiter (2000, 222) suggests that "the theory of optimal currency areas is unfortunately one of the low points of post-world war two monetary economics," and Ishiyama holds (1975, 378) that "the theory of optimum currency areas is primarily a scholastic discussion which contributes little to practical problems of exchange rate policy and monetary reform." P. Krugman (1993b) notes that "it is arguable that the optimum currency area issue ought to be the center piece of international monetary economics." In another analysis P. Krugman (P. Krugman, 1993a, 3) eloquently mentions,

> We have some suggestive phrases-reduced transaction costs, improvement in the quality of the unit of account-to describe what we think are the benefits of fixed rates and common currencies. We even have a loose-joined theory of optimum currency areas that stresses the tension between these hypothesized benefits of fixity and the more measurable costs of lost monetary autonomy. What we do not have, however, is anything we can properly call a model of the benefits of fixed rates and common currencies.

The seminal contributions of Mundell (1961), McKinnon (1963), and Kenen (1969) led the foundations of classical OCA theory and were followed by other scholars underlining a wide spectrum of endogenous and exogenous OCA traits that are necessary and desirable for states looking to adopt a common currency. Modern approaches to OCA have also stressed that monetary integration implies transfer of sovereignty (exchange rate policy and monetary policy) from states to a supranational authority and thus it does have political dimensions.

Despite the fact that it is not possible to do justice with the vast literature on OCAs the chapter underlines the major tenets of OCA theory and underlines complementarities, interactions, and linkages between OCA and EMU.

## THE MAJOR TRAITS OF THE OCA THEORY

### Friedman on OCAs

Friedman (1953a) argued in favor of flexible exchange rates believing that they can absorb negative shocks. According to his analysis as state's wages are rigid and international factor mobility is low, flexible exchange rates swings (currency depreciation/appreciation) could bring national economies back to equilibrium overcoming balance of payments problems. On the contrary, a fixed exchange rates regime could not face effectively inflationary pressures and unemployment. Thus, factor mobility and monetary integration are linked with flexible exchange rates and adjustment process.

Studying the sterling area and the option to fixed exchange rates in the area as well as the flexible exchange rates between sterling area and other national currencies, he concludes (1953a, 193) that

> in a sense any flexible exchange system is such a mixed system, since there are rigid rates between the different sections of one nation-between say the different states of the United States. The key difference for present purposes between the different states of the united states on the one hand and the different members of the sterling area on the other is that . . . the latter are not all effectively subject to a single fiscal and monetary authority-the federal government-having ultimate fiscal and monetary powers.
>
> In addition . . . the latter have not effectively surrendered the right to impose restrictions on the movement of goods, people or capital between one another. This is a major factor explaining why a central monetary authority is able to operate without producing serious sectional strains.

Further, analyzing the differences between the sterling area and the USA he underlines (1953, 194) that

> the problem of maintaining exchange rates within the sterling area without restrictions on trade differs only in degree from the corresponding problem of the world as a whole. In both cases the area included a number of sovereign political units with independent final monetary and fiscal authority. In consequence, in both cases the permanent maintenance of a system of fixed rates without trade restrictions requires the harmonization of internal monetary and

fiscal policies and a willingness and ability to meet at least substantial changes in external conditions by adjustments in the internal price and wage structure. Many of these differences are of course themselves the product of the prior existence of fixed and stable exchange rates. Whatever their cause can be, I think be little doubt that on balance they mean that a system of fixed exchange rates has more chance of surviving without trade restrictions in the sterling area than in the world as a whole.

## Mundell's Contribution to OCA Analytical Framework

Mundell underlined four major traits which were often downplayed in 1970s and 1980s. First, it is highly important for a currency area to be as enlarged as possible with a maximum at a global scale. Thus, there is a trade-off between the currency area with a high factor mobility, though sometimes very small, and the convenience of money as he called it. It seems that this position leads to broad dollarization or large OCAs if the quality of money is poor and the area of its use is strongly limited as compared to the benefits of factor mobility.

Second, Mundell warned against the notion of many small currency areas. He stressed that the exchange markets might be too thin and therefore subject to single speculators which could distort the exchange rates. In small areas, the money illusion of workers might be less pronounced, so that the depreciation of the currency would trigger immediate wage increases to offset the increased costs for imported goods (Mundell, 1961).

Third, he mentioned seven conditions for the effectiveness and efficiency of flexible exchange rates underlining that "an international price system . . . is dynamically stable after taking speculative demands into account" (Mundell, 1961, 663) based on flexible rates. Overall, he seemed to believe in the absence of strong exchange rate fluctuations under a regime of flexible exchange rates suggesting (Mundell, 1961, 661) that "currencies are . . . an expression of national sovereignty . . . currency reorganizations would be feasible only in areas where political organization is in a state of flux such as in ex-colonial areas and in Western Europe."

This in fact stipulates that currency areas that comprise several nations should include a supranational state or the merging of states. But is this a necessary precondition, a derived result, or a desirable precondition? Why didn't Mundell shed more light on these major points?

In his concluding argument (1961, 663) he underlines that "the subject of flexible exchange rates can logically be separated into two distinct questions. The first is whether a system of flexible exchange rates can work effectively and efficiently in the modern world economy . . . the second concerns how the world should be divided into currency areas."

Thus, Mundell not only highlights the arguments concerning flexible and fixed exchange rates but he contributes on the definition of the optimal size of a currency zone. As he mentions (1961, 661),

> The argument for flexible exchange rates based on national currencies is only as valid as the Ricardian assumption about factor mobility. If factor mobility is high internally and low internationally a system of flexible exchange rates based on national currencies might work effectively enough. If regions cut across national boundaries or if countries are multiregional than the argument for flexible exchange rates is only valid under the condition that currencies are reorganized on a regional basis.

More precisely, he assumes two entities (1961, 658) A and B which are in equilibrium as far as it concerns balance of payments and employment and have their national currencies. Within such a framework the two states can change their monetary strategy whenever necessary. He then considers a shift of demand from B to A. He notes (1961, 658), "To the extent that prices are allowed to rise in A the change in the terms of trade will relieve B of some of the burden of adjustment. But if A tightens credit restrictions to prevent prices from rising all the burden of adjustment is thrust onto country B . . . what is needed is a reduction in B's real income and if this cannot be effected by a change in the terms of trade . . . it must be accomplished by a decline in B's output and employment."

He then supposes that the world consists of two countries Canada and USA each of which has separate national currencies. He also assumes a division into two regions which do not correspond to national boundaries, the east which produces goods like cars and the west which produces goods like lumber products. A shift in demand from cars to lumber increases the unemployment rate in the east, pushes upward inflation rates in the west and provokes payment imbalances between the regions. He underlines that (1961, 660) "finally the burden of adjustment can be shared between east and west with some unemployment in the east and some inflation in the west. But both unemployment and inflation cannot be escaped."

The flexible exchange rates could address payment imbalances between the two states but not between the two regions. Mundell eloquently concludes that (1961, 660) "the logic of the argument can in fact be rescued if national currencies are abandoned in favor of regional currencies." Thus, high labor mobility within a specific region gives the ability to the region to have a fixed exchange rate within its border and flexible exchange rates with other countries. However, in the absence of significant labor mobility within the region it does not matter what exchange regime the respective state has.

So, which are the key tenets of Mundell's analytical framework?

a. He underlines the functions of money as a medium of exchange and as a unit of account which is enforced the wider a currency is accepted. He states (1961, 662) that "money is a convenience and this restricts the optimum number of currencies. In terms of this argument alone the optimum currency area is the world regardless of the number of regions of which it is composed." According to his analysis the greater the number of currencies is the higher the informational and transaction costs of money.
b. Mundell underlines the differences in the adjustment strategy between a single currency zone and a currency zone with many national currencies and fixed exchange rates (1961, 658). As he mentions (1961, 658), "The policy of surplus countries in restraining prices therefore imparts a recessive tendency to the world economy on fixed exchange rates or (more generally) to a currency area with many separate currencies." On the other hand (1961, 659), "In a currency area comprising many regions and a single currency the pace of inflation is set by the willingness of central authorities to allow unemployment in deficit regions."
c. Although J. E. Meade and Tibor Scitovsky (Mundell, 1961, 661) underline the importance of factor mobility in a single currency zone it is Mundell who focuses on labor mobility as a key pillar of OCA since such mobility counterbalances the necessity of nominal exchange rate adjustment as a tool to combat external imbalances. If there is high mobility of labor force from region A to region B there will be no more unemployment or inflationary pressures and thus no need for possessing their own exchange rates but on the contrary a common monetary strategy will be satisfactory for both regions.

## The Endogeneity-Exogeneity View on Ocas

De Grauwe (2007) starts with a simple but always relevant question concerning the essence of OCA. Do the economists know for sure the link between economic integration and occurrence of asymmetric shocks?

De Grauwe (2007) argues that the relation between the two can be analyzed as follows. On the vertical axis of figure 6.1 we set out the degree of symmetry in the movements of output and employment between a group of states which are candidates for a monetary union and on the horizontal axis of the same figure we set out the degree of trade integration between these states. This measure could be the mutual trade of these states as a share of their GDP. He states that the resulting so-called EC view is represented by an upward sloping line underlining that as the degree of economic integration between states rises, asymmetric shocks will take place less frequently

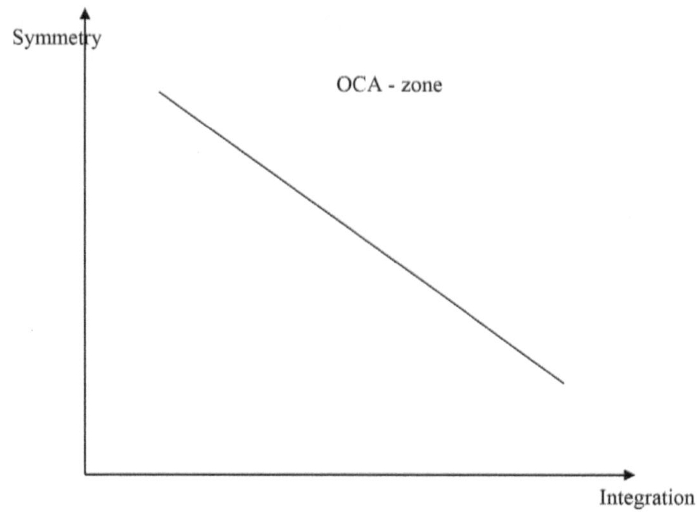


**Figure 6.1 Symmetry and integration as optimum currency area criteria.**

(so that income and employment will tend to be more correlated between the countries involved). Thus, symmetry increases.

On the other hand, there are those who argue that when economic integration rises, the states involved become more specialized so that they will be subjected to more rather than fewer asymmetric shocks and thus symmetry declines. De Grauwe claims it is reasonable that a presumption exists in favor of the EC approach (De Grauwe, 2007, 26). He argues that relevant regions in which some activity is centralized will transgress one or more borders. Thus, although integration leads to concentration effects, he underlines that national borders will increasingly be less relevant in producing a clear impact on concentration and regions may be influenced by asymmetric shocks. Conclusively, he states that monetary union intensifies economic integration and integration reduces asymmetric shocks (2007, 27).

According to De Grauwe et al. (2004, 17) a common currency precludes competitive devaluations, promotes reciprocal trade, economic and financial integration, and fosters business cycle synchronization among the countries sharing the currency.

De Grauwe et al. (2004) argue that

> the group of states is initially on the left of the OCA line. If these states form a union such as the European Union, both trade integration and income correlation within the group will rise. If the same states were to set in motion a currency zone (i.e. EMU) the degree of trade integration and income correlation within this group would rise even further and the group would subsequently find itself on the right of the OCA line.

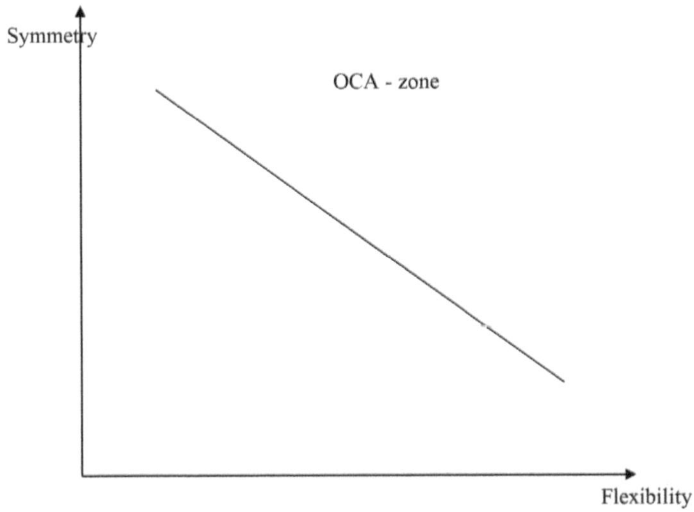


**Figure 6.2 Symmetry and flexibility as optimum currency area criteria.**

Overall, the new version of OCA underlines the endogeneity of the theoretical framework stressing that closer trade integration leads to better synchronized business cycles and similar production structures. Instead of asking which states are ready to join a monetary union the new dynamic approach underlines how effectively and speedy a new monetary union fulfills OCA criteria. Thus, the new version of OCA focuses on the degree of openness in a currency area (i.e., reciprocal trade between the members of such an area which tends to rise after the launch of a new currency) and on the positive interaction between income correlation and trade integration in a monetary union.

Frankel and Rose (1997) stressed that monetary union facilitates deepening of reciprocal trade and as far as it concerns euro area "countries which join EMU, no matter what their motivation may be, may satisfy OCA properties ex post even if they do not ex ante." De Grauwe and Mongelli (2005) analyzed further the concept focusing on the endogeneity of financial integration or equivalent of insurance schemes provided by capital markets, on the endogeneity of symmetry of shocks and on the endogeneity of labor and product market flexibility.

Cesarano (2006, 206) also concludes in his analysis that

> the notion of optimality is therefore endogenous in that the very operation of a common currency heightens those features underlining the optimality criteria. The equilibrium approach thus turns the received view of optimum currency areas on its head. The areas do not stem from preexistent optimizing features; rather, the features themselves are the product of an equilibrium process set off by the introduction of the common currency.

There is also a flourishing of studies based on the exogeneity of OCA, arguing that states which do not attain specific OCA criteria are under supervision and pressure to forward necessary structural reforms so as to ameliorate macroeconomic results. Such pressure is exerted officially through a network of rules, principles, norms, and decision-making procedures (i.e., the six packs in euro area).

Thus, EMU may not be an OCA according to the criteria of the classical version of the theory but it could be optimized through significant reforms leading to real wage flexibility.

## The McKinnon Approach on OCAs

McKinnon (1963) contribution complements Mundell's optimality criteria for a currency zone. Although he accepts Mundell's argument for factor mobility he underlines the degree of openness as a fundamental pillar of OCAs and defines the latter as the ratio of tradables to non-tradables sector. The more open an economy is the better is to adopt a fixed exchange rate. The higher the openness the most severe the changes in international prices would influence domestic prices in a country. For McKinnon (1963) optimum is a "single currency area within which monetary-fiscal policy and flexible external exchange rates can be used to give the best solution of three objectives."

In McKinnon's analytical framework, swings in exchange rates are not effective and put into danger the stability of prices. Further, if the economy is open, flexible exchange rates are not sufficient to ameliorate trade imbalances. As he stresses "In the extreme case where the economy is completely open . . . the only way the trade balance can be improved is by lowering domestic expenditures . . . changes in the exchange rate will necessarily be completely offset by internal price-level repercussions with no improvement in the trade balance." Moreover, money stability is conditio sine qua non for economic development since "the process of saving and capital accumulation in a capitalistic system is greatly hampered unless a suitable numeraire and store of value exists."

## The Kenen's Contribution on Ocas

Although Kenen underlines himself that mobility of factors of production is a key issue that delineates an optimum currency zone he suggests (1969, 49) that "diversity in nation's product mix, the number of single product regions contained in a single country, may be more relevant than labor mobility."

Consequently, diversifying a state's export base is fundamental since (1969) "the law of large numbers will come into play . . . its aggregate exports then are sure to be more stable than those of an economy less thoroughly diversified."

Evidently, highly diversified economies are better members for currency zones than less diversified economies in the meaning that export diversification protects an economy from industry- and sector-specific asymmetric shocks and attains adjustment without deliberate nominal exchange rate swings. Of course, in the case of unexpected and severe macroeconomic disturbance the negative impact on the export sector is inevitable and diversification could not absorb the total shock.

Kenen also notes that the higher the level of fiscal integration between two regions the grater the capacity to absorb asymmetric shocks through fiscal transfers from an area with low unemployment rate to an area with high unemployment rates. Of course, this could take place under the condition of a well-defined risk-sharing scheme which requires certain traits of political integration.

## CONCLUSIONS AND POLICY IMPLICATIONS

Many empirical and theoretical studies attempted to assess the advantages, costs, and risks of adopting a common currency based on the criteria of OCA framework. Most of them shed light on traits of OCA such as the degree of labor mobility, the system of fiscal transfers, the extent and specialization of trade, the similarity of national business cycles/economic structures, and the extent of asymmetric shocks. They tried to test feasibility and desirability of a common currency as well as to examine how close the EU states were to meet predetermined OCA criteria.

The results face significant analytical and methodological hurdles since many advantages and costs of OCAs are not tangible or permanent and depend on the economy structure, size, and policy credibility. Many questions are still raised and include the following: Is there a clear threshold of OCA traits beyond which OCA is verifiable? Is it time to focus more on intranational and regional levels of analysis in euro area looking for analogous adjustment mechanisms which optimize OCA criteria fulfillment at such geographical level? Why institutional framework is so much under graded in the effort to enforce collective action to adjust price/wages? Why certain traits of OCA optimality gained exorbitant preponderance (inflation, nominal convergence) relative to the other traits of OCA framework? Is anti-inflationary credibility enough per se to achieve real economic/productive convergence in all regions of euro area in the long term? Is OCA an elegant methodological-analytical vehicle for legitimatizing austerity policies within EMU governance or is it a framework to tying one's hands in macroeconomic policy as Giavazzi and Pagano suggest (1988)? Could endogeneity of OCA act per se as a tool to cure all aforementioned weaknesses in the meaning that a single currency puts in place strong and de facto irreversible processes which enforce euro area states integration and interdependence ameliorating OCA traits and OCA optimality in its totality?

Bayoumi, Eichengreen et al. (1997) underlined that "OCA theory while providing a useful template for research and helping to structure the debate over EMU, it remains difficult to estimate the project benefits and costs." Eichengreen (1996) also suggested that it was not possible to conclude whether the advantages and costs dominate for a specific state or a group as a whole.

Frieden (1998) is also skeptical on the application of classical OCA framework in EU because of the inability to measure the welfare impact of a common currency. Further, Ishiyama (1975) argues that the difficulties of delineating an OCA based on specific traits enforce the argument that each state should assess the advantages, costs, and benefits of joining a currency zone from the viewpoint of advantages of its own national interest and welfare.

The complexity of OCA operationalization put into question the validity of the theory for EU because OCA focused on the option between fixed exchange rates and floating exchange rates whereas EU states had to accommodate the option between the common currency (euro) and the quasi-fixed exchange rates of EMS. Further, there is the problem of inconclusiveness (Tavlas, 1994) as different features of OCA may send confusing signals over OCA optimality. A state might have trade openness relative to other states in the currency zone favoring fixed exchange rates while the same state might not have adequate labor mobility with partner states in the currency zone rendering flexible exchange rate regime feasible.

Equally important, there are significant differences in the financial structures of euroarea states (Berg et al., 2005) concerning maturity of national debt, household/enterprises wealth/debts as well as bank recapitalization needs (Angeloni et al., 2003) which have not been adequately addressed by classical OCA analysis.

Despite all aforementioned objections and reservations the key traits of OCA theory are still central in the debate of EMU. To start with, Mundell's arguments influenced EMU logic heavily. The deflationary bias thesis served as the basis of German monetary rationale and of ECB independence as well as the legitimating factor for the preponderance of price stability target over all other targets. Further, it becomes evident that currency zones that include many states with different production/export structures should involve a supranational organizational framework for attaining adjustment, convergence, and shock absorption.

Fiscal policy is also crucial in Mundell's paradigm. In the surplus regions of east, authorities can gather revenue through taxation so as to diminish Eastern demand and facilitate conveyance of the surplus to the Western regions. Of course, strong, transparent, and flexible fiscal rules are needed to avoid moral hazard problems in capital flows from developed to less developed regions of a monetary union.

Construction bubble in Spain, consumption spending in Portugal, and persistent government deficit in Greece were financed by low lending rates during the first decade of euro, creating unsustainable disequilibria in national current accounts. Indeed, in the absence of macroeconomic and banking surveillance, capital flows and lending procedures could create significant distortions and permanent asymmetric shocks. This presupposes further political unification in euro area which could enforce centralization of diversified national fiscal policies, maximizing the real convergence of productive/competitiveness structures of all regions.

Mundell's thesis on labor mobility also faces fierce problems in its application in EU. Interregional migration of workforce in EU is lower than USA due to diverse reasons such as higher mobility costs, differences in professional qualifications requirements, limitations on public sector employment and cultural barriers. Moreover, post 2010 migration in EU set in motion a brain drain of high skilled workers from European periphery to the core distorting the perspective of economic recovery and influencing negatively competitiveness drivers.

On the other hand, Kenen's contribution to product diversification is appropriate as a criterion for OCA in Europe under the condition that there is no asymmetrical industrial concentration in specific European regions. Thus, highly diversified regions are more suitable for currency zones than less diversified regions permitting control of negative industry shocks. However, is it possible to track product differentiation easily when it is beyond dispute that it is the outcome of several enterprises acting in different value added stages and within transnational clusters?

Tavlas (1994) highlights that small states which have strong trade openness and thus are in favor of fixed exchange rates with their trading partners in a currency zone are perhaps not enough differentiated in their production structures than larger states (problem of inconsistency). This again presupposes not just a common European currency but also an efficient fiscal transfer mechanism to address negative asymmetric shocks during adjustment of national industrial structures. Thus, the stronger a fiscal integration between areas, the better the competence to face negative shocks through capital transfers.

In any case, one should also mention that from a political economy point of view EMU is not a technical macro experiment but it is part of a broader, path-dependent, and highly complex process of economic-financial integration in Europe and as such it involves political traits of an evolving integration framework. Evidently, it is not possible to ignore institutional features of an OCA. Thus, productive inefficiency, regional divergence, and productive sub-optimality come up in the absence of a dynamic and steadily evolving integrative framework in an operation OCA since the institutional and economic vacuum provoked by national monetary sovereignty abandonment has to be filled by strong transparent and independent OCA institutions.

This also means that those states that de facto exert leadership or hegemony in a common currency area should bear proportionately not only the benefits but also the cost of such solidarity providing critical resources which enforce developmental aspects of OCA instead of maximizing short-term national advantages. In the end, when shocks in EMU prove to be permanently asymmetric and large, political criteria should come in overarching solidarity and unity within EMU common destiny than beggar-thy-neighbor autonomous monetary and economic strategies.

As Eichengreen and Frieden (1994) eloquently note that "the decision to create a single currency and central bank is not made by a beneficent social planner weighting the cost and benefits to the participating nations. Rather it is the outcome of a political process of treaty negotiation, parliamentary ratification and popular referenda." Fiscal transfers are crucial for the cohesion of the common currency area and should take into account two conditions namely the content/intensity of asymmetric shocks and the member state willingness to undertake structural/macroeconomic reforms that rearrange the distribution of fiscal transfers toward the tradables sector of economies/regions in trouble.

One should also bear in mind that automatic stabilizers do not perform effectively during cyclical downturns. Determining optimality of OCAs should take into consideration key developmental and structural traits of involved states so as to preserve capability for real convergence and not to perpetuate lock-in asymmetries and risks associated with national/regional productive macroeconomic and structural weaknesses and inconsistencies. Structural reforms do play a crucial role in adjustment process of national productive frameworks.

However, it remains to be seen, what is the efficient mixture of reforms in labor/product markets, their sequence and the way they are linked to macroeconomic stabilization strategies in lagged EU regions. More light should be shed also on microeconomic risks, advantages, and costs involved in delivering of structural reforms.

Finally, the role of ECB as lender of last resort as well as the role of single supervisory mechanism as a mechanism for bank surveillance should be further incorporated in OCA analysis. Debt and bank sustainability are crucial for efficient operation of a currency zone and should not be viewed as sui generis and temporary outcomes of economic cycle downturns.

Establishing a currency or a monetary union without efficient budgetary integration and without rule-based macroeconomic coordination is problematic and risky. Adjustment of member states economies to asymmetric shocks is based on an effective and consensual mixture of structural reforms-price flexibility, strategy-factor mobility policy, and interregional fiscal transfers guaranteeing synchronization of national business cycles and real economic convergence in the long term.

**Table 6.1 The Benefits of Eurocurrency According to Bibliography**

| | | | | |
|---|---|---|---|---|
| Avoidance of exchange rate risks | Enhancement of price transparency | Avoidance of the cost of currency hedging | Reduction of information costs in economy | Reduction of transaction costs in economy |
| Discouragement of price discrimination | Reduction of market segmentation | Promotion of competition | Stronger role of common currency as a medium of exchange | Stronger role of common currency as a unit of account and as international currency |
| Avoidance of beggar-thy-neighbor competitive devaluations | Facilitation of capital/ investment inflows | Promotion of trade flows | Stabilization and synchronization of national business cycles | Facilitation of labor market flexibility |
| Transparency of economic transactions | Lower interest rate costs | Pressure for coordination of national fiscal policies | Credibility to EMU | |

## BIBLIOGRAPHY


Angeloni, I and Ehrmann, M. 2003. *Monetary transmission in the Euro area: Early evidence.* ECB working paper no. 240. Frankfurt: ECB Publications.

Bayoumi, Tamim., Eichengreen, Barry., and Hagen von Jurgen. 1997. "European monetary unification: Implications of research for policy, implications of policy for research". *Open Economies Review,* 8: 71–91.

Berg, J., Grande M., and Mongelli, F. P. 2005. *Elements of the euro area: Integrating financial markets.* Aldershot: Ashgate Publishing.

Buiter, W. H. 2000. "Optimal currency areas: Why does the exchange rate regime matter? With an application to UK membership n EMU". *Scottish Journal of Political Economy,* 47(3): 213–250.

Cesarano, F. 2006. "The equilibrium approach to optimum currency areas". *BNL Quarterly Review,* LIX(237): 193–209.

De Grauwe, P and Mongelli, Francesco. 2004. *The enlargement of the Euro area and optimum currency areas.* Paper prepared for the 8th CERP/ESI annual conference on EMU Enlargement to the east and the West. September 24–25. Budapest.

De Grauwe, P and Mongelli F. P. 2005. *Endogeneities of optimum currency areas: What brings countries sharing a single currency closer together*? ECB working paper no. 468, Frankfurt: ECB Publications.

De Grauwe, P. 2007. *Economics of Monetary Union.* Oxford: Oxford University Press.

Eichengreen, Barry and Frieden, Jeffrey. 1994. "The political economy of European monetary integration: An analytical introduction". In *The political economy of European monetary unification,* eds. B. Eichengreen and Jeffrey Frieden, 1–21. Boulder: Westview Press.

Eichengreen, Barry. 1996. "Lessons from the gold standard for European monetary unification". In *Modern perspectives on the gold standard,* eds. T. Bayoumi, B. Eichengreen and M. Taylor, 365–387. New York: Cambridge University Press.

Frankel, J and Rose, A. 1997. *The endogeneity of the optimum currency area criteria.* CEPR discussion paper no. 1473. London: CEPR.

Frieden, Jeffrey. 1998. "The Euro: Who wins? who loses?" *Foreign affairs,* 112: 24–40.

Friedman, M. 1953. "The case for flexible exchange rates". In *Essays in positive economics,* ed. Friedman Milton, 157–203. Chicago: University of Chicago Press.

Giavazzi, G and Pagano, M. 1988. "The advantages of tying one's hands: EMS discipline and central bank credibility". *European Economic Review,* 32: 1055–1082.

Ishiyama, Y. 1975. "The theory of optimum currency areas: A survey". *IMF staff papers,* 22: 344–383.

Kenen, P. 1969. "The theory of optimum currency areas: An eclectic view". In *Monetary problems of the international economy,* eds. R. Mundell and A. Swoboda, 41–60. Chicago: University of Chicago Press.

Krugman, P. 1993a. *What do we need to know about the international monetary system?* Essays in international finance no. 190. Princeton: Princeton University, International Finance Section.

Krugman, P. 1993b. "Six skeptical propositions about EMU". *Greek Economic Review*, 15: 93–104.

McKinnon, R. 1963. "Optimum currency areas". *The American Economic Review*, 53(4): 717–725.

Mundell, R. A. 1961. "A theory of optimum currency areas". *American Economic Review*, 51(4): 657–665.

Tavlas, G. S. 1994. "The theory of monetary integration". *Open Economies Review*, 5(2): 221–230.

## FURTHER DISCUSSION

1. How much real convergence does a monetary union demand?
2. Does OCA theory provide a suitable analytical framework to assess the merits and costs of EMU?
3. Could immigrants solve the labor mobility rigidities in euro area?
4. Which should be the major pillars of a federal budget to deal with negative asymmetric shocks within euro area? How such a budget could be organized institutionally?
5. Can we draw on a robust modern theory of OCA when talking about regional integration?
6. What is an OCA as compared to a currency (or monetary) union? What is an "area" in this context?
7. Does an OCA, even more so a monetary union, need a common state and thus political unification?
8. Is it likely enlargement of euro area to raise the risk of asymmetric shocks?
9. How one can define optimality in terms of several OCA traits in EMU?

# *Chapter 7*

# The Challenge of Economic Adjustment in Eurozone

(This chapter is based on four earlier articles and chapters of the author published in 2015, 2016, 2017, and 2018.)

Economic adjustment, the effectiveness of fiscal policy and the crowding out results of expansionary public economics on private investments are not a new issue but have been examined since 1960s.

However, from 2008 onward sovereign and deficit crises in some members of the eurozone as well as the derived consolidation efforts in Portugal, Ireland, Greece, and Cyprus triggered once more the academic and policy interest on fiscal and structural adjustment issues (Gros and Alcidi, 2013; Sapir et al., 2014; Pisany-Ferry et al., 2013). Accordingly, the scope and speed of national consolidation efforts have been analyzed thoroughly (Blanchard and Leigh, 2013, 5) and the political-institutional aspects of APs have received rising attention (Featherstone, 2011).

Hungary was the first to accept financial support from both IMF and EU (November 2008) and paved the way for new procedures of IMF-EU cooperation (initially for Latvia in December 2008, Romania in May 2009, and later for Greece in May 2010, Ireland in December 2010, Portugal in May 2011, and Cyprus in May 2013).

## THE CONTENT OF ECONOMIC ADJUSTMENT POLICIES IN EUROAREA

Fiscal policy seeks to accommodate macroeconomic stability, provision of public goods, limitation of market failures, and effective distribution of income. Within fiscal planning, tax and spending measures do have an impact on product-labor markets and on how distribution of benefits-costs in national reforms is taking place. How fiscal adjustment is linked to structural reforms?

States are induced to apply structural reforms when confronted with an aggravation in economic terms activating the so-called crisis-induces-reform hypothesis (Drazen and Grilli, 1993). However, reforms are delayed and adjustment becomes ineffective when political fragmentation insists and when political parties try to enhance their influence through blocking reform initiatives (Alesina and Drazen, 1991; Roubini and Sachs, 1989). Moreover, when crises hit, fast or slow, adjustment critically depends on the electoral cycles (Mierau et al., 2007).

Already in the 1970s, Barro (1974) put the fundamentals of the EFC theorem, arguing that for rational economic agents, any increase in public deficits means higher taxation in the future and thus postponement of private investment and growth. Therefore, a fiscal contraction with lower public consumption and taxation could be expansionary if it is permanent, credible, and leads to lower taxes (Barro, 1979).

Feldstein (1982) further contributed to the formation of EFC thesis arguing that permanent reduction of public expenditure may be expansionist if it signals future reductions of taxation and thus shapes expectations for a permanent rise of incomes.

Fels and Froehlich (1986, 184–85) also emphasized for the West German economy in the 1980s that "fiscal consolidation had a benign impact on expectations . . . [An] important explanation is the way fiscal consolidation was actually brought about. Rather than raising taxes, the deficit was reduced by keeping a lid on expenditure growth . . . . By absorbing a smaller share of GNP, the public sector made room for the private sector to expand."

Policy experience shows that adjustment is attained either externally through a depreciation or devaluation of the nominal exchange rate or internally through reforms and fiscal consolidation which lead to reduction of demand and restoration of external competitiveness (Hazakis, 2017). Economic adjustment is thus a process of restoring macroeconomic fundamentals through deliberate economic/institutional action, intended to bring about concrete-measurable results over a specified time frame (Hazakis, 2015; Hazakis, 2018).

Which is the best way to achieve fiscal consolidation? The EFC theorem stresses that fiscal restrictions enforce private consumption, investment expenditures, exports dynamics, and thus an economy may expand contrary to standard Keynesian analysis (Alesina and Perotti, 1995; McDermott and Wescott, 1996; Perotti, 2012; Ardagna, 2004).

More specifically, Alesina et al. (1997), as well as Alesina and Ardagna (1998, 489), insist that fiscal adjustments are long lasting when focused on public expenditure rather than on tax increases. Two types of fiscal consolidation are possible (Alesina and Perotti, 1997a; 1997b).

In type 1 adjustment, the budget deficit is reduced through social expenditures cuts (i.e., subsidies for unemployed, minimum income subsidies, and other welfare programs) as well as cuts in wages of public servants. In type 2 adjustment, the budget deficit is realized through taxes on labor income and through cuts in public investment expenditures. They further argue that the fiscal episode of Ireland (1987–1989) is considered a type 1 adjustment, while Denmark fiscal consolidation (1983–1986) is considered a type 2 adjustment.

Although economists are not sure about the impact of fiscal consolidation on growth (i.e., the fiscal multipliers and how much a dollar of tax cuts or expenditure increase leads to a rise in GDP), tax reductions are perceived as more expansionary.

Eyraud and Weber (2013) and Mineshima et al. (2014) suggest that the mixture of revenue-expenditure fiscal measures does have a serious impact on the level of debt reduction attained through fiscal austerity while De Mooij and Keen (2012) underline that fiscal devaluation, meaning taxing more consumption rather than production, enforces export growth and leads to reduction of debt. Broadbent and Daly from Goldman Sachs (2010) also agree that expenditure reduction lowers bond yields and leads to positive growth rates above OECD average. Following an analysis of 44 fiscal adjustments over the last 35 years in OECD countries, they found that fiscal adjustment can be expansionary.

EFC theory also argues that fiscal consolidation restores trust in public finance reduces real interest rates of sovereign bonds and contributes to de-escalation of public deficits and public debt stocks. Moreover, rationalization of public wages, according to productivity levels, leads to internal devaluation, improvements in RULC, and enforcement of external competitiveness.

But how EFC is implemented in a common currency area where exchange rates are irrevocably fixed? According to EFC theorists' internal devaluation thesis is the only solution meaning rationalization of household incomes and wage salaries so as to restore external competitiveness (for an analysis see Hazakis, 2018). Flexible wages deregulated labor, product, and financial markets and reduction of unemployment benefits are considered critical prerequisites.

As Germany's ex federal minister of finance, Wolfgang Schauble, mentioned in Financial Times (2011), "Austerity is the only cure for the eurozone and thus states faced with high levels of debt and deficits need to cut expenditures and remove the structural hindrances in their economies, however politically painful." The triple economic recipe which emerges is "reduction of fiscal deficits, internal devaluation of incomes, higher direct/indirect taxes" in order to counterbalance the collapse of capital inflows and the imbalances in national current accounts.

It is also suggested that fiscal consolidation influences in a positive manner private households and companies, through the "expectation channel." Front-loaded fiscal consolidation creates optimistic expectations by anticipating tax reductions and increases in private agents' disposable income in the future (demand side). Equally important, it enforces investment and raises current consumption increasing rather than reducing national income. The emerging fiscal policy regime "eliminates the need for larger, maybe much more disruptive adjustments in the future" (Giavazzi and Pagano, 1990, 111).

Is the EFC theorem a sufficient methodological/policy framework for adjustment irrespective of the national economic cycle and irrespective of a country's economic structure?

Already in 2010, IMF underlined the methodological problems of the standard cyclical adjustment and mentioned that Alesina and Ardagna EFC framework "biases the analysis toward downplaying contractionary effects and overstating expansionary ones" (2010, 94).

Indeed, the common monetary policy did not deliver real economic convergence, and did not solve country-specific shocks (Pisani-Ferry, 2011). Fiscal and external imbalances, labor market and price rigidities, and low labor mobility persisted. Further, policy experience indicates that fiscal retrenchment had contractionary effects on economic activity and led to higher unemployment rates and high levels of national debt (Hazakis, 2018).

Although many empirical studies focused on the scope and speed of adjustment process, a number of critical questions remain on different issues of EFC theorem. First, how consumers overpass the liquidity constraints due to inadequate bank capital and falling household incomes and opt for more consumption? In an IS-LM model with fixed exchange rate, the financial channel is not delivering the anticipated results. Apparently, efficient and properly working banking and financial markets are conditio sine qua non for realization of positive consumers' expectations.

Already in 1930s, Keynes mentioned (1936, 210),

> An act of individual saving means—so to speak—a decision not to have dinner today. But it does not necessitate a decision to have dinner or to buy a pair of boots a week hence or a year hence or to consume any specified thing at any specified date. Thus, it depresses the business of preparing today's dinner without stimulating the business of making ready for some future act of consumption. It is not a substitution of future consumption-demand for present consumption-demand—it is a net diminution of such demand.

Apparently, if domestic credit is absent and if growth rates are anemic due to high taxes and economic uncertainty, domestic demand is weak, incomes fall, private debts cannot be paid, and banks face deteriorating balance sheets. The inability of banking institutions to extend non-performing loans and the deteriorating results of a low-wage labor market undermine Ricardian expectations and rationalization in the decision-making process of households. For example, Greek banks faced a vicious circle of capitalization needs as low incomes increased non-performing private loans and thus uncertainty led to bank run psychology of depositors in the years 2015–2016.

Second, how firms address the uncertainty over future demand due to persistent contraction and how they choose to invest rather than to adopt a wait and see policy? Samuelson underlined in 1948 (353–354) that "you can lead a horse to water, but you can't make him drink. You can force money on the system in exchange for government bonds . . . but you can't make the money circulate against new goods and new jobs . . . . You can tempt businessmen with cheap rates of borrowing, but you can't make them borrow and spend on new investment goods."

Indeed, if firms forecast a sluggish demand for their products/services, even a 0% interest rate won't stimulate their investment activity. In the same manner, if consumers are uncertain about their incomes and jobs, lower prices cannot stimulate their demand. Apparently, zero inflation and zero interest rates do not automatically deliver sustainable growth. Despite low interest rates, investment levels are low and output is below capacity. Further, horizontal spending reduction on all government investments (i.e., infrastructure, research, and development) is not only contractionary but sends the wrong signals to both firms and households (Hazakis, 2018).

Conclusively, uncertain expectations of firms/households about future income levels are more detrimental to investment/consumption patterns than tax levels. Uncertainty renders economic agents unable to calculate adjustment process impact and time horizon and leads if combined with a persistent deflationary policy to a disastrous "wait and see" policy both for consumption and investment decisions. As a result, the theory of rational expectations cannot enforce savings and investment decisions in the economic stages of persistent contraction.

Third, can internal devaluation and reduction of household incomes restore external competitiveness in all states of a monetary union irrespective of their trade and economic openness ratio and irrespective of the degree of states' integration in global productive networks? Is competitiveness improvement possible through fiscal consolidation only?

Without the existence of sustainable international/regional demands, RULC improvements cannot maximize their benefits. For example, German economy retrieved its competitiveness in the early 2000s based on strong demand by other euroarea countries. Similarly, if a state in adjustment has a high degree of trade integration with other states of a monetary union but none of these states is able or willing to sustain an increase of demand from the first state then current account imbalances will not be restored.

Obviously, if the surplus states deny to play in the medium term the role of a "locomotive machine" in the absorption of increased exports from the countries in adjustment then there is no way to sustain primary fiscal surpluses and to pay back debt (Hazakis, 2015). The deficit states need external demand from the surplus states so as to restore exports in sustainable levels and so as to ameliorate their terms of trade.

Moreover, combining competitiveness only with labor nominal wage is a part of the adjustment leaving aside the main question how to combine adjustment with non-price and structural supply-side variables such as the accumulation of productive capital, the state's specialization in regional/global trade, the adjustment of the local productive networks to the demands of international competition, the improvement of product quality, and the integration of local productive networks to the global/regional supply chains.

All of the abovementioned necessities presuppose capital and institutional support not suppression of wages. Equally important, EFC theorem wrongly argued for a reduction of unit labor cost in all sectors while the priority should have been the application of productivity reforms and RULC improvements in the non-tradables sectors of the eurozone economies.

In the same manner, even if one accepts the internal devaluation theorem a dramatic reduction in the incomes without an equal dramatic reduction in prices is not only antigrowth but also against any sense of economic justice. The deficit states need capital to modernize their equipment and to enforce the tradables sector so as to improve RULC through real productivity channels and not through salary reduction only. Is there such a mechanism in euroarea? Are there transfer mechanisms to compensate the deficit states for the negative impact of income-based adjustment on employment and welfare in the painful transition period? In Greece, for example, wages adjusted much more than prices, implying higher-than desirable purchasing power losses and a lower-than-desirable improvement in competitiveness (Hazakis, 2015).

Does internal devaluation deliver automatically higher exports to GDP? Since 2010 exports in the three of the four countries (Greece, Portugal, and Cyprus) under examination have contributed to GDP growth, lower than expected. Eurostat data (2017) clearly demonstrate that contribution of net exports to GDP growth deteriorated in Greece (from 3.1% in 2009 to −0.3% in 2016), in Portugal (from 0.7% in 2009 to −0.8% in 2015), and in Cyprus (from 5.7% in 2009 to −1.3% in 2015) while the only exception to negative trends was Ireland, (from 4.1% in 2009 to 1.4% in 2016). In the case of Greece, current account balances have been improved not through exports but through collapse of imports and internal demand.

Fourth, can one anticipate the same level of fiscal multipliers in countries with significant and persistent divergences in economic structure and institutional settings? How much are investment and consumption outputs affected by fiscal contraction?

Fiscal multipliers level is linked to the content and duration of a fiscal shock, to the specific traits of the economic environment, and to the economic policy framework. A multiplier of less than unity means a quick adaptation of the economy to fiscal consolidation priorities (i.e., consumer behavior, firms pricing, wages adaptation) while an above-unity multiplier means degradation of GDP and thus cancelling of investment and consumption decisions.

While the EFC theorem anticipates a perfect knowledge on the impact of fiscal multipliers, several economists raised doubts on the ability to estimate fiscal multipliers (Blanchard, 2015) irrespective of the economic cycle and without taking into consideration the path dependency of an economy, the structural deficiencies of an economy, the responsiveness of consumption and investment to income shifts, and the trade-economic integration patterns of an economy within a monetary union. Undeniably, fiscal and investment multipliers are quantitatively and qualitatively different in economies with persistent levels of high unemployment and unused production capacity.

Similarly, wrong predictions on fiscal multipliers have a disastrous effect on macroeconomic predictions and thus on the ability to implement fiscal consolidation programmes. The IMF's Independent Evaluation Office studied 133 IMF programmes in 70 countries and noted that "a tendency to adopt fiscal targets based on over-optimistic assumptions about the pace of economic recovery is leading inevitably to fiscal under performances" (IMF, 2003, vii). Economic agents do not automatically fill the output gap and compensate for GDP contraction (IMF, 2003, 6). A reversed crowding out hypothesis (meaning that a reduction in fiscal spending leads to higher expenditure of private economic agents) did not occur.

Thus, in contradiction with the Keynesian principles (highly flexible wages and prices tend to be destabilizing rather than stabilizing) the uncertainty about the size and content of fiscal multipliers undermined the positive spillovers of EFC theorem. In the same manner, excessive taxation (through the Luffer curve effect) combined with front-loaded collapse of all major GDP components undermine market and consumer confidence, breaks off social cohesion, and ends up in a strong recession trap where deflation is combined to low GDP performance making national debt unsustainable (Hazakis, 2018).

Fifth, how can a monetary union without a fiscal union address asymmetric shocks which occur simultaneously in more than two states when there are differences in national economic structures, in national business cycles, in national trade patterns, in trade specialization, and absence of perfect mobility of factors of production? Are there strong and highly coordinated economic institutions in euroarea to administer transfer of funds from richer to poorer euroarea regions and to attain insurance and risk sharing against macroeconomic shocks and sovereign debt crises?

The experience in euroarea demonstrates a preference for national fiscal consolidation only and not for the application of effective mechanisms to transfer investment capital from richest to poorer regions. The euroarea crisis also made apparent the lack of a strong Eurozone lender of last resort with the institutional-regulatory ability to provide all necessary long-term liquidity to eurozone market.

Sixth, can policymakers in states following APs identify and support efficient adjustment mechanisms? Experience demonstrates that it depends on a number of variables, including the institutional-productive capacity of a state as well as the ability to decide which social groups will be asked to make the sacrifices necessary to resolve the macroeconomic disequilibria (Hazakis, 2015).

Indeed, national adjustment trajectories differ with respect to which organizational traits are involved in the adjustment process, how economic institutions are modified, and which policy terms are proper to accommodate APs rationale. The asymmetry between front-loaded structural reforms and back-loaded realization of benefits creates political difficulties since weak political support (and thus pressure to minimize necessary transactions for the reforms) undermines the essence of the reforms.

Elites and voters only gradually come to believe that reforms will be applied in a steady and long-term way, and consequently learning and adaptation mechanisms cannot deliver results instantly. If one notes the asymmetry between budgetary measures and measures concerning employment and social cohesion then it is easily understood why well-entrenched vested interests enlarge their influence against adjustment through usual populist game theory tactics. IMF underlined in its January 2013 report (IMF, 2013a) for Greece that "the mounting sense of social unfairness was undermining support for the programme." Apparently, the results of structural reforms occurred with a significant time lag especially in economies trapped at the lower phase of the economic cycle (Hazakis, 2015).

Thus, although the impact of the quality of institutions on growth is stressed in the literature (Rodrik, 2000; Acemoglou et al., 2004; Acemoglou et al., 2012), identifying issues such as good governance, efficient administrative capacities, effective policy design and implementation, trust and credibility of policy, ability to apply fiscal measures in a consensual manner, and control of corruption, EFC seems to take them for granted downgrading the peculiarities and imperfections in government and institutional decision-making in many states (Hazakis, 2018).

Seventh, why structural reforms did not have an equal foot to fiscal consolidation in the euroarea fiscal consolidation programs? Adjustment experience confirms that domestic distortions persist if reforms are based upon expenditure cuts only, leaving domestic production structures and vested interests unaffected. Given the path-dependent specific circumstances-weaknesses of each eurozone country one should put the question what type of structural reforms are needed each time, which is the relevant hierarchy/priority, how structural reforms are applied, and how the burden of adjustment is distributed in society. The focus and priority of structural reforms should be to shift capital-labor from non-tradables to tradables sector of a national economy.

Lastly, does adjustment solve the national debt problem? Since EFC does not reshape the macroeconomic fundamentals in such a way so as to deliver an export-led and capital-intensive growth and since rescheduling of national debt is out of question in EFC economic decision-making, debt problems are not solved. The evidence is provided in this chapter when considering the application of euroarea consolidation programmes in Greece, Cyprus, Ireland, and Portugal.

## THE CAUSES OF ECONOMIC ADJUSTMENT IN EUROZONE

Most authors highlight two main groups of causes for the euroarea crisis (Buti and Carnot, 2014; Fernandes and Paulet, 2014; Hazakis, 2016). They understand eurozone crisis either as a result of national policy failures or as a result of the euroarea architecture. There are also some authors who underline the interaction of the two aforementioned groups of causes which finally lead to the "sudden stop" in current account balances, meaning the inability to finance deficits through lending (Alcidi et al., 2011). Baldwin and Giavazzi (2015), for example, underline as major causes of crisis, the lack of a central bank to provide a sovereign lender of last resort support, as well as the rigidity of labor and product markets in crisis countries, and the absence of a central management mechanism in the euro area.

In the "national economic policy failures" argument, the blame is put on the lack of fiscal discipline, the failure to carry out structural reforms, the weaknesses of the tradables sector of the national economies, and the external borrowing that was not productively invested but led to the construction bubble.

In the "European architecture failure" argument, the blame is put on design imperfections of euroarea (Mongelli, 2010; De Grauwe, 2015). Indeed, euroarea sovereign debt crisis did not provoke immediate actions and favored ad hoc adjustment strategies and mechanisms for its members. EEG not only failed to anticipate the timing, complexity, and magnitude of Eurozone debt crisis but delayed to provide adequate institutional solutions (failure to prevent/control systemic risk). In the first two years of the crisis (2009–2010) the profound asymmetry and tension between the urgent macroeconomic-financial priorities of Eurozone, the structural economic deficiencies in eurozone periphery, and the institutional-management capacity of EEG were crystal clear (Hazakis, 2016).

Indeed, EEG intervention in national economic adjustment has developed in an ad hoc way which from an institutional point of view involves high transaction cost, systemic uncertainty, and coordination vacuum. Although eurozone states were characterized by different economic structures, diversified trade accounts, and idiosyncratic business cycles, economic APs through troika supervision enforced a "one size fits all" policy linking conditionality to debt installments (Hazakis, 2015). Further, the terms of the economic APs that troika (IMF, ECB, EC) enforced in Portugal, Greece, Ireland, and Cyprus (and incorporated in MOU) from 2010 onward did not favor structural and real convergence to euro area average but mainly attained nominal convergence with Eurozone average in fundamental macroeconomic targets (Hazakis, 2015).

More specifically, as far as it concerns the inadequacies of euroarea architecture with an impact on adjustment policies one can note the following:

a. Euroarea institutions anticipated a small interconnectedness of national banks in euroarea downplaying the contagion effects of the banking crisis in the European economy. The failure to identify the linkages between the sovereign debt and banks accounts further maximized the systemic risk in eurozone.
b. The euroarea institutions underestimated the systemic risk of a sovereign debt or bank crisis in the small economies of the euroarea and focused only on the large economies.
c. The euroarea authorities anticipated real convergence irrespective of structural reforms and central economic coordination at eurozone level. As a result, in the first years of the euro, financial markets perceived sovereign debt as mutually guaranteed and deprived of risk in all euroarea states. They also expected a centrally coordinated and financially sound plan if systemic risk emerged.

Turning to the national policy problems and macroeconomic failures one can observe many similarities and differences in states implementing APs. Based on macroeconomic data one easily perceives that the four states under examination had at the beginning of the crisis common economic traits but also differed enormously (Hazakis, 2017).

Portugal and Greece shared three common traits, namely, high external debt, low rate of national savings, and low competitiveness. Ireland had a much lower debt ratio, possessed higher savings rate but was heavily exposed to financial market because of a construction bubble. In Cyprus, Greek, PSI caused heavy losses in the two largest banks of the country (Hazakis, 2017). The aforementioned facts linked with the housing and credit bubbles deteriorated the ability of the private sector to pay back and as a consequence provoked the necessity for Cypriot state to follow APs.

Greek banks were also exposed to the domestic public sector because of public bonds. As a result, the implementation of the PSI programme in early 2012 in Greece had a negative impact on pension funds that held Greek government bonds obliging them to adjust pension payouts. At the same time the weakening of the banking system, concerns about bank balance sheets, and a possible debt haircut created an atmosphere of bank run with massive deposit outflows in Greece in years 2010 and 2015.

Equally important, the four countries had to address similar constraints as they were members of a monetary union (with no possibility of currency depreciation or devaluation), they could not apply for sovereign debt restructuring because of euroarea rules and the amount of euroarea financing was limited.

As far as it concerns fiscal policy in the four countries, it was until 2008 procyclical stimulating disposable income and consumption, through credit. Indeed, precrisis growth rates were robust in Greece (3.5% on average 1999–2008), in Spain (4%), and in Ireland (6%). Further, in Greece productivity gains were realized through bank loans and domestic demand and not through exports. The decline of interest rates and the credit expansion led housing boom in Ireland and Spain and enforced construction growth, house purchases, and domestic demand. Between 1999 and 2008, housing prices in Greece rose by 110% and in Spain and Ireland by 150%. The debt of households also rose from 17% of GDP in 1999 in Greece (compared to about 50% in Spain and 62% in Portugal) to 52% in 2007 while growth of loans to households averaged 28% in the years 1999–2007.

On the critical issue of inflation levels in the four countries, data illustrate that they were bigger then in north states as the average inflation rates in Portugal, Ireland, Spain, and Greece ranged between 2.9% and 3.4% compared with only between 1.6% and 1.8% in Germany, Finland, Austria, and France between 1999 and 2007.

A fundamental issue has also been the openness ratio where with the exception of Ireland (80%) the other economies did not perform as expected (in 2007, exports of goods and services were 23% of GDP in Greece, 25% in Spain, and 30% in Portugal).

As a result, the increase in domestic demand led to a steady reallocation of the factors of production to domestically oriented sectors aggravating further macroeconomic developments. With regard to Greece, the current account balance rose from 5.1% of GDP in 1999 to nearly 15% of GDP in 2008 making the economy vulnerable to economic cycles and highly dependent on foreign loans.

## ANALYZING THE CONTENT AND LOGIC OF THE APS IN EUROZONE

According to regulation 472/2013/EU, three types of economic surveillance are implemented in adjustment, namely, enhanced surveillance, programme-based surveillance, and post-programme surveillance.

There are significant differences in conditionality between the three aforementioned types which range from an organized macroeconomic AP to implementation of specific eligibility terms. The content of surveillance depends on the seriousness of the financial difficulties of the euroarea country concerned and the type of the financial assistance it receives and takes into account the measures of economic policy coordination provided for in the TFEU.

Which adjustment route was chosen by the countries in examination in the years 2010–2017? On March 25, 2010, euro area leaders took the decision to support the Greek economy through bilateral loans with the involvement of IMF, and on April 11, they specified the terms of support (European Commission, 2010). Greece officially requested EU-IMF financial assistance on April 23, 2010 and the so-called troika was activated (the IMF, EC, and the ECB).

A second package of financial assistance of 130 billion euros followed in March 2012 (European Commission, 2012a), with a specific set of prior actions. It included a haircut on privately held Greek public debt (the well-known PSI). Indeed, Greece exchanged bonds worth 199.2 billion euros in face value and attained a relief of about 100 billion euros in present value terms.

In August 2015, the Hellenic Republic concluded a third agreement with the ESM for three years (August 2015–20th August 2018) and total financing of 86 billion euros (European Commission, 2015b). Again the country signed a MOU with the EC with specific conditionalities. The latter were evaluated at regular reviews focusing on four key issues namely restoring fiscal sustainability, guaranteeing financial stability, safeguarding growth, competitiveness, and investment and enforcing a modern public administration.

Ireland was the second country to apply for APs with the troika. It agreed in November 2010, to a rescue package of 85 billion euros in order to recapitalize its banking sector which suffered from non-performing loans

(European Commission, 2011a). Portugal followed in May 2011 due to significant macroeconomic and current account imbalances and received assistance of 78 billion euros (European Commission, 2011b).

Spain received assistance in July 2012 also to recapitalize the banking-financial sector (European Commission, 2012b) and Cyprus followed in April 2013 receiving 10 billion euros for recapitalization needs as its banks had unexpected losses from the PSI programme in Greece (European Commission, 2013).

Clearly, the IMF had an active participation in all aforementioned programmes (three-year extended arrangement approved in December 2010 for Ireland, three-year extended arrangement approved in May 2011 for Portugal, and three-year extended arrangement approved in May 2013 for Cyprus).

Which was the institutional process for national APs implementation in euroarea? In all programmes, negotiations of the states concerned with officials from the EC, the ECB, and the IMF took place and MOUs as well as specific conditionalities attached to the programmes followed. A Memorandum of economic and financial policies analyzed the targets and measures to be applied, a MOU provided programme details, and a Technical MOU illustrated the content of key definitions for the programmes.

Which were the pillars of euroarea adjustment logic in the MOUs? The basic pillars of the euroarea adjustment rationale (although the list is not meant to be exhaustive) were the following (Hazakis, 2015):

a. The rational expectations hypothesis which mentions that all diverging eurozone countries will eventually converge on a correct macroeconomic model of a balanced and surplus economy.
b. Priority of adjustment is given to the application of an extensive front-loaded fiscal adjustment to cut excessive domestic demand, restore fiscal primary surpluses, and restore market confidence. The adjustment includes reduction in state/municipal subsidies of all categories as well as redesign of the tax base.
c. Adjustment in euroarea level means provision of clear and rigid rules for all participants. Within this framework, IMF strengthens its surveillance role and becomes de facto a key player in the adjustment process (see provisions of regulation no. 472/2013, articles 1b, 3(1), 3(5), 7(1)).
d. The causes of Eurozone sovereign debt are not systemic but are national. Sound fiscal policies are considered vital to sustain recovery and to provide policy flexibility against new economic shocks.
e. Last, structural reforms (Vogel, 2014) in diversified sectors such as health, pensions, protected professional activities, and labor and product markets are considered key ingredients of adjustment (Bouis and Duval, 2011) targeting productivity and RULC improvements (D'Auria et al., 2009; Varga

> et al., 2013). Structural policies, thus, seem to gain an important, although not equal, status to fiscal stabilization in order to restore exports and growth and remains in states to limit adverse adjustment burdens/risks.

One can theoretically analyze the content of euroarea APs in the period 2010–2016 at three levels.

At the first level, there are basic concepts and routines of economic adjustment which are apparent in all programmes. The concepts define the cognitive conditions that lead to compliance or to noncompliance with Euroarea adjustment framework, reflect and shape the macroeconomic priorities of states in memoranda influencing how economic assistance is distributed, how conditionality is structured, and what kind of economic action is taken. Obviously, the question of how to institutionalize expansionary austerity (Scott, 2014) principles at the domestic level retains the essence of adjustment action. The tetralogy "fiscal stabilization—low inflation—primary surplus—structural reforms" determines national economic decision-making (Hazakis, 2015).

Within this framework, eurozone economic asymmetries are considered to be of a transitional nature and are linked to temporary disequilibria and imbalances generated by domestic fiscal and banking crises. National structural deficiencies, internal policy failures, national economic mismanagement, and incomplete structural reforms end up in national economic failures and are the key obstacles to national effective insertion in Eurozone core.

Likewise, sharp adjustment is considered sufficient if it addresses fiscal and external deficits and if it ameliorates access to international capital markets (Belke, 2013). As a result, the priority of fiscal stabilization overrules all other targets of adjustment irrespective of national macroeconomic cycle dynamics. Although article 9 of the TFEU underlines that in applying its policies and activities the EU takes into account requirements linked to the promotion of a high level of employment; the guarantee of adequate social protection; the fight against social exclusion; and a high level of education, training, and protection of human health, APs gave priority to fiscal consolidation. Despite the fact that article 7 (para 7, subpara 2) of regulation 472/2013/EU states that at the initiative of the EP any macroeconomic AP should take into account "the need to ensure sufficient means for fundamental policies, such as education and healthcare" social inclusion policies are downgraded in the APs (Hazakis, 2015).

The second level of content analysis concerns institutional arrangements which influence national economic agent motives and risks/profits/burdens in an AP implementation. Accordingly, financial assistance provided in the four countries was conditional and provisional (see regulation 472/2013/EU). Through the conditionality clause, the troika was not only engaged in design and surveillance of programmes but also in the micromanagement of fundamental domestic public policies (governance-related conditionality).

As article 136 (para 3, TFEU) underlined "the granting of any required financial assistance under the mechanism will be made subject to strict conditionality." Eurozone states that accepted assistance was required "to prepare in agreement with the commission acting in liaison with the ECB and where appropriate with the IMF, a macroeconomic adjustment programme" (regulation 472/2013/EU, article 7, para 1, subpara 1). In this way, reforms and installments were linked and financial support depended on compliance of member states to budgetary, structural, and macroeconomic targets of memoranda.

Besides, ECB intervention was ad hoc, exceptional, and subject to price stability targets. In the exceptional case that ECB adopted a strong stance, the instrument of intervention was used judiciously given its implications for monetary policy (Draghi, 2015). Moreover, such an intervention was based on a clear and consistent national assessment of the economic fundamentals (Hazakis, 2016).

The third level of content analysis concerns not only the institutions per se but the structure of adjustment surveillance and the functional interconnectedness of the troika institutions. The synergies between all key institutions to face Eurozone debt crisis were embedded in the previously mentioned tetralogy of EFC framework. Monitoring compliance with the policy terms of MOU as well as European Council decisions application was assigned to the troika (ESM treaty article 13, para 7) and its reports were connected with loan tranches (ESM treaty, article 15, para. 5).

In this way the overall emphasis of APs shifted from the question of how to reorganize Eurozone/national institutional hierarchies so as to attain the OCA criteria, to if national economic logic guaranteed macroeconomic equilibrium and full compatibility with technical targets of the adjustment paradigm. Moreover, programmes were based on a sanction-driven adjustment and not on an incentive-driven rationale which could provide necessary time for adjustment.

## THE ASSESSMENT OF ECONOMIC APS IN EUROAREA

Many researchers analyzed thoroughly the constraints, benefits, and failures of the APs in eurozone (i.e., Sapir et al., 2014). It seems that adjustment efforts in euroarea faced two key problems (Hazakis, 2015).

First, time lag existed between adjustment efforts-reforms and deliverable results distorting a clear link of reforms to adjustment and competitiveness. Further, the asymmetry in APs between correction of fiscal imbalances (which are based on a specific set of budgetary tools) and the ineffectiveness of structural reforms was elusive in certain cases (i.e., Greece).

Second, not only the delay effected but also the nature of crisis in euroarea periphery prevented an ongoing evaluation of APs. Indeed, in states with collapsed internal demand, limited liquidity for private and public investment and diminished GFCF, accurate projections for structural adjustment and competitiveness improvements (which were vital for debt sustainability) were impossible (Hazakis, 2018).

A critical overview of the literature on APs in euroarea underlines the following key lessons from the AP implementation in euroarea in the years 2010–2017.

a. In Greece and to a lesser extent in Portugal, the programmes proved to be overoptimistic about the governmental ability to implement a large number of politically difficult reforms. As Olivier Blanchard (Blanchard, 2015) stressed for the Greek programmes, they "only served to raise debt and demanded excessive fiscal adjustment," they were "used to repay foreign banks," and as a result "growth-killing structural reforms, together with fiscal austerity, have led to an economic depression."
b. The fiscal multiplier which was the base of programmes turned out to be too small in Greece (0.5) and Portugal (see also Hondroyiannis and Papaoikonomou, 2015). IMF itself underlined in October 2012 that actual fiscal multipliers were larger than the ones assumed by the economists (Blanchard et al., 2013).

   Taking into consideration the inability to devalue the currency and the structural problems of most countries in adjustment it was naïve to expect a small impact of fiscal consolidation on fundamental economic activities and national demand.
c. Likewise, the assessment of public debt sustainability was based on unrealistic assumptions undermining the risks linked with the projections (GDP growth and privatization receipts) and downgrading structural and institutional problems of countries with APs. However, the bulk of the increase of public debt in Greece was due to growth underperformance despite enormous fiscal consolidation.

   Indeed, the APs did not put a brake on debt dynamics of the economies in APs (Hazakis, 2015) and they did not address the problems of private and bank debt. Even in the best performing Ireland, the weight of the debt stock or debt servicing costs on total tax revenue remained significant. The private sector indebtedness was high (nonfinancial private sector non-consolidated debt stood at 322.3% of GDP at the end of 2015) and the non-performing loans ratio for domestic banks stood at 14.7% at the end of June 2016 (among the highest in the eurozone).

**Table 7.1 General Gross Government Debt as a Percentage of GDP (2009–2016), October 1, 2017, European Commission**

| *Year* | *Greece* | *Cyprus* | *Portugal* | *Ireland* | *EU-28* | *Euroarea-19* |
|---|---|---|---|---|---|---|
| 2009 | 126.7 | 53.4 | 83.6 | 61.7 | 72.8 | 78.4 |
| 2010 | 146.2 | 55.8 | 96.2 | 86.3 | 78.4 | 83.9 |
| 2011 | 172.1 | 65.2 | 111.4 | 109.6 | 81.1 | 86.1 |
| 2012 | 159.6 | 79.3 | 126.2 | 119.5 | 83.8 | 89.5 |
| 2013 | 177.4 | 102.2 | 129.0 | 119.5 | 85.7 | 91.4 |
| 2014 | 179.7 | 107.1 | 130.6 | 105.3 | 86.7 | 92.0 |
| 2015 | 177.4 | 107.5 | 129.0 | 78.7 | 84.9 | 90.3 |
| 2016 | 179.0 | 107.8 | 130.4 | 75.4 | 83.5 | 89.2 |

*Source*: European commission, 2017.

It is well worth noting that high public debt implies a smaller fiscal margin for maneuver to absorb adverse macroeconomic shocks and cope with possible rises in interest rates.

d. The programmes applied an enormous front-loaded fiscal adjustment without taking into consideration the effects on local economic structures and productive networks. The programmed primary balance reached 3.5% points of GDP for Greece, 8.2% points for Ireland, and 4.8% points for Portugal (Eurostat, 2017). As the Greek case illustrated, high levels of taxation did not contribute to reduction of transaction costs since they favored tax evasion and grey economy disorganizing effective networks of firms (Hazakis, 2017; 2018). This means that the average annual fiscal adjustment required was larger than in Latin American programmes in the 1980s and 1990s.

Primary surpluses were not attained by the same manner. Greece managed to achieve fiscal surpluses through high direct and indirect taxation while privatization revenues were below expectations. The issue concerns the balance between tax increases or reduction of government expenditure. In the Greek case it proved to be all shock but not fiscal therapy due to a false policy mixture of higher taxes and unconditional horizontal expenditure cuts.

Indeed, a sustainable adjustment should address with the same rigor and in the same time the three fundamental imbalances of an economy (Hazakis, 2018), namely, private saving (S) to private investment (I), exports (X) over imports (M), and government spending (G) over tax revenues (T). If a policy focuses only in one of the aforementioned three dimensions, there could be no effective equilibrium and there is negative impact of a fiscal policy on the other two dimensions especially on firm performance, on employment rates, and on welfare levels (Hazakis, 2015).

e. Along with fiscal consolidation, the programmes did not succeed in many cases to promote structural reforms. The multiplicity of targets in different

**Table 7.2 IMF, World Development Indicators, Gross Domestic Product per Capita, Constant Prices, National Currency**

| *Country* | *2009* | *2010* | *2011* | *2012* | *2013* | *2014* | *2015* | *2016* |
|---|---|---|---|---|---|---|---|---|
| Cyprus | 20.787 | 20,490 | 20,051 | 18,916 | 17,711 | 17,600 | 18,128 | 18,613 |
| Germany | 30,709 | 32,001 | 33,197 | 33,362 | 33,468 | 33,860 | 34,066 | 34,233 |
| Greece | 21,553 | 20,327 | 18,464 | 17,173 | 16,742 | 16,919 | 16,989 | 17,001 |
| Ireland | 38,401 | 38,988 | 38,853 | 38,301 | 38,598 | 41,745 | 52,377 | 54,615 |
| Portugal | 16,663 | 16,971 | 16,686 | 16,079 | 15,984 | 16,214 | 16,535 | 16,832 |

*Source*: IMF database, October 1, 2017.

policy areas and the lack of prioritization created too often policy confusion (Kopits, 2016). Instead, adjustment process should have targeted transaction costs at all levels of economic action, improvement of corporate governance/conduct, minimization of systemic/sectoral risks, and enforcement of structural competitiveness.

Evidence illustrates that Greece, for example, made little progress with politically difficult measures, including competitiveness-related measures such as privatization and rationalization of the public sector activities (Wyplosz and Sgherri, 2016). Moreover, the troika overestimated the administrative capacity of the Greek government and underestimated the opposition that structural reforms would face from vested interests.

On the contrary, structural reforms had better results in Portugal and even much better in Ireland. In the former, most structural reforms were linked to labor-product market reforms and government expenditure while in Ireland political conditions permitted the implementation of product and labor market reforms in the country.

f. The programmes downgraded the role of institutions in adjustment although non-effective institutions and political conflict postpone or downgrade structural reforms, blocking reform legislation (Roubini and Sachs, 1989; Alesina and Drazen, 1991; Rodrik, 2000). Too often, policy gaps emerged between the intentions of the economic AP designers and the capabilities of institutions undermining adjustment performance.
g. Troika conditions focused on fiscal consolidation, downgrading the necessity for an explicit growth policy. Economic stagnation means that fiscal deficit/GDP and national debt/GDP ratios remain high due to a falling denominator. As GDP falls, more bank assets become non-performing deteriorating the sovereign debt crisis and further undermining banks position.

   Here again a number of variables are responsible for this trend among others: the larger-than-expected fiscal multipliers, the deterioration in the external environment and in investor confidence, an optimistic evaluation of the initial macroeconomic conditions, an overestimation of the state administration capabilities, and a lack of political ownership.

h. There was no clear demarcation of responsibilities between the IMF and its European partners in the first years of APs, and their areas of competence overlapped considerably. As noted in the IMF's ex-post evaluation of Ireland's Extended Arrangement, "A unified approach would have helped communicate the program objectives more effectively and avoid possible uncertainties and mixed signals" (IMF, 2015).
i. Equally important, APs deteriorated social deprivation. Thus, there was not an ongoing evaluation about how APs' benefits, burdens, and responsibilities should be distributed between social groups in euroarea countries following austerity programmes. A key negative spillover of the AP policy has been the rising inequality in income distribution due to collapse of incomes and deteriorating labor market terms (Hazakis, 2017; 2018).

As a result, intra-Euro divergence persisted and rose. The GDP per capita rate of Greece was 70.87% of the German GDP in 2009 but only 52.4% in 2016 and the same negative trend holds true for all the other states under examination namely Cyprus, (66.1% in 2009 but 48.6% in 2016), Portugal (55.2% in 2009 but 48.23% in 2016), and Ireland (123% in 2009 but 120% in 2016).

According to IMF data (IMF database, 2017) which highlight economic divergence of Eurozone periphery states vis-à-vis north euroarea states, the ratio of per capita income (in constant prices) of Germany relative to Greece although steadily narrowing in 1990s to a low of 1.53 worsened to 2.12 in 2013 and for Italy and Spain it also worsened to 1.36 and 1.38 in 2013, respectively. This is alarming because widening gap in euroarea per capita incomes not only undermines European cohesion but undermines the provision of public goods such as education and health. The result is widening of income inequality as the poorer rely mainly on wages, state benefits, and public goods provision while the richest get a much higher percentage of their income from capital.

**Table 7.3 Unemployment Rates, Number of Unemployed as a Percent of Total Labor Force (2007–2016)**

| *Year* | *Greece* | *Cyprus* | *Portugal* | *Ireland* | *Euro Area* |
|---|---|---|---|---|---|
| 2010 | 12.7 | 6.3 | 12.0 | 13.9 | 10.2 |
| 2011 | 17.9 | 7.9 | 12.9 | 14.7 | 10.2 |
| 2012 | 24.5 | 11.9 | 15.8 | 14.7 | 11.4 |
| 2013 | 27.5 | 15.9 | 16.4 | 13.1 | 12.0 |
| 2014 | 26.5 | 16.1 | 14.1 | 11.3 | 11.6 |
| 2015 | 24.9 | 15.0 | 12.6 | 9.4 | 10.9 |
| 2016* | 24.7 | 13.4 | 11.6 | 8.2 | 10.3 |

*Source*: Eurostat, October 1, 2017 (for 2016* the data are preliminary).

**Table 7.4 People at Risk of Poverty or Social Exclusion (As a Percent of Total Population)**

| | *2009* | *2010* | *2011* | *2012* | *2013* | *2014* | *2015* | *2016* |
|---|---|---|---|---|---|---|---|---|
| European Union (28 countries) | n.a. | 23.7 | 24.3 | 24.7 | 24.6 | 24.4 | 23.8 | n.a. |
| Italy | 24.9 | 25.0 | 28.1 | 29.9 | 28.5 | 28.3 | 28.7 | n.a. |
| Germany (until 1990 former territory of the FRG) | 20.0 | 19.7 | 19.9 | 19.6 | 20.3 | 20.6 | 20.0 | n.a. |
| Ireland | 25.7 | 27.3 | 29.4 | 30.0 | 29.5 | 27.6 | 26.0 | n.a. |
| Greece | 27.6 | 27.7 | 31.0 | 34.6 | 35.7 | 36.0 | 35.7 | 35.6 |
| Cyprus | 23.5 | 24.6 | 24.6 | 27.1 | 27.8 | 27.4 | 28.9 | n.a. |
| Portugal | 24.9 | 25.3 | 24.4 | 25.3 | 27.5 | 27.5 | 26.6 | 27.9 |

*Source*: European commission, October 1, 2017.

APs' negative spillovers were also apparent in employment and risk of poverty indicators. The common ground for all four countries included austerity measures that were not socially balanced and included downward real wage adjustments. It is no coincidence that in 17 of the EU countries the number of people at risk of poverty or social exclusion has raised since 2008.

As a result, two types of poor emerged in euroarea countries in memoranda. The chronically poor consisting of people whose poverty predates fiscal stabilization and are below poverty line as a direct result of public expenditure rationalization. The new poor comprising of those who have been pushed into poverty by the anti-development tetralogy of lower incomes, higher taxes, higher domestic goods/services prices, and high household loan installments. For both groups there is a need to guarantee stability on the provision of fundamental public goods during recession and to provide mechanisms for individual capabilities reorganization. This definitely leads not to horizontal cuts in government expenditure but to changes in inter- and intra-sectoral government expenditure allocation to preserve certain levels of fundamental public goods at the time of front-loaded fiscal stabilization.

Conclusively, APs were deprived of a well-designed, properly financed, front-loaded, and unconditional poverty reduction policy framework (PRPF).

j. Finally, ownership of the programmes defined as "a willing assumption of responsibility or an agreed program of policies" (IMF, 2001) was different in the countries which implemented APs.

In Greece, there was a lack of ownership (Kopits, 2016) while Ireland had from the beginning of its programme a high degree of ownership putting in

**Table 7.5 Labor Cost Adjustment Indicators (2009–2016)**

| | *Real Unit Labor Costs 2009–2016* | *Real Unit Labor Costs 2009–2016* | *Real Unit Labor Costs Shift from 2000–2009 Relative to Euro-19* |
|---|---|---|---|
| *Country* | *%* | *Score* | *%* |
| Greece | −7.7 | 6.1 | 13.8 |
| Ireland | −15.4 | 10.0 | 24.8 |
| Spain | −6.9 | 5.6 | 5.0 |
| Portugal | −10.8 | 8.4 | 3.2 |
| Cyprus | −8.4 | 6.6 | 13.1 |
| Italy | −2.1 | 2.1 | 6.2 |
| Germany | −0.7 | 1.0 | −5.8 |
| Euro-19 | −2.3 | 2.2 | 0.0 |

Values: Cumulative change in real unit labor costs in percent, 2009–2016.
*Source*: Euro plus monitor, The Lisbon Council, October 2017.

place reforms before the negotiations with the troika (i.e., the target of the national recovery plan in November 2010 to reduce the budget deficit target to 3% of GDP by 2014). Portugal also had a strong ownership to implement the extended arrangement with the IMF (Kopits, 2016).

Accordingly, the main achievements of APs concern primary fiscal balances, current account balances, and RULC. According to the Lisbon Council, (The Euro Plus Monitor, September 2017), from 2010 to 2017, the states that adjusted the most as far as it concerns deficits were Greece (No. 1), Ireland (No. 4), Cyprus (No. 9), Portugal (No. 10), and Spain (No. 13) while on the critical issue of labor cost the states that adjusted more were Ireland (No. 1), Greece (No. 2), Cyprus (No. 3), Spain (No. 4), and Portugal (No. 5).

Concerning the current account balances, in Spain and Portugal, the trade balance adjusted by about 8.5% points of GDP, with the contribution of exports being 8 and 11% points and that of imports 0.5 and −2.5%, respectively. In Ireland too, the improvement of the trade balance was the result of an increase in both exports (60 pp.) and imports (43 pp.). Finally, Greek adjustment took place through a massive contraction in imports, while the export sector played a minor role.

On the other hand, the level of public and private debt is higher than in 2009, across the eurozone. Productivity rates in the eurozone are lagging behind that of the USA. Total factor productivity growth had been particularly weak in the four countries (Greece, Italy, Portugal, and Spain) that had the lowest labor productivity in 1999 (IMF, July 2017).

During the core of euro area crisis (2010–13) strong divergence also took place in the dispersion of GDP per capita levels. The main adjustment channels (trade, labor, and capital flows) did not produce the expected convergence dynamics in euroarea. Further, labor mobility continues to be low

**Table 7.6 Current Account Balance as Percent of Gross Domestic Product**

| | *2009* | *2010* | *2011* | *2012* | *2013* | *2014* | *2015* | *2016* |
|---|---|---|---|---|---|---|---|---|
| Spain | −4.3 | −3.9 | −3.2 | −0.2 | 1.5 | 1.1 | 1.4 | 2.0 |
| Italy | −1.9 | −3.4 | −3.0 | −0.4 | 1.0 | 1.9 | 1.4 | 2.6 |
| Germany | 5.7 | 5.6 | 6.1 | 7.0 | 6.7 | 7.5 | 8.6 | 8.3 |
| Ireland | −5.6 | −2.0 | −2.4 | −2.6 | 2.1 | 1.6 | 10.0 | 4.6 |
| Greece | −12.3 | −11.4 | −10.0 | −3.8 | −2.0 | −1.6 | 0.1 | −0.6 |
| Cyprus | −7.7 | −11.3 | −4.1 | −6.0 | −4.9 | −4.3 | −2.9 | −5.3 |
| Portugal | −10.4 | −10.1 | −6.0 | −1.8 | 1.6 | 0.1 | 0.1 | 0.8 |

*Source*: October 1, 2017, European Commission.

**Table 7.7 Net Lending (+)/Net Borrowing (–) as Percent of GDP**

| | *2009* | *2010* | *2011* | *2012* | *2013* | *2014* | *2015* | *2016* |
|---|---|---|---|---|---|---|---|---|
| European Union (28 countries) | −6.6 | −6.4 | −4.6 | −4.3 | −3.3 | −3.0 | −2.4 | −1.7 |
| Euro area (19 countries) | −6.3 | −6.2 | −4.2 | −3.6 | −3.0 | −2.6 | −2.1 | −1.5 |
| Germany (until 1990 former territory of the FRG) | −3.2 | −4.2 | −1.0 | 0.0 | −0.2 | 0.3 | 0.7 | 0.8 |
| Ireland | −13.8 | −32.1 | −12.6 | −8.0 | −5.7 | −3.7 | −2.0 | −0.6 |
| Greece | −15.1 | −11.2 | −10.3 | −8.9 | −13.1 | −3.7 | −5.9 | 0.7 |
| Cyprus | −5.4 | −4.7 | −5.7 | −5.6 | −5.1 | −8.8 | −1.2 | 0.4 |
| Portugal | −9.8 | −11.2 | −7.4 | −5.7 | −4.8 | −7.2 | −4.4 | −2.0 |

*Source*: Eurostat. October 1, 2017.

relatively to USA, with only around 2% of the EU-15 working-age population living in another EU-15 country.

Despite the fact that eurozone institutional imperfections persist and that senior proposals have been made for the necessity of reforms (i.e., the Five Presidents' Report on "*Completing Europe's Economic and Monetary Union*" in 2015 and the EU Commission paper on the "*Deepening of the Economic and Monetary Union*" in 2017, which argues in favor of completing the banking union, creating a capital markets union, and creating a European Treasury and a European Monetary Fund), institutional inertia prevails.

## IS THERE AN ALTERNATIVE TO EFC THESIS?

Figure 7.1 proposes an ideal AP type underlining the operational/cognitive linkages between adjustment targets and tools as well as the required catalysts for effective implementation of the adjustment strategy (Hazakis, 2015). The proposed holistic adjustment framework treats macroeconomic, microeconomic, financial, and structural reforms not as isolated issue areas but rather as interdependent and mutually vulnerable issue areas.

Such an analysis stresses the complexities of national decision-making structures and their embeddedness within a specific path-dependent institutional and political context. It is further suggested that APs should be based on an exclusively European surveillance mechanism, which takes into account transparency, accountability, European cohesion, and national ownership of programmes.

Within this policy framework APs' effectiveness refers to a triple challenge namely to identify the core pillars of macro and micro economic imbalances in a country, to induce corrective action with long-term positive results, and to balance economic effectiveness with social equity at the domestic level (Hazakis, 2015). Effectiveness of APs is linked to specific structural/fiscal problems and the ability to solve them taking into account the necessity of European social and economic cohesion. Obviously, it involves identification of problems, hierarchy of issue areas priorities, and corrective actions to face them. In sum, the effectiveness of APs targets is assessed according to six criteria:

a. Strength of APs targets meaning degree of compliance to specific and well-defined economic/structural/social indicators.
b. Organizational effectiveness of flexible, adequate, and transparent APs mechanisms to enforce achievements of aforementioned targets, limiting systemic/market risks associated with national sovereign default.
c. Internal consistency of APs scope meaning ability to simultaneously achieve all aforementioned targets as well as institutional ability to enforce results.
d. Legitimized and effective distribution of risks/burdens/benefits of APs policies in citizens.
e. Restoration of states capacity to access autonomously the international capital market.
f. Resumption of precrisis GDP growth rates and achievement of potential GDP.

As it is evident in the first column of the diagram, the scope of APs depends on specific initial conditions of the state and covers eight fundamental macro and micro economic issue areas. APs target to restoration of economic fundamentals, to full restoration of state ability to access international markets, and to full restoration of private agents/firms inclusion in international production/commercial networks.

Equally important, APs success in the eight major targets depends on realistic benchmarks against which failure/success is evaluated. A scoreboard assesses effectively the implementation of policies and permits of surveillance with enough policy flexibility. The key is not to use a "one size fits all" threshold regardless of states precrisis traits but rather to define benchmarks taking into consideration path dependence and initial conditions of each state. Although differences in country-specific targets and implementation horizons limit the potential of cross-country comparison, they do not undermine the essence of fundamental targets giving enough flexibility and adequate national ownership in economic APs.

As it is well known that adjustment policies always influence macroeconomic aggregates with different impact and time lag. For example, measures aimed at improving the fiscal balance/fiscal deficit (column 1, number 3) translate rather rapidly into fiscal discipline/figures while structural reforms (reduction of transaction costs, employment measures) may impact real GDP with a delay of at least three to four years. Thus, time horizon for APs differs from country to country and as euroarea experience shows, front-loaded fiscal adjustment and structural reforms demand enough time to reap benefits. It is suggested that a four-year horizon is compatible with present euroarea experience and seems practical because picking up a longer period makes the links between adjustment and economic outcomes more tenuous and difficult to estimate.

Finally, one should remember that effective application of an AP programme is not important only for national stabilization/growth but it has an additional value within euro zone which is linked with European economic-social cohesion as well as with the avoidance of euroarea financial-economic asymmetries/disturbances.

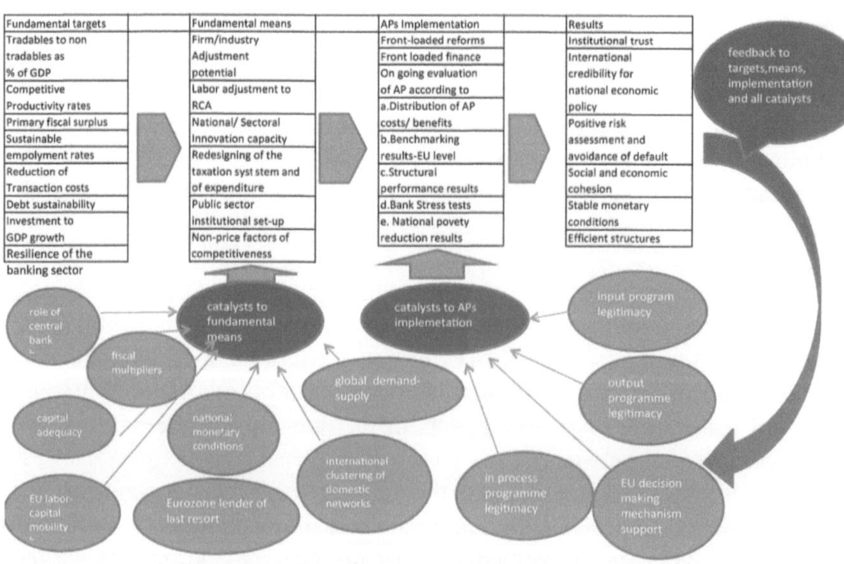


**Figure 7.1 An ideal type for economic adjustment in Eurozone.**

Beginning with the prerequisites of a successful AP (column 1), a key priority is to shift labor-capital-entrepreneurship from non-tradables to tradables sector for three reasons (Hazakis, 2015).

First, failure to counterbalance the internal devaluation of tradables and non-tradables sector salaries with internal devaluation of prices in goods/services acts against purchasing power of workers and creates an anti-reform block. Second, most of non-tradables goods/services are inputs for tradables sector and consequently preservation of high prices in non-tradables sector prevents reduction of cost in tradable sector. Finally, evidence clearly links competitiveness results with divergences in unit labor cost growth in tradables and non-tradables sector, underlining that in states with memoranda, salaries cost growth in non-tradable was higher than in tradables sector (Hazakis, 2015).

Thus, the problem is not "high wages—low productivity" in all sectors of an economy but "high wages—low productivity—lower returns on capital" in the non-tradables sector of an economy. Consequently, in order to restore Balassa-Samuelson positive results, adjustment should favor a programme of tax incentives to shift critical resources toward export-oriented sectors of an economy. This also means that incentives should favor stronger operational synergies of propulsive export-oriented units of production with local subcontractors.

The non-tradable sectors (i.e., public sector and retail trade) are used as inputs for the production of tradable goods and thus rising prices in the provision of their services exert a negative impact on the tradables sector and erode international competitiveness. This corresponds to a reverse Balassa-Samuelson effect where rising wages in the non-tradable sector trigger increases in the value-chain of tradable sector leading to competitiveness problems. In addition, increases in prices in the non-tradable sector had a direct negative impact on inflation destabilizing further macroeconomic stability (Kyrkilis and Hazakis, 2014).

Thus, one should examine the unit labor cost and the productivity rate especially in the non-tradable sector and consequently reforms of the AP should target this sector. The problem is that indirect taxes, administrative prices, and the persistence of rents in protected sectors usually contribute to keeping prices high. In Greece, for example, wages adjusted much more than prices, implying higher-than desirable purchasing power losses and a lower-than-desirable improvement in competitiveness.

The second fundamental issue for a successful AP is achieving sustainable productivity rates. Usually, weak productivity performances in states with memoranda are due to inadequate national-sectoral competition (Bourles et al., 2010), overregulation, and lack of international productive/commercial linkages of domestic firms. Further, low-productivity rates in the non-tradables sector exert negative influence on export-oriented firms' performance. Equally important, lack of strong private investment as percentage of total GFCF and as percentage of GDP reduces innovation capability of local firms.

It is also worth noting that productivity in states with memoranda is vital since the rate of retirement exceeds by far employment growth; thus with more citizens consuming and not actively participating in national production the only way to preserve per capita levels is through productivity improvements. Finally, productivity is linked with national competitiveness and as a consequence is linked to sustainable trade surpluses which are conditio sine qua non for current account surpluses and for primary fiscal surpluses (Hazakis, 2015).

A third target is the achievement of primary fiscal surplus based on rationalization of state expenditure and on positive rates of growth and not on internal devaluation of incomes and higher direct/indirect taxes. It is argued that the fiscal adjustment should be gradual and should be based on expenditure cuts, preserving taxes to precrisis levels in order not to undermine investment activity. Furthermore, there is a need to reschedule from zero all-state expenditure based on cost-result logic and to redesign the national taxation system. This does not mean that there will be a deterioration of the provision of public goods but a better design of the means and targets in each issue area of the public goods.

In this way, international credibility of government is strengthened and both producers and consumers are not completely deprived of disposable incomes in the medium term. Excessive taxation (Luffer curve effect) combined with front-loaded collapse of all major GDP components undermines market and consumer confidence, breaks off social cohesion and ends up in a strong recession trap where deflation is combined to low GDP performance making debt reduction unsustainable.

A crucial component of an AP is also the sustainability of national debt. But how one defines debt sustainability and what is the acceptable range of deviation from a monetary union?

Reinhart and Rogoff (2010; 2014) argued that if a government's debt level is above 90% of GDP, there are serious macroeconomic problems in an economy. Economists suggest that any model of debt sustainability should take into account the financial needs for interest payments and GDP forecasts, comparing debt stock with exports/budget revenues so as to assess payment capacity of the state in future. The contribution a policy measure can make to improve fiscal sustainability depends on how it affects the three factors that drive the debt-to-GDP ratio namely the primary balance, the interest rate, and the GDP growth rate.

It is beyond dispute that debt solvency is achieved when primary surpluses are enough to pay back principal debt and interest. Too often policy uncertainty leads to a vicious circle that goes from fear of debt non-sustainability to higher interest rates and thus to higher probability of non-sustainability (Hazakis, 2015).

Although picking up a specific threshold for debt-to-GDP ratio involves a significant degree of arbitrariness, it is useful to set a target. The lack of a viable debt-to-GDP ratio undermines any adjustment effort since markets are uncertain for future sustainability of national macroeconomic performance. It is suggested that national debt-to-GDP ratio should target in the long-term the eurozone debt average (currently 89.5% in euroarea, August 2017) excluding loans for capitalization of national systemic banks and state guarantees for public infrastructure projects. This requires as far as debt is concerned five priorities:

a. Reprogramming national interest installments based on a constant interest rate.
b. Reprogramming national interest installments based on annual GDP rate performance. Achieving debt sustainability requires maintaining gross financing needs at low levels for a prolonged period (below 10%) of GDP and without further rise to the debt/GDP ratio.
c. Linking annual primary national surpluses with European cohesion funds flows based on incentive-driven compliance logic to adjustment targets.
d. Incorporating bank recapitalization in ESM since single supervisory mechanism in in place.
e. Establishing a reliable lender of last resort in eurozone which presupposes permanent role of ECB in primary market of bonds under the condition of implementation of eurozone rules and principles.

The main objective of the aforementioned framework of public debt management is to ensure that the government's financing needs and its payment obligations are met at the lowest possible cost over the medium to long run. The idea is not to shift from a stock (debt-to-GDP) to a flow (gross financing needs) framework, but how to combine the two in the long-term—meaning a longer horizon for debt installments and lower-constant interest rates. It also means that certain expenditures such as public investment in infrastructure and research and development should be excluded from expenditure reduction so as to restore the growth fundamentals.

Equally important, for a successful AP is the reduction of transaction costs in national economies. Transactions occur either as market exchange between firms or as administrative-hierarchical decisions within firms. Consequently, transaction costs involve the costs of establishing and administering economic relations within and between companies/private economic agents. There are also additional costs of formulating and safeguarding the terms of exchanges as well as enforcing/monitoring compliance with agreed market rules. The target of APs is to ameliorate transaction cost at all levels of economic action and behavior, to reduce systemic/sectoral risks, and to enforce competitiveness (Hazakis, 2015).

Full employment should also be a key target of adjustment and income redistribution should be a secondary medium-term target strictly linked with sustainable GDP growth rates, sustainability of national debt levels, and productivity performance. Equally important, active labor market policies such as better education and vocational training to enforce skills of labor force and apprenticeships are considered a priority for sustainable jobs in tradables sector.

Statistics in euroarea states with memoranda show that slump investment leads to anemic domestic demand and to high unemployment rates. Evidently, it is crucial to provide low interest rate loans through a European growth fund in selected export-oriented national firms that proved to be relatively resistant to economic depression.

Finally, APs' success strongly depends on domestic banks performance since macroeconomic stability/growth is affected by developments in financial/banking sectors. The capitalization of systemic banks and the protection of depositors are necessary not only for systemic contagion reasons but also for the restoration of a sustainable deposit level for future investment financing. This clearly suggests a front-loaded application of best international practices in both operational and procedural issues of distressed credit areas and mechanisms to facilitate settlement of borrower arrears. In addition, there is a need for improvement of corporate governance in national banking-financial sectors targeting efficient regulation and minimization of distortive practices in the future (Hazakis, 2015).

## WHICH ARE THE FUNDAMENTAL MEANS TO ACHIEVE THE AFOREMENTIONED TARGETS?

Firm/industry adjustment is closely linked to lower transaction costs, to reduce barriers to entry in protected sectors, and to better innovation capability of industrial clusters. This means that quality, cost, and availability of key intermediate inputs for tradables sector are significantly improved raising productivity through real competitiveness changes.

Equally important, for adjustment is the enforcement of revealed comparative advantage through RULC improvements. Experience showed that in some cases, absence of a coherent competitiveness strategy in existing APs resulted in decline of RULC in tradables sector more than the decline in non-tradables sector although the trend during precrisis period in APs states was the opposite. Moreover, RULC adjustments have not always been followed by improvements in export price competitiveness (i.e., in Greece). It is no coincidence that the price of exports relative to the price of goods produced in APs markets has improved in Ireland but deteriorated in Portugal and Greece.

National innovation capacity is also vital for sustainable adjustment and refers to improvements in workforce skills and in technology content of products/services so as to increase global market share of a country in medium and high value added products-services. This presupposes significant investment in research and development of the tradables sector and could be realized through a European venture capital fund with enough resources for such a long-term and high-risk effort.

Reorganization of national institutions is also a conditio sine qua non for sustainable adjustment. Several authors (Pisani et al., 2013) and IMF (IMF, 2013b) underline that implementation of an AP depends on the efficiency of state mechanism. Regulation 472/2013/EU also (article 7, para 11) provides technical assistance when member experiences "insufficient administrative capacity or significant problems in the implementation of the programmes."

More precisely, there are at least five functions that institutions could play in euroarea states with memoranda. First, institutions offer efficient administration and coordination in imperfect markets or markets with negative externalities. Second, institutions provide learning and adjustment mechanisms for national economic agents in situations of bounded rationality and uncertainty. Third, institutions provide a stable safety net for the less privileged citizens, strengthening social cohesion during the adjustment period. Fourth, institutions could provide the necessary framework for developing human capabilities and thus lowering barriers to entry in information/knowledge for all citizens. Fifth, they put in action a level playing field for all economic agents preventing private/state monopolies and sectoral interest groups influence.

The last precondition for successful AP implementation underlines non-price aspects of competitiveness (i.e., specialization of exports, local production networks cooperation and structure, quality traits of exported products/services, institutional barriers, efficiency of sales networks, after-sales services) which are important in supporting export growth. Exports can be classified as having high, medium-high, medium-low, or low technology content, based on the intensity of the research and development (R&D) invested. Thus, having a high level of technical specialization can work in favor of a country's export performance as high-tech products, which are innovative and made up of high value added components, and can achieve higher prices than low-tech, undifferentiated products/services.

Overall, the second pillar of the proposed ideal type of AP is heavily dependent on catalysts as exemplified in diagram 7.1, the most influential of which is multipliers.

Multipliers do play a crucial role and vary considerably depending on whether the fiscal adjustment is conducted via expenditure reduction or tax increases, with different levels of expenditure and taxes yielding different multipliers. Multiplier effects are also enhanced because of the time horizon of a programme meaning that they are low if consumers/investors incomes are temporarily affected but are high if consumers and investors perceive that adjustment is long-term and thus uncertainty over incomes is strong. Significant reduction of incomes-state expenditure through internal devaluation as well as high taxation creates asymmetrical and unanticipated negative effects in different aspects of GDP, investment, employment, and consumption. Experience in euroarea shows that all affected aspects of GDP reinforce negatively each other in a much faster way than predicted. Moreover, if exports do not compensate for losses in fiscal consolidation and if investment does not offset collapse of government expenditure they add to the drag on consumption/demand.

The third pillar of a successful AP deals with implementation procedures. Unfortunately, APs in euroarea are deprived of input and output legitimacy and target basically Eurozone systemic stability priorities (input legitimacy relies on national participation in all stages of an AP and output legitimacy concerns effectiveness of AP results). Thus, without a concessional framework, political instability and social conflict undermine any type of necessary and time-bound adjustment. Such an environment offers tremendous opportunities for extreme right wing and extreme left wing populist mobilization along issues related to corporatist politics.

In the four states under examination, APs favor adjustment learning without adjustment adaptation mechanisms and thus several social groups face practical and ideological problems to adopt stabilization policies (Hazakis, 2017). However, as IMF (2001, 52) mentioned, national commitment to reform programmes is critical in the success of failure of bank- or fund-supported APs.

Unavoidably, successful AP implementation demands a strong domestic reform block ready to define the limits of national bargaining power and the available negotiating trade-offs. Clearly, the limits include recipient country's financial needs, availability of financing alternatives, creditors' internal structure, and credibility of European noncompliance measures as well as quality traits of domestic negotiating team.

Taking into consideration that a state in complex debt, liquidity, structural-cyclical crisis opts for choices within inelastic financial constraints, there is a need for solutions based on European solidarity and cohesion and against unilateral actions of noncompliance to commonly agreed rules of EEG. Collective intentionality of all involved EU institutions in APs is the basis of success and covers not only common economic intentions of EU institutions and agents but also collective beliefs and commonly agreed content, scope and speed of adjustment. A successful adjustment on its turn reinforces EU collective intentionality further since mutual gains to all involved agents and joint commitment to commonly accepted rules, strengthen EU group identity and credibility, and face policy uncertainty (Hazakis, 2015; 2017).

Conclusively, when international credibility is strengthened, trust of international lenders and investors is clearly reflected in FDI portfolio inflows as well as in the ratio of GFCF to GDP. Thus, APs serve as a signaling device of a state which is both willing and capable to apply substantive reforms and to keep fiscal balances irrespective of electoral cycles. This further reduces risk of default, and self - reinforces macroeconomic fundamentals.

## CONCLUDING REMARKS

The chapter raises several doubts about the effectiveness of APs in euroarea in the years 2010–2017. Although APs succeeded in many aspects of fiscal consolidation they did not contribute to long-term sustainable growth rates, to intra-Eurozone real economic convergence, and to a viable de-escalation of private and sovereign debt danger.

More specifically, APs proved in many cases to be ineffective because of four failures: failures of policy mix (simultaneous application of expenditure reduction and tax increases as well as implementation of wrong fiscal and investment multipliers), inadequate knowledge of national economic/structural terms (national economic path dependency as well as national economic priorities for development), and overestimation of national administration capabilities and overestimation of political will (thus underestimation of vested interests with rent-seeking behavior). Moreover, APs downgraded the impact of non-performing loans on national systemic banks.

Ultimately, there are four conclusions. First, it is evident that internal politics of the participating countries have a major impact on APs implementation and thus any successful combination of fiscal-structural policies should seriously consider internal political variables. This involves not only the issue of which social groups gain or lose from different adjustment strategies, thus the distributional effects, but also how constellations of interest form and disintegrate, how they learn from adjustment experience, how they develop identity and strategy through learning (adjustment process of economic actors), and of course how specific vested interests are translated into policy preferences and bargaining power.

Second, asymmetric information and loose commitments on adjustment burden at EU national level multiply economic uncertainty and raise transaction cost in the absence of efficient domestic-European economic institutions.

Third, effective assignment of AP targets without national ownership of programmes and long-term euroarea collective intentionality on integration seems highly fragile. On the procedural side, it is further argued that IMF participation in surveillance and monitoring is not appropriate for European monetary union and consequently stronger EEG is considered sufficient for such a role.

Fourth, a new type of AP in Eurozone should focus more on "flexible enforcement" (incentive-driven compliance), domestic ownership of programmes (in all stages of APs), accountability of surveillance mechanisms to EP (through relevant modifications in EEG decision-making), and transparency of programme policies.

Enhancing accountability and transparency presupposes not only elimination of creative national accounting and misreporting but strong institutional reforms in EEG and national economic decision-making systems to guarantee the process against executive power manipulation. The two pillars (intentionality plus domestic ownership) create a common cognitive framework and link in a legitimate and predictable way the ordering of adjustment norms/targets to the ordering of adjustment actions/policies. This clearly presupposes proper adaptation/learning/adjustment mechanisms so as to make rule-following, national self-interest, and eurozone collective macroeconomic intentionality mutually compatible.

On the other hand, a penalty-driven conditionality lacks flexibility and does not permit compliance to EEG rules. Tranches should not be conditional upon all targets of an agreed adjustment framework but should take into consideration hierarchy of issue areas and policy priorities. Moreover, time lag between intermediate troika assessment, the delivering of APs tranches, and the dynamics-priorities of national macroeconomic frameworks should be avoided since they often lead to a non-orderly application of APs.

As it has emerged in the course of previous discussion, three challenges in EEG policymaking on macroeconomic adjustment emerge. First, the challenge is how to accommodate the objectives of EFC-inspired adjustment, the neglected interests of euroarea periphery states, and the necessity for new decisional arrangements in EEG architecture. There is a clear long-term debate around two competing logics, namely, the politics of enlarged coordination among all euroarea states and the politics of a la carte inclusion in core euroarea decision-making mechanisms. Reconciling the abovementioned logics rests on a new social purpose of equitable European development and deeper economic integration.

Increasing economic cohesion in Eurozone can be realized through a more balanced interaction between EEG structures, national economic interests of euroarea states, and European economic-political integration priorities. Without radical institutional reforms, organizational failures and institutional inertia will continue to create low institutional performance and ineffective decision-making in emerging issue areas of eurozone.

Second, the exit strategy of states from APs should be revisited. On the one hand, there needs to be a highly cautious approach on which expansionary fiscal actions are sufficient or excessive. Downplaying fiscal-structural policies and ignorance of primary fiscal surpluses can impose a "W curve," in recovery.

On the other hand, it is also obvious that fiscal expansion without structural reforms, growth-oriented policies, and poverty reduction programmes cannot generate employment and cannot reduce market imperfections and asymmetric negative externalities. Without prudential APs which encourage euroarea systemic stability and face systemic risk and transaction cost, the idea of a sustainable and equitable euroarea economic development seems non-pragmatic.

Third, there is a need to develop a policy framework that redraws the interconnections between Eurozone structures, Eurozone institutions, and EEG regime objectives while recognizing the importance of contingent factors at the national level. The scope of all issue areas in APs will be reached if there are efficient trade-offs so as to ensure real convergence while preventing adjustment from becoming unmanageable and too complex.

In conclusion, long-term euroarea fiscal austerity and income collapse have become part of the problem, not of the solution. This does not mean that fiscal discipline is not important but that it must be exercised within a growth-oriented policy programme taking into consideration the idiosyncrasies of the states. It becomes evident that adjustment should equally target from the beginning of structural and fiscal consolidation, enforcement of local productive networks (and their ability to competitively export), taking into consideration the necessity to protect the most vulnerable social groups in an economy.

It looks like that euroarea states should apply new normative and cognitive rules for adjustment giving an end to a vicious circle of depression. Whether this trajectory is more effective and politically more acceptable is unclear, as eurozone economies are at the beginning of a long adaptation and convergence process. However, as time passes and euroarea cooperative momentum fades, the space for concerted efforts by EEG nexus on the regulatory agenda may be constrained in a significant way and the window of opportunity for a new economic regime in eurozone may disappear.

## BIBLIOGRAPHY


Acemoglou, D., Johnson, S., and Robinson, J. 2004. *Institutions as the fundamental cause of long-run growth,* NBER working paper 10481. Washington, D.C.: National Bureau of Economic Research.

Acemoglou, D and Robinson, J. 2012. *Why nations fail: The origins of power, prosperity and poverty.* New York: Crown Business.

Alesina, A. 1997. "Fiscal adjustments in OECD countries: Composition and macroeconomic effects", *IMF Staff papers*. Washington, D.C.: IMF.

Alesina, A and Ardagna, S. 1998. "Tales of Fiscal Policy". *Economic Policy,* 13(27): 489–545.

Alesina, A and Drazen, A. 1991. "Why are stabilizations delayed?" *American Economic Review,* 81: 1170–1188.

Alesina, A and Perotti, R. 1995. "Fiscal expansions and fiscal adjustments in OECD Countries". *Economic Policy,* 10(21): 205–248.

Alesina, A and Perotti, R. 1997a. "The welfare state and competitiveness". *American Economic Review,* 87(5): 921–939.

Alesina, A and Perotti, R. 1997b. "Fiscal adjustments in OECD countries: Composition and macroeconomic effects". *International Monetary Fund Staff papers*, 44(2): 210–248.

Alcidi, C and Gros, D. 2011. *Adjustment difficulties and debt overhang in the eurozone periphery,* CEPS working document 347. May. Brussels: CEPS.

Ardagna, S. 2004. "Fiscal Stabilizations: When do they work and why". *European Economic Review,* 48(5): 1047–1074.

Baldwin, R and Gavazzi, Fransesco. 2015. *The Eurozone crisis: A consensus view of the causes and a few possible solutions.* London: CEPR.

Barro, R. J. 1974. "Are government bonds net wealth?" *Journal of Political Economy,* 82 (November/December): 1095–1117.

Barro, R. J. 1979. "On the determination of public debt". *Journal of Political Economy,* 7(5): 940–971.

Belke A. 2013. "Towards a genuine economic and monetary union-comments on a roadmap". *Politics and Governance,* 1: 48–65.

Blanchard, O and Leigh D. 2013. *Growth forecasts errors and fiscal multipliers,* IMF working paper 13/1. Washington, D.C.: IMF.

Blanchard, O. 2015. *Greece: past critiques and the path forward.* IMF Blog, 9th July. Washington, D.C.: IMF.

Bourles, R., Cette, G., Lopez, J., Mairesse, J., and Nicoletti, G. 2010. *Do product market regulations in upstream sectors curb productivity growth? Panel data evidence for OECD countries.* National bureau of economic research, working paper 16520. Washington, D.C.: NBER.

Bouis, R and Duval, R. 2011. *Raising potential growth after the crisis: A quantitative assessment of the potential gains from various structural reforms in the OECD area and beyond.* OECD economics department working papers 835. Paris: OECD Publishing.

Broadbent, B and Daly, K. 2010. *Limiting the fall out from fiscal adjustments, Goldman Sachs Global economics*. Global economics paper 195. April. New York: Goldman Sachs.

Buti, Marco and Carnot, Nicholas. 2012. "The EMU debt crisis: Early lessons and reforms". *Journal of Common Market Studies,* 50(6): 899–911.

D'Auria, F., Pagano, F. A., Ratto, M., and Varga J. 2009. "A comparison of structural reform scenarios across the EU member states: Simulation –based analysis using the QUEST model with endogenous growth" *European economy*. Economic paper 392. Brussels: European Commission.

De Grauwe, P. 2015. "Design failures of the eurozone". In *The Eurozone crisis: A consensus view of the causes and a few possible solutions.* eds. R. Baldwin and Fransesco Gavazzi, 99–108. London: CEPR.

De Mooij, R and Keen, M. 2012. '"Fiscal devaluation and fiscal consolidation: The VAT in troubled times" *IMF working paper 12/85.* Washington, D.C.: International Monetary Fund.

Draghi, M. 2015. *Introductory statement to the ECB press conference.* 22 January, Frankfurt am Main: ECB.

Drazen, A and Grilli, V. 1993. "The benefit of crises for economic reforms". *American Economic Review,* 83(3): 598–607.

European Council and European Parliament. 2013. "Regulation 472 on the strengthening of economic and budgetary surveillance of the member states in the euroarea experiencing or threatened with serious difficulties with respect to their financial stability", *Official Journal of the European Union*. 27-05-2013. Brussels: European Council and European Parliament.

European Commission. 2010. "The economic adjustment programme for Greece". *Occasional Papers, 61*. Brussels: European Commission.

European Commission. 2011a. "The economic adjustment programme for Ireland". *Occasional Papers, 76*. Brussels: European Commission.

European Commission. 2011b. "The economic adjustment programme for Portugal". *Occasional Papers, 79*. Brussels: European Commission.

European Commission. 2012a. "The second economic adjustment programme for Greece". *Occasional Papers, 94.* Brussels: European Commission.

European Commission. 2012b. "The financial sector adjustment programme for Spain". *Occasional Papers, 118.* Brussels: European Commission.

European Commission. 2013. "The economic adjustment programme for Cyprus". *Occasional Papers, 149*. Brussels: European Commission.

European Commission. 2014a. "The economic adjustment programme for Portugal", eleventh review. Economic and financial affairs. *Occasional paper, 191*. April. Brussels: European Commission.

European Commission. 2014b. "The second economic adjustment programme for Greece", fourth review. Economic and financial affairs. *Occasional paper, 192*. April. Brussels: European Commission.

European Commission. 2014c. "Post programme surveillance for Ireland report", Economic and financial affairs. *Occasional paper, 195.* June. Brussels: European Commission.

European Commission. 2014d. "The economic adjustment programme for Cyprus", fifth review. Economic and financial affairs. *Occasional paper,* 209. December. Brussels: European Commission.

European Commission. 2015a. *Debt sustainability analysis*. August. Accessed http://ec.europa.eu/economy_finance/assistance_eu_ms/greek_loan_facility/pdf/debt_sustainability_analysis_en.pdf. Brussels: European Commission.

European Commission. 2015b. *Memorandum of Understanding between the European Commission acting on behalf of the European Stability Mechanism and the Hellenic Republic and the Bank of Greece.* 19 August. Brussels: European Commission. Accessed http://ec.europa.eu/economy_finance/assistance_eu_ms/greek_loan_facility/pdf/01_mou_20150811_en.pdf

Eurostat. 2017. *Eurostat online database*. Brussels: European Commission.

Eyraud, L and Weber, A. 2013. "The challenge of debt reduction during fiscal consolidation". *IMF working paper, 67.* Washington, D.C.: IMF.

Featherstone, K. 2011. "The JCMS annual lecture: The Greek sovereign debt crisis and EMU: A failing state in a skewed regime". *Journal of Common Market Studies,* 49: 193–217.

Feldstein, M. 1982. "Government Deficits and Aggregate Demand". *Journal of Monetary Economics,* 9(1): 1–20.

Fels, G and Froehlich, H. P. 1986. "Germany and the world economy: A German view". *Economic Policy,* 4, April: 178–195.

Fernandez, S and Paulet, T. 2014. "Adjustment programs in the euroarea: Mission accomplished?" *Synthesis,* Notre Dame Jacques Delors Institute. 22 May: 1–14.

Giavazzi, F and Pagano, M. 1990. "Can Severe Fiscal Contractions be Expansionary? Tales of two small European countries". *NBER Macroeconomics Annual,* 5: 75–111.

Gros, D and Alcidi C. 2013. "Country adjustment to a sudden stop: Does the euro make a difference?" *European economy.* Economic paper 492, April. Brussels: European Commission.

Hazakis, K. 2015. "The political economy of economic adjustment programs in the Eurozone: A detailed policy analysis". *Politics and Policy,* 43(6): 822–854.

Hazakis, K. 2016. "The economic governance crisis in the Eurozone and itsimlications for the management of greece'spublic debt". In *The Greek political economy 2010-2015,* eds. S. Roukanas and P. Sklias. 269–286. Amsterdam: Eburon - Wilfried Martens Center for European Studies.

Hazakis, K. 2017. "An institutional proposal for economic adjustment in euroarea". *Journal of Sustainable Development, Culture and Traditions,* 1a: 82–100.

Hazakis, K. 2018. *The expansionary fiscal consolidation theorem in doubt: Its tragic implications and why it should be avoided.* Forthcoming.

Hondroyiannis, G and Papaoikonomou, D. 2015. "When does it pay to tax? Evidence from state-dependent fiscal multipliers in the Euro area". *Economic Modelling,* 48: 116–128.

IMF. 2001. *Conditionality in fund supported programs-policy issues.* Washington, D.C.: IMF.

IMF. 2003. *Fiscal adjustment in IMF supported programs.* Independent evaluation office. Washington, D.C.: IMF.

IMF. 2010. "Will it hurt? Macroeconomic effects of fiscal consolidation". *World Economic Outlook,* Chapter 3, October: 93–124.

IMF. 2013a. *Staff Country reports, first and second reviews under the extended arrangement for Greece.* IMF country report 13/20. Washington, D.C.: IMF.

IMF. 2013b. *Greece ex post evaluation of exceptional access under the 2010 stand-by arrangement.* Washington, D.C.: IMF.

IMF. 2015. *Ireland: Ex post evaluation of exceptional access under the 2010 extended arrangement.* IMF country report 15/20. Washington, D.C.: IMF.

IMF. 2017. *Euroarea selected issue.* IMF country report 17/236. IMF publications Washington, D.C.: IMF.

Keynes, John Maynard. 1936. *The general theory of employment, interest and money.* London: Macmillan.

Kopits, George. 2016. *The IMF and the euro area crisis: The fiscal dimension.* BP/16-02/07 International Monetary Fund, Washington, D.C.: IMF.

Kyrkilis, D and Hazakis, K. 2014. *The impact of economic adjustment programs on Greek competitiveness.* working paper. South and east European development center. 4 April. Volos: SEED.

McDermott, C and Wescott, R. 1996. "An empirical analysis of fiscal adjustments". *International Monetary Fund Staff Papers,* 43(4): 725–753.

Mierau, J., Jong-A-Pin, R., and De Haan, J. 2007. "Do political variables influence fiscal adjustment decisions? New empirical evidence". *Public Choice,* 133: 297–319.

Mineshima, A., Poplawski - Ribeiro, M., and Weber, A. 2014. "Size of fiscal multipliers". In *Post-Crisis Fiscal Policy,* eds. C. Cottarelli, P. Gerson, and A. Senhadji. chapter 3. Cambridge, MA: MIT Press.

Mongelli, F. 2010. "The OCA theory and the path to EMU". In *The euro: The first decade,* eds. M. Buti, S. Derrose, V. Gaspar, and J. Martins. 115–142. Cambridge: Cambridge University Press.

Perotti, Roberto. 2012. "The Austerity Myth: Gain without Pain?". In *Fiscal policy after the financial crisis*, eds. Alberto Alesina and Francesco Giovazzi, 307–354. Chicago: University of Chicago Press.

Pisani-Ferry, Jean., Sapir, André., and Wolff, G. B. 2011. *TSR external study: An IMF surveillance of the Euro area,* July. Washington, D.C.: International Monetary Fund.

Pisani-Ferry, Jean., Sapir, André., and Wolff, G. B. 2011. 2013. "EU-IMF assistance to euro-area countries: An early assessment". *Blueprint, 19.* Brussels: Bruegel.

Reinhart, C and Rogoff, K. 2010. "Growth in a time of debt". *American Economic Review,* 100(2): 573–578.

Reinhart, Carmen M and Rogoff, Kenneth S. 2014. "Recovery from financial crises: Evidence from 100 episodes". *American Economic Review,* 104(5): 50–55.

Rodrik, D. 2000. "Institutions for high-quality growth: What they are and how to acquire them". *Studies in Comparative International Development,* 35(3): 3–31.

Roubini, N and Sachs, J. 1989. "Political and economic determinants of budget deficits in the industrial democracies". *European Economic Review,* 33: 903–933.

Samuelson, P. 1948. *Economics: An introductory analysis*. New York: McGraw-Hill.
Sapir, André., Wolff, G. B., de Sousa, Carlos., and Terzi, Alessio. 2014. *Committee study on the Troika and financial assistance in the Euro area: Successes and failures,* Study at the request of the Economic and Monetary Affairs Committee. February. Brussels: European Parliament.
Schauble, Wolfgang. 2011. Why austerity is only cure for the Eurozone. *Financial Times.* September 5. Accessed https://www.ft.com/content/97b826e2-d7ab-11e0-a06b-00144feabdc0
Scott, G. 2014. "Structural adjustment comes to Europe: Lessons for the Eurozone from the conditionality debates". *Global Social Policy,* 14(1): 51–71.
The Lisbon Council. 2014. *Euro plus monitor report.* December. Brussels: The Lisbon Council.
The Lisbon Council. 2017. *Euro plus monitor report.* September. Brussels: The Lisbon Council.
Varga, J., Roeger, W., and Veld, J. 2013. "Growth effects of structural reforms in southern Europe: The case of Greece, Italy, Portugal and Spain". *European economy.* Economic paper 511, December: 1–68.
Vogel, L. 2014. "Structural reforms at the zero bound". *European economy.* Economic papers 537, November. Brussels: European Commission.
World Bank. 2017. World Bank online database. Washington, D.C.: World Bank.
Wyplosz, Charles and Sgherri, Silvia. 2016. *The IMF's role in Greece in the context of the 2010 Stand-By Arrangement* BP/16-02/11, Washington, D.C.: International Monetary Fund.

## FURTHER READING

Agnello, L., Castro, V., Jalles, J. T., and Sousa, R. M. 2014. "Fiscal adjustments, labour market flexibility and unemployment". *Economic Letters,* 124(2): 231–235.
Anderson, D., Hunt B., and Snudden, S. 2014. "Fiscal consolidation in the Euroarea: How much pain can structural reforms ease?" *Journal of Policy Modeling,* 36: 785–799.
Blyth, M. 2013. *Austerity: The history of a dangerous idea.* New York: Oxford University Press.
Boyer, R. 2012. "The four fallacies of contemporary austerity policies: The lost Keynesian legacy". *Cambridge Journal of Economics,* 36(1): 283–312.
Canton, E., Grilo I., Monteagudo, J., Pierini, F., and Turrini, A. 2014. "The role of structural reform for adjustment and growth" European Commission. *ECFIN economic brief*: 1–6. Brussels: European Commission.
Carnot, N. 2014. "Evaluating fiscal policy: A rule of thumb" *European economy.* Economic paper 526, August: 1–41. Brussels: European Commission.
Corsetti, G., Meier, A., and Muller, G. 2012. *What determines government spending multipliers?* IMF working paper 150. Washington, D.C.: IMF.
Ilzetzki, E., Mendoza, E., and Végh, C. 2013. "How big (small?) are fiscal multipliers?" *Journal of Monetary Economics,* 60(2): 239–254.

Lane, Philip R. 2012. "The European sovereign debt crisis". *Journal of Economic Perspectives,* 26: 49–68.

Larch, M., Magnusson, K., and Tatar, B. 2014. "Hard work and more: How to successfully conduct adjustment with official assistance" *European Economy,* Economic paper 514, February. Brussels: European Commission.

Williamson, J. 1994. *The political economy of policy reform.* Institute for International Economics. Washington, D.C.: IIE.

## QUESTIONS

1. Why real economic convergence matters in eurozone?
2. Compare the failures and successes of the Portuguese, Greek, and Irish APs in euroarea.
3. Is there a synchronization of national business cycles in eurozone?

## *Chapter 8*

# The Common Agricultural Policy

Policymaking, including the agricultural sector, is of idiosyncratic nature and differs widely from country to country. EU's CAP is also considered a very special case which is in no way comparable to the agricultural policy regime in any other country because of its sui generis stance within EU institutional mechanism.

In particular, the specificity of the CAP is due to several reasons, including the path dependency of European integration process, the historical origin of agricultural policymaking in Europe, the unique process of EU decision-making mechanism, the peculiarities and complexities of the financing regime for agriculture, and the significant weight of the EU's agricultural sector in global agricultural trade.

The abovementioned specificity is clearly mirrored in the unusually large share of the EU budget that is devoted to agricultural sector (41% in 2011 and approximately 38% in 2015 of the EU budget which means that 0.4% of the Union's GDP is spent on agriculture and rural development).

Historically, the CAP is unique as a highly politicized regime in the sense that it has not evolved smoothly over a long period, but it evolved through intense political debates among member states since 1960s. Undeniably, the decision to include agriculture issues in the common internal market of the EEC, taking into consideration diverging agricultural policies of the six founding states, was perceived necessary to achieve a kind of a political balance (Tangermann, 1992) between the advantages accrued by Germany in the industrial sector and France's interest in realizing a larger market for its agricultural exports.

According to OEEC (1956), the main type of farm in Europe at 1950s was a fairly small-scale, family-owned farm with major and chronic structural problems. Further, different patterns of economic development among the six countries (Tracy, 1982, 5–17) imposed diversified national agricultural policies. Enforcing production outcome was perceived as the answer to the farmers' income problem and in all six countries a price policy combined with structural policy tools was picked up as the way to achieve this target. Thus, in Belgium, France, Germany, and Luxembourg the policy was applied through market organizations for the key products, with governments intervening in the market to achieve a higher price than the international market price.

Although the Treaty of Rome established a CAP, it left enough space for policy maneuvering to the states. Very soon, it became evident that implementing a CMO for the fundamental agricultural commodities was not enough and that protection and support of agriculture products was also crucial in EEC market. Indeed, the CAP is along with European trade policy among the most intensely integrated policy domains in the EU, where countries have given up a significantly large degree of national sovereignty.

Mansholt (1963) mentioned four major motives for CAP in EC. First, it was not possible to isolate agricultural sector from European integration process because of its multiple linkages with industrial sector. Second, agricultural sector was considered important and had a major role in the economies of the six countries in the 1960s, taking into account its contribution to national trade balances. Third, food prices were influenced by agricultural policy and did impact on their turn in the total cost of products in the non-agricultural sector. Last but not least, adjustments in the agricultural sector were crucial for economic growth (Mansholt, 1963, 83–89).

Overall, the EU agricultural policy until 1992 considered essential to protect intra-Community trade in agricultural products against price fluctuations of the world market and implemented a system of market organization based on considerable support to producers. The family farm was the cornerstone of European agriculture, and it was believed that price support and structural measures could preserve farmers' income relative to other social categories of EU economy.

The chapter analyzes the economics and the decision-making process of CAP focusing on the latest reform of 2013. The main objectives of the CAP are a decent standard of living for agricultural producers and plentiful supply of high-quality food for European citizens.

## THE ECONOMICS OF CAP

Several political economy surveys highlight the logic of governmental strategy in the agricultural sector (i.e., De Gorter and Swinnen, 2002; Swinnen, 2008; Anderson, Rausser and Swinnen, 2013). For many economists, the main problem in the agricultural sector is the misallocation of resources, in other words the use of too many resources in agricultural production relative to other goods and services. To the farmer, the problem is that despite hard work and significant capital investment, the result is low and unstable incomes (Hathaway, 1963, 81).

Equally important, EU member states' national interests diverge, mirroring different political agendas and diversified structures of primary sector, putting an additional layer of interaction between agents to the already existing of agricultural producers versus consumers or EU taxpayers. Moreover, to capture the evolutionary path of CAP one should underline the impact of the interplay of economics, politics, and institutions on implementation and financing of CAP.

Economic models of agricultural sector underline the fundamental influence exerted by taxpayers, producers, consumers, and institutions (Swinnen et al., 2013). Among the explanatory variables analyzed in surveys are collective action costs, public choice reasons, interest groups and voters' options, institutional impact, the cost of market distortions, and international and domestic economic changes (Roederer and Schimmelfennig, 2012; Greer and Hind, 2012; Coleman et al., 1996).

Other studies, (Runge and von Witzke, 1987; Pokrivcak, Crombez, and Swinnen, 2006; Cunha and Swinbank, 2011) focused on trade policy issues as well as on incomes and prices in the agricultural sector in order to analyze thoroughly the evolutionary path of CAP reforms.

Grant (2008) groups the vital factors of influence on agriculture under the headings of agency, structure, and context. Agency refers to a wide range of EU institutional actors like the Commissioner for agriculture and rural development, the DG for Agriculture and the rest of the Commission, the EP and the member states while structure refers to all decision-making procedures of the EU vis-à-vis CAP. Finally, context refers to all variables existent during a specific period of CAP shaping the conditions for CAP reforms.

Survey results demonstrate that at the micro analytical level market failures means that economic agents are rent-seekers in the political-economic system and enhance state failures. Price support, production quotas, set-aside restrictions, direct payments linked to production and an uneven support across sub-sectors all have more or less obvious impacts on allocation efficiency, on transfer efficiency, and on the overall welfare of society.

Thus, it is no coincidence that in EU, price support and intervention schemes have been for a long time at the core of member state policies protecting domestic agricultural producers (market price support policies included import duties and levies, antidumping taxes, export subsidies, price and buying guarantees, production quotas).

Before analyzing diagrammatically the economics of agriculture it is useful to underline the main traits of the supply of farm products. First, the farms are many and are geographically spread with consequences on the cost of collection, transportation, and process. Second, the factors of production are characterized by immobility and inflexibility in response to price changes. Third, the supply of farm products is characterized by high risks and volatility due to biological and climate-related variables. Finally, the demand for agricultural goods is characterized by low-income elasticity.

To begin with, the target of a typical variable levy system is to ensure that non-EU agricultural suppliers will not lower high prices for EU agricultural products. Figure 8.1 shows supply and demand curves for agricultural products in a net-importing country in a simple price/quantity framework. One should mention that the supply curve of the agricultural product is based on many factors among others the state of technology in farming, the acreage in use, the stock of capital, and the weather conditions. It is also affected by EU high target prices (Px) since such decisions create incentives for farmers to enter the market or to use extra acreage and capital in the sector pushing supply curve S upward. The target price (Px) is that price with which agricultural producers are able to keep or raise their standard of living. It is considered a key price for the system directly linked with the other three prices and usually it is administratively politically fixed.

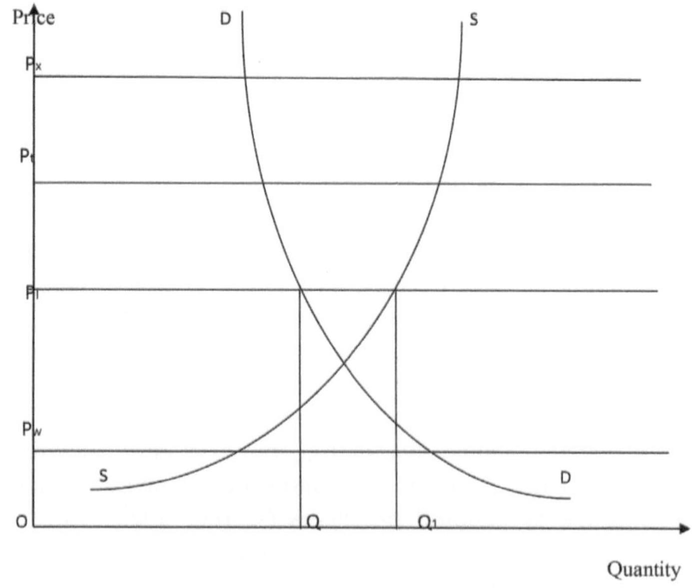


**Figure 8.1 The economics of variable levies in agriculture.**

The threshold price (Pt) is a price for CU usage and it is the target price (Px) minus the transport and handling cost of the agricultural product from EU frontier to consumption centers. The difference between threshold price and the world price (Pw) is the variable levy. It is called variable because both Pt and Pw may vary.

The intervention price or floor price (Pi) is the minimum price for agricultural producers that is guaranteed by EU and gives the ability to EU member states to act whenever there is excess supply in the product. Thus, prices are not allowed to be under Pi. The consumers lose since demand is lower at price Pt (welfare loss) relatively to world price (Pw) and the higher price serves de facto as an income policy since it raises income of EU agricultural producers.

The world price (Pw) is the price at which consumers would buy in a competitive free market. However, the application of variable levies on imports pushes the import price upward to the threshold price. One should underline that before MacSharry reforms, the EU tried several times to dispose surpluses of agricultural products at price OPw with an export subsidy given by the difference of Pi-Pw.

The final outcome is that through price support, producer's gain is financed by EU consumers, since the latter pays a higher price than the equilibrium price for their products. In the deficiency payments case the producers' gain is paid by the taxpayers, because the difference between the target price and the equilibrium price is transferred directly to the farmers from the fiscal budget. The option of price support thus allows the CAP to help with respect to both the production objective and the income objective.

In figure 8.2 the analysis focuses on the new CAP. One first observes that the agricultural market is characterized by inelastic supply and demand curves, shown in figure 8.2 by S and D, respectively. The example concerns an agricultural product where EU a net exporter. In the absence of CAP reform, it is considered that all surpluses go to global market. The cost of the latter is given by the difference between the price floor and the global price (the area b+c+d). In order to keep the higher price only for EU farmers, the global price plus the imposed tariff of EU should be over the price floor.

The CAP reform brings down the price faced by EU producers and EU consumers from the price floor to the global price and as a result EU consumption goes up while agricultural production of EU goes down from Z to Z'. The consumers of EU face lower prices and their total gain is given by the area a+b, while agricultural farmers profits go down and their total loss is given by the area a+b+c.

Equally important, the total benefit for EU budget equals to the area b+c+d. In the case that agricultural producers are fully compensated, the payments allocated to them are given by the area a+b+c. Thus, the new CAP reforms

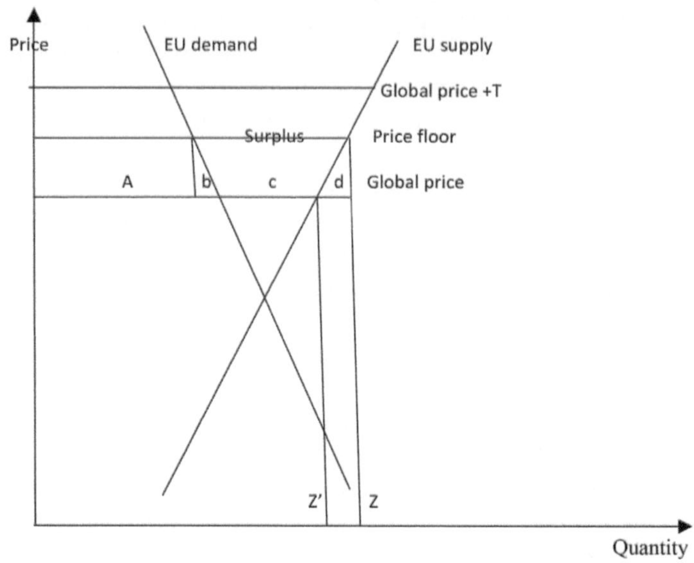


**Figure 8.2 The economics of new common agricultural policy in EU.**

target the disappearance of agricultural production surplus and taking into account the linkage of payments to environmental terms, the respect for environment.

The preceding analysis uncovers three fundamental distributional effects of the CAP which are the following:

a. Transfer of welfare from EU consumers to EU agricultural producers since consumers should pay higher prices and do not have full access to cheaper imports from third countries. Moreover, there is a transfer of welfare from consumers to the member states' government in the form of higher taxes needed to finance the CAP budget.
b. Transfer of welfare from one member state to another since CAP payments is not allocated equitably across each country of the EU. Some member states receive more payments under the CAP framework than they contribute to the EU budget as a whole.
c. Distribution of benefits between large and small-scale agricultural producers within the EU—because, on average, the EU farms with the highest gross (profit) margins occupy the largest agricultural area and receive the greatest financial support. Evidently, scale of production and capital intensity do matter in agriculture enforcing the link between farm size and farm income in the EU.

## THE FUNDAMENTALS TRAITS OF EU AGRICULTURAL SECTOR

Which are the fundamental indicators for present EU agriculture? In a total of 4,463,213 million square kilometers of EU territory, rural regions cover almost 52% of the EU territory while intermediate regions cover 38.2% of the area (the highest percentages of around 50% of intermediate territory are in Denmark, Germany, Spain, the Netherlands, and Sweden) and urban regions account only for 9.8%. Of course, there are significant differences between member states as rural areas cover almost 80% (and more) of the territory in some states (Estonia, Ireland, Greece, Croatia, Austria, Portugal, and Finland) while other countries (Malta, the Netherlands, Belgium) are more urbanized (Eurostat, 2016). Thus, in a total population of 506,847,612 million (EU-28), 112,918,244 citizens are considered as rural population (Eurostat, 2016).

As far as it concerns agricultural land, there were 13.7 million agricultural holdings within the EU-28 in 2014 and the UAA was 178.4 million hectares. Hence, the average holding was almost 12.6 hectares (the USA has 2 million farmers and an average farm size of 180 hectares). Of course, there is great heterogeneity in this average since agro climatic terms in the EU vary widely from Finland to Spain and agricultural structures and production patterns are also varied.

Undeniably, agriculture is a relatively small sector in the economy of the EU-28. Although CAP represents a major part of EU budget, only 22.2 million people were involved in agriculture (5.2% of all employment in 2013) on a regular basis in the EU-28 (of which 20.2 million people were either holders or members of the holder's family). Member states like Romania (6.5 million), Poland (3.5 million), and Italy (2.1 million) contributed more than 50% to this result (Eurostat, 2016). If one adds Spain, Greece, and Hungary then the six member countries together represented 73% of persons working in agriculture in the EU-28 (forestry employed 0.5 million people and represented 0.3% of total employment in the EU-28).

More specifically, Slovenia, Romania, Greece, Poland, Croatia, Malta, Cyprus, Ireland, and Italy have a high percentage of family farmers (above the EU average) in the total labor workforce, while the Czech Republic and Slovakia have less than 50% of family labor in the total labor force. Thus, there is great diversity which has become even greater with the arrival of the new member countries of Central and Eastern Europe.

It is also worth noting that the share of agricultural employment in total employment decreased over the from period 2009 to 2014 (more than one million employees) mostly in the EU-15 (−1.6%/year). The people employed in agriculture increased in Luxemburg, in the UK, in Malta, in Cyprus, and in Ireland over the period from 2009 to 2014 but decreased in most states of the EU. However, the food industry which is linked strongly to agricultural sector employed 5 million people in 2014 (2.3% of total employment in the EU-28) while Germany only accounted for around 20% of total employment in the sector in the EU-28.

There are also large differences in per hectare productivity. At one hand, there are member states like the Netherlands which produce almost 7% of the EU's agricultural output on just over 1% of its agricultural area, implementing intensive production techniques and high-value products (flowers, bulbs).

On the other hand, there are states like Bulgaria with almost three times as much agricultural land as the Netherlands which produce less than 20% of the Netherlands agricultural output. Evidence clearly shows that some member countries possess many farms but a low share of UAA, leading to a small average farm size in physical terms while other states have a small number of relatively large farms. Moreover, more than 70% of UAA is in EU-15 countries, while the agricultural labor force is divided roughly equally between the old and new member states.

However, most farms are considered rather small in physical terms since two-thirds of them have less than 5 ha of UAA and only 6.7% had more than 50 ha of UAA in 2013 (the average economic size is 61,916 euros in EU-15). Comparing USA and EU reveals that EU agriculture includes family companies and that many farmers and farm workers perform farming as a part-time activity or as a seasonal activity.

As far as it concerns the average labor input per agricultural holding, the Czech Republic is at the top with 4.0 AWU per holding (far higher than the EU-28 average which is 0.9 AWU/holding), followed by the Netherlands (2.3 AWU/holding), and Slovakia (2.1 AWU/holding).

Investing in machinery is a vital factor for labor productivity and thus GFCF, which measures how much of the value added is invested rather than consumed, is a fundamental prerequisite for competitiveness. Between 2006 and 2013, GFCF in agriculture in the EU-28 increased at an average annual rate of 1.3%. More specifically, in 2013, the agricultural sector in the EU-28 invested 58 billion euros, accounting for 30% of the total agricultural GVA. However, 52.2 billion euros, or 90% of the total, was invested in the EU-15, especially in France, Italy, and Germany while the lowest levels of investments in agriculture occurred in Cyprus and in Slovakia.

Looking at the agricultural production output, the gross value of EU-28 of crop output in producer prices fluctuates and was 170.3 billion euros in 2009, 212.1 billion euros in 2013, and 201.8 billion euros in 2014 while EU-28 gross animal output in producer prices was raised from 134.7 billion euros in 2009 to 167.9 billion euros in 2014.

Lastly, on the critical issue of CAP financial flows, the evolution of the structure of expenditure on the CAP from 1980 to 2015 clearly indicates that CAP expenditure is primarily born by taxpayers in the EU member countries and partly by the users of products imported into the EU from third states.

The international significance of the EU's agricultural policy is also a crucial factor for the analysis of CAP resulting from the size of EU output volume and import-export flows. The international trade of agricultural products reveals that the total value of imports and exports of agricultural goods between the EU-28 and the rest of the world was 235 billion euros in 2013, representing about 7% of total extra-EU trade (close to 75% of all EU agricultural trade is carried out within the EU-28 countries). Vegetable products represented almost half (47%) of EU-28 import, 35% were foodstuff products while animal products accounted for the smallest portion of agricultural imports (18%).

Exports of agriculture products from the EU-28 to non-EU countries had a similar trend and thus in 2013, the export of animal products was 20% of total agricultural exports, foodstuffs represented more than half of exports (54%), and vegetables accounted for 26% of exports of agricultural products. In 2013, beverages, spirits, and vinegar alone, with a value of 25 billion euros, represented more than one-fifth of all exports of agricultural merchandize from the EU-28.

With the exception of 2013, in the period from 2002 to 2013 the export value of all agricultural products from the EU-28 to extra-EU countries was less than imports. From 2002 to 2013 animal products' exports more than doubled while imports increased by 38%. As far as it concerns vegetable products imports had a slower growth (90% from 2002 to 2013) than exports (130% from 2002 to 2013). Further, during the period from 2002 to 2013 (Eurostat, 2016), EU-28 exports of foodstuffs exceeded imports and exports have increased at a faster rate (103%) than imports from non-EU countries (62%).

Eurostat data (2016) clearly indicate that the EU is the largest partner in international trade of agricultural products and that the EU-28 imports simple unprocessed agricultural goods and exports processed food products. Brazil was the leading supplier of agricultural products (11% share of EU-28 imports in 2013) and USA follow with a 9% share. Norway was the largest exporter of animal products (22% of the total in 2013 mostly fishes) followed by China and New Zealand (9% and 6% of total, mostly fishes).

The shares of EU-28 imports of vegetable products from the USA, Indonesia, and Ukraine were all over 5% in 2013, while Brazil, the USA, and Argentina together supplied one-third of EU-28 imports of foodstuffs. In 2013, the USA was the main recipient of EU-28 exports of agricultural goods with 13% of the total, followed by Russia and Switzerland.

More specifically, while the USA had a 16 billion US dollars agricultural trade surplus with the rest of the world in 2015, it recorded a 12 billion dollars trade deficit in farm and food products with the EU and it imported 25 billion dollars in food and agricultural products in 2015. As far as it concerns US exports to EU, low commodity prices and a strong US dollar resulted in a decline of 4% to US performance to fewer than 13 billion dollars. China, Japan, Norway, Saudi Arabia, Algeria, and Hong Kong represented another 20% of exports of agricultural products from the EU-28. The main products for export in these countries were foodstuffs (beverages, spirits, and vinegar) and tobacco.

As far as it concerns animal products the main recipient states were Russian Federation, China, the USA, Japan, Hong Kong, Switzerland, and Saudi Arabia and included products such as meat and dairy produce, birds' eggs and natural honey. It is worth noting that in 2013 the EU-28 exported almost 30 billion euros worth of vegetable products to extra-EU countries (edible fruit and nuts, peel of citrus fruits, or melons).

What are the implications of the aforementioned descriptive economic statistics for agricultural policymaking in the EU?

a. Despite EU enlargement process, the share of CAP expenditure as a share of the EU budget is falling rapidly over the past 25 years, from 73% in 1985 to 39% in 2014 due to CAP reform and to the rising importance of other EU policies. Equally important, the content of CAP has altered dramatically.

   As a share of GDP, CAP expenditure has been stabilized and despite successive enlargements, overall CAP spending has actually decreased from 0.66% in the 1990s to 0.39% in 2015. Equally important, in the 1980s, CAP spending was mainly price support through market mechanisms (intervention and export subsidies) which rose by the end of the decade due to agricultural surpluses.

   However, soon after the 1992 CAP reform market price support was constrained and replaced by producer support in the form of direct payments. Agenda 2000 implemented rural development policy as a second pillar, and after the 2003 reform most direct payments had been decoupled production as they were based on the farmer's historical receipts. The 2008 Health Check also limited market support (European commission, 2016).
b. EU producers are highly dependent on public support (direct payments, rural development). The EU average share of direct payments in agricultural factor income from 2010 to 2014 stood at 28% although there are striking differences between EU countries, ranging from 15% or less in Cyprus, Malta, the Netherlands, and Romania to more than 40% in Ireland, Luxembourg, Slovakia, and Sweden (Eurostat, 2016).

**Table 8.1 MFF Ceiling from 2014 to 2020 (in Billion Euros)**

| | *2014–2020 Ceiling (Current Prices)* | *2014–2020 Ceiling (2011 Prices)* |
|---|---|---|
| Pillar 1 | 312,74 | 277,85 |
| Pillar 2 | 95,58 | 84,94 |
| Total CAP | 408,31 | 362,79 |

*Source*: European commission, 2016.

Taking all subsidies into consideration, total public support in agricultural income was 33% of agricultural income on average in the EU. According to EC analysis this variation in the share of public support in agricultural income mirrors the distribution of support across member countries (based on historical levels of production in EU-15 and on farm structure and eligible land in the EU-13). Further, one should not underestimate the fact that specialization of EU countries and competitiveness of agriculture are highly differentiated throughout the EU-28.

c. Distribution of support is still very imbalanced between beneficiaries, mirroring the distribution pattern of the beginning of the 1990s. In 2013, on average, 84% of support went to 21% of the beneficiaries, underlining a differentiation between member countries characterized by productive systems that are relatively more homogeneous in terms of support and member countries which are highly determined to preserve the historical distribution of support in favor of the old beneficiaries of the CAP.
d. Between 2007 and 2013, the farm labor force in the exception of Ireland, Hungary, and Malta fell in all of the EU countries with the largest falls recorded in Slovakia, Italy, Cyprus, and Bulgaria. Moreover, among regular workers, the division between full-time and other workers varied significantly between the EU states.
e. The level of agricultural income is generally lower than the average income in the economy and the hourly agricultural earnings in the EU-15 have fluctuated between 54% and 63% of average earnings with the exception of 2009.
f. The CAP and its protectionism, as well as export subsidization measures, have been an issue of strong criticism by EU's trading partners, and too often GATT/WTO negotiations on farm issues have been intense. Indeed, during the Uruguay round (1986–95), USA and the Cairns Group exerted all their influence toward EU for the limitation of trade-distorting CAP policies.

Non-EU agricultural producers underlined that export subsidization of EU agricultural products in third markets distorted global competition (Mahler, 1991, 35; Daugbjerg and Swinbank, 2007) and significantly suppressed prices (Kenyon and Lee, 2006). This means that the links between the CAP and the WTO are very important for the smooth operation of the global trading system (Daugbjerg and Swinbank, 2007; Daugbjerg and Swinbank, 2009).

The aforementioned conclusions suggest that farm structures, agricultural production patterns, and productivities are heterogeneous across EU member states and consequently the agricultural policy interests of EU countries are also heterogeneous. This heterogeneity complicates decision-making process and implies difficult compromises in EU agricultural negotiations. Equally important, farm structures in the EU are dual. Small farms exist parallel to large farms in all sectors with different levels of productivity and performance. This makes decision-making complex since policymakers have to consider the priorities of both groups of producers within a restricted budget.

## CAP DECISION-MAKING: HOW IT WORKS

With the signing of the Treaty of Rome in 1957 and the establishment of the EEC on January 1, 1958, the CAP came into being. CAP decision-making is unique, involving several idiosyncratic elements. One should initially mention that the wording has little changed since the Treaty of Rome, signed in 1957 despite significant territorial and institutional diversification of EU.

The durability of CAP targets is evident in their regular citation in legal texts (regulations and directives) as well as in the usual reference in ECJ decisions on agricultural issues. However, fundamental changes in EU and international socioeconomic environment put greater attention to environmental and social issues of agriculture, contributing to policy shifts in CAP and to new forms of producer support.

The legal and institutional foundations of the EU are laid down in treaties. Title III of that Lisbon Treaty (which entered into force on December 1, 2009) deals with EU policies relating to agriculture and fisheries issues. Its article 39(1) states the major targets of the CAP as follows:

"The objectives of the common agricultural policy shall be:

a. To increase agricultural productivity by promoting technical progress and by ensuring the rational development of agricultural production and the optimum utilization of the factors of production, in particular, labor
b. Thus to ensure a fair standard of living for the agricultural community, in particular by increasing the individual earnings of persons engaged in agriculture
c. To stabilize markets
d. To assure the availability of supplies
e. To ensure that supplies reach consumers at reasonable prices."

The aforementioned targets of European CAP can be divided into two broad groups referred to income and production. The production dimension targets productivity, market stabilization, and the availability of supplies. The income dimension targets a reasonable income for agricultural population as well as a supply of food products for consumers at reasonable prices.

An interesting issue is the complexity of the decision-making process in CAP. The EC collaborates with all key stakeholders (through its advisory groups) and its proposals are decided by the Council of agriculture ministers of the EU states, acting together with the EP. The EU Court of auditors supervises CAP expenditure and EU states are responsible for daily running of CAP issues. Equally important, article 4(2d) of TFEU underlines that competence in agricultural issues is shared between the EU and the EU countries.

Until 2010 EU treaties prescribed a different policymaking procedure which comprised Commission proposal, an opinion delivered by the EP and the EESC, and a Council decision taken by a qualified majority. Thus, Parliament did not have a crucial role in decision-making and was de facto limited to use non-binding methods, such as own-initiative reports and resolutions. However, the Lisbon Treaty (article 42, para 1, and article 43 para 2) laid down co-decision as the ordinary legislative procedure for the CAP empowering EP's role as co-legislator in the agricultural policy issues.

This policy shift permitted parliament to exert its influence in several occasions through resolutions (i.e., resolutions of July 8, 2010 and June 23, 2011 on the future of the CAP after 2013, OJ C 351 E, 2.12.2011 and OJ C 390 E, 18.12.2012) responding to the new challenges facing the agricultural industry, such as product quality, public health, sustainable development, economic, social and territorial cohesion, environmental protection.

Indeed, the Lisbon Treaty laid down a distinction between delegated acts and implementing acts. The adoption of delegated acts is governed by the relevant basic legislative act while the adoption of implementing acts is subject to the rules provided by regulation no. 182/2011 of the EP and of the Council of February 16, 2011 (OJ L 55, 28.2.2011). Within this process a key role is attributed to the COPA and the COGECA advisory groups.

## THE DYNAMICS OF CAP REFORMS FROM 1962 TO 2016

Looking at the history of the EU's CAP one can easily perceive its complex dynamics, (Moyer and Josling, 1990; Swinnen, 2008; Buckwell, 2009), its incremental change and the concentration of major policy reforms in the last three decades (1992, 2003 and 2013 reforms). As a result, CAP is not a *sensu stricto* issue area policy but a multidimensional and enlarged policy, incorporating in all its stages, (strategy, implementation), environmental, rural, territorial, and social traits.

Did EU try to reform the highly protected agricultural sector before 1990s? In 1968 a significant proposal for a structural policy reform of the CAP has been presented (COM (68) 1000, European Commission, 1968). The target was to apply measures that could ease structural adjustment in European agricultural sector, reducing the quantities of farms, land and dairy cows in the agricultural sector so as to limit total production. However, European farmers and key politicians in the majority of EEC member countries were not ready for structural policy reforms in the 1960s. The remaining of the chapter examines the successive milestones in CAP and focuses on the last CAP 2013 reform.

In the early 1990s, the need for deeper reform in CAP became inevitable. Significant domestic and international economic events exerted strong influence toward reform in EU agricultural policymaking (Swinbank and Tanner, 1996; Tangermann, 2004). The application of CAP measures became more complex due to bureaucracy involved as well as due to distributive imbalance in CAP expenditure between continental and Mediterranean products. Further, CAP's implementation was considered too costly and its importance in European integration was put into question by different political forces across Europe.

The aforementioned issues made farm Commissioner Ray MacSharry to propose a substantial reform of the CAP in February 1991. The MacSharry reform represented a fundamental shift in the CAP (Council Regulation (EEC) no. 1765/92; Council Regulation (EEC) no. 2066/92) process because it put into doubt coupled support to production and introduced the direct payments (OECD, 2011).

More specifically, the MacSharry reforms reduced the level of market price support and introduced direct support including production limits to address surplus reshuffling the political economy balance in EU agricultural policymaking. It also introduced rural development measures with an environmental focus and mandatory land set-aside. The crucial policy changes took place in the arable sectors while the reforms in the beef and sheep sectors were more moderate. Thus, domestic support in these sectors was partially transformed from price support to direct payments, decoupling them from production output.

## The AGENDA 2000 Reform

Agenda 2000 CAP reform was adopted in March 1999 (Council Regulation (EC) no. 1251/1999; Council Regulation (EC) no. 1254/1999) and can be perceived as a deepening of the MacSharry reform as it further reduced the guaranteed minimum prices and enforced direct payments (Buckwell, 2009; Tangermann, 2011).

More specifically, Agenda 2000 reforms attained a further fall in market distortions. Reforms also imposed an environmental focus encouraging single EU countries to apply a comprehensive rural development policy and to set in motion the seven-year rural development plans. The latter gave enough discretion and flexibility to CAP finance without violating EU regulations or distorting inter-EU trade. Further, a new rural development policy was introduced as a second pillar of the CAP. This new policy direction encouraged EU farmers to diversify as well as to restructure their businesses.

Thus, Agenda 2000 explicitly established economic, social, and environmental targets within a reformulated CAP consistent with the requirements of the Amsterdam treaty. It also put the framework of a European model of agriculture taking into account the need to preserve the diversity of farming systems across EU including areas with specific problems. The Agenda 2000 objectives included many targets among others more market orientation and increased competitiveness, food safety and quality, stabilization of agricultural incomes, integration of environmental concerns into agricultural policy, development of rural areas, and simplification of procedures, and decentralization of payments.

## The Fischler (2003) Reform

The Fischler reform (Council regulation (EC) no. 1782/2003) was adopted as a result of the mid-term review of Agenda 2000 and was a milestone for the evolution of the CAP. It introduced significant changes in the way the EU provided support to the agricultural sector and applied fundamental instruments to improve the functioning and legitimacy of CAP (Sorrentino et al., 2011; Cooper et al., 2009).

The reform did not only apply decoupling direct payments and cross-compliance but it further enforced rural development policies through modulation. Thus, the 2003 CAP reform was a clear reassessment of the orientation of the CAP, targeting a market-oriented agriculture where prices provide the signals for production and consumption and sustainable agriculture is based on rural development, agri-environmental, and ecological terms.

The implementation of such flexibility meant the transformation of the CAP from a "product-specific policy" to a "producer-specific policy" (Cooper et al., 2009). The 2003 reform decoupled some direct payments from production and enforced rural development policy. The reform decoupled direct payments from production and transformed them into a flat-rate, SFP. It further allowed member states to tie up to 25% of the direct payments to production and to select from among various options for coupled payments in the beef cattle and sheep sectors.

Evidently, direct payments lost their function of support to production and were linked to the farmer income, without any direct link to the production for which they were obtained in the past. In sum, decoupling, modulation, and cross-compliance are the three key points around which the Fischler reform has rotated.

In sum, the content of 2003 CAP reforms was highly influenced by the WTO trade negotiations (reexamination of agricultural support within the global agricultural trade regime set out in the Uruguay round agreement on agriculture, see Daugbjerg and Swinbank, 2009), the necessity for reductions in budget expenditure, the enlargement of EU with 10 states in May 2004, and of course the pressure for improved food and environmental standards because of successive food safety and environmental crises during 1999 and 2001.

As far as it concerns the enlargement of 2004, it definitely reshuffled the CAP framework since the newcomers had large farm sectors and great interest over the agricultural prices. The Copenhagen package agreement of December 2002, regulating the access to the EU of the 10 new countries laid down the criteria for implementing the CAP to the newcomers. As a result, parallel to the phasing in of the direct payment system, the agreement gave the opportunity to temporarily apply a simplified scheme, the SAPS, before shifting toward the classical direct payment scheme existing in EU before accession of May 2004.

More specifically, regulation 1782/2003 put in place a SPS that combined the various support mechanisms into a single scheme of DP to agricultural producers. Further, the direct payments were combined to standards in the areas of plant and animal health, animal welfare, and agri-environmental measures under the cross-compliance system.

Thus, the Fischler reform was a major policy shift, whereby the idea of a single policy for the whole EU retreats in favor of a mechanism that focuses on greater involvement of the EU countries. CAP policy shifted from one provided the opportunity to each EU country to pick up the tools best suited for attaining its targets and to transform them according to its sector and territorial priorities (Sorrentino et al., 2011).

In sum, Fischler reform redefined the "first pillar" of the CAP and deepened the decoupling process of the farm support that had started with the MacSharry reform through the SPS and the SAPS. It also linked support to the ownership of land and to the exercise of farm activity in compliance with cross-compliance requirements. The EU's domestic markets for agricultural products had also become much more open to international competition and as a result agricultural prices became more variable. Market and incomes policy (Pillar 1 of the CAP) became complemented by structural policies under the heading of rural development (Pillar 2 of the CAP), which expanded to around 20% of CAP.

However, even CAP 2003 reform did not properly address crucial issues such as the necessity for a more balanced distribution of support among EU countries and a widely acceptable justification for the overall generous financial support, calling for a new reform (Swinnen, 2008).

## The Health Check Reform (2008)

When the farm ministers adopted the Fischler reform in June 2003 they mandated a review of key traits of the CAP in 2007/2008 (Daugbjerg and Swinbank, 2011, 131). Mariann Fischer Boel (EU agriculture Commissioner) proposed a new reform agenda, comprising two stages—the first of which was the requirements of the "Health Check" (European Commission, 2007). The "Health Check" reform agreed by the farm ministers in November 2008 put in place the dismantling of the partial coupling option for the main arable crops by 2010 and for many of the livestock payments by 2012 (Daugbjerg and Swinbank, 2009; Swinbank, 2012, 41).

More specifically, the 2008 CAP "Health Check" agreement involved three Council Regulations:

- Regulation (EC) No. 72/2009 for adjustments in commodity programmes under the CMO (intervention system for different productions, expected end of quota systems for milk and sugar)
- Regulation (EC) No. 73/2009 establishing common rules for direct income support schemes
- Regulation (EC) No. 74/2009 on support for rural development by the dedicated fund (EAFRD).

In sum, the Health Check reform limited further direct payment through "modulation" and enforced cross-compliance (the system which reduces income support payments to farm producers if they do not respect specific criteria of environmental care, animal welfare, and public health).

## The CAP 2013 Reform

CAP 2013 reforms took place within a complex international and European economic environment characterized by budgetary limits posed by EU member states, the WTO criticism for EU protectionism in agriculture, and the post-accession problems of May 2004 enlargement.

The debate after the Fischler reform and the Health Check reform focused mainly on two relevant aspects. First, the extent to which direct payments were able to ameliorate the production of public goods in agriculture. Second, the question of whether the production of public goods in agriculture was best delivered at EU or member state level. Relevant to this discussion was the content of direct payments and the terms according to which these payments should be applied.

The CAP 2013 reform put in place a simpler, fairer, more efficient, and effective agricultural policy, reshuffling distribution of direct payments both between and within EU countries. Equally important, the reform targeted a greener and more aligned (with the Europe 2020 goals) policy of smart, sustainable, and inclusive growth (Anania et al., 2015; Burns et al., 2013).

Further, the purpose of CAP reforms was also to simplify bureaucratic procedures and to legitimize implementation in the eyes of EU taxpayers and consumers, through greater transparency. Among the achieved results of this process had been the transformation of the CAP from a product-specific policy to a producer-specific policy and the possibility of member states to tailor the CAP according to their specific needs, within a general common framework of regulations. It was also the first time that the EP acted as co-legislator with the Council.

More specifically after a fierce public debate, the Commission presented on November 18, 2010 a Communication on "The CAP towards 2020," which suggested options for the future CAP and initiated discussions with the other stakeholders and institutions. On October 12, 2011 the Commission presented proposals targeted at making EU agricultural policy more effective and EU agriculture more competitive in international terms. On June 26, 2013 a political agreement on the reform of the CAP has been reached between the European Commission, the European Parliament, and the European Council and on December 16, 2013 the Council of EU agriculture ministers formally adopted the four basic regulations for the reformed CAP as well as the transition rules.

The negotiations proved to be intense because of the difficult social and economic European context, the policies of fiscal austerity pursued within EU, the implementation of the ordinary legislative procedure for CAP reform, and the highly diversified positions forwarded by EU countries and the European institutions. Further, the discussions took into consideration the overall EU budgetary framework from 2014 to 2020, the MFF, which provided the funds for CAP.

According to the regulations of CAP reform the better targeted instruments of the first pillar of CAP were complemented by regionally tailor-made and voluntary measures of the second pillar of the CAP. Based on the Commission proposals the agreement relates to four basic EP and Council regulations for the CAP which are the following:

- Regulation (EU) No. 1305/2013 for support for rural development by the EAFRD;
- Regulation (EU) No. 1306/2013 on the financing, management, and monitoring of the CAP;
- Regulation (EU) No. 1307/2013 establishing rules for direct payments under support schemes within the framework of the CAP;
- Regulation (EU) No. 1308/2013 establishing a common organization of the markets in agricultural products.

To ensure a smooth transition, regulation 1310/2013 determined transitional provisions concerning the application of the four basic regulations in the year 2014.

In detail, the CAP reform agreement on the direct payments regulation allows seven schemes, three of which are mandatory and four of which are optional. However, with each of the mandatory and optional schemes there are options to be made by EU countries concerning application. For example, in mandatory components of direct payments, the EU countries have the option to determine how the components are to be applied (i.e., how per-unit payments are calculated), how to fix practices eligible for green direct payments, and whether to implement more restrictive standards to identify the farmers entitled to specific payments, such as payments for young farmers.

The mandatory elements of the direct payments regulation is related to the BPS, GPS, and YFS, while the optional schemes are related to VCSS, SFS, RPS, and ANCS.

It is also important to underline that the share of the national direct payments financial ceiling that is allocated to the BPS depends on the share of the national direct payments financial ceiling allocated to the other mandatory and optional schemes (direct payments is financed with a portion of the national ceiling set out for each EU country in annex II of regulation (EU) no. 1307/2013).

## Direct Payments

The new system of direct payments replaced the SPS (and the SAPS in new EU countries) introduced by the 2003 Fischler reform (Bureau and Witzke, 2010; Swinbank, 2012). Moreover, it provides aid to persons, natural or legal, for which agricultural activity is not marginal (the so-called active farmers).

The internal convergence terms of the reform target the elimination or reduction by 2019 of any differences in the per hectare basic payment received by agricultural producers in those EU countries in which the SPS was applied. Indeed, regulation 1307/2013 implements a system of multi-objective payments with two fundamental traits namely a basic payment per hectare (BPS) to help farm income subject to a convergence procedure among and between EU countries and a "greening" dimension to compensate for the burden of providing environmental public goods.

But who is considered an active farmer? The system performs this task by defining who is not an active farmer. A farmer (whether a natural or legal person) is considered "non-active" ( and consequently is not entitled direct payment ) when his farm lies in an area naturally kept in a state suitable for grazing or cultivation and when he does not carry out in that area the minimum activity defined by the EU country. The reform defines a list of entities that cannot be considered "active farmers" and include entities operating airports, railway services, waterworks, real estate services, and permanent sport- recreational grounds.

However, EU countries may add other standards to identify active farmers that relate to the importance the agricultural activity has on their overall economic activity. There is also the ability for potential beneficiaries who do not qualify as "active farmers" to receive direct payments if these do not exceed 5,000 euros per year. Additionally, EU countries can lower this threshold (and differentiating it among regions) rendering the definition of "active farmer" even more restrictive.

In addition to "degressivity" (i.e., the reduction of support to larger beneficiaries under the condition that they can be efficient with lower levels of support, given their possibility to adjust), the reform puts in place a more uniform distribution of the per hectare basic farm payments (internal convergence), payments for young farmers, a "redistributive payment" (shifting support from larger farms to smaller ones), and payments for farms located in areas with natural constraints (European Commission, 2015a; European Commission, 2015b). Further, all direct aid is paid to agricultural producers under the term that they keep to strict standards relating to the environment, food safety, plant and animal health-animal welfare, and also keep their farm in good productive condition (cross-compliance clause). If these rules are not complied with, payments may be suspended and the farmer agricultural producer might face penalties. In sum, the major provisions of the CAP-2013 reform are the following:

a. BPS: The new CAP from 2014 to 2020 implements a new single BPS. Under the conditions of this scheme, EU countries dedicate up to 70% of their direct payments national envelope to the BPS (minus capital transfers committed for extra payments such as the young farmer top-ups, LFA top-ups, the redistributive payment) and "coupled" payments. For the EU countries that apply SAPS, the end-date for the simpler, flat-rate SAPS system is extended until 2020. Thus, with the reform, direct payments have been expanded to include almost all active farmers.

b. GPS: According to the scheme each agricultural holding receives a payment per hectare tied to the objective of the basic payment for implementing specific farm practices beneficial for the environment and the climate. The provisions give EU countries the opportunity to use 30% of their national envelope in order to pay for this. This is compulsory and violation of the greening requirements results in reductions and penalties which might in some cases go beyond the greening payment. The green payment is granted for those regions that comply with the terms (i.e., being eligible for BPS or SAPS, respect of greening obligations).
c. YFS: The reform favors new entrant young farmers (no more than 40 years of age) and provides an additional payment available for a period of maximum five years (linked to the first installation).

   A young farmer is defined as a natural person who (a) becomes the head of an agricultural holding for the first time, or who has become the head of a holding during the five years preceding the first submission of an application under the BPS, and (b) is no more than 40 years of age in the year of the submission.

   EU countries may introduce additional criteria to be satisfied in terms of appropriate skills and/or training requirements. This is in addition to other measures available for young farmers under rural development programmes. EU member states also have the right to revise the percentage of the national ceiling devoted to the payment for young farmers and in the case that the budget necessary to cover all requests of young farmers applying for payment is not sufficient they could use the national reserve.
d. ANCs/ LFAs: The reform gives the right to EU countries (or regions) to provide an additional payment for areas with natural constraints (as defined under rural development rules) of up to 5% of the national envelope. This is optional and does not exert any influence on the ANC/LFA options available under rural development. The target is to guarantee the presence of agricultural producers in these regions by providing aid that is additional to that foreseen in rural development policies.

   Agricultural producers are entitled to receive this component of the direct payments if their farms are located in "areas with natural constraints," as determined by the member state according to rural development rules. However, only agricultural producers entitled to receive the basic payment are eligible for this support. The amount of the annual payment for eligible hectares is calculated by dividing the portion of the national ceiling committed to this payment by the number of eligible hectares in those regions with natural constraints for which the EU country activates the payment.
e. VCSS: EU countries have the choice of providing limited amounts of "coupled" payments, that is, a payment linked to a specific product so as to

preserve present levels of production in sectors or regions where specific types of farming or sectors face hurdles and are considered crucial for economic, social, or environmental reasons. This constrained up to 8% of the national envelope, or up to 13% if the current level of coupled support in an EU country is higher than 5%. However, the Commission has the flexibility to approve a higher rate where justified.

f. RPS: In order to enforce small farms, EU countries can take up to 30% of the national envelope and redistribute it to farmers on their first 30 hectares (or up to the average farm size if higher than thirty hectares).
g. SFS: This simplified scheme reduces bureaucracy both for the farmers and for the public sector when small payments are involved. According to the scheme, any agricultural producer claiming support may participate and thereby receive an annual payment fixed by the EU country of normally between 500 euros and 1,250 euros irrespective of the farm size. EU states may use different methods to estimate the annual payment including an option whereby agricultural producers would simply receive the amount they would otherwise receive.

   Additionally, the scheme exempts the producers both from "green payment" requirements and from cross-compliance controls and sanctions. The total burden of the SFS may not be more than 10% of the national envelope with some exceptions. There is also rural development funding for advice to small agricultural producers for economic development and restructuring grants for regions with many such small farms.

   An important novelty of the CAP reform provisions is the establishment of a national or regional reserve with a deduction of the ceiling for the basic payment no higher than 3%. However, if the reserve is insufficient to face the aforementioned targets, the percentage of deduction may be higher than 3%. The target of the reserve is to allocate payment entitlements to young farmers and new farmers.

   EU member states may use the national/regional reserve to allocate payment entitlements for five reasons, namely, to avoid abandonment of the land, to compensate farmers for specific disadvantages, to provide aid to farmers that cannot have payment entitlements as result of force majeure or exceptional circumstances, to address specific situations in SAPS, and to provide a linear increase, on permanent basis, of the value of all entitlements of the BPS if the national/regional reserve exceeds 0.5% of the respective annual ceiling for the basic payment.
h. Degressivity: Targeting the reduction of subsidies to large agricultural enterprises the reform imposes a compulsory reduction of the payments for individual farms above 150,000 euros. As a result, the amount of support that a farm holding receives as basic payment will be reduced by at

least 5% for the amounts above 150,000 euros (after the deduction of salary costs). This reduction is not obligatory for EU countries which apply the "redistributive payment" under which at least 5% of their national envelope is held back for redistribution on the first hectares of all farms.

i. Reserve for crises: Regulation no. 1306/2013 (article 25) establishes a new reserve for crises in EU agriculture using deductions from direct payments, with unused payments reimbursed to agricultural producers. The first experience of using the reserve is to "compensate" the negative outflows of the Russian embargo on EU agriculture.
j. Transferring funds between pillars: EU states have the right to transfer up to 15% of their national envelope for direct payments (Pillar 1) to their rural development envelope. These amounts will not need to be co-funded.

Evidently, the share of BPS in the 2015 direct payments envelope of member countries varies between 12% and 68%.

## THE MARKET MANAGEMENT MECHANISMS OF THE NEW CAP

Regulation 1308/2013 (common organization of the markets) presents a list of aid schemes to various sectors as well as risk management tools such as insurance and mutual funds for fruits, vegetables, and wine.

The CAP reform ended the sugar quota regime on September 30, 2017 ensuring improved competitiveness for EU producers on the domestic and world market alike (as EU exports are limited by WTO rules under quotas). Supply on EU domestic markets at reasonable prices also benefits the intermediate and final users of sugar. However, in order to provide added security, standard provisions for agreements between sugar factories and growers are maintained and most developing countries keep enjoying unlimited duty-free access to the EU market.

Reforms to the CMO provisions target enforced competition on global markets and enhanced safety for producers in the context of external uncertainties. Equally important, rules related to the recognition of POs and inter-branch organizations are covering all sectors—with further options for establishing such organizations now transferred to rural development funding. The existing systems of public intervention and private storage aid are revised to be more responsive and more efficient, for example, with technical adjustments for beef and dairy.

Moreover, new safeguard clauses are introduced for all sectors in order to enable the EC to adopt emergency measures to respond to general market disturbances such as the measures taken during the crisis from May to July 2011.

More specifically, regulation (EU) no. 1308/2013 is divided into six parts dedicated respectively to introductory provisions, internal market (market intervention and specific provisions for individual agricultural sectors), trade with third countries (including export refunds), competition rules, general provisions (for exceptional measures against market disturbance), and delegation of power and implementing provisions.

Crucially important for the success of the new CAP is the enhancement of issue areas where EU countries offer advice to farmers cover (farm advisory service), such as cross-compliance, the green direct payments, the conditions for maintenance of land eligible for direct payments, the water framework and sustainable use of pesticides directives, and certain rural development measures.

## THE CAP PROVISIONS FOR RURAL DEVELOPMENT

According to CAP reform, measures will not be classified at EU level into axes with associated minimum spending requirements per axis but it will be up to EU countries/regions to determine which measures they use (and how) so as to attain objectives in six broad priorities. The six priorities refer to fostering knowledge transfer and innovation; enhancing competitiveness of all types of agriculture and the sustainable management of forests, promoting food chain organization (including processing and marketing and risk management); restoring, preserving, and enhancing ecosystems; promoting resource efficiency and the transition to a low-carbon economy; and promoting social inclusion, poverty reduction, and economic development in rural areas.

Moreover, EU countries have to allocate at least 30% of their rural development funding from the EU budget on specific measures related to land management and the fight against climate change, and at least 5% on the LEADER approach.

Equally important, rural development policy operates in closer coordination with other policies through an EU level common strategic framework and through partnership agreements at national level covering all aid from ESI funds (the EAFRD, ERDF, cohesion fund, ESF, and EMFF) in the EU country concerned. Additionally, EU countries/regions have the option to apply thematic sub-programmes in issues such as young farmers, small farms, and mountain areas; women in rural areas; climate change mitigation/adaptation; biodiversity; and short supply chains.

## The Main Advances of the New CAP

Which are the fundamental traits of the complex CAP 2013 reform?

a. The objective of a more competitive agricultural sector is promoted through a new scheme of direct payments, better targeted, greener, and more equitable. In addition to the basic payment, the green direct payment and possible additional support for ANCs contribute to specific environmental and territorial objectives. Moreover, direct payments are better targeted by limiting aid to those who are actively engaged in farm activities.

   The level of direct payments per hectare is progressively adjusted with the introduction of a minimum national average direct payment per hectare across all EU countries by 2020. The objective of past reforms to enhance the market orientation of EU agriculture is continued by adapting the policy instruments to further encourage farmers to base their production decisions on market signals.
b. The new CAP continues the policy shift from product to producer support and to a more land-based approach. This corresponds fully to the challenges facing the agricultural sector, many of which are driven by variables that are external to agriculture. The key facts that are taken into account are not only economic (i.e., food security, a declining rate of productivity growth, price volatility, high input prices to the production chain, and deteriorating position of farmers in the food supply chain), but also environmental (i.e., resource efficiency, soil and water quality, threats to biodiversity), and territorial (i.e., deindustrialization). This is why CAP targets viable food production, sustainable management of natural resources and climate action, and balanced territorial development.
c. The reform puts in place a simplified and more targeted cross-compliance, representing the compulsory basic layer of environmental requirements and obligations to be met in order to receive full CAP funding. Additionally, the CAP introduces a new policy instrument in first pillar, the green direct payment accounting for 30% of the national direct payment envelope and rewards farmers for respecting three obligatory agricultural practices, namely maintenance of permanent grassland, ecological focus areas, and crop diversification.

   As the green direct payment is compulsory it has the benefit of introducing actions that are advantageous for the environment and climate on most of the UAA. The focus of the second pillar on sustainability is clearly visible by the fact that at least 30% of the budget of each rural development programme must be reserved for voluntary measures that are beneficial for the environment and climate change. These include agri-environmental-climate measures, organic farming, Areas of Natural

Constraints, Natura 2000 areas, forestry measures, and investments which are beneficial for the environment or climate. All these measures contribute significantly to environmental enhancement and climate change because they are adapted to local needs.

Further, a new policy instrument of the first pillar (greening) is directed to the provision of environmental public goods, which constitutes a major change in the policy framework. Equally important, the inclusion of environmental criteria in the CAP has a direct impact on both agricultural producers and EU consumers as well as on the agenda of agricultural vested interests (Hodge, 2013).

d. The key traits of the EU rural development policy do not change but rural development policy focuses more on increasing competitiveness and promoting innovation. The policy is applied through national and regional RDP's which, for a seven-year period, set out the actions to be undertaken and the relevant funding for these actions.

e. There is new flexibility for EU countries in the budgeting and application of first pillar instruments, taking into consideration the diversity of agriculture, the redistributive target of the reform, agronomic production potential, climatic-environmental terms as well as socioeconomic terms, and priorities across the EU territory. The most innovative element is not so much the transfer of funds from direct payments to rural development programmes (which could take place also by means of the compulsory modulation applied with the Fischler reform and by means of the voluntary modulation of Agenda 2000) as the transfer of funds from rural development to direct payments.

Undeniably, it is a significant tool, because it permits better distribution of financial resources between pillars, and among EU countries allowing each country to shift resources between the two policies in keeping with its own development strategy, programming skills, and spending capacity. Accordingly, the common targets and interactions between the two pillars are being strengthened and the two pillars interact in financial terms, with possible transfers between both, preventing double-funding. In this way, EU countries can rebalance payments with the introduction of the redistributive payment, voluntary capping, and degressivity (reduction) of payments, beyond the mandatory cuts which apply to the Basic Payment above a specific threshold.

f. The market management mechanisms become simpler and competitiveness is ameliorated by reforms to market mechanisms, particularly the removal of production constraints. All of the existing restrictions on production volumes for sugar, dairy, and the wine sector end and facilitate agricultural producers' adaptation to growing world demand.

Moreover, the reform applies under the second pillar restructuring and modernization measures at farm level as well as start-up aid for young agricultural producers. The farm advisory system and the training and innovation programmes further enhance competitiveness and agricultural productivity. The establishment of farm advisory system in EU countries covers obligations of statutory management requirements and standards for good agricultural and environmental conditions of land, the agricultural practices for the climate, and the environment and measures for farm modernization, competitiveness, innovation, market orientation, and entrepreneurship.

Equally important, the system may also cover the promotion of conversions of farms and the diversification of their economic activity, risk management, and the introduction of appropriate preventive actions (so as to address natural disasters, catastrophic events, and animal and plant diseases), the minimum requirements set by EU countries' laws on agri-environment-climate, and organic farming measures and the information related to climate change mitigation, biodiversity, and protection of water.

The two pillars of CAP further accommodate producer cooperation and ameliorate agricultural competitiveness by improving access to credit, promoting product differentiation, enforcing quality, and reducing total costs. The legal provisions for producer organizations and the financial incentives under the second pillar include support for setting up producer groups and supply chains.

g. CAP reform provides adequate safety net measures and enforces EU's crisis management. This is taking place through market measures to address potential threats of market disturbances as well as through more flexible exceptional measures. The new crisis reserve secures adequate financial resources needed in case of crisis, through deductions from direct payments, with unused amounts reimbursed to agricultural producers in the consecutive budget years. In addition, a new risk management toolkit is put in place under the provisions of the second pillar, including insurance schemes for crops, animals, and plants, as well as mutual funds and an income stabilization tool.
h. A common and coherent overall EU policy framework is established for all ESI funds including EAFRD to improve coordination between them and enforce the complementarities of the different programmes.
i. EU countries have the option to further target direct payments through other optional schemes. A redistributive payment can be attributed to the first hectares of the farms, to give more targeted support to small and medium-sized agricultural producers. Further, specific and simplified support scheme for small farmers facilitates their ability to benefit from direct

payments and to limit administrative burden. EU countries may also grant coupled support to secure the future of potentially vulnerable sectors. It is beyond dispute that the reduction in disparities of the level of direct payments between EU countries, known as external convergence strengthens the credibility and legitimacy of the support system at EU level.

j. Transparency is further enhanced since EU states provide full transparency to all beneficiaries with the exception of those farms which are eligible for the SFS. Additionally, legitimization of CAP is enforced through new processes for monitoring and evaluation of the CAP. According to these provisions the Commission will present a report before the end of 2018 (and every four years) on the performance of the CAP with respect to the targets of viable food production, sustainable management of natural resources, and balanced territorial development. Moreover, the target is also to eliminate fraud which according to data from the OLAF accounted on average for 0.02% of the CAP's budget from 2006 to 10.
k. Finally, the CAP 2013 provides EP the ability to fully participate in all stages of the decision-making process in agricultural policy.

## FINANCING THE CAP OF EU

For the last 50 years the CAP has been the most important policy of EU. This easily explains why it has absorbed a significant portion of EU's budget, although the percentage has reduced in recent years. Member countries of EU pay close attention on how financial flows of CAP are distributed and on the maximization of possible returns in the form of payments directed at their own farmers (i.e., the large financial flows involved in the direct payments). Consequently, net surplus/deficit position vis-à-vis the EU budget is de facto given an equal foot to economic efficiency and rationality of CAP.

Although in 1992 market management represented over 90% of total CAP expenditure due to export refunds and intervention purchases by the end of 2013 it dropped to just 5% as market intervention was limited and direct payments became the key tool of support (94% are decoupled from production). Thus, CAP costs have been falling since 1984 while the successive enlargements of the EU since 1992 ended in a doubling of farmers.

According to new CAP provisions, EU Council and the EP work within a multiyear financial framework and prepare each year the budget. Within heading two of the multiyear framework (entitled "Sustainable growth–natural resources"), a maximum ceiling for the first pillar of the CAP (direct payments and market support measures) is implemented. Further, rural development actions within the second pillar of the CAP are funded from the amount available in heading two.

On December 2, 2013, the Council adopted regulation (EU) 1311/2013 laying down the MFF (the annual ceilings for the financial resources given to the priorities of the EU) for the period from 2014 to 2020. The regulation entered into force on January 1, 2014. In order to maximize effectiveness and transparency in CAP, the Commission consults stakeholders and citizens and conducts independent studies on the performance of the CAP's tools.

The CAP is financed by two funds which are part of the EU's budget and are the following:

1. The European Agricultural Guarantee Fund (EAGF) which primarily finances direct payments to agricultural producers and measures regulating or supporting agriculture.
2. The European Agricultural Fund for Rural Development (EAFRD) which finances the EU's contribution to rural development programmes.

According to the provisions for the financial management of the CAP, the EC is responsible for the management of the EAGF and the EAFRD. However, the principle of shared management gives the duty for payments to the beneficiaries to member states who themselves work through national or regional paying agencies. The paying agencies are accredited on the basis of a set of criteria laid down by the Commission and the exact checks to be carried out are analyzed in the different sector regulations of the CAP and differ from one sector to another. The expenditure delivered by the paying agencies is then reimbursed by the EC to the EU countries, in the case of the EAGF on a monthly basis and in the case of EAFRD on a quarterly basis. In any case reimbursements are subject to corrections which the EC may make under the clearance of accounts.

In 2014, the EAFRD was incorporated into the new common strategic framework together with the ERDF, the ESF, the EMFF to accomplish the targets of the Europe 2020 strategy (sustainable, smart, and inclusive growth). All funds for rural development can be used for both farmer and non-farmer activities, based on the following priorities:

a. Fostering knowledge transfer and innovation
b. Enhancing competitiveness, promoting food chain organization and risk management
c. Restoring, preserving, and enhancing ecosystems
d. Promoting resource efficiency and transition to a low-carbon economy
e. Promoting social inclusion, poverty reduction, and economic development in rural areas.

Additionally, a new role is attributed to the EGAF. The EGAF is a fund outside the MFF providing temporary aid to workers (including those in agriculture) who have lost their jobs as a result of major changes in trade patterns brought about by disruptive effects of the globalization process on a specific sector in an EU country. Resources allocated to the EGAF from 2014 to 2020 amount to 1,050 million euros (in 2011 prices), an important reduction (−70.6%) relative to the allocation from 2007 to 2013.

In order to promote competitiveness and avoid market distortion, payments are not based on how much a farmer produces, but on how much land he uses and how he uses it. Within this framework rural development programmes provide co-funding for projects with economic, environmental, or social targets, primarily favoring farms and SMEs in rural areas. Thus, CAP budget is allocated via tailor-made measures designed to match local priorities and opportunities. It also becomes clear that the CAP expenditure is tied to performance with target indicators and monitoring, which effectively demands EU countries and regions to deliver well-defined results in order to keep the budget allocation.

The common monitoring and evaluation framework provide crucial data on the performance and policy implementation of the CAP. Based on the indicators of this framework the EC will deliver annual reports on the performance of the CAP, the first report being due in 2018.

From 2014 to 2020, some 365,000 farmers are expected to benefit from funding in order to restructure and modernize their farms. During the same period 22.6 billion euros from the EAFRD will be given for investment in the rural regions supported also by private capital investment flows. EU states will also take advantage of their rural development allocations to put in place financial tools such as loans, guarantees, and equity.

Overall, 362,787 billion euros are projected from 2014 to 2020 of which 277,851 billion euros are foreseen for direct payments and market-related expenditure (Pillar 1) and 84,936 billion euros for rural development (Pillar 2) in 2011 prices. Furthermore, the share of expenditure between pillars may change between 2014 and 2020, with the possibility to transfer up to 15% of their national envelopes between pillars enabling EU countries to better target spending to their specific priorities.

Total financial resources allocated in the MFF for the EU-28 amounted to 959,988 million euros (in 2011 prices), corresponding to 1% of the Gross National Income (3.5% lower than that in MFF for the period 2007–2013). Heading 1 ("Smart and inclusive growth") and Heading 2 ("Sustainable growth, natural resources"), account for 86% of the financial resources in the MFF from 2014 to 2020.

More specifically, Heading 1, which includes policies to forward "competitiveness for growth and jobs" and "economic, social and territorial cohesion," has been allocated 47% of the total resources. Heading 2 total allocations for the MFF is reduced from 42.3% in the previous MFF to 38.9%. In particular, policy measures in first pillar ("Market related expenditure and direct payments") are allocated 27,7851 million euros, amounting to a share of 28.9% of the total financial resources of the MFF (as compared to a 32.1% share of the MFF for 2007–2013), while policy measures in second pillar 2 ("rural development policies") are assigned 84,936 million euros, amounting to a share of 8.8% (as compared to 9.6% for the previous MFF). Overall, therefore, the CAP accounts for 37.8% of the MFF 2014–2020 budget, as compared to 41.7% of the MFF 2007–2013 budget.

A common critique of CAP by non-European analysts is that it does not promote targets of increased productivity stated in para 1 of article 39 through activities such as R&D so as to promote technical progress innovation and improvement of factor mobility but rather focuses subsidies toward farmers irrespective of their performance. There are agricultural sectors where due to rising production costs (i.e., the price of fertilizers or energy cost) consumer prices rise without farmer's incomes improvements.

## CONCLUSIONS-POLICY IMPLICATIONS

The chapter analyzes the main traits of CAP. The analysis of the rationale of the CAP reform and of its decision-making system gives an interesting and thorough picture. The most substantial reforms to the CAP began in 1992 and intensified in 2013, when the link between subsidies and production was interrupted.

Overall, the new CAP reform offers the EU countries greater flexibility (the distribution of funds between the first and second pillar of the CAP), leaving it to them to decide on which payments to forward. Further, the rural development policy helps agricultural producers to restructure their farms without undermining environmental standards. Equally important, the new second pillar underlines knowledge transfer and innovation giving the opportunity to family farms to apply new technologies and reap the economic advantages. Although the capital available for the innovation and farm advisory schemes is important, the success is highly dependent on the level of agricultural producers' participation and so efforts will be required to enforce participation.

However, six challenges lie ahead of CAP and will definitely determine the success or failure of CAP 2013 reform. First, the CAP's ability to include specificities and priorities of EU member states in a common policy framework taking into consideration the differences in socioeconomic conditions and the traits of their agricultural sectors. The complex procedure of fine-tuning of the tools at national level should continue, in order to offer even more flexibility and effectiveness in the following years of implementation of the reform to the EU countries.

Second, there is still the issue of how to achieve an enlarged policy agenda within an economic-financial crisis with reduced financing. At an analytical level there is no doubt that policy measures need to be properly targeted to well-defined objectives and that the number of policy measures applied needs to match the number of targets pursued. Simplifying and improving the manageability of CAP implementation in regional level is crucial.

Third, the decision-making system needs to reexamine farm competitiveness and full application of the green measures on farms while attaining in the same time equity and fairness within agricultural population.

Fourth, there is still room for more transparency and control of subsidies allocation. The European taxpayer too often considers that these capitals are not correctly spent. It is therefore of crucial importance that management and checking systems are in place which gives reasonable assurance that the subsidies are allocated properly and that any irregular payments are detected and recovered.

Fifth, price volatility of several agricultural products is likely to continue as a key threat to the economic viability of family farms. Domestic policies such as multiyear tax smoothing as well as CAP policies such as the income stabilization scheme and the crisis reserve fund are useful tools to insulate agricultural producers from price risk. Finally, despite CAP improvement in decision-making there are problems in the linkages of CAP policy with other crucial policies in EU such as energy, trade, health, climate action policy; thus deprive CAP from maximizing its potential in a highly volatile, dynamic, and complex world agricultural market.

In general, a proper and effective system of monitoring the implementation of the CAP would be welcome as it would facilitate CAP procedures, adjustment of agricultural producers to global changes, and rationalization of EU agricultural production.

## BIBLIOGRAPHY

Anania, G., Pupo, M. R., and D'Andrea, M. R. 2015. "The 2013 reform of the Common Agricultural Policy". In *The Political Economy of the 2013 CAP Reform*, ed. Jo Swinnen. Brussels: CEPS.

Anderson, K., Rausser, G., and Swinnen, J. 2013. "Political economy of public policies: Insights from distortions to agricultural and food markets". *Journal of Economic Literature,* 51(2): 423–477.

Buckwell, A. 2009. *Elements of the post 2013 CAP.* Brussels: European Parliament–Directorate General for Internal Policies.

Bureau, J. C and Witzke, H. P. 2010. *The Single Payment Scheme after 2013: New approach –New targets*. Study for the European Parliament, Directorate General for Internal Policies. IP/B/AGRI/IC/2009_038, March, http://capreform.eu/wpcontent/uploads/2010/05/EST31208.pdf

Burns, C., Rasmussen, A., and Reh, C. 2013. "Legislative co-decision and its impact on the political system of the European Union". *Journal of European Public Policy,* 20(7): 941–952.

Coleman, W., Skogstad, G., and Atkinson, M. 1996. "Paradigm shifts and policy networks: Cumulative change in agriculture". *Journal of Public Policy,* 16(3): 273–301.

Cooper T., Hart K., and Baldock, D. 2009. *The Provision of public goods through agriculture in the European Union.* Report for DG agriculture and rural development. London: Institute for European Environmental Policy.

COPA-COGECA. 2015. *Member states' choices for the implementation of direct payments in 2014-2020.* PAC (14)2758:17 FB, 16 April.

Cuhna, A and Swinbank, A. 2011. *An inside view of the CAP reform process, explaining the MacSharry, Agenda 2000 and Fischler reforms.* Oxford: Oxford University Press.

Daugbjerg, C and Swinbank, A. 2004. "The CAP and EU enlargement: Prospects for an alternative strategy to avoid lock-in of CAP support". *Journal of Common Market Studies,* 42: 92–119.

Daugbjerg, C and Swinbank, A. 2007. "The politics of CAP reform: Trade negotiations, institutional settings and blame avoidance". *Journal of Common Market Studies,* 45(1): 1–22.

Daugbjerg, C and Swinbank, A. 2009. *Ideas, institutions and trade. The WTO and the curious role of EU farm policy in trade liberalization.* Oxford: Oxford University Press.

Daugbjerg, C and Swinbank, A. 2011. "The budget and the WTO: Driving forces behind the health check?" In *The common agricultural policy after the Fischer reform: National implementations, impact assessment and the agenda for future reforms,* eds. Sorrentino Alesandro, Roberto Henke and Simone Severini. UK: Ashgate.

De Gorter, H and Swinnen, J. 2002. "Political Economy of Agricultural Policy". In *Handbook of Agricultural Economics.* eds. G. Gardner and G. Rausser. vol. 2, Elsevier Science.

DG AGRI. 2011. *Evaluation of effects of direct support on farmers' income – Common Agricultural Policy Evaluations.* Brussels: European Commission. Accessed http://ec.europa.eu/agriculture/eval/reports/income/leaflet_en.pdf

European Commission. 1968. *Memorandum of the reform of agriculture in the European Community*, DG VI/COM (68) 1000. Brussels: European Commission.

European Commission. 2007. *Preparing for the 'Health Check' of the CAP reform.* Communication from the Commission to the Council and the European Parliament, COM (2007) 722, 20 November. Brussels: European Commission.

European Commission. 2015a. *Agriculture in the European Union. Statistical and economic information report.* DG agriculture and Rural Development, December, Accessed http://ec.europa.eu/agriculture/statistics/agricultural/2013/index_en.htm

European Commission. 2015b. *The CAP towards 2020: Implementation of rural development policy. State of play of RDPs.* European Commission. DG Agriculture and rural development. February. Brussels. Accessed http://ec.europa.eu/agriculture/rural-development-2014-2020/countryfiles/ common/implementation-state-of-play_en.pdf

European Commission. 2016. *Rural Development in the EU: Statistical and Economic Information, Report 2013.* DG agriculture and Rural Development. December, Brussels: European commission. Accessed http://ec.europa.eu/agriculture/statistics/rural-development/2013/full-text_en.pdf

European Union. 2013. "Regulation No 1306/2013 of the European parliament and of the council of 17 December 2013 on the financing, management and monitoring of the common agricultural policy and repealing Council Regulations (EEC) No 352/78, (EC) No 165/94, (EC) No 2799/98, (EC) No 814/2000, (EC) No 1290/2005 and (EC) No 485/2008" *Official Journal of the European Union.* L 347/549, 20.12.2013.

European Union. 2013. "Regulation No 1307/2013 of the European parliament and of the council of 17 December 2013 establishing rules for direct payments to farmers under support schemes within the framework of the common agricultural policy and repealing Council Regulation (EC) No 637/2008 and Council Regulation (EC) No 73/2009" *Official Journal of the European Union.* 20.12.2013. L 347/608, Brussels.

European Union. 2013. "Regulation No 1308/2013 of the European parliament and of the council of 17 December 2013 establishing a common organization of the markets in agricultural products and repealing Council Regulations (EEC) No 922/72, (EEC) No 234/79, (EC) No 1037/2001 and (EC) No 1234/2007" *Official Journal of the European Union* L 347/671. 20.12.2013.

European Union. 2013. "Regulation No 1310/2013 of the European parliament and the council of 17 December 2013 laying down certain transitional provisions on support for rural development by the European Agricultural Fund for Rural Development (EAFRD), amending Regulation (EU) No 1305/2013 of the European Parliament and of the Council as regards resources and their distribution in respect of the year 2014 and amending Council Regulation (EC) No 73/2009 and Regulations (EU) No 1307/2013, (EU) No 1306/2013 and (EU) No 1308/2013 of the European Parliament and of the Council as regards their application in the year 2014" *Official Journal of the European Union* L347/865. 20.12.2013.

European Union Council. 2013. "Council regulation (EU, EURATOM) No 1311/2013 of 2 December 2013 laying down the multiannual financial framework for the years 2014-2020" *Official Journal of the European Union.* 20.12.2013, L 347/884.

Eurostat. 2016. *Database for agriculture.* October. Accessed http://ec.europa.eu/eurostat/web/agriculture/data/database

Grant, W. 2008. "Implications for future reforms". In *The perfect storm: The political economy of the Fischler reforms of the common agricultural policy,* ed. J. F. M. Swinnen. Brussels: Centre for European Policy Studies.

Greer, A and Hind, T. 2012. "Inter-institutional decision-making: The case of the common agricultural policy". *Politics and Society,* 31(4): 331–341.

Hathaway, D. 1963. *Government and agriculture–economic policy in a democratic society.* New York: The MacMillan Company.

Hodge, Ian. 2013. "Agri-environment policy in the era of lower government expenditure: CAP reform and conservation payments". *Journal of Environmental Planning and Management,* 56(2): 254–270.

Kenyon, D and Lee, D. 2006. "The struggle for trade liberalization in agriculture: Australia and the cairns group in the Uruguay round". *The foreign affairs and trade files* n.4. Barton. ACT: Department of Foreign Affairs and Trade.

Mahler, V. A. 1991. "Domestic and international sources of trade policy: The case of agriculture in the ` and the United States". *Polity,* 24(1): 27–47.

Mansholt, S. 1963. "Regional agreements for agricultural markets". Proceedings of the eleventh international conference of agricultural economics. London: Oxford University Press.

Moyer, H. W and Josling, T. E. 1990. *Agricultural policy reform: Politics and process in the EC and the USA.* New York, London, Toronto, Sydney, and Tokyo: Harvester Wheatsheaf.

OEEC. 1956. *Agricultural policies in Europe and North America–First report of the ministerial committee for agriculture and food.* Paris: Organisation for European Economic Cooperation.

OECD. 2011. *Evaluation of agricultural policy reforms in the European Union.* Paris: OECD.

Pokrivcak, J., Crombez, C., and Swinnen, J. 2006. "The status quo bias and reform of the common agricultural policy: Impact of voting rules, the European Commission, and external changes". *European Review of Agricultural Economics,* 33(4): 562–590.

Roederer-Rynning, C. and Schimmelfennig, F. 2012. "Bringing co-decision to agriculture: A hard case of parliamentarization". *Journal of European Public Policy,* 19(7): 951–968.

Runge, C. F and Von Witzke, H. 1987. "Institutional change in the common agricultural policy of the European community". *American Journal of Agricultural Economics,* 69(2): 213–222.

Swinbank, A. 2012. *"New direct payments scheme: Targeting and redistribution in the future CAP"* Directorate General for Internal Policies. Policy department B: Structural and Cohesion Policies. Agriculture and rural development. Note IP/B/AGRI/CEI/2011-097/E003/SC1. Brussels: Directorate General for Internal Policies.

Swinbank, A and Tanner, C. 1996. *Farm policy and trade conflict: The Uruguay round and CAP reform.* Ann Arbor: The University of Michigan Press.

Swinnen, J. 2008. *The perfect storm: The political economy of the Fischler reforms under the common agricultural policy.* Brussels: Centre for European Policy Studies.

Swinnen, J., Knops, L., and Van Herck, K. 2013. *Food price volatility and EU policies, UNU*-WIDER working paper 2013/032.

Tangermann, S. 1992. "European integration and the common agricultural policy". In *Industry, services and agriculture: The United States faces a united Europe,* eds.

C. E. Barfield and M. Perlman. Washington, D.C.: American Enterprise Institute for Public Policy Research.

Tangermann, S. 2004. "Agricultural policies in OECD countries: An agenda for reform". In *The global competitiveness report 2004-2005,* ed. A. Lopez-Claros, 173–186. Houndsmills and London: Palgrave Macmillan.

Tracy, M. 1982. *Agriculture in Western Europe–Challenge and response 1880-1980.* London: Granada.

US Department of agriculture. 2016. *Data and analysis, foreign agricultural service. Department of agriculture.* Accessed http://www.fas.usda.gov/data October.

Zobbe, Henrik. 2001. *The economic and historical foundation of the CAP in Europe.* The royal veterinary and agricultural university, working paper 2001/12.

## FURTHER READING

Crombez, C., Knops, L., and Swinnen, J. 2012. "Reform of the common agricultural policy under the co-decision procedure". *Intereconomics,* 47(6): 336–342.

## FURTHER QUESTIONS

1. What is the overall impact of the EU CAP on farmers in developing states?
2. Compare US and EU agricultural policy and mention the similarities and differences.
3. To what extent have the reforms of the CAP been driven by international pressures (i.e., WTO) and intra-EU political and economic pressures?
4. Taking into consideration the costs/benefits to consumers/taxpayers, which are the most robust arguments in favor of price support system for European agriculture?
5. Is there any type of subsidy to EU farmers which has no trade-distorting impact on European consumers?

*Chapter 9*

# The Economics of the European Single Market

EU's internal market is considered a crucial asset of EU integration process encompassing 28 states, 500 million consumers, and 21 million SMEs. The transformation of the EEC into a common market started with the abolition of customs duties and quantitative restrictions in 1958 and with the application of a CET in 1968 (Egan, 2001). However, this transformation constituted only the first part of a long-term process toward more and deeper integration.

According to article 3 of the European union treaty (para. 1a–1e) the EU has exclusive competence in the areas of CU, the establishment of the competition rules necessary for the functioning of the internal market, the monetary policy for the EU countries whose currency is the euro, the conservation of marine biological resources under the common fisheries policy and the common commercial policy.

The Single Market is a milestone in this process (Pelkmans, 2006), because it abolished NTBs to the free movement of goods and services, namely, physical (borders), fiscal (taxes), legal (access restrictions, import quotas), and technical (product standards) barriers.

Undeniably, the present environment in which the Internal Market operates is very different from the 1980s. Services constitute the major part of European economy accounting for 73.6% of the EU total gross value added in 2013 (71.5% in 2003) but a much smaller share of intra-EU trade (20%), indicating their low tradability within the EU. This relatively low figure reflects not only the low tradability of services in general but also the continued existence of regulatory barriers within the Internal Market. Obviously, there is a need to upgrade global tradability of services as well as productivity growth of European service sector.

Equally important, as many sectors of services (e.g., telecommunications, transport, energy, and financial services) provide inputs to other economic activities their performance has major impact for European competitiveness. Indeed, due to their intangibility, services tend to be affected by more complex regulatory barriers than trade. In addition, foreign firms often face additional costs due to a lack of knowledge of EU regulations. Further, the regulation heterogeneity severely restricts the realization of economies of scale in complying with regulations within the EU.

From a competition perspective, the negative consequences of the low tradability of services can to a certain extent be offset by ensuring the freedom of establishment for service providers and by forwarding a simplification and harmonization of regulatory requirements. The services directive, which was adopted at the end of 2006, aims to enhance competition and growth by encouraging the cross-border provision of services, either via trade or via the local establishment of competing service providers.

Finally, EU enlargement process also influenced heavily the content and speed of internal market evolution. In particular, the accession of 10 new countries in May 2004 and Bulgaria-Romania in 2007 substantially increased the pool of consumers and provided companies with key opportunities to reap comparative advantages characterizing the new EU countries.

## THE MAIN CORNERSTONES OF THE EUROPEAN SINGLE MARKET

Consecutive political, economic, and monetary crises in 1970s set in motion euro-pessimism and delayed European integration momentum. The EC's 1985 White Paper on the SMP was an effort to surpass this standstill and aimed to remove physical, technical, and fiscal barriers so as to create a SEM.

More specifically, EC President, Jacques Delors, and Internal Market Commissioner, Lord Cockfield, put together a package of proposals that targeted the implementation of the Single Market by 1992. The EC White Paper entitled "Completing the Internal Market" contained 300 proposals (Cecchini et al., 1988) and focused on specific trade and welfare benefits from trade intensification. Which were the major traits of this effort?

First, the size and content of reforms for intra-EU liberalization were unprecedented. Second, the issue areas under reform were part of national competence for many years and thus constituted a delicate area of negotiation (i.e., implementing common regulations and mutual trust in veterinary and phyto-sanitary issue areas). Third, the whole process was based mostly on regulatory mutual recognition.

Indeed, in 1986, Lord Cockfield, on behalf of the EC, invited Professor Paolo Cecchini (then Deputy Director-General for internal markets and industrial affairs at the EC) to organize a detailed study into the likely economic impact of completing the programme of actions set out in the 1985 *White Paper* on the single market. A large number of economic experts and research institutes contributed to the effort and the final report was published in 1988.

According to the estimates, the potential economic gain was 200 billion ECUs constituting 5% of the European Community's GDP. This calculation included not only the savings made by removing the barriers which directly affect intra-EC trade (essentially frontier formal ties and related delays) but also the impact of removing barriers which hinder new market entrants (Cecchini report, 5). Besides static growth impact, Cecchini report also expected dynamic effects meaning that as competition intensifies companies could adapt their strategies to the new terms, which would enforce innovation and productivity.

Microeconomic and macroeconomic analyzes calculated a potential wealth effect from 4.25 to 6.5% of GDP for the 12 member states (at 1988 prices for the 12 member states at that period the gains amounted to a range of 170 to 250 billion ECU; see Cecchini report, 5). They further estimated that enhanced competition between companies could reduce prices by 6% and put in place two million new jobs while in the long-term 5 million additional jobs and a 7% rise in GDP would also occur.

A decade later, Baldwin (1989) estimated that these dynamic effects could generate an annual growth stimulus from 0.2% to 0.9% of GDP arguing that the Cecchini report not only did not overestimate expected positive results but in fact it underestimated their impact by at least 40%.

According to Cecchini report the main costs of the lack of a single market were the following:

a. "Customs-related costs put a charge on companies equal to a major portion of their profits from intra-EC trade; first in effect pay a penalty dividend (around 25% of profits in many sectors) to national border controllers for the privilege of going European.
b. industry in areas like motor manufacturing and telecommunications is losing billions of ECUs because of inefficiencies imposed by divergent product standards or protectionist procurement.
c. smaller companies are to a significant extent debarred from transborder business activity by administrative costs and regulatory hassles.
d. a bewildering array of price differences faces consumers of essential services: car insurance may vary by as much as 300% between high and low

price countries; tariffs for telephone services can vary 50% from one EC country to another; the range of price differences for some key financial services can be even greater.

e. the public authorities, year in year out, pay around 17,500 millions ECU more than they should in purchasing the goods and services they need, because of protective procurement systems over which they themselves preside."

Moreover, Cecchini report divided NTBs into three broad types namely, physical barriers (i.e., customs controls), technical barriers (i.e., differing product standards, or protectionist public procurement policies), and fiscal barriers (i.e., differing rates of VAT and excise duties).

Overall, the Cecchini report underlined European firms' relatively weak specialization in sectors with high growth potential and argued that the result of this hysteresis was low-productivity performance in those sectors and significant losses in world market export shares.

But which integration logic lies behind the Single Market initiative?

Intergovernmentalists argue that the institutional dynamics that favor the Single Market initiative were the outcome of a convergence of policy preferences in 1980s (Moravcsik, 1991). Political parties that favor liberal market reforms came to power in Britain, Denmark, and Belgium arguing that Keynesian anti-recession policies did not yield the expected results. Garrett (1992) further suggested that in important areas of legal activity, the European Court anticipated reactions from European states and favored their interests (especially those of the most powerful member states) in rendering its judgments. Majone (1995) further suggested that non-majoritarian institutions (such as courts) can better promote single market targets than other agents such as political parties and interest groups. Moreover, the impact of single market policies on EU regions and economic sectors uncovered the non-benign facets of single market policies and was illustrated in several research efforts (Scharpf, 1999; Hirst and Thompson, 1996; Amin and Tomaney, 1995).

On the other hand, the neo-functionalist academic camp underlined the importance of supranational agents (Burley and Mattli, 1993) in the single market initiative. Sandholtz and Zysman (1989) highlighted the role of the EC as an innovative policy actor in forming the European agenda. Further, the European Court advanced its supranational authority over national courts in order to favor supranational initiatives which refer to free trade (Egan, 2001; Shapiro, 2002) when European Community losses momentum.

Cameron (1997) synthesized the two theoretical groups and insisted that the single European reform was the outcome of the complex interaction of different institutions and agents which served at the same time economic integration purposes and intergovernmental bargaining priorities among European Community countries.

Other studies highlighted that European policies were the outcome of different instruments and institutional arrangements (Héritier, 2002). Within this framework, the European Single Market is the policy vehicle to constrain transaction costs and face problems of heterogeneity through collective action and coordination.

Thus, Single Market success presupposes strong political support and legitimacy as well as institutional capabilities and effectiveness. Overall, Single Market integration has revealed the fierce and continuous tension among national interests and EU priorities about how to stabilize and regulate markets and the necessity to find compromise through flexible bargaining and effective trade-offs.

## THE ECONOMICS OF THE SINGLE MARKET

Single Market is based on the idea of an open market economy with free competition. This is translated in the Europeanization of the fundamental types of markets, which together are the foundation of every economy. In other words, goods, services, and factors of production (labor, capital, and knowledge and codified technology) should be free, allowing for actual and credible mobility across intra-EU borders (Pelkmans, 2012).

Since markets are often heavily regulated at the national or regional level, a single market demands that free movement and the right of establishment have to be unrestricted and that EU regulation applies in order to overcome market failures and distortive interventions by national authorities in many economic sectors. Variables that restrain market integration include natural barriers which are inherently difficult to overcome (i.e., geographic distance or language) and artificial NTBs which are the outcome of unnecessary national regulation or even hidden state aid.

Differences in legal systems and provisions related to FDI are also considered as barriers to trade if they represent an additional cost for firms willing to sell their products in other EU member states.

Nobel Laureate Jan Tinbergen (1954) underlined the positive and negative facets of integration. The former reduces all intra-EU barriers which prevent free movement of factors of production while the latter sets the rules/principles of common policies at EU level (i.e., common competition policy, common trade policy, but also mutual recognition, harmonization).

In theory, two cases emerge. One is that in which comparative advantage can be reaped through trade. Emerson et al. (1988, 35) eloquently demonstrate the two cases in figures 9.1 and 9.2. The removal of specific market

**Table 9.1 Degrees of Economic Integration**

| *Traits* | *Free Trade Area (NAFTA)* | *Customs Union (MERCOSUR)* | *Single Market (European Union)* | *Currency Union (Eurozone)* |
|---|---|---|---|---|
| Abolition of customs duties for goods produced within the area | + | + | + | + |
| Abolition of tariff trade barriers within the area | + | + | + | + |
| Common customs policy relative to third states | – | + | + | + |
| Reduction of nontariff trade barriers within the area | – | – | + | + |
| Reduction of barriers relating to establishment and mobility | – | – | + | + |
| Common currency | – | – | – | + |

barriers and distortions leads to the relative price of a specific commodity at price P2, compared to the higher protected price P1 in state x, and the lower price P3 elsewere, prevailed earlier.

Based on the fact that state x is a net importer from EU, comparative advantage is in EU and comparative disadvantage lies in state x. Consumers gain a total benefit given by areas A+B and producers surplus is reduced by area A. In the rest of EU, producers gain to the extent of areas C+D, while consumers loose to the extent of area C. The total benefits to the EU are the sum of the area B+D and thus producers and consumers make net gains in the economy as a whole.

The second case is also illustrated by Emerson et al. (1988, 35), in figure 9.3 and refers to enhanced competition with no comparative advantage between states involved. The removal of barriers gives the importers the ability to reduce their prices from P2 because of the direct costs saved. Domestic suppliers of the same product also reduce their prices in order to save their market share through reductions in wages and profits and elimination of inefficiency of different types (i.e., excess manning and inventories, overhead costs).

As prices decline demand goes up beyond Q1, creating opportunities for investment and economies of scale plus further price reductions. This evolution triggers more competition and obliges firms to restructure their operations over a number of years (not only further investments but also mergers and acquisitions) until the price falls to the lower equilibrium level of P2 and output increases to Q2. In that case consumer surplus equals the area P2D1D2P1. Producers offset price cuts with cost reductions and face some

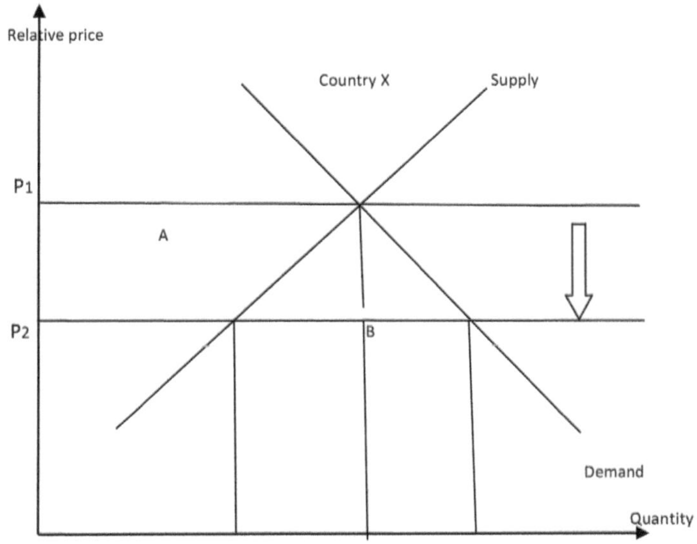


**Figure 9.1** The impact of reducing market obstacles and distortions for a given commodity.

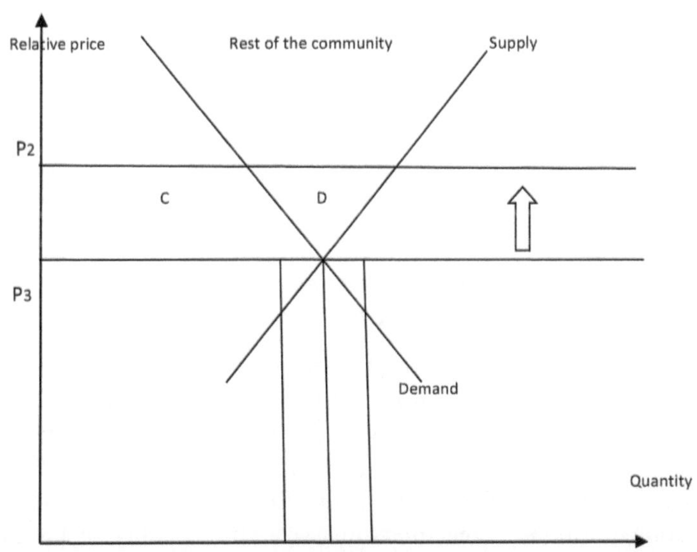


**Figure 9.2** The impact of reducing market obstacles and distortions for a given commodity (Comparative advantage can be exploited by trade).

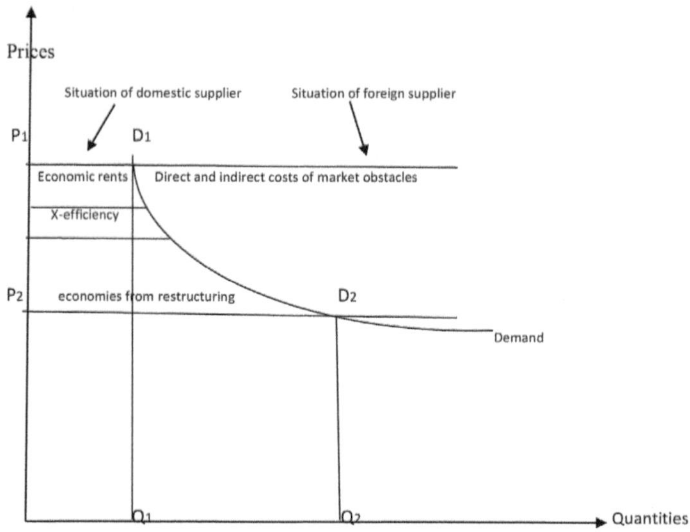


**Figure 9.3 The impact of limiting cost increasing trade obstacles (enhanced competition with no comparative advantage between states).**

losses of economic rents (excess profits or wages in the protected firms) illustrated in figure 9.3.

However, the fact that they become more competitive gives them the ability to sell their products outside EU thereby increasing production and profits. Of course, there is always the danger to lose a portion of EU market since home market penetration by suppliers from non-EU states may benefit not only other EU suppliers but also firms from non-EU states. The total welfare gain for the economy amounts to the consumer gain less the loss of protected profits.

## Which are Considered the Advantages of State Involvement in a Single Market Effort?

First, there are competition effects. Indeed, the dismissal of barriers to free circulation of factors of production in EU area gives rise to stronger inter-brand competition and to more competitive firms. Transparency in cross-border transactions improves efficiency in production planning and limits price discrimination tactics of firms. Inefficient firms are squeezed out by more efficient competitors and consumers enjoy a better quality of products-services and better prices. This also reduces the mark-ups in protected national markets and puts in motion a price convergence.

Equally important, harmonization of production and quality standards enables products to be marketed more easily within the EU. Mutual recognition principle in internal market also ensures that a product which is already approved in one state can also be sold in all EU states. Further, simplification of cross-border mobility of labor force and the freedom of movement without any discrimination gives the ability to all EU citizens to settle in another single market state.

Second, there is a strong impact of single market on firms' behavior. Companies' reaction to enforced competition is realized through economies of scale (i.e., profitability increases when the production volume rises due to high fixed costs) and scope (the same production inputs might be used for multiple purposes), product differentiation, innovation in operations and marketing and fierce battle over market shares. Firms operating across borders can maximize their output by establishing international manufacturing networks and by using comparative cost benefits (i.e., they acquire stakes in foreign firms, merge with them, and relocate links in the production chain within the single market).

Third, single market does influence the structure of industry. Indeed, the reduction in EU transaction costs promotes interindustry specialization among EU countries. Moreover, the reallocation of factors of production may under specific terms smooth the national economic adjustment process resulting in a shift in market shares toward most efficient firms.

However, "New Economic Geography" arguments (i.e., Paul Krugman, 1991a; 1991b) underline that due to the exploitation of agglomeration economies, production may also become more concentrated in already developed regions which are closest to the largest markets. Thus, industrial specialization and geographic concentration should be carefully analyzed so as to permit the development of competitive advantages of all regions in EU.

Fourth, single market creates innovation at micro- and macroeconomic level. Competition stimulates innovation because the risks of being eliminated from the market are higher in a single market. Besides, internal market gives the opportunity of writing off the fixed R and D costs over a larger volume of production and allows technology transfer through FDI flows.

Finally, the liberalization of capital flows and the implementation of financial integration make cross-border financial transactions easier and cheaper. As a result, EU consumers gain access to a larger variety of financial products.

## Which Costs Does the Single Market Generate?

At first, community overregulation, inefficient national bureaucracy, and deficient allocation of tasks between the administrative levels of the federal system do impact negatively on firms. Further, the greater opening of national markets leads to adjustment costs for those countries and regions, whose companies are less competitive than their foreign rivals.

More specifically, there are trade diversion losses which create the necessity for proper adjustment within a transition period for all firms as they find it difficult to survive in new competition terms. Companies that previously had a protected status in national markets suddenly had to contend with more efficient competitors from other states. Thus, transfer schemes (and fiscal cost) are crucial so as to guarantee that integration leads to a Pareto improvement, in which nobody is worse off.

Evidence on productivity distribution in European industries demonstrates that there is still a high degree of misallocation of resources and that low-productivity firms coexist with high-productivity firms (Criscuolo et al., 2014). It also indicates the existence of barriers to competition in the goods and services markets.

Equally important, there is a significant retreat of sovereign autonomy and policymaking on competitiveness issues. Further, there are substantial process costs on national and community institutions. To what extent the Single Market gives rise to additional bureaucratic and regulatory costs also depends on how efficiently the national administrative systems adapt the content of new regulations.

Taking into account the aforementioned benefits and costs of a single market which are the prerequisites of successful market integration? The intra-EU trade intensity is a crucial factor since the greater the volumes of external trade with the other EU member states, the greater the benefits thanks to lower costs and trade barriers. Indeed, exports into the EU make up over half of total exports in nearly every country, and in some countries the share even exceeds 70%.

The external trade intensity (exports plus imports as a percentage of GDP) tends to be higher for small states, which is why they take advantage more from trade liberalization. On the other hand, firms that operated in a larger national market are initially better positioned to take advantage of the single market and could better exploit economies of scale and scope. Their competitive advantage has both a price component (i.e., unit labor costs) and a non-price component (i.e., innovative and technological strength).

Firm size is also a vital factor, as bigger firms are on average more export-oriented and thus reap more benefits from trade liberalization. On the consumers' side, in highly protectionist countries the advantages are greater than in those states that already enjoy a relatively high degree of liberalization.

Another influential factor in the achievement of single market full potential is the tax system. As EU countries are free to design their corporate, personal, and VATs according to their preferences there is no harmonization of the national tax regimes. The implementation of 28 different tax systems, however, puts barriers to the mobility of factors and creates high transaction costs.

Finally, the states could not optimize the internal market potential without significant structural reforms. This is also true for euro area countries where the absence of national monetary policy leads to an adjustment process through the so-called competitiveness channel. Within this process, the role of structural reforms is clearly to rearrange wage and price setting behavior. Thus, forwarding a more integrated and competitive Internal Market, particularly in services, ensures that prices adjust more rapidly to changing supply and demand conditions and closes the productivity gap with other developed states.

## HOW EUROPEAN SINGLE MARKET WORKS

The TFEU establishes the objective of "a highly competitive social market economy" and stresses the key traits of the internal market. The treaty also makes explicit reference to the joint responsibility of EU and EU countries to work toward achieving single market targets.

The cornerstones of the SEM are the four freedoms:

a. Free movement of goods which also implies the abolition of state subsidies, discriminatory taxes on imported goods, and preferential tax treatment for exports.
b. Free movement of people which gives all EU citizens the right to work in another country of EU without discrimination due to their nationality.
c. Free movement of services as providers of services may conduct their business in all EU countries without having to be settled there.
d. Free movement of capital and payments which means that capital controls and restrictions on the amount of currency that may be imported or exported are abolished.

More specifically, TFEU states in its article 26 (2) that "the internal market shall comprise an area without internal frontiers in which the free movement of goods, persons, services and capital is ensured." In article 28 it notes, "The Union shall comprise a customs union which shall cover all trade in goods and which shall involve the prohibition between member states of customs duties on imports and exports and of all charges having equivalent effect, and the adoption of a common customs tariff in their relations with third countries" while articles 45 and 46 mandate freedom of movement for workers.

Articles 34 and 35 prohibit quantitative restrictions on imports and exports between EU countries, article 101 prohibits practices that may affect trade between EU states or prevent free competition within the internal market, and article 102 prohibits the abuse of dominant position from undertakings within the internal market. Which are the instruments of single market to realize its targets?

The implementation of internal market directives is the key policy tool for setting in motion a better functioning Internal Market. However, all directives need to be efficiently applied by the EU countries. The latter have the responsibility for transposing European Community directives into domestic legislation and for guaranteeing effective implementation. Here again, there are notable differences between EU states in terms of speed and efficiency of transposition. To face this challenge, the Commission publishes twice in a year an Internal market scoreboard, which reports on progress made by the EU countries in limiting their transposition deficit.

The application of agreed standards and the implementation of the mutual recognition principle are two tools for reducing TBTs between EU states. Both favor producers since they forward compatibility and interoperability of the traded products, they reduce trade costs and they put in place economies of scale. Consumers also take advantage since agreed standards and the implementation of the mutual recognition principle limit uncertainty and costs of purchase decisions by facilitating comparisons.

More specifically, under mutual recognition, there is agreement at an EU-wide level that EU countries will accept the rules and standards imposed by other states. Thus, "Any product imported from another member state must in principle be admitted to the territory of the importing member state if it has been lawfully produced, that is, conforms to rules and processes of manufacture that are customarily and traditionally accepted in the exporting country and is marketed in the territory of the latter."

The legal principle of mutual recognition within Europe first arose in the Cassis de Dijon case (European court of Justice, February 20, 1979). In that case, the firm Rewe-Zentral AG sought to import a liqueur from France into Germany but was unable to realize it because of a German law forbidding the sale of spirits with alcohol content below 32%, while Cassis de Dijon had only from 15 to 20%. The decision of ECJ ruled that barriers to free trade within the Community included "any national measure capable of hindering, directly or indirectly, actually or potentially, intra-Community trade" and that this included technical and commercial rules. So, rules differ in EU states but under mutual recognition each EU country accepts imported products produced under the rules other states imposed. Of course, mutual recognition can lead to regulatory dumping competition since a member state which is willing to impose the laxest rules will attract all the firms to relocate in its territory and from there export to the rest of the EU.

The second instrument of single market policy is "harmonization." When rules are harmonized across EU's member states, EU Directive or EU Regulation requires all EU countries to apply the same rules.

Finally, the EU chooses often a third way to forward single market proceeding through mutual recognition for a certain time period until there is a policymaker consensus as to what constitutes best practice, and only then it forward with harmonization.

## STATE AID WITHIN THE EUROPEAN SINGLE MARKET

State aid control is an integral part of EU competition policy and an important safeguard to promote effective competition and free trade in the Single Market. Several market failures (i.e., negative externalities, imperfect or asymmetric information, institutional rigidities, imperfect factor mobility, subsidization of foreign competitors) are relevant to the analysis of state aid. In order to understand the logic of state aid one should underline the impact of subsidies and aid on prices and firm behavior.

In the figure 9.4 the state intervenes with regulations to limit price to average cost. A subsidy may also be implemented to cover the gap between marginal cost and average cost. In a monopolistic situation, the monopoly is obliged to reduce prices from Pm to the average cost price (Pac) and thus to

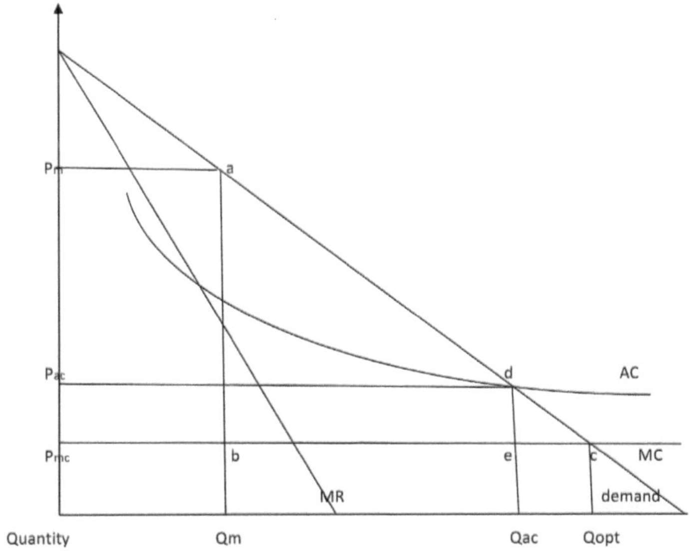


**Figure 9.4 Economies of scale-production aid.**

reduce inefficiency from abc to cde. A subsidy, given by the difference Pac-Pmc, induces the monopoly to keep the price at marginal cost and eliminates the distortion. However, there is extra taxation in the whole economy for gathering the capital destined to subsidy and governments may have limited information on company costs since firms may exaggerate to attain higher support in the form of subsidies.

In figure 9.5 state aid is given to facilitate entry of a company in a monopolistic market. The monopoly price is at Pm. The equilibrium is attained at price level P2, with the new firm producing Qc, a third of the total output of the two companies. However, this is taking place because a subsidy (CDEP2) is provided representing the difference between the entrant's total revenue and total cost. Consumers ameliorate their position by the amount represented by the area PmABP2 but the monopolistic firm revenues fall.

In figure 9.6 the states' subsidy favors the fixed costs of a company producing a new product. Taking into consideration that the average cost curve is above the demand curve, the absence of a subsidy could deter entry of the firm in the market. The welfare is enhanced if the consumer surplus (ACP2) exceeds the subsidy (P1BCP2) by an amount adequate to compensate for inefficiencies caused elsewhere in the economy.

The treaty emphasizes in article 107(1) that state aid which distorts or threatens to distort competition is prohibited in so far as it affects trade

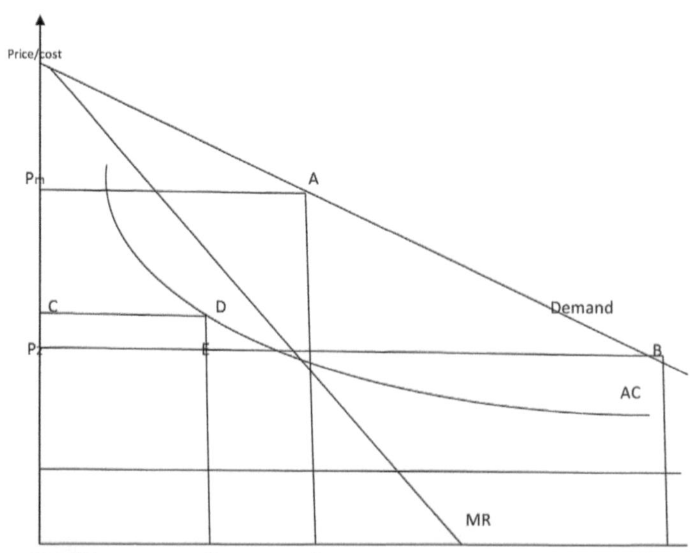


**Figure 9.5 Aid for entry into a monopolistic market.**

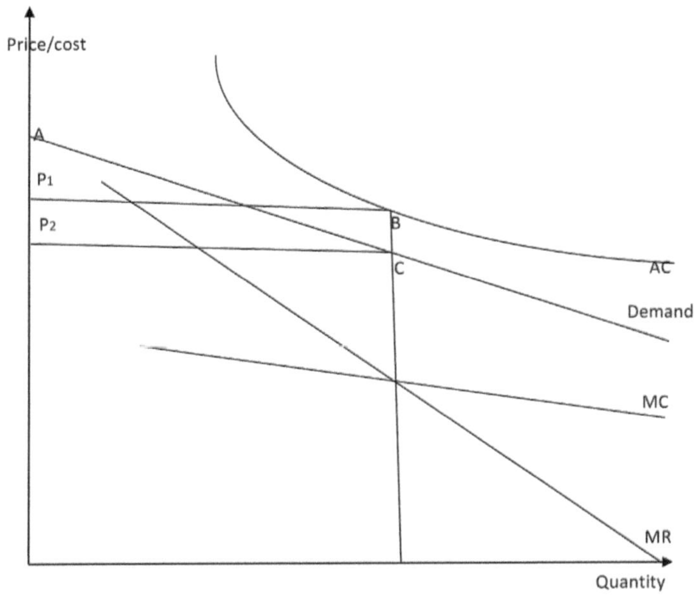


**Figure 9.6 Aid through economies of scale for a new product.**

between EU countries. However, it also notes in article 107(3) that state aid, which contributes to well-defined objectives of common European interest without unduly distorting competition between undertakings and trade between EU states, may be considered compatible with the internal market. So the targets of Commission's control of state aid activity are to ensure that aid is growth-enhancing, effective, and it does not restrict competition but addresses market failures to the benefit of society as a whole.

Taking into account that 32% of state aid is delivered under block-exempted schemes which are not examined by the EC prior to their entry into force, it is highly important for the EC to control that EU countries implement the schemes rightly and that they only give aid when all necessary terms are in place. This is why the EC applied in 2006 a regular control of existing aid schemes ("monitoring") which initially covered only 20 schemes and 10 EU countries in each monitoring cycle but reached 75 schemes in the 2014 review.

Equally important, the 2014 cycle covered all EU countries, all key categories of aid approved as well as block-exempted schemes and as a result by December 31, 2014, the amount of illegal and incompatible aid recovered from beneficiaries had reached 9.6 billion euros, from 7.3 billion euros in December 2004.

### But What Makes an Aid Measure Compatible with the Internal Market?

First, the aid measure must aim at a target of common interest. Second, it must be targeted toward a situation where aid can result in a material improvement that the market cannot deliver itself (i.e., addressing market failure). Third, it must be an appropriate policy instrument to face the target of common interest. Fourth, the aid must change the behavior of the undertaking(s) concerned in such a way that it engages in additional activity that it would not carry out without the aid. Fifth, the aid amount must be limited to the minimum needed to induce the additional investment or activity. Sixth, all negative results on competition and trade between EU countries must be sufficiently limited. Last but not least, the relevant acts and information about aid awards must be transparent (all EU countries publish full information on individual aid awards above 500,000 euros). Indeed, by providing third parties access to information about aid granted, transparency improves control of practices from civil society and other market agents.

As already mentioned, one of the pillars of the state aid modernization reform is the GBER which makes aid granting procedures easier for EU countries by authorizing without prior notification a significant range of actions fulfilling horizontal common interest targets. Since July 1, 2014, evaluation is required for large GBER schemes in specific aid categories and is also provided for some notified schemes under the new generation of state aid guidelines.

It is perfectly true that GBER does influence aid beneficiaries and granting authorities, permitting faster access to the aid (through avoidance of the notification process), and reduction of administrative obstacles (simpler conditions for demonstrating the incentive effect). Moreover, it also enforces EU countries in state aid control, including designing state aid actions to fit the rules, taking responsibility for compliance of the aid they grant, and putting in place transparency and evaluation requirements. Overall, according to the national expenditure reports for 2014, EU-28 states spent 101.2 billion euros (0.72%) of GDP on state aid.

## THE SINGLE MARKET AND MERGER CONTROL

Effective merger control stimulates innovation and efficient distribution of resources through competition enforcement and guarantees that firms maintain access to critical input at competitive prices (Council Regulation no. 139/2004 of January 20, 2004 on the control of concentrations between undertakings and Commission regulation no. 802/2004 of April 21, 2004 implementing Council Regulation no. 139/2004 on the control of concentrations between undertakings).

The regulation considers illegal all mergers and acquisitions which would significantly reduce competition in the Single Market (i.e., creating dominant firms that are likely to raise prices for consumers). Thus, mergers are prohibited if the merging firms are major competitors or if the merger would otherwise significantly weaken competition in the market, creating or strengthening a dominant player. It is worth noting that regulation provisions apply to all mergers no matter where the merging firms have their registered headquarters, activities, or production facilities taking into consideration that mergers between firms based outside the EU may have an impact on markets in the EU. Thus, EC must be notified of any merger intention with an EU dimension prior to its application and consequently firms contact the commission to see how to best prepare their notification.

According to article 101 (ex-article 81 TEC), "agreements between undertakings, decisions by associations of undertakings and concerted practices which may affect trade between member states and which have as their object or effect the prevention, restriction or distortion of competition within the common market are prohibited as incompatible with the internal market" and in particular those which:

a. Directly or indirectly fix purchase or selling prices or any other trading conditions
b. Limit or control production, markets, technical development, or investment
c. Share markets or sources of supply
d. Apply dissimilar conditions to equivalent transactions with other trading parties, thereby placing them at a competitive disadvantage
e. Make the conclusion of contracts subject to acceptance by the other parties of supplementary obligations which, by their nature or according to commercial usage, have no connection with the subject of such contracts.

Similarly, article 102 (ex-article 82 TEC) seeks to limit any distortion to the effective functioning of the single market and stresses that "any abuse by one or more undertakings of a dominant position within the internal market or in a substantial part of it shall be prohibited as incompatible with the internal market in so far as it may affect trade between member states." Such abuse consists in:

a. Directly or indirectly imposing unfair purchase or selling prices or other unfair trading conditions;
b. Limiting production, markets, or technical development to the prejudice of consumers;

c. Applying dissimilar conditions to equivalent transactions with other trading parties, thereby placing them at a competitive disadvantage;
d. Making the conclusion of contracts subject to acceptance by the other parties of supplementary obligations which, by their nature or according to commercial usage, have no connection with the subject of such contracts.

Moreover, according to article 106 (ex-article 86 TEC), "In the case of public undertakings and undertakings to which member states grant special or exclusive rights, member states shall neither enact nor maintain in force any measure contrary to the rules contained in the Treaties, in particular to those rules provided for in article 18 and articles 101 to 109." Further, paragraph two of the same article holds that undertakings entrusted with the operation of services of general economic interest or having the character of a revenue-producing monopoly shall be subject to the rules contained in the treaties, in particular to the rules on competition, in so far as the application of such rules does not obstruct the performance, in law or in fact, of the particular tasks assigned to them. The development of trade must not be affected to such an extent as would be contrary to the interests of the EU.

Based on aforementioned articles of the treaty as well as on the EU regulations, the EC examines larger mergers with an EU dimension involving merging companies which reach certain turnover thresholds. According to EU provisions there are two ways to reach turnover thresholds for EU dimension which are either a combined worldwide turnover of all the merging firms over 5,000 million euros, and an EU-wide turnover for each of at least two of the firms over 250 million euros (first), or a worldwide turnover of all the merging firms over 2,500 million euros, a combined turnover of all the merging firms over 100 million euros in each of at least three member states, a turnover of over 25 million euros for each of at least two of the firms in each of the three EU countries, and EU-wide turnover of each of at least two firms of more than 100 million euros (second).

However, smaller mergers which do not have an EU dimension are under the jurisdiction of EU countries' competition authorities but there is a referral mechanism which permits the EU countries and the EC to transfer the case between them. Of course, not all mergers which significantly impede competition are prohibited and this means that even if the EC considers that a proposed merger could distort competition, the firms may commit to taking all appropriate measures to try to correct distortive effects. If the EC considers that the firms maintain competition in the market (i.e., the firms sell part of the combined business or license technology to other market players, protecting consumer interests), it gives permission for the merger to take place and go ahead keeping an eye to application of firms commitments.

The merger simplification package (December 2013) came in force on January 1, 2014 widened the scope of the simplified procedure to review unproblematic mergers and limited the administrative burden for parties notifying mergers to the EC. Equally important, the directive on antitrust damages actions entered into force in 2014 and allow citizens and firms to claim damages if they are victims of an infringement of the EU antitrust regime, such as cartels or abuses of dominant market positions. The directive includes substantive and procedural rules on key issues of antitrust damages actions, such as limitation periods for bringing an action, joint and several liabilities of the infringers.

## ASSESSMENT OF THE FUNCTIONING OF THE EUROPEAN SINGLE MARKET AND WOULD BE POTENTIAL

Empirical evidence clearly underlines that more can still be attained in terms of efficiency and innovation in EU market. The internal market is comprised of several reforms in microeconomic issue areas the aggregate impact of which are do have a major impact on several sectors of economic activity.

Some authors measure the macroeconomic impact of EU-15 market integration in manufacturing by simulating the competition and innovation results as analyzed in the literature on the impact of the SMP. Others focus their simulation on the macroeconomic impact of the opening up to competition-specific issue areas (i.e., electricity and telecommunication markets) while others underline the competition and innovation effect of the increased trade in all EU states.

Soon after the Cecchini report, many studies tried to evaluate the impact of integration and the elimination of all border and standardization costs on European economy (Boltho and Eichengreen, 2008; Britain's HM Treasury, 2005; Griffith et al., 2006). However, one should be cautious as comparisons between surveys on single market effects are often built on different concepts and variables (Blanchard and Giavazzi, 2003).

Harrison et al. (1994) quantified the direct effect of single market at just 0.5% of EU GDP underlining that the biggest potential winners were those states with high intra-EU trade intensity, (Belgium and the Netherlands), with potential growth more than 6% of GDP (for most other states such as Italy and Germany they considered 2% growth to be feasible).

Ilzkovitz et al. (2007) evaluated additional income stemming from the Single Market initiative at 2.2% between 1992 and 2006 and the growth of new job positions in the EU at around 1.35%. Straathof et al. (2008), taking into account data from the period 1958 to 2005 assessed that European integration, has enforced GDP in the EU from 2 to 3% (the overall effect stranded at 4–6% for the Netherlands because of stronger trade integration) and also concluded that exports and imports are 8% higher than they would have been if there had been no integration. Moreover, they identified that EU membership boosted bilateral FDI stock of countries within the EU by 28%.

The Copenhagen Economics (2012) report reached the conclusion that Single Market actions in four issue areas (i.e., taxes, services, public procurement, and mutual recognition) might have generated more than anticipated growth in GDP while Sousa et al. (2012) assessed that in 2007 around 25 million jobs (or 10.3% of all jobs in the EU) were directly dependent on exports to non-EU states (15.7 million have been created in manufacturing sector and 8.5 million jobs in services sector).

The Bertelsmann Stiftung institute based on a calculation of cumulative gains in real GDP per capita found that between 1992 and 2012, every EU country with the exception of Greece achieved important income benefits within the European integration framework. The regression analysis was conducted on 14 selected EU countries' economies (EU-15, except Luxembourg) and found that a rise of 1% of the EU integration index could lead to a growth rate of 0.08% points of real GDP per capita. Equally important, the research revealed that the better an EU country is integrated into the single market, the more GDP gains can be accrued (the greatest GDP gains were recorded in Denmark and Germany).

Kox and Lejour (2006) estimated that the trade and FDI effects of the EU services market liberalization could forward GDP from 0.5 to 1.5% while Sørensen's study found that EU average welfare gains from tax coordination ranged from 0.18% to 0.94% of GDP and the benefits from coordinating corporate taxes in Europe reached to 1.42% of GDP.

All simulations point out that the macroeconomic benefits coming from the Internal Market could have been larger if services markets had been fully liberalized. The application of the services directive could enforce trade and investment flows in services, resulting in a further from 0.5% to 1% increase in GDP while the potential benefits from increased tax cooperation could lead to a 0.2% rise of GDP. Fully integrated financial markets could also reduce the cost of capital for EU firms by 0.5% points boosting GDP by 1.1% in the long run while liberalizing energy market would give a rise of GDP from 0.6 to 0.8%.

Egger and Pfaffermayr (2004) estimated in their analysis that the Single Market and the enlargement in 1995 resulted in substantial anticipation effects, and Badinger (2007) found that mark-ups fell in manufacturing and to a lesser degree in the construction sector.

Which is the real picture of present European single market? The first conclusion is that trade integration in services is lower than for goods and thus the deepening of the internal market in services has been slow despite the enactment of the services directive and the limitation of regulatory heterogeneity in professional services between 2008 and 2013 (in 2012 interstate trade in manufactured goods was approximately 21% of GDP in EU-28 while it was 35% of GDP in the USA, see also Fournier, 2015). Further, intra-EU exports of services (EU-28) were below 7% in 2014 (Eurostat, 2016).

Second, the crisis had a considerable but short-lived impact on the international exchange of goods in 2009 which was overturned in 2010 as the level of trade integration for goods reached a level that was above that recorded in 2008.

Third, the data eloquently demonstrate that the Single Market led to a rise in international trade within the EU and with the rest of the world. Indeed, intra-EU trade intensity increased between 1992 and 2012 from 12% to 22% of GDP and exports to non-EU states grew faster than intra-EU exports, which mirror the high competitiveness of the export-oriented companies in the EU.

Fourth, empirical evidence also highlights that the Single Market has enforced GDP in the EU from 2 to 3%. The elimination of trade obstacles put in place cost advantages, enforced competition in the European Single Market, and boosted exports. In the same manner, the delimitation of intra-EU trade obstacles has also put in place more investment opportunities for foreign firms.

However, on the vital issue area of public procurement, there is a need for deep reforms to generate important and sustainable economic advantages. While public procurement accounts for around 16% of EU GDP, direct cross-border procurement accounts only 3% of the total number of bids. Equally important, only 22% of public procurement is published and thus open to competition when research suggests that greater cross-border public procurement (Zsolt Pataki, 2014) could potentially yield annual savings from 36 to 66 billion euros (0.3–0.5% of EU GDP).

Thus, after increasing noticeably in the late 1990s, integration, as measured by the ratio of intra-EU trade flows of goods to GDP, lost momentum. Indeed, the ratio of intra-EU-25 manufacturing trade to GDP rose in the second half of the 1990s (particularly from 1998 onward) was based on trade flows between the EU-15 and the Central and Eastern European states. A rise of intra EU-15 trade as a share of GDP was also evident until 2000, which was the outcome of the gradual application of the internal market acquis. Since 2000 the positive trade impact of the enlargement process lost momentum and the ratio of intra-EU-15 trade to GDP in 2005 was below the 2000 peak.

The euro also exerted a positive influence on trade integration as several studies assessed that it increased intra-euro-zone trade from 5% to 10%. The positive trade effect of the introduction of the euro has however been far less important than the trade impact of enlargement as highlighted by the decreasing ratio of intra euro-zone trade to intra-EU-25 trade since 1998. Regulation rigidities in the services sector delay price convergence in the euro area and enforce price dispersion in the euro area.

Equally important, the indicator of product market regulation underlines important delays between 2008 and 2013 in the EU as a whole. As data clearly indicate price levels for food, beverages, and tobacco vary across the EU countries (Eurostat database, 2016). In 2015, the prices for food and non-alcoholic beverages in Poland were 63% of the EU average while in Denmark were 145% of the EU average.

The 2015 Eurostat-OECD purchasing power parities programme expressed in price level indices provides a comparison of countries' price levels of approximately 440 comparable products, relative to the EU average. The EU average is given by the weighted average of the national PLIs, weighted with expenditures from EU countries' national accounts, corrected for price level differences.

If the price level index exceeds 100, the state concerned is considered expensive compared to the EU average, while if the price level index is lower than 100, then the state is considered cheap. Among the EU countries, Denmark is the most expensive state for food and non-alcoholic beverages and Ireland has the highest price level for alcoholic beverages in the EU, while the lowest prices for food are noted in Poland and for alcoholic beverages and tobacco in Bulgaria.

Within the EU, Denmark is the most expensive state for bread and cereals, meat and fish, while Cyprus is the most expensive for milk, cheese, and eggs. It is well worth noting that that for each main group of products dispersion in 2015 was lower than in 2003.

Accordingly, there is little doubt that the Single Market provided a convergence in the price level of household goods in the second half of the 1990s, due to stronger competition but also due to an income effect in states with lower per capita incomes, whose influence is all the greater the more mixed the group of countries observed.

Indeed, across most high income EU-15 countries inflation levels followed a downward trend and price levels also converged downward toward the EU-25 average, influenced among others by ECB monetary policy, cheaper non-EU imports and increased price transparency after euro launch.

On the other hand, price levels have moved upward toward the EU-25 average in new EU countries and in the lower income EU-15 EU countries. It also looks like that price levels in the euroarea are more harmonized than across the EU and dispersion is linked with differences in indirect taxation, transportation costs, and differences in consumer patterns. Of course, firms do not compete on price alone since there are markets with differentiated products where companies can differentiate from competitors through actual or supposed quality differences. Similarly, there are economic sectors where price differences persist and cannot be explained by product differentiation, for example, the telecommunications sector, where regional price differences are evident despite homogeneous products.

Still, financial and banking markets in the EU are fragmented with negative spillovers to SMEs borrowing costs. Capital markets in the EU are less integrated than in the USA and thus policies to encourage banks to reach an optimal size relative to the European market is a priority.

Huge differences are also observed in the issue area of taxation. As a percentage of GDP, EU-28 and EA-19 tax revenue followed a downward trend every year from its 2007 peak but started to rise in 2011. In 2014 tax revenue as percentage of GDP, including net social contributions, accounted for almost 40.0% of GDP in the EU-28 and 41.5% of GDP in the euro area. More specifically, in 2014 (Eurostat online data, 2016), tax revenue accounted for almost 89% of total general government revenue in the EU. More specifically, the ratio of 2014 tax revenue to GDP was highest in Denmark (50.8%), Belgium and France (47.9%) while the lowest shares were recorded in Romania (27.7% of GDP), Bulgaria (27.8%), and Lithuania (28.0%).

Thus, in percentage points, the highest increases in % of GDP from 2013 to 2014 were recorded by Denmark (48.1–50.8% GDP), Cyprus (2.6 p.p.), and Malta (1.4 p.p.). Among the countries that joined the EU since 2004, Hungary and Slovenia had the highest tax revenue-to-GDP ratios in 2014, at 38.4% and 37.0% of GDP, respectively. Government tax revenue varied due to changes in economic activity and in tax legislation (affecting tax rates, the tax base, thresholds, exemptions) influencing revenue as well as levels of GDP. Further, the crisis and the measures of fiscal policy adopted in the member states influenced the level and composition of tax revenue from 2009 to 2014, although the results had already become evident from the third quarter of 2008. Of course, one should mention that the impact of changes in legislation or economic activity follows a time lag and thus reforms tend to have a delayed impact on tax revenue.

Macroeconomic and sovereign debt crises also exerted negative influence on tax revenue from 2007 onward. The ratio of tax revenue to GDP in the EU-28 decreased to 38.5% in 2010, while the ratio for the euroarea also decreased from 40.0% in 2007 to 39.2% in 2010. During the period, tax revenue in terms of GDP moved upward due to tax policies applied by EU countries to restore their government deficits, such as VAT rate increases and new taxes (i.e., taxes on property and bank levies). Apparently, the proportional rise in tax revenue was higher than the proportional rise in GDP, which led to the upward trend in the tax-revenue-to-GDP ratio in both the EU and the euro area.

Similarly, taxes and social contributions received by state and local governments made up 16.3% of total tax and social contribution revenue in 2014 in the EU-28, taxes on production and imports accounted for 13.6% of GDP, and current taxes on income and wealth, stood at 12.8% of GDP. Tax revenue increased in absolute terms in all EU countries in the exception of the Czech Republic (−3.4%, following on from decreases since 2012), Croatia (−0.7%) and Sweden (−1.5%).

According to Eurostat, tax revenue can be classified into three main types, namely, indirect taxes (taxes linked to production and imports such as VATs), direct taxes (taxes on income and wealth), and net social contributions (including actual social contributions for social security purposes and social insurance projects) as well as imputed social contributions (relating to the property income of certain social insurance schemes) deemed as being an additional contribution to the scheme (D.614 households' social contribution supplements), and imputed output of certain social insurance schemes (D.61 social insurance scheme). Following the EU classification (ESA 2010), these categories correspond to the following transactions:

a. Taxes on production and imports (code D.2): Taxes on production and imports (D.2) are divided into taxes on products (D.21) and other taxes on production (D.29). Taxes on products are further split into VAT (D.211), taxes and duties on imports excluding VAT (D.212), and taxes on products except VAT and import taxes (D.214). The most important type of taxes on production and imports is VAT.
b. Current taxes on income, wealth (D.5): Current taxes on income, wealth include taxes on income (D.51) and other current taxes (D.59). Taxes on income cover both taxes on individual or household income and the income or profits of corporations and include taxes on holding gains.
c. Capital taxes (D.91): Capital taxes (D.91) are taxes levied at irregular and infrequent intervals on the net worth or value of assets owned or transferred in the form of legacies or gifts.
d. Net social contributions (D.61).
e. Actual social contributions (D.611 and D.613 representing respectively employers' and households' actual social contributions) are the main component of net social contributions and cover the compulsory and voluntary contributions payable to government by employees, employers and self-and non-employed persons.

Taxes on production and imports have increased between 2009 and 2014 due to increases in the VAT rates in many states and the application of new taxes. The highest ratios of taxes on production and imports were recorded (Eurostat, 2017) in Sweden (22.1%), Croatia (18.8%), Hungary (18.6%), and Denmark (16.6%), while the lowest ratios of these indirect taxes were recorded for Slovakia (10.8%) and Germany (10.9%).

In 2014, revenue from taxes on products in the EU-28 accounted for about 82.1% and VAT for around 51.4% of the total taxes on production and imports. Current taxes on income wealth as a ratio to GDP amounted to 12.8%, while taxes on household income accounted for the largest share of this (9.4% of GDP). The comparatively high ratio for Denmark is due to welfare spending being financed via taxes on income; thus the figures for net social contributions are very low relative to other EU countries while Lithuania (5.1% of GDP in 2013) and Bulgaria (5.3% of GDP) had relatively small revenue from these taxes (Eurostat, 2017). Tax revenue in the EU-28 remained equally distributed between net social contributions (13.4% of GDP), taxes on production and imports (13.6%), and current taxes on income, wealth (12.8%).

For the EU-28, the share of current taxes on income, wealth has decreased from 2007, but moved upward between 2011 and 2013 and stagnated between 2013 and 2014 due to an increase in taxes on profits of companies, rather than tax-raising measures such as the implementation of property taxes. One should also mention that direct taxes (taxes on the income of individuals and firms) are highly vulnerable to economic swings.

Actual social contributions had the highest ratios in GDP terms in France (17.1%), Germany (15.4%), and the Netherlands (14.8%) and for the lowest shares in Denmark, Sweden (0.8%, 3.6%, respectively).

Capital taxes (D.91) accounted for 0.3% of GDP in the EU-28 in 2014, with low ratios recorded for some of the new EU countries and they varied from 1.0% of GDP in Belgium and 0.5% in Spain and France to being very small in other EU states (Eurostat, 2017).

Tax revenue (including social contributions) of central government accounted for 53.0% of total tax and social contribution revenue in 2014 (EU-28), while state government recorded a share of 5.9% of total tax revenue and local governments recorded 10.4% of the total. Social security raised important revenues in France (51.2% of the total), Slovakia (42.3%), Lithuania (39.7%), the Netherlands (39.1%), and Germany (39.0%), while Denmark had the lowest share (1.5% of the total). The local government raised important revenues in Sweden (32.2% of the total), Denmark (24.6%), and Finland (23.5%) while it raised less than 5% of total tax revenue in Bulgaria, Estonia, Ireland, Greece, Cyprus, Lithuania, Luxembourg, the Netherlands, Austria, Romania, and Slovakia.

A fundamental issue area of single market is also that of labor. Labor mobility favors cyclical stabilization and acts as a shock-absorber and a risk-sharing mechanism (De Grauwe, 2014). However, the freedom to find a job in any EU country has not led to a major increase in mobility within the EU-15. Despite the fact that the free movement of labor between countries of the European Community was introduced in 1968 and was one of the principles underlying the 1992 SMP, labor mobility has remained in low levels due to linguistic and cultural differences, the absence of harmonization of social security systems and of professional qualifications, and other fundamental legal and administrative hurdles (OECD, 2014a).

Statistical data clearly highlight that in the EU-15, 0.1% of the working-age populations change their country of residence in a given year when in the USA, about 3% of the working-age population moves to a different state every year. Enlargement process in 2004 (ten states) and in 2007 (Bulgaria and Romania) brought to surface the differences in income between the new eastern European countries and the EU-15 and activated incentives for mobility. In the same manner, EU sovereign debt crisis led to high unemployment in southern Europe and enforced an increase in employment-driven migration.

During 2014, 3.8 million people immigrated to one of the EU-28 countries (1.6 million citizens of non-member countries) and 2.8 million emigrants have left an EU country (Eurostat, 2016). The largest total numbers of immigrants (884.9 thousand) in 2014 were reported in Germany, the UK (632.0 thousand), France (339.9 thousand), Spain (305.5 thousand), and Italy (277.6 thousand). It is worth noting that 15 of the EU countries reported more immigration than emigration in 2014, but in Bulgaria, Ireland, Greece, Spain, Croatia, Cyprus, Poland, Portugal, Romania, Slovenia, and the three Baltic states, the number of emigrants was greater than the number of immigrants (Eurostat, 2016).

Taking into account the size of the resident population, the highest rates of immigration in 2014 occurred in Luxembourg (40 immigrants per 1,000 persons), Malta (21 immigrants per 1,000 persons), and Ireland (15 immigrants per 1,000 persons) while Cyprus (28 emigrants per 1,000 persons), Luxembourg (20 emigrants per 1,000 persons), and Ireland (18 immigrants per 1,000 persons) had the highest rates of emigration in 2014. In Germany, Austria, and Luxembourg national immigration accounted for 10.0% of their total immigration in 2014 (Eurostat, 2016).

Equally important, in 2014, there were an estimated 1.9 million immigrants to the EU-28 from non-member countries. Luxembourg had the largest share of immigrants coming from another EU country (91% of its total number of immigrants in 2014), followed by Slovakia (80%) and Romania (75%) while Bulgaria (19% of all immigrants), Italy, and Sweden (both 29%) reported low shares.

Data also reveal (Eurostat, 2016) that as far as it concerns the gender distribution of immigrants in 2014, there were slightly more men than women (53% compared with 47%) and that the median age of immigrants to EU-28 was 28 years.

In 2015, the number of people living in the EU-28 who were citizens of non-member countries was 19.8 million, while the number of people living in the EU-28 who had been born outside of the EU was 34.3 million. Finally, the largest numbers of non-nationals living in the EU countries by January 1, 2015 were reported in five states (collectively represented 76% of the total number of non-nationals living in all of the EU member states), namely, Germany (7.5 million persons), the UK (5.4 million), Italy (5.0 million), Spain (4.5 million), and France (4.4 million). However, in relative terms, the countries with the highest share of non-nationals were Luxembourg (non-nationals accounted for 46% of its total population), Cyprus, Latvia, Estonia, Austria, Ireland, and Belgium (10% or more of the resident population). One should mention that immigrant flows are among other things highly influenced by the regime of residency permits which is differentiated across EU.

Are there policies to enhance labor mobility within the EU? The Erasmus programme facilitates foreign language learning and enforces cross-border mobility but it included less than 5% of graduates in 2012 and 2013 (European Commission, 2015a). Enforcement of all procedures on the issue of recognition of professional qualifications (amended Directive 2005/36/EC) is also vital since it introduces training frameworks targeting common competences.

Similarly, European professional card can limit administrative hurdles linked with recognition of professional qualifications. Finally, there is a need to focus on services since they are affected by more complex regulatory barriers than trade. The duplication of regulatory requirements and burdens (national social security schemes for the staff, different administrative, and tax procedures) since services demand business processes and the presence of the provider in both EU countries (in that of the service provider and in that of the delivery) complicates labor mobility choices.

The impact of EU economic integration on FDI flows is not easy to trace. The Internal Market Programme and the Eurozone conditions limit trade costs and may lead to higher geographic concentration of production in certain industries. If productive companies firms locate previously dispersed economic activities in the place that they consider to be the most appropriate, it goes without saying that intra-EU FDI flows rise.

Eurostat data show that the Internal Market programme had a positive impact on the accumulated stocks of inward and outward FDI in the last 10 years. Inward FDI also accounts for an important percentage of GDP in the new EU countries (around 40% in 2004/5). Competition enforcement also favored consolidation and restructuring in many industries through mergers and acquisitions.

More specifically, the share of the euro-area in the total number of cross-border acquisitions by euro zone firms rose from 34% in 1999 to 42% in 2004 reversing the declining trend reported since the early 1990s. The 2004 enlargement process also led to an increase of mergers and acquisitions operations in the new EU countries.

Finally, a key issue area where little progress has been made is that of public procurement. The EC indicators (based on notices published in the tenders electronic daily database under the general, sectoral, and defense procurement directives) underline major differences between EU states on several issues of public procurement (EU open data portal, 2016).

However, EC's Scoreboard provides a partial analysis of EU states' public procurement since performance indicators are affected by state-specific variables such as what is actually being bought, the structure of the economies concerned, and the links between different tendering choices, none of which are taken into consideration. The scoreboard is based on six indicators which are the following (European commission, 2016):

a. Indicator 1 (one bidder) which mirrors several aspects of procurement including competition and bureaucracy. More bidders are better, as this means the public buyers have more choices, and can get better value for money.
b. Indicator 2 (no calls for bids) which reflects the proportion of procurement procedures that were negotiated with a company without a call for tender.
c. Indicator 3 (aggregation) which mirrors how often public buyers buy together.
d. Indicator 4 (award criteria) which shows how public buyers choose the companies they award contracts to and whether they decide only on the basis of price, or give preponderance to quality.
e. Indicator 5 (decision speed) which mirrors the speed of the public buyers' decision-making. The indicator reflects the mean decision period which is the time between the deadline for receipt of offers and the award of the contract.
f. Indicator 6 (reporting quality) which reflects the quality of information provided by public buyers. A higher indicator score means firms can make better bidding decisions and consumers know how their money is being spent.

Thus, overall performance is a weighted average of all the performance indicators.

**Table 9.2 Scoreboard Indicators (European Commission, 2017)**

| | | |
|---|---|---|
| (1) One Bidder | ≤10% | >20% |
| (2) No calls for Bids | ≤5% | ≥10% |
| (3) Aggregation | ≥10% | <10% |
| (4) Award Criteria | <80% | ≥80% |
| (5) Decision speed | <120 days | ≥120 days |
| (6) Reporting quality | ≤3% | >3% |

*(all six indicators combined)*
*Source*: European commission website, 2017.

Equally important, timely transposition of EU directives by member countries is also measured by the EC. Transposition monitoring unveils the transposition deficit (the difference between the number of Single Market directives adopted by the EU and those transposed in EU states) and the compliance deficit (number of incorrectly transposed directives). EC evidence illustrates that the average transposition delay significantly increased.

To estimate the transposition deficit of each EU state, the EC includes directives for which no transposition measures have been communicated and directives considered as partially transposed by EU countries after they notified some transposition measures. However, the transposition deficit does not include directives for which transposition actions are still under analysis by the EC.

In 2016 outstanding directives are late by 10.1 months on average (up from 7.4). More specifically, 22 of the EU states increased their average delay while 5 decreased it and 1 remained the same (European commission, 2016). Delays increased in Ireland, France, the Netherlands, Romania, and Finland, while 11 EU countries with the lowest delays have no directives overdue for 2 years or more.

However, it should be noted that the EU average deficit has been decreasing steadily for the last 18 years (since 1997). Thus, EC political commitment to transposition in most of its countries (European Council set targets of 1.5% and 1%), as well as the introduction of effective administrative procedures and improved coordination, seem to deliver results.

The most problematic areas seem to be financial services (9 non-transposed directives out of 78 in force), environment (10 out of 113), transport (9 out of 123), and employment and social policy (5 out of 75).

## CONCLUSIONS AND POLICY IMPLICATIONS

Since 1970s integration of EU countries' markets faced significant political, economic, ideological, and cultural barriers. Regulatory heterogeneity, private law and tax issues, language barriers, informational asymmetries hold up single market forces. Although a new Single Market strategy was set in motion by the EC on October 28, 2015 in order to deliver a deeper and fairer single market and to enforce growth, it is common truth that the Single Market did not reach its full potential and economic benefits. The comparison with the USA indicates that national borders in Europe still play a key role (Pacchioli, 2011). Indeed, the trade between individual US states is nearly 40% of GDP, whereas in the EU-27 it is just 20%.

Which are the major obstacles for the full achievement of single market advantages?

First, implementation and effectiveness should be given an equal foot to bargaining and negotiation and thus procedures of enforcement and compliance with single market directives should be strengthened. This means that delays in the implementation of harmonized rules in EU countries' legal frameworks, as well as infringements of single market regulations, should be faced in a systematic way. Equally important, enforcement of the rules of the European Single Market should be assessed moving from a sanction-oriented enforcement toward an incentive-driven approach.

Second, there is a need to prioritize key issue areas which lag behind in liberalization and to focus on the interconnections of different issue areas and economic sectors with the purpose to maximize single market potential. For example, improving effective competition in network industries has wider benefits, as these sectors provide inputs to a large number of other economic activities. While significant progress has been made in terms of market liberalization (particularly in the air transport and telecom sectors and to a lesser extent in postal services, energy and rail transport), the goal of full market integration seems to be far away reflected in the still significant price differences between EU countries.

The first step in fostering market integration in network industries is to ensure that the physical infrastructure for integration is in place. This is the case in air travel, telecommunications, and postal services where a well-established Europe-wide network already exists. Limiting obstacles on international transport and cross-border provision of services (cabotage) and better enforcement of existing rules could help significantly (European Commission, 2014). Single Market directives can only attain their intended results if they are completely and correctly transposed into member countries' national law. On the other hand, electricity and gas sectors are currently deprived of this priority as interconnection capacity between EU countries is still insufficient.

More specifically, there is a need to promote harmonization in key issue areas like financial services (i.e., retail banking, mortgages and cross-border mergers), professional services (qualifications and mutual recognition rules for some professions), security services, e-payments, and public procurements (differences in governance models and levels of proficiency in public procurement in EU countries).

Third, there is a need to enforce labor mobility by limiting the administrative burden linked with recognition of professional qualifications and legislating effective portability of supplementary pension rights.

Finally, economic and capital integration, properly regulated, is a major policy vehicle to achieve not only absorption of asymmetric economic shocks but also equity and welfare for European society as a whole. Unavoidably, the achievement of full integration on a sustainable basis presupposes that the European institutional framework evolves together with increased integration and EU states apply all necessary structural reforms in their national markets.

## BIBLIOGRAPHY


Amin, A and J. Tomaney. 1995. *Behind the myth of European union: Prospects for cohesion. London.* New York: Routledge.

Badinger, H. 2007. "Has the EU's single market programme fostered competition? Testing for a decrease in markup ratios in EU industries". *Oxford Bulletin of Economics and Statistics,* 69(4): 497–519.

Baldwin, R. 1989. On the growth effects of 1992. *NBER working paper 3119.* USA: NBER.

Bartelsman, E., Scarpetta S., and Schivardi, F. 2006. "Comparative analysis of firm demographics and survival: Micro-level evidence for the OECD countries", *OECD working paper no. 348.* Paris: OECD.

Bertelsmann Stiftung. 2014. 20 years of the European single market: Growth effects of EU integration. *Policy brief* 2014/02.

BIS. 2011. The economic consequences for the UK and the EU of completing the single market, *BIS economics paper no. 11.* Switzerland: BIS Department for Business, Innovation and Skills.

Blanchard, O and Giavazzi, A. 2003. "Macroeconomic effects of regulation and deregulation in goods and labour markets". *Quarterly Journal of Economics,* 122(58): 349–402.

Boltho, A and Eichengreen B. 2008. "The economic impact of European integration". *CEPR discussion papers no 6820.* London: CEPR.

Burley, Anne-Marie and Mattli, Walter. 1993. "Europe before the Court: A political theory of legal integration." *International Organization,* 47: 41–76.

Cameron, D. 1997. "Economic and Monetary Union: Underlying imperatives and third-stage dilemmas". *Journal of European Public Policy,* (4): 455–485.

Cecchini, P., Catinat, M., and Jacquemin, A. 1988. *The European challenge 1992. The benefits of a single market.* Wildwood house. Accessed http://ec.europa.eu/economy_finance/emu_history/documentation/chapter12/19880301en127eurochalle nge92_a.pdf

Copenhagen Economics. 2010. *The Economic impact of a European digital single market. Final report.* Copenhagen: Copenhagen Economics.

Criscuolo, C., Gal, P., and Menon C. 2014. "The dynamics of employment growth: New evidence from 18 countries". *OECD Science, technology and industry policy papers* no. 14. Paris: OECD.

De Grauwe, P. 2014. *Economics of Monetary Union*, tenth edition. Oxford: Oxford University Press.

Egan, M. 2001. *Constructing a European market. Standards, regulation and governance.* Oxford: Oxford University Press.

Egger, P and Pfaffermayr, M. 2004. "Foreign direct investment and European integration in the 1990s". *The World Economy,* 27: 99–110.

Emerson, Michael., Aujean, Michel., Catinat, Michel., Goybet, Philippe., and Jacquemin, Alexis. 1988. *The economics of 1992. An assessment of the potential economic effects of completing the internal market of the European Community.* Brussels: Directorate-General for Economic and Financial Affairs.

European Commission. 2011. *Towards a better functioning Single Market for services–building on the results of the mutual evaluation process of the Services Directive.* Brussels: Directorate-General for Economic and Financial Affairs.

European Commission. 2015a. *Erasmus–facts, figures and trends: The European Union support for student and staff exchanges and university cooperation in 2013-14.* Brussels: European Commission.

European Commission. 2015b. "*Better regulation for better results: An EU agenda*", Communication COM (2015) 215 final. Brussels: European Commission.

European Commission. 2015c. "*Upgrading the single market: more opportunities for people and business*", COM (2015) 550 final. Brussels: European Commission.

European Commission. 2015d. *Assessment of the economic impact of the services directive: Update of the 2012 study.* Brussels: European Commission.

European Commission. 2015e. *Economic impact of the Services Directive: A 2014 update.* Brussels: European Commission.

European Commission. 2016. *EU open data portal.* Accessed https://www.europeandataportal.eu/

European Parliament Research Service. 2014. *The cost of non-Europe in the Single Market (Cecchini revisited): An overview of the potential economic gains from further completion of the European Single Market.* September. Strasbourg: European Parliament.

Garrett, Geoffrey. 1992. "International cooperation and institutional choice: The European community's internal market". *International Organization,* 46: 533–560.

Griffith, R., Harrison, R., and Simpson, H. 2006. "The link between product market reform, innovation and EU macroeconomic performance", *European Commission economic papers, n. 243.* Brussels: European Commission.

Harrison, G., Rutherford T., and Tarr, D. 1994. Product standards, imperfect competition, and completion of the market in the market in the European Union, *World Bank Policy Research Working Paper No. 1293.* Washington, D.C.: World Bank.

Héritier, A. 2002. "New modes of governance in Europe: Policy-making without legislating?" In *Common goods: Reinventing European and international governance,* ed. Héritier, A. Lanham: Rowman and Littlefield.

Hirst, P and Thompson, G. 1996. *Globalisation in question.* Cambridge: Polity Press.

Ilzkovitz, F., Dierx, A., Kovacs, V., and Sousa, N. 2007. "Steps towards a deeper economic integration: the internal market in the 21st century: A contribution to the single market review". *European Economy No. 271.* Brussels: European Commission.

Kox, H and Lejour, A. 2006. "The effects of the services directive on intra-EU trade and FDI". *Revue Economique,* 57(4): 747–769.

Krugman, P. 1991a. *Geography and trade.* Cambridge, MA: MIT Press.

Krugman, P. 1991b. "Increasing returns and economic geography". *Journal of Political Economy,* 99: 483–499.

Majone, G. 2005. *Dilemmas of European integration.* Oxford: Oxford University Press.

Meiklejohn, R. 1999. "The economics of state aid" *European economy issue 3.* Brussels: European Commission.

Monti, M. 2010. *A new strategy for the single market: At the service of Europe's economy and society.* Study prepared for the European Commission, May. Brussels: European Commission.

Moravcsik, A. 1991. "Negotiating the single European act: National interests and conventional statecraft in the European Community". *International Organization,* 45(1): 19–56.

OECD. 2014a. *OECD Economic surveys: European Union.* Paris: OECD Publishing.

Pacchioli, C. 2011. "Is the EU internal market suffering from an integration deficit? Estimating the home-bias effect", *CEPS working document No. 348.* Brussels: CEPS.

Pacchoili, C. 2011. "Is the EU internal market suffering from an integration deficit? Estimating the home-bias effect". *CEPS working document no. 348.* London: CEPR.

Pelkmans, J. 2006. *European integration, methods and economic analysis,* third edition. London: Financial Times Management.

Pelkmans, J. 2012. The economics of single market regulation. *European economic policy briefings, issue 25.* Bruges: College of Europe.

Sandholtz, W and Zysman, J. 1989. "1992 recasting the European bargain". *World Politics,* 42(1): 95–128.

Scharpf, F. 1999. *Governing in Europe. Democratic and efficient?* Oxford: Oxford University Press.

Shapiro, C. 2002. "Competition policy and innovation," Directorate for Science, Technology, and Industry" *OECD, STI working paper no. 2002/11.* Paris: OECD.

Sørensen, P. B. 2000. "The case for international tax coordination reconsidered". *Economic Policy,* 31: 431–461.

Sousa, N., Rueda-Cantouche, J. M., Arto, I., and Andreoni, V. 2012. *Extra-EU exports and employment.* European Commission. DG Trade chief economist note. Brussels: European Commission.

Spulber, Daniel F. 1989. "Product variety and competitive discounts". *Journal of Economic Theory,* 48(2): 510–525.

Straathof, B., Linders, G.J., Lejour, A., and Möhlmann, J. 2008. *The internal market and the dutch economy: Implications for trade and economic growth.* Netherlands: CPB Netherlands Bureau for Economic Policy Analysis.

Tinbergen, J. 1954. *International economic integration.* Amsterdam: North Holland Publ.

Zsolt, Pataki. 2014. *The Cost of Non- Europe in the Single Market Cecchini Revisited: An overview of the potential economic gains from further completion of the European Single Market.* European Parliamentary Research Service European added value unit, September CoNE 1/2014. Strasbourg: European Parliament.

## FURTHER READING

Cafiso, G. 2009. *Sectorial border effects in the European Single Market: An Explanation through industrial concentration.* European Central Bank working paper series no. 1116. Frankfurt: ECB.

Fournier, J., Domps, A., Gorin, Y., Guillet, X., and Morchoisne, D. 2015. "Implicit regulatory barriers in the EU single market: New empirical evidence from gravity models". *OECD Economics department working papers, no. 1181.* Paris: OECD. Accessed http://dx.doi.org/10.1787/5js7xj0xckf6-en

Fournier, J. 2015. "The heterogeneity of product market regulations". *OECD Economics department working papers no. 1182.* Paris: OECD. Accessed http://dx.doi.org/10.1787/5js7xhxwrnwd-en

Neary, J. P. 2002. "Foreign direct investment and the single market". *The Manchester School,* 70(3): 291–314.

Salgado, R. 2002. "Impact of structural reforms on productivity growth in industrial countries", *IMF Working Paper.* January. Washington, D.C.: IMF.

Sauner-Leroy, J. B. 2003. "The impact of the implementation of the single market Programme on productive efficiency and on mark-ups in the European manufacturing industry" *Economic papers, no 192.* Economic and financial affairs Directorate-General of the European Commission. Brussels: European Commission.

## QUESTIONS

1. What are the main barriers to trade in the EU?
2. What type of policy instruments has the EU used to integrate national markets?
3. How successful has the EU been in establishing a single market free of restrictions to trade and commerce?
4. What were the driving forces behind the "relaunch" of the Single Market project in the 1980s?

5. How have different theories and approaches been used to explain the SMP?
6. What role has the ECJ played in addressing barriers to trade?
7. Explain the different types of regulatory strategy used to tackle barriers to trade in Europe. What accounts for their success or failure?
8. What are the main challenges the EU faces in making the Single Market operate efficiently and effectively?
9. To what extent is the environment in which the Internal Market operates today different from that of the late 1980s to early 1990s?
10. What is the latest empirical evidence on the economic impact of the Internal Market?

# *Chapter 10*

# The Regional Policy of European Union

## THE ARGUMENTS FOR A EUROPEAN REGIONAL POLICY

Regional disparities have been a main issue in the economic literature in the last decades (Romer, 1986; Lucas, 1988; Krugman, 1991; Barro and Sala-i-Martin, 1995; Fujita, Krugman and Venables, 1999). Equally important, the issue of intraregional and interregional disparities within different forms of regional economic integration has been at the center of academic and political debates (Camagni, 1992).

Based on neoclassical perception some scholars argue that economic integration leads in the long term to a limitation of regional disparities and to greater social and economic cohesion through intensification of trade relations, mobility of labor, and capital and diffusion of technology. In other words, economic convergence could be realized (Solow, 1956; Swan, 1956) through constant returns to scale, (constraining marginal productivity of capital) substitutability between production factors and technological progress.

According to writers of neoclassical school (i.e., Heckscher, [1919] 1991; Ohlin, 1933; Samuelson, 1949) each region exports goods that use intensively its abundant factors of production and imports goods that use intensively its scarce factors and thus trade integration leads product and factor prices to converge. Similarly, other neoclassical thinkers claim that a free factor movement of factors of production paves the way for equalization of factor prices as low-wage, less advanced regions attract capital, and more advanced regions attract labor.

Conversely, non-neoclassical approaches (Myrdal, 1957; Hirschmann, 1958) underline that regional divergence is the result of market dynamics and consequently the advanced areas are expected to reap more benefits, while lagging areas benefit less. Thus, internal and external economies of scale and technological progress enforce regional divergences.

More specifically, the endogenous growth theories (Romer, 1986; Lucas, 1988; Barro, 1990) argue that investment in human resources and knowledge lead to increasing returns to capital and divergence.

In the same manner, the new economic geography school (Krugman, 1991) insists that increasing returns to scale, monopolistic competition, completely liberalized factors of production mobility, and non-zero transportation costs lead to uneven concentration of economic action and agglomeration economies (Henderson, 1986) in specific regions, which exceed a critical development threshold.

Agglomeration economies create incentives for the concentration of firms in large urban areas (Carlino, 1979) and generate differential rates of growth (Krugman, 1993). On the contrary, remote regions cannot attract investment (Limao and Venables, 2001) and thus spatial imbalances are increasing (Ciccone, 2002).

Williamson (1965) also underlined the role of labor migration, capital migration, interregional linkages, and central government policy in regional convergence/divergence inequalities. Imperfect competition favors industry concentration and enforces regions that already possess a critical mass of factors of production.

Empirical studies and theoretical models (Brülhart, 1998) tested the aforementioned methodological views at EU level (Magrini, 1999; Barca, 2009) but concluded different results and thus no consensus has been reached on the causes of economic convergence and territorial cohesion (Barro and Sala-i-Martin, 1992; Geppert et al., 2005; Armstrong, 1995; Neven and Gouyette, 1995; Carrington, 2003).

Oil crises have been blamed for economic divergence in the studies of Button and Pentecost (1995) and Magrini (1999) while other studies linked the metropolitan areas' developmental status to specific drivers of economic convergence (Dunford, 1994; Abraham and Van Rompuy, 1995; Puga, 2002; Lopez-Balaz, 1996; Minassian and Totev, 1996; Lopez-Bazo et al., 1999; Terrasi, 1999).

Although EU cohesion policy has proved to be largely effective in terms of enforcing the long-run growth performance of many EU regions (Pellegrini et al., 2013), intraregional disparities in member states persisted in many cases (Dunford, 1994; Puga, 2002). The productive system in advanced regions is more likely to be characterized by economies of scale, positive externalities and agglomeration, higher levels of R&D, a higher quality of human resources, and an advanced market structure. In sum, four crucial points are raised for the study of EU regional policy.

First, the path dependency of member states and regions as well as the institutional and market traits of regions and cities do influence convergence/divergence patterns in EU. Second, agglomeration economies and urban economies of scale do impact on concentration of economic activities, and consequently EU areas with significant external scale effects have higher and faster rates of growth. Third, there is a critical threshold to achieve sustainable growth targets involving medium and high value added activities and thus there is a need for policy intervention on critical areas such as infrastructure, education, and research. Finally, structural traits of the regions influence the speed and content of convergence of poorer regions to advanced EU areas. This further means that more advanced regions are characterized by intensified trade and economic openness as well as by better integration to European productive networks.

Likewise, the theory suggests that there is a need for structural similarity at regional level which would improve the expansion of intra-industry trade, and technology diffusion (Bernard and Jones, 1996; Ruffin, 1999; Best, 1990; Budd, 1998). This means that building regional institutional capacity, improving poor areas accessibility to public goods and services, enforcing regional innovation and entrepreneurship do matter for regional growth and thus targeted, and time specified policy interventions are important to set the basics for economies of scale and innovation at regional level.

## THE EVOLUTION OF EUROPEAN REGIONAL POLICY

The rationale of EU cohesion policy is embedded in the dynamics and evolving needs of European integration. From 1970s the European regional policy acted as a mechanism not only to finance weaker areas but also to put in place the fundamentals of regional growth. However, the coevolving processes of deepening/enlargement in European integration set in motion challenges that were not predicted by the European regional policy designers (Krugman and Venables, 1995).

The origins of regional policy are traced in 1957, in the Treaty of Rome founding the EEC. A first Communication was applied by the EC in 1965, and in 1968 the DG for regional policy of the EC was created. The Thompson report, published by the EC in 1973, highlighted that "although the objective of continuous expansion set in the Treaty has been achieved, its balanced and harmonious nature has not been achieved."

During the period from 1957 to 1988, the ESF (1958), the EAGGF (1962), and the ERDF (1975) co-financed projects for regional development. However, it is interesting to note that the ERDF had a budget of only 1,300 million euros to address severe regional imbalances occurred due to industrial change and structural unemployment. In that period the ERDF could finance actions eligible for up to 50% of public expenditure, such as investments in small enterprises creating at least 10 new jobs and infrastructure investments in less developed areas.

Although European Community promoted initiatives to face regional disparities it was the SEA of 1986 that put the pillars for the cohesion policy so as to mitigate the effects of the single market on the less-favored regions of the Community. Indeed, from 1989 to 1993, EEC focused more on programmes than on projects.

The admission of Greece (1981), Spain, and Portugal (1986) in European Community created the need for more and better organized resources in cohesion policy based on the principles of prioritizing the poorest and most backward regions, forwarding a multi-annual programming promoting strategic orientation of investments and enforcing the participation of regional and local partners in the process. A milestone had been reached in March 1988 when the European Council in Brussels allocated 64 billion ECUs to the structural funds while on June 24, 1988 the Council adopted the first regulation integrating the structural funds in the framework of cohesion policy.

The efficiency of the cohesion resources again came under severe critique in the early 1990s and as a result the Maastricht treaty (February 7, 1992) put into action the cohesion fund, the committee of regions, and the principle of subsidiarity. The new period in regional policy lasted from 1994 to 1999, characterized by a significant rise of the resources (168 billion ECUs) for the structural and cohesion funds (almost a third of the EU budget).

Targeting at consolidation of European Community experience in regional policy the cohesion policy regulations adopted by the Council on July 20, 1993 enforced the principles of concentration, programming, additionality (additionality is defined as positive development outcomes that would not have been possible without the cohesion policy intervention), and partnership and included the financial instrument of fisheries guidance, and the cohesion fund. The accession of Austria, Finland, and Sweden on January 1, 1995 led to further amendments of regional policy regulations so as accommodate the needs of low populated areas of Finland and Sweden.

Taking into consideration previous reports and findings (OECD, 2005), the Barca (2009) report criticized sharply the content of EU cohesion policy underlining that it was deprived of an ongoing monitoring-evaluation, it did not use data for regional analysis in an organized way, and it confused efficiency-social inclusion targets—concluding that without a system of incentives and sanctions, regional policy could not set in place the terms for EU regional growth.

It also argued that the national authorities responsible for the implementation of regional policy should apply specific binding agreements concerning the provision of data and the policy objectives without disregarding transparency. The report further suggested that sanctions should have implemented only for absence of clarity of expected results, data provision, transparency, stakeholder engagement, and a lack of monitoring.

The proposed regional policy underlined the necessity for place-based approaches which integrate in a single context, innovation, environment, and inequality (EC, 2010a). The aforementioned findings led to the Europe 2020 Growth Strategy of "smart, sustainable and inclusive growth," which was adopted by the community in 2010 (EC, 2010b).

There is little doubt that EU cohesion policy after 2013 was heavily influenced by Barca report findings in issues such as innovation (poorer states have more infrastructure funding), ongoing assessment, funding concentration and result-oriented logic (Barca and McCann, 2011), transparent performance information (EC, 2011c; EC, 2011d), and necessity for networking between regions to facilitate coordination.

However, the true challenges to regional policy came in between 2000 and 2006 not only due to urgent institutional and development priorities of EU but also because of a unique enlargement of the EU (in 2004, 10 states became members of EU increasing its population by 20% and its GDP by 5%). In 2000, the Lisbon strategy prioritized growth, jobs, and innovation and cohesion policy mirrored this shift. Unavoidably, the EU had to face disparities in income and employment in the new member states as their average GDP per head was under half of the EU average and only 56% of their population was in active employment. This meant that the new EU countries' territory fell under Objective 1 of regional policy, eligible for the highest possible level of support from the structural and cohesion funds.

In the period from 2007 to 2013, the EU faced again the challenge to ameliorate the developmental status of the poorest countries and regions and to set in motion sustainable growth, jobs, and innovation. The EU applied simplified rules and structures and promoted transparency in the allocation of resources.

However, the evidence clearly indicated that disparities hold between the poorest and the richest regions (i.e., between the richest region is Inner London and the poorest region in north-East of Romania). This led the European Council in December 2005 to allocate 347 billion euros on structural and cohesion funds (of which 81.5% were planned in the "Convergence" regions category).

More specifically, the convergence target was financed by the European Fund for Regional Development, the European Social Fund, and the cohesion fund, the regional competitiveness and employment objective by ERDF and ESF and the ETC objective by ERDF.

The convergence objective (282.8 billion euros) targeted conditions leading to real convergence for the least developed member states and regions and covered 18 EU countries (84 regions) with a population of 154 million, and per capita GDP at less than 75% of the Community average (on a "phasing out" basis another 16 regions were added with a total of 16.4 million inhabitants).

Under the regional competitiveness and employment objective, 168 regions were eligible (representing 314 million inhabitants with a budget of 55 billion euros). The actions targeted development programmes which promoted innovation, entrepreneurship, the protection of the environment, and the improvement of their accessibility as well as programmes to support the labor force.

Finally, the ETC target (covering 181.7 million people or 37.5% of the total EU population) strengthened cross-border cooperation based on joint (local and regional) initiatives, interregional cooperation, and exchange of knowledge. However, its budget was rather low (8.7 billion euros or 2.5% of the total).

## THE MECHANISM OF EU REGIONAL POLICY FROM 2014 TO 2020

According to article 174 of the TFEU, the EU aims at reducing disparities between the levels of development of the EU regions and the backwardness of the least favored regions or islands, focusing especially on rural areas, areas undergoing industrial transition, and regions with severe and permanent natural or demographic problems.

How does EU regional policy realize this target? The policy is applied by national and regional bodies in cooperation with the EC. The budget and the rules (covering the structural and investment funds) for the regional policy are decided by the European Council and the European Parliament (based on a proposal from the EC). One should mention that the principles and priorities of cohesion policy are the outcomes of continuous consultation between the EC and the EU states. Further, each country proposes a draft partnership agreement which includes among others the national strategy and the list of programmes (the states also produce proposals for cooperation programmes involving more than one member states).

The EC negotiates with the member state authorities on the final content of the partnership agreement, as well as for the content of each programme. It also allocates the funds to each member state. Finally, in order to guarantee the transparent and efficient implementation of programmes, the EC monitors each programme and submits reports throughout the programming period.

A crucial role during many stages of regional policy decision-making is attributed to the European CoR. Established in 1994, the European CoR has 350 members who are elected representatives, mayors, and regional presidents in the member states of EU. The committee collaborates with the European Commission, the European Parliament, and the Council of the European Union so as to promote multilevel governance; economic, social, and territorial cohesion; decentralization; and effective application of the principles of subsidiarity and proportionality at a local level.

Current EU cohesion policy is established for a period of seven years (2014–2020), has a budget of 352 billion euros (32.5% of the total EU budget) and targets the reduction of disparities between EU regions and the achievement of balanced and sustainable territorial development.

The policy is delivered through three funds, namely, the European regional fund, the cohesion fund, and the ESF. If one adds the EAFRD and the EMFF, the five funds constitute the ESI investment funds.

Cooperation and coordination between the ESI funds are realized through the common provisions regulation for the ESI funds (Regulation (EU) 1303/2013), which has rules that implement to all five. Indeed, the common rules promote stronger focus on results (measurable targets for better accountability), simplification (common set of rules for five funds), and conditionality to financing.

Separate rules apply also to each fund and are the following:

- the ERDF Regulation (No. 1301/2013)
- the ESF Regulation (No. 1304/2013)
- the Cohesion fund Regulation (No. 1300/2013)
- the EAFRD Regulation (No. 1305/2013)
- the EMFF Regulation (No. 508/2014)

Moreover, the ETC regulation (no. 1299/2013) applies to cooperation programmes co-financed by the ERDF.

The principles of intervention (already existed before 2014) include complementarity and consistency, shared management and coordination, partnership, proportionality and subsidiarity, compliance with EU, and the national law relating to its application, equality between men and women, nondiscrimination, and sustainable development.

From 2014 to 2020 the cohesion policy has set 11 thematic objectives which are the following:

a. Strengthening research, technological development, and innovation
b. Enhancing access to, and use and quality of, information and communication technologies

c. Enhancing the competitiveness of SMEs
d. Supporting the shift toward a low-carbon economy
e. Promoting climate change adaptation, risk prevention, and management
f. Preserving and protecting the environment and promoting resource efficiency
g. Promoting sustainable transport and improving network infrastructures
h. Promoting sustainable and quality employment and supporting labor mobility.
i. Promoting social inclusion, combating poverty, and any discrimination
j. Investing in education, training, and lifelong learning
k. Improving the efficiency of public administration

Investment from the ERDF supports all 11 objectives (although 1–4 are the main priorities for investment) while the ESF supports targets from 8 to 11 (and in certain cases objectives 1–4) and Cohesion Fund supports objectives from 4 to 7 and 11.

Equally important the cohesion policy is based on four principles:

a. Concentration, which is analyzed as concentration of resources (70% structural fund resources for 2014–2020 are concentrated on the poorest areas and countries), concentration of effort (the focus is on growth priorities such as R&D, small and medium-sized enterprises, low-carbon economy), and concentration of spending (at the beginning of each programming period, annual funding is allocated to each programme).
b. Programming, in the meaning that cohesion policy finances only multi-annual national programmes aligned with EU priorities.
c. Partnership, in the meaning that each programme involves authorities and partners at European, regional and local level during all phases of the programming process (design, management, implementation, monitoring, evaluation).
d. Additionality, in the meaning that European structural funds do not replace national spending by an EU country. In this regard, the EC agrees with each state on the allocated financial aid throughout the programming period and controls the compliance in the middle of the programming period and at the end (2022) so as to ensure that contribution of the structural funds does add value.

The resources available for each region are strictly linked on each region's average GDP per capita. More specifically, there is a distinction between three groups of regions instead of the previous two (convergence and regional competitiveness and employment in the period 2007–2013) which are the following:

a. Less developed regions whose GDP per capita is less than 75% of the average GDP of the EU-28
b. Transition regions where GDP per capita is between 75% and 90% of the average GDP of the EU-28
c. More developed regions where GDP per capita is above 90% of the average GDP of the EU-28

The more interesting point of the present regional policy is its direct link to the Europe 2020 strategy. The latter sets five targets by 2020 in the issue areas of employment (rise the employment rate among those aged 20–64 to at least 75%), R&D (increase combined public and private investment in R&D to 3% of GDP), climate change and energy sustainability (reduce greenhouse gas emissions by at least 20% compared with 1990 levels, increase the percentage of renewable energy in final energy consumption to 20% and achieve a 20% increase in energy efficiency), education ( reduce the rate of early leavers from education and training to less than 10% and rise the proportion of those aged 30–34 having completed tertiary education to at least 40%), and fighting poverty and social exclusion.

The EC (COM(2014) 130 final, March 5, 2014) put in place specific policy tools to achieve the aforementioned targets and grouped them under three headings namely smart growth, sustainable growth and inclusive growth. The EC also proposed (March 2015) the broad guidelines for the economic policies of the EU and of the member countries (COM (2015) 99 final) including four main targets which are boosting investment, enhancing growth through the application of structural reforms in the EU states, removing obstacles to growth and jobs at an EU level, and improving the sustainability and growth-friendliness of public finances.

Similarly, the Commission applies the guidelines for the employment policies (COM (2015) 098 final) targeting strong demand for labor enforcement of labor supply and skills, better functioning of labor markets, combating poverty, and promoting equal opportunities which are linked to Europe 2020.

Eligibility for the funds is defined according to the NUTS classification (regulation no. 1319/2013). Already in place since the 1970s, NUTS divides EU territory in geographical terms for the purposes of regional policy. The NUTS level to which an existing administrative level corresponds is determined on the basis of the average population size of its administrative units and is presented in table 10.1.

Thus, NUTS 1 level refers to major regions (i.e., German Länder), NUTS 2 level refers to basic regions for the implementation of regional policies (i.e., Belgian provinces), and NUTS 3 level refers to small regions (i.e., Bulgarian provinces). One should observe that the NUTS does not cover the municipalities level as well as that where the population of an EU country as a whole

**Table 10.1 NUTS Categorization According to European Union**

| *Level* | *Minimum Population* | *Maximum Population* |
|---|---|---|
| NUTS 1 | 3 million | 7 million |
| NUTS 2 | 800,000 | 3 million |
| NUTS 3 | 150,000 | 800,000 |

is below the minimum threshold for a given NUTS level, the country itself constitutes a NUTS territorial unit of that level. The current NUTS classification (from January 1, 2015) lists 98 regions at NUTS 1 level, 276 regions at NUTS 2 level, and 1,342 regions at NUTS 3 level.

The EU also applies a number of legal and institutional requirements (the so-called ex ante conditionality), which should be realized upon submission of the partnership agreements and programmes. The conditionality is either thematic (associated with investment or EU priorities underlined in the fund regulations) or general (not associated with investment or EU priorities).

## THE EUROPEAN REGIONAL DEVELOPMENT FUND

Regulation (EU) no. 1301/2013 (December 17, 2013) specifies that ERDF should promote the harmonious, balanced, and sustainable development of the EU focusing also on problems of naturally disadvantaged regions (island, mountainous, or sparsely populated) and outermost areas. The eligible regions are defined in terms of their GDP as a percentage of an EU average (more developed regions a GDP of more than 90%, transition regions a GDP of 75%–90%, and less developed regions a GDP less than 75%).

More specifically, the ERDF has a budget of over 185 billion euros and focuses on four key issue areas, namely, innovation and research, information and communication technologies, support for small and medium-sized enterprises, and promoting a low-carbon economy. Although all EU states' regions are eligible the amount granted depends on EU priorities and the type of region.

## THE EUROPEAN SOCIAL FUND

According to ESF regulation all EU member states are eligible for financing. The ESF focuses on several social issue areas including employment and labor mobility, social inclusion and poverty, education and lifelong learning, and institutional capacity of public administration.

**Table 10.2 Allocation of Cohesion Policy Funds for the Programming Period 2014–2020 (Million Euros)**

| | *ERDF-ESF* | *ERDF-ESF* | *ERDF-ESF* | | | |
|---|---|---|---|---|---|---|
| | *Less Developed Regions* | *Transition Regions* | *More Developed Regions* | *Cohesion Fund* | *Total Cohesion Policy* | *Share of EU-28 Cohesion Policy Funds (%)* |
| EU-28 | 182171.8 | 35381.1 | 54350.5 | 63399.7 | 351854.2 | 100.0 |
| Belgium | – | 1039.7 | 938.6 | – | 2283.9 | 0.6 |
| Bulgaria | 5089.3 | – | – | 2278.3 | 7588.4 | 2.2 |
| Czech republic | 15282.5 | – | 88.2 | 6258.9 | 21982.9 | 6.2 |
| Denmark | – | 71.4 | 255.1 | – | 553.4 | 0.2 |
| Germany | – | 9771.5 | 8498.0 | – | 19234.9 | 5.5 |
| Estonia | 2461.2 | – | – | 1073.3 | 3590.0 | 1.0 |
| Ireland | – | – | 951.6 | – | 1188.6 | 0.3 |
| Greece | 7034.2 | 2306.1 | 2528.2 | 3250.2 | 15521.9 | 4.4 |
| Spain | 2040.4 | 13995.5 | 11074.4 | – | 28559.5 | 8.1 |
| France | 3407.8 | 4253.3 | 6348.5 | – | 15852.5 | 4.5 |
| Croatia | 5837.5 | – | – | 2559.5 | 8609.4 | 2.4 |
| Italy | 22324.6 | 1102.0 | 7692.2 | – | 32823.0 | 9.3 |
| Cyprus | – | – | 421.8 | 269.5 | 735.6 | 0.2 |
| Latvia | 3039.8 | – | – | 1349.4 | 4511.8 | 1.3 |
| Lithuania | 4628.7 | – | – | 2048.9 | 6823.1 | 1.9 |
| Luxembourg | – | – | 39.6 | – | 59.7 | 0.0 |
| Hungary | 15005.2 | – | 463.7 | 6025.4 | 21905.9 | 6.2 |
| Malta | – | 490.2 | – | 217.7 | 725.0 | 0.2 |
| Netherlands | – | – | 1014.6 | – | 1404.3 | 0.4 |
| Austria | – | 72.3 | 906.0 | – | 1235.6 | 0.4 |
| Poland | 51163.6 | – | 2242.4 | 23208.0 | 77567.0 | 22.0 |
| Portugal | 16671.2 | 257.6 | 1275.5 | 2861.7 | 21465.0 | 6.1 |
| Romania | 15058.8 | – | 441.3 | 6935.0 | 22993.8 | 6.5 |
| Slovenia | 1260.0 | – | 847.3 | 895.4 | 3074.8 | 0.9 |
| Slovakia | 9483.7 | – | 44.2 | 4168.3 | 13991.7 | 4.0 |
| Finland | – | – | 999.1 | – | 1465.8 | 0.4 |
| Sweden | – | – | 1512.4 | – | 2105.8 | 0.6 |
| UK | 2383.2 | 2617.4 | 5767.6 | – | 11839.9 | 3.4 |

*Source*: European commission, Directorate general for regional, and urban policy, 2017.

## THE COHESION FUND

According to its regulation (1300/2013) the cohesion fund provides aid for the poorer areas of the EU targeting employment and sustainable development. Every region whose gross national income is less than 90% of the EU average is eligible for funding. Its budget for the years 2014 to 2020 reaches 63.4 billion euros and covers a wide range of issues such as the shift toward a low-carbon economy, climate change adaptation, and risk prevention, protecting the environment and promoting resource efficiency, enforcing sustainable transport and network infrastructures, and enhancing institutional capacity. The budget for cohesion policy and the principles linked with its allocation are decided by the Council and the EP.

Is the new regional policy framework efficient? In the new period, the linkages between policy targets and the method of allocating the regional policy resources have been redefined. Cohesion policy is linked with the Europe 2020 strategy which means that all regions can reap the benefits of intervention (investment priorities for the funds) but to different degrees as defined by the principles on thematic concentration.

Overall, EU regional policy from 2014 to 2020 is results-oriented, is integrated with the Europe 2020 strategy, and is embedded within European economic policy coordination. The new regional policy framework enhances the coordination between the funds, defines common standards for all programmes, and promotes effectiveness, sound financial management, and legal certainty through transparent rules, easier reporting, and reduction of the administrative burden on beneficiaries.

Thematic concentration ensures that investments focus on a limited array of priorities linked to the Europe 2020 strategy. Last, the regional policy associates funds to the European semester and thus links financing to socio-economic challenges in each member state.

## EU ECONOMIC GEOGRAPHY: TRENDS AND INEQUALITIES

Demography should be taken into account in regional analysis not only because it influences regional competitiveness and social cohesion but also because it is part of the solution for addressing spatial imbalances. One also should be cautious that regional development traits and economic evolution in EU are different from those in North America and other developed states. EU urban growth patterns also present unique traits and consequently EU spatial changes are different from those of USA/Canada.

More specifically, each EU country maintains a number of specific characteristics in its historical path, institutional setting, administration, and policy agenda.

The population of the EU-28 was 508.5 million in 2015. Across the whole of the EU-28, inhabitants aged between 0 and 19 accounted for 20.9% of the total population, inhabitants aged between 20 and 64 accounted for 60.2% of the population, while people aged 65 and above accounted for the remaining 18.9% (Eurostat, 2017). Literature suggests that population shifts are mainly the outcome of two variables in a peacetime namely natural population change and net migration flows.

As far as it concerns the first dimension, high birth and fertility rates lead to high shares of young inhabitants in EU (i.e., many Irish areas). After a peak in 1964 (when there were 3.6 million more births than deaths) in EU, birth rates started to fall and life expectancy increased, leading to a low natural rate of population growth (in 2003 the number of births exceeded the number of deaths by less than 100,000).

According to the Eurostat in 2014, 17 NUTS level 3 regions had a fall in population by more than 15.0 per 1,000 inhabitants (among them seven regions in Bulgaria and three regions in Croatia) while the biggest fall took place in the Greek region of Kentrikos Tomeas Athinon (24.9 per 1,000 inhabitants).

Turning to the second main reason of population shift, migratory flows were balanced during the 1960s and 1970s (except in the years 1991 and 1997) but after 1988 positive net migration exceeded half a million people each year and reached 1.7 million in 2013. In 2014, 430 NUTS level 3 regions in the EU-28 had a negative migration trend (more persons left an area than arrived in it).

As far as it concerns birth rates and fertility rates there are also considerable regional variations. In 2014, the EU-28 crude birth rate was just 10.1 births per 1,000 inhabitants (14.6 births per 1,000 inhabitants in Ireland while less than 7.0 births per 1,000 inhabitants in five regions of Italy, Portugal, and Spain). Fertility follows the pattern of most developed states and member states of EU are not an exception to the downward trend (1.58 in 2014 when 2.10 live births per woman are considered to be the natural replacement rate). However, infant mortality rates also follow a declining trend (infant mortality rate stands at 3.7 deaths per 1,000 live births, compared with a rate of 5.3 a decade earlier).

Life expectancy (average 78.0 years) has improved due to better socioeconomic and environmental terms and higher standards of medical treatment and care (Eurostat, 2017). The lowest life expectancy at birth in 2014 (across NUTS level 2 regions) was recorded in one of the poorest regions of EU—the Bulgarian region of Severozapaden (73.0 years).

GDP per capita trends also uncover considerable income variations between east and west EU regions, south and north EU regions, as well as intraregional differences within each EU state. Nominal economic convergence was achieved in many cases for less developed regions but the financial-economic crisis stopped or even reversed the real convergence process. In 2014, in all of the multiregional EU countries there was at least one NUTS level 2 region that had an average level of GDP per capita that was below the EU-28 average (in Bulgaria, Greece, Croatia and Slovenia all NUTS level 2 regions had an average GDP per capita below the EU-28 average). Likewise, GDP per capita was below the EU-28 average in several NUTS 2 regions where in 2008 was above it (i.e., in certain regions of Greece, Italy and Finland, Spain, Cyprus, Slovenia, UK and Sweden). With relatively low levels of GDP per capita 21 regions of the 78 regions (19 were located in Eastern Europe) had a level of economic output per capita that was less than half the EU-28 average (average GDP per capita in 2014 for Inner London West was 18 times as high as in Severozapaden in Bulgaria which recorded only 30% of the EU-28 average GDP per capita).

On the other hand, in 2014, 15% of the 276 NUTS level 2 areas had a GDP per capita at least 25% higher than the EU-28 average (i.e., regions in western and southern Germany, western Austria and northern Italy, and in the UK). Commuters also influence the GDP performance in many cases (i.e., Inner London West, Luxembourg, the Région de Bruxelles-Capitale/Brussels Hoofdstedelijk Gewest, Hamburg, and Inner London East).

Another crucial finding of regional statistics is the existence of wide disparities in wealth creation between areas of the same state (i.e., in the UK, GDP per capita in Inner London West was almost eight times as high as in West Wales). The same holds true for areas in Slovakia and France; while wealth creation was better spread across the Netherlands, Austria, Spain, Croatia, Portugal, and Ireland in the meaning that in each of the aforementioned countries, the recorded average GDP per capita in the area with the highest value was never more than double that recorded in the area with the lowest value (Eurostat, 2017).

The faster growing areas (NUTS level 2) during 2008 and 2014 were located in Poland (7 of its 16 regions), Austria (3 of its 9 regions), Germany (12 of its 38 regions), Lithuania and Luxembourg. On the other hand, 38 regions recorded a dramatic fall between 2008 and 2014 in their GDP per capita relative to the EU-28 average (i.e., in Greece, Cyprus, Spain, and Italy due to financial crisis spillovers).

GDP per capita grew at a faster pace than the EU-28 average in every area of Hungary, Poland, Romania, and Slovakia and every region except for one in Denmark and Germany. In France, Portugal, and the UK the results are mixed, with the bulk of areas growing slower than the EU-28 average.

Taking into account the rapid ageing of the EU's population, high employment rates are crucial for European welfare, social security contributions, and public finances. The financial crisis led to a reduction of employment rate in EU-28 to 68.4% in 2012 although the policies of EU succeeded to partly reverse the trend (70.0% in 2015). There are states that already attained the Europe 2020 target (in 2015 the Netherlands, Estonia, Denmark, the UK, and

**Table 10.3 Gross Domestic Product at Current Market Prices in Selected NUTS 2 Regions, (Million Euros)**

| | *2000* | *2005* | *2008* | *2014* |
|---|---|---|---|---|
| European Union (28 countries) | 9.561.961 | 11.517.668 | 12.995.762 | 13.959.739 |
| Belgium | 258.222 | 311.481 | 354.066 | 400.643 |
| Région de Bruxelles-Capitale/Brussels Hoofdstedelijk Gewest | : | 59.418 | 64.667 | 73.381 |
| Vlaams Gewest | : | 178.583 | 204.547 | 233.433 |
| Prov. Brabant Wallon | : | 11.197 | 13.567 | 15.484 |
| Prov. Luxembourg (BE) | : | 5.214 | 5.873 | 6.425 |
| Prov. Namur | : | 9.391 | 10.883 | 12.207 |
| Bulgaria | 14.300 | 24.002 | 37.373 | 42.751 |
| Severna i yugoiztochna Bulgaria | 7.043 | 10.527 | 14.832 | 16.677 |
| Severoiztochen | 1.709 | 2.689 | 4.205 | 4.759 |
| Yugoiztochen | 2.183 | 3.285 | 4.536 | 5.327 |
| Czech Republic | 66.649 | 109.394 | 160.962 | 154.739 |
| Praha | 15.132 | 26.846 | 41.190 | 37.673 |
| Severozápad | 6.111 | 9.667 | 13.614 | 12.288 |
| Denmark | 178.018 | 212.907 | 241.087 | 260.582 |
| Hovedstaden | 64.706 | 79.438 | 87.846 | 102.153 |
| Nordjylland | 16.887 | 19.203 | 22.018 | 23.028 |
| Germany (until 1990 former territory of the FRG) | 2.116.480 | 2.300.860 | 2.561.740 | 2.915.650 |
| Baden-Württemberg | 309.104 | 335.893 | 380.876 | 440.057 |
| Bayern | 358.601 | 396.832 | 436.645 | 524.064 |
| Niederbayern | 27.228 | 31.109 | 34.488 | 41.522 |
| Berlin | 85.162 | 87.052 | 99.177 | 117.750 |
| Brandenburg | 44.728 | 48.785 | 54.965 | 62.150 |
| Bremen | 22.348 | 25.082 | 27.658 | 30.360 |
| Hamburg | 77.867 | 87.831 | 95.200 | 103.566 |
| Eesti | 6.171 | 11.262 | 16.517 | 19.963 |
| Ireland | 108.360 | 169.978 | 187.547 | 189.046 |
| Border, Midland, and Western | 19.250 | 31.623 | 34.400 | 33.186 |
| Southern and Eastern | 89.110 | 138.355 | 153.147 | 155.860 |
| Greece | 142.976 | 199.242 | 241.990 | 177.559 |
| Ionia Nisia | 2.719 | 3.789 | 4.522 | 3.137 |
| Attiki | 64.921 | 94.039 | 116.717 | 85.579 |
| Spain | 646.250 | 930.566 | 1.116.207 | 1.041.160 |
| La Rioja | 4.890 | 6.855 | 8.275 | 7.727 |
| Comunidad de Madrid | 114.203 | 166.139 | 202.035 | 196.118 |
| Este (ES) | 201.081 | 288.170 | 344.706 | 320.763 |

(*Continued*)

**Table 10.3 (*Continued*)**

| | *2000* | *2005* | *2008* | *2014* |
|---|---|---|---|---|
| Comunidad Valenciana | 62.532 | 90.535 | 108.508 | 97.430 |
| Ciudad Autónoma de Melilla (ES) | 922 | 1.209 | 1.411 | 1.406 |
| France | 1.485.303 | 1.771.978 | 1.995.850 | 2.132.449 |
| Île de France | 421.009 | 497.045 | 595.566 | 649.101 |
| Auvergne | 27.094 | 31.707 | 33.568 | 35.046 |
| Corse | 4.930 | 6.316 | 7.441 | 8.771 |
| Guyane | 1.982 | 2.807 | 3.317 | 4.469 |
| Croatia | 23.582 | 36.508 | 48.130 | 43.020 |
| Jadranska Hrvatska | 7.311 | 11.686 | 15.392 | 13.731 |
| Kontinentalna Hrvatska | 16.271 | 24.822 | 32.738 | 29.288 |
| Italy | 1.239.759 | 1.490.409 | 1.632.933 | 1.613.859 |
| Piemonte | 100.506 | 120.079 | 129.225 | 122.936 |
| Veneto | 112.752 | 136.254 | 147.291 | 147.498 |
| Emilia-Romagna | 107.042 | 127.276 | 142.919 | 144.140 |
| Sardegna | 25.306 | 30.683 | 33.941 | 33.256 |
| Cyprus | 10.750 | 14.946 | 18.822 | 17.394 |
| Latvia | 8.606 | 13.711 | 24.318 | 23.581 |
| Lithuania | 12.491 | 21.002 | 32.696 | 36.444 |
| Luxembourg | 23.201 | 29.734 | 37.647 | 48.898 |
| Hungary | 51.186 | 90.543 | 107.503 | 104.239 |
| Közép-Magyarország | 21.967 | 41.510 | 51.655 | 49.740 |
| Dél-Dunántúl | 3.736 | 6.049 | 6.965 | 6.412 |
| Malta | 4.388 | 5.131 | 6.116 | 8.091 |
| Netherlands | 448.061 | 545.609 | 639.163 | 662.770 |
| Groningen | 16.534 | 22.221 | 29.806 | 28.563 |
| Flevoland | 6.875 | 9.665 | 11.625 | 12.042 |
| Utrecht | 39.340 | 47.144 | 54.894 | 58.412 |
| Zeeland | 7.559 | 9.306 | 11.244 | 11.429 |
| Austria | 213.196 | 253.009 | 291.930 | 329.296 |
| Wien | 57.601 | 67.051 | 76.251 | 84.211 |
| Kärnten | 12.335 | 14.468 | 16.606 | 17.937 |
| Vorarlberg | 9.515 | 11.460 | 13.372 | 15.642 |
| Poland | 186.376 | 244.822 | 363.692 | 410.845 |
| Lódzkie | 11.357 | 15.308 | 22.663 | 25.055 |
| Mazowieckie | 38.049 | 50.823 | 75.615 | 91.188 |
| Region Poludniowy | 38.770 | 50.999 | 75.653 | 83.006 |
| Podlaskie | 4.330 | 5.702 | 8.290 | 9.213 |
| Opolskie | 4.356 | 5.616 | 8.505 | 8.672 |
| Portugal | 128.466 | 158.653 | 178.873 | 173.446 |
| Algarve | 4.979 | 6.741 | 7.848 | 7.348 |
| Centro (PT) | 24.944 | 30.244 | 33.236 | 32.708 |
| Área Metropolitana de Lisboa | 47.386 | 59.469 | 67.279 | 64.010 |

*(Continued)*

**Table 10.3 (*Continued*)**

| | *2000* | *2005* | *2008* | *2014* |
|---|---|---|---|---|
| Região Autónoma dos Açores (PT) | 2.428 | 3.264 | 3.761 | 3.731 |
| Romania | 40.797 | 80.226 | 142.396 | 150.230 |
| Bucuresti-Ilfov | 9.117 | 19.070 | 37.846 | 40.453 |
| Sud-Vest Oltenia | 3.539 | 6.561 | 11.074 | 11.288 |
| Vest | 3.831 | 7.842 | 14.128 | 14.285 |
| Slovenia | 21.923 | 29.235 | 37.951 | 37.303 |
| Vzhodna Slovenija | 10.168 | 13.107 | 16.821 | 16.416 |
| Slovakia | 22.347 | 39.220 | 65.840 | 75.561 |
| Bratislavský kraj | 5.549 | 10.688 | 17.299 | 21.075 |
| Západné Slovensko | 7.336 | 12.772 | 21.656 | 24.064 |
| Stredné Slovensko | 4.628 | 7.595 | 13.369 | 14.877 |
| Finland | 136.261 | 164.387 | 193.711 | 205.268 |
| Manner-Suomi | 135.323 | 163.280 | 192.555 | 203.848 |
| Helsinki-Uusimaa | 50.242 | 60.178 | 72.791 | 78.461 |
| Åland | 806 | 1.048 | 1.086 | 1.354 |
| Sweden | 281.859 | 313.218 | 352.317 | 430.642 |
| Östra Sverige | 121.680 | 136.739 | 154.010 | 197.255 |
| Stockholm | 80.917 | 91.242 | 103.156 | 135.631 |
| Södra Sverige | 113.068 | 124.249 | 141.182 | 168.067 |
| Mellersta Norrland | 10.671 | 11.623 | 12.465 | 14.314 |
| UK | 1.685.975 | 1.945.624 | 1.908.370 | 2.254.297 |
| North West (UK) | 160.024 | 188.771 | 183.548 | 209.557 |
| Cumbria | 10.637 | 12.123 | 12.856 | 15.027 |
| Lancashire | 31.925 | 36.900 | 34.720 | 38.687 |
| Cheshire | 24.706 | 31.209 | 31.249 | 36.079 |
| East Yorkshire and Northern Lincolnshire | 19.348 | 23.388 | 22.608 | 24.447 |
| Lincolnshire | 13.500 | 15.463 | 15.757 | 18.919 |
| London | 337.585 | 392.558 | 393.767 | 509.402 |
| Inner London West | 123.303 | 151.998 | 156.040 | 193.762 |
| Outer London South | 32.417 | 35.326 | 34.207 | 40.027 |
| North Eastern Scotland | 14.786 | 16.747 | 20.186 | 25.639 |
| Highlands and Islands | 10.235 | 12.770 | 11.995 | 13.956 |
| Northern Ireland (UK) | 38.656 | 44.593 | 43.869 | 48.078 |

*Source*: Eurostat, 2017.

Germany were above the target of 75% and in Sweden it was 80.5%) while other countries lag behind the target (less than 65% in Spain, Croatia, Italy, and Greece). Overall, there were 100 NUTS level 2 regions in EU where the employment rate in 2015 was greater than or equal to the critical threshold of 75% (Eurostat, 2017).

As far as it concerns education, the percentage of early leavers (2015) was high in Spain (20.0%), Malta (19.8%), Italy (14.7%), Portugal (13.7%),

Romania (19.1%), Bulgaria (13.4%), Hungary (11.6%), and Estonia (11.2%) while other EU member states had achieved their Europe 2020 national target (Lithuania and Cyprus). In total, there were 158 NUTS level 2 regions across EU where the percentage of early leavers from education and training was below the EU-28 average of 11.0%. Considerable differences exist across EU as more than half of all young people (aged 30–34) had achieved a tertiary level of educational attainment in Lithuania, Cyprus, Luxembourg, Ireland, and Sweden, while the share was significantly lower in other member states (Eurostat, 2017).

Eurostat data (2017) also underline that 24.5% of the EU-28 population was at risk of poverty or social exclusion in 2014 (122.2 million persons). Romania, Bulgaria Greece, Latvia, and Hungary had percentages over 30% and the share was higher in rural areas for most of the Baltic, eastern, and southern member states.

In like manner variations exist in EU-28 R&D ratio to GDP (average 2.03% in 2013). Of the 266 regions at NUTS level 2 there were only 30 regions where R&D expenditure as a share of GDP was above the Europe 2020 target of 3.00% in 2013. Capital city regions also had some of the highest levels of R and D expenditure as a share of GDP.

Labor productivity (gross value added per employee) at NUTS level 2 also shows the large differences between EU member states. In 2014, Luxembourg had the highest gross value added per person employed and its performance was twice as high as the EU-28 average (Luxembourg also had the second highest level of GDP per inhabitant). One should mention that high levels of labor productivity are associated to the efficient use of factors of production and to specific sector traits of an economic activity (i.e., financial services). Among the regions with the highest levels of labor productivity were areas in east and south Ireland, three Belgian regions (the capital city region and its neighboring regions) and the Danish, French, and Swedish capital city areas. Quite interesting is to note that no region from the 2004 enlargement states had a level of gross value added per person employed above the EU-28 average.

The capital city regions of Spain, Italy, Hungary, and Finland recorded disposable income per inhabitant that was above their respective national averages, although there was at least one other region in each of these EU countries which recorded a higher level of disposable income per inhabitant. On the other hand, the largest variations in disposable income per inhabitant across areas of the same EU countries were recorded in Italy, France, and Spain (Eurostat, 2017). The biggest contractions in disposable income occurred in the EU countries most affected by the financial and economic crisis (i.e., the nine regions with the largest falls were Greek).

**Table 10.4 People at Risk of Poverty or Social Exclusion (% of Total Population)**

| | *2005* | *2010* | *2014* | *2015* |
|---|---|---|---|---|
| EU (changing composition) | – | – | 24.4 | 23.7 |
| EU (28 countries) | – | 23.7 | 24.4 | 23.7 |
| EU (27 countries) | 25.8 | 23.7 | 24.4 | 23.7 |
| Euro area (19 states) | 22 | 22 | 23.5 | 23.1 |
| Euro area (18 states) | 21.8 | 21.9 | 23.5 | 23 |
| Belgium | 22.6 | 20.8 | 21.2 | 21.1 |
| Bulgaria | – | 49.2 | 40.1 | 41.3 |
| Czech Republic | 19.6 | 14.4 | 14.8 | 14 |
| Denmark | 17.2 | 18.3 | 17.9 | 17.7 |
| Germany | 18.4 | 19.7 | 20.6 | 20 |
| Estonia | 25.9 | 21.7 | 26 | 24.2 |
| Ireland | 25 | 27.3 | 27.5 | 25.9 |
| Greece | 29.4 | 27.7 | 36 | 35.7 |
| Spain | 24.3 | 26.1 | 29.2 | 28.6 |
| France | 18.9 | 19.2 | 18.5 | 17.7 |
| Croatia | – | 31.1 | 29.3 | 29.1 |
| Italy | 25.6 | 25 | 28.3 | 28.7 |
| Cyprus | 25.3 | 24.6 | 27.4 | 28.9 |
| Latvia | 46.3 | 38.2 | 32.7 | 30.9 |
| Lithuania | 41 | 34 | 27.3 | 29.3 |
| Luxembourg | 17.3 | 17.1 | 19 | 18.5 |
| Hungary | 32.1 | 29.9 | 31.8 | 28.2 |
| Malta | 20.5 | 21.2 | 23.8 | 22.4 |
| Netherlands | 16.7 | 15.1 | 16.5 | 16.4 |
| Austria | 17.4 | 18.9 | 19.2 | 18.3 |
| Poland | 45.3 | 27.8 | 24.7 | 23.4 |
| Portugal | 26.1 | 25.3 | 27.5 | 26.6 |
| Romania | – | 41.5 | 40.3 | 37.4 |
| Slovenia | 18.5 | 18.3 | 20.4 | 19.2 |
| Slovakia | 32 | 20.6 | 18.4 | 18.4 |
| Finland | 17.2 | 16.9 | 17.3 | 16.8 |
| Sweden | 14.4 | 15 | 16.9 | 16 |
| UK | 24.8 | 23.2 | 24.1 | 23.5 |

*Source*: Eurostat, 2017.

Business demography data in EU also reveal the complex mosaic of EU economic landscape. There were 22.6 million enterprises active in the EU-28's nonfinancial business economy in 2013 with almost 133 million employees. The degree of geographical concentration and specialization of these activities varies and depends on the availability of natural resources, access to skills, cost of production, infrastructure facilities, and access to markets.

Eastern EU regions specialize more in industry as a result of low labor costs and natural resource endowments. Many German and Belgian areas were relatively specialized in the production of chemicals and pharmaceuticals, with Rheinhessen-Pfalz the most specialized region for chemicals manufacturing and the Prov. Brabant Wallon for pharmaceutical products. Tourist areas (i.e., in Greece, Italy, Portugal, and Spain) were among the most specialized in accommodation services and food and beverage service activities while Inner London West is the most specialized area in the EU for real estate legal and accounting activities.

The EU's birth rate for new firms in the business economy was estimated below 10% for 2013 (however in Lithuania it reached 23.6%). The lowest enterprise birth rates (below 8%) were recorded in 16 Italian regions, 3 Spanish regions, and 2 Hungarian regions, as well as in Cyprus and Malta. Among member states regions, the largest differences between the highest and lowest regional enterprise birth rates were recorded in Italy (9.5% in Campania while 5.0% in Valle d'Aosta/Vallée d'Aoste). Enterprise birth rates tended to be higher than average in capital cities in 2013 because of market size, better educated employees, and agglomeration economies.

Concerning survival rates of enterprises Sweden and Belgium, Italy (nine regions), Cyprus and Luxembourg, Ireland, the Netherlands, Austria, and Slovenia perform better than the other states.

One can measure the competitiveness differences of EU regions based on the RCI. The index measures at NUTS 2 level, regions performance and is a weighted composite measure of eleven dimensions which are aggregated into three sub-indices of competiveness and an overall composite index.

The most competitive regions in the EU in 2013, as measured by the RCI, were mainly located in the northwest of Europe, comprising most regions in the Benelux countries, Denmark, Germany, Austria, Sweden, and Finland, while high levels of regional competitiveness were also found in southeast of the UK and northern France. In contrast, the least competitive regions were generally located in the southeast of Europe (Bulgaria, Greece, and Romania) as well as in some of the French overseas areas (Eurostat, 2017).

The data further reveal a complex economic landscape within each member state (i.e., a north-south divide in Italy and a north-west-south-east divide in the UK). In most of the EU countries, the region containing the capital city had a higher level of competitiveness than any other area within the same state. The highest ranking region in 2013 was Utrecht, in the Netherlands (which was also the highest ranking region in 2010) and the least competitive region was Severozapaden (in Bulgaria).

Of the 10 most competitive regions in the EU-28 (2013), 7 were either capital regions or regions that included large cities. No region in Bulgaria, Greece, Croatia, Hungary, Poland, or Romania had an RCI above the EU-28 average in 2013. On the contrary, all areas in Belgium, Denmark, Germany, the Netherlands, Austria, Finland, and Sweden were more competitive than the EU-28 average in 2013.

The basic sub-index of RCI consists of an aggregated score based on the assessment of the quality of institutions, macroeconomic stability, infrastructure, and health and basic education. Basic competitiveness was below the EU-28 average in each and every area of the Czech Republic, Ireland, Croatia, Italy, Hungary, Poland, Portugal, Slovenia, Slovakia, Bulgaria, Greece, and Romania.

The second group of indicators (efficiency sub-index) is based on performance in higher education and lifelong learning, labor market efficiency, and market size. Many of the regions with low scores in the basic aspects of competitiveness were also low performers for the efficiency aspects of RCI. The level of efficiency competitiveness was below the EU-28 average in each and every region of Bulgaria, Ireland, Greece, Croatia, Italy, Hungary, and Poland, while in the Czech Republic, Portugal, Romania, and Slovenia, only the capital region had a score above the EU-28 average. The highest scores were observed in Denmark, Sweden, the UK, Finland, and the Netherlands (2013). Capital regions were again among the best performers in higher education and lifelong learning.

The last group of RCI dimensions (innovation sub-index) includes measures relating to the level of technological readiness of enterprises and households, business sophistication, and innovation. All the regions in Denmark, Germany, Ireland, and the Netherlands had an innovation score above the EU-28 average while Île de France and the London area were outstanding innovation locations. On the contrary, all the areas in Bulgaria, Greece, Poland, and Romania were below the EU-28 average.

The aforementioned analysis illustrates the critical role of capital cities in European economic geography. In the 1990s, the role of specific city regions in EU economy has been further strengthened (Fujita, Krugman, and Venables, 1999; Glaeser, Scheinkman, and Shleifer, 1995) and accessibility-connectivity to EU interregional networks acquired a new status (Dijkstra, Garcilazo, and McCann, 2012).

It is no coincidence that many of the 10 NUTS level 3 regions in the EU with the highest shares of their inhabitants being aged between 20 and 64 were capital city regions. On the other hand, the regions with the highest shares of elderly inhabitants are rural (i.e., regions in Greece, Spain, France, Portugal, and eastern Germany), relatively remote, and with reduced employment opportunities. Capital regions performed better in the business sophistication dimension which mirrors the agglomeration and urban economies in capital cities.

## CONCLUSIONS

Regional demography statistics reveal the specific traits in each EU region and uncover the complex interaction between intraregional and interregional inequalities (Herrmann-Pillath, Kirchert, and Pan, 2002). Agglomeration economies, geography, economic integration, and path dependency are the critical drivers of regional growth in Europe. Agglomeration economies favor growth in large urban concentrations geography favors areas with high levels of accessibility and connectivity within the European market while path dependency specifies the local/regional economic and institutional capabilities. It remains to economic integration mechanism to address all distortions, identifying the prerequisites of growth at regional level through a place-based approach (OECD, 2005).

## BIBLIOGRAPHY

Abraham, F and Van Rompuy, P. 1995. "Regional convergence in the European monetary union". *Papers in Regional Science,* 74(2): 125–142.

Angeriz, A., McCombie, J., and Roberts, M. 2008. "New estimates of returns to scale and spatial spillovers for EU regional manufacturing, 1986–2002". *International Regional Science Review*, 31: 62–87.

Armstrong, H. 1995. "Convergence among regions of the European Union". *Papers in Regional Science*, 74(2): 143–152.

Barca, F. 2009. *"An agenda for a reformed cohesion policy: A place-based approach to meeting European Union challenges and expectations*". Independent Report prepared at the request of the European Commissioner for Regional Policy, Danuta Hubner, Brussels: European Commission.

Barca, F and McCann, P. 2011. Methodological note: Outcome indicators and targets–towards a performance oriented EU cohesion policy. European commission. Regional policy. Brussels. Accessed http://ec.europa.eu/regional_policy/sources/docgener/evaluation/performance_en.htm

Barca, F., McCann, P., and Rodrigues-Pose, A. 2012. "The case for regional development intervention: Place-based versus place-neutral approaches". *Journal of Regional Science*, 52: 134–152.

Barro, R. 1990. "Government spending in a simple model of endogenous growth". *Journal of Political Economy*, 98: 103–125.

Barro, R and Sala-i-Martin, X. 1995. *Economic growth.* Boston, MA: McGraw-Hill.

Bouayad-Agha, S., Turpin, N., and Vedrine, L. 2011. "Fostering the development of European regions: A spatial dynamic panel data analysis of the impact of cohesion policy". *Regional Studies*, 47: 1573–1593. doi:10.1080/00343404.2011.628930.

Barro, R and Sala-i-Martin, X. 1992. "Convergence". *Journal of Political Economy*, 100(2): 223–251.

Bernard, A and Jones, C. 1996. "Comparing apples to oranges: Productivity convergence and measurement across industries and countries". *American Economic Review*, 86(5): 1216–1238.

Best, M. eds. 1990. *The new competition: Institutions of industrial restructuring*. Cambridge: Policy Press.

Budd, L. 1998. "Territorial competition and globalization: Scylla and Charybdis of European cities". *Urban Studies*, 35(4): 663–685.

Button, K and Pentecost, E. 1995. "Testing for convergence of the EU regional economies". *Economic Inquiry*, 33(4): 664–671.

Camagni, R. 1992. "Development scenarios and policy guidelines for the lagging regions in the 90s". *Regional Studies*, 26(4): 361–374.

Carlino, G. 1979. "Increasing returns to scale in metropolitan manufacturing". *Journal of Regional Science*, 19: 363–373.

Carrington, A. 2003. "A divided Europe? Regional convergence and neighborhood spillover effects". *Kyklos*, 5(3): 381–394.

Ciccone, A. 2002. "Agglomeration effects in Europe". *European Economic Review*, 46: 213–227.

Combes, P. P and Overman, H. 2004. "The spatial distribution of economic activities in the European Union". In *Handbook of urban and regional economics*, eds. V. Henderson and J.-F. Thisse, 2845–2910. Amsterdam: North Holland.

Dunford, M. 1994. "Winners and losers: The new map of economic inequality in the European Union". *European Urban and Regional Studies*, 1(2): 95–114.

European Commission. 2010a. "Delivering smart, sustainable and inclusive growth". *Panorama Inforegio 36,* 2010/2011. Directorate-General for Regional Policy, Brussels: European Commission.

European Commission. 2010b. *Europe 2020: A European strategy for smart, sustainable and inclusive growth.* Luxembourg: Publications office of the European Union.

European Commission. 2011c. "The role of regional policy in the future of Europe". *Panorama Inforegio, Autumn 39.* Directorate–General for regional policy. Luxembourg: Publications office of the European Union.

European Commission. 2011d. "Investing in Europe's regions". *Panorama Inforegio, 40, Winter 2011/2012,* Directorate - General for regional policy, Publications office of the European Union, Luxembourg.

European Union. 2016. Eurostat regional yearbook 2016. Luxemburg: Eurostat. Accessed http://ec.europa.eu/eurostat/documents/3217494/7604195/KS-HA-16-001-EN-N.pdf/76c007e9-6c1d-435a-97f8-e5ea700aa149

Eurostat. 2017. Eurostat online database. Luxembourg: Eurostat. Accessed http://ec.europa.eu/eurostat

Fujita, M., Krugman, P., and Venables, A. J. 1999. *The spatial economy: Cities, regions and international trade*. Cambridge, MA: MIT Press.

Glaeser, E. L., Scheinkman, J., and A. Shleifer. 1995. "Economic growth in a cross-section of cities". *Journal of Monetary Economics*, 36: 117–143.

Geppert, K., Happich, M., and Stephan, A. 2005. *Regional disparities in the European Union: Convergence and agglomeration*. DIW Discussion paper 52.

Giannetti, M. 2002. "The effects of integration on regional disparities: Convergence, divergence or both?" *European Economic Review*, 46: 539–567.

Heckscher, E. 1919. 1991. "The effect of foreign trade on the distribution of income". In *Heckscher–Ohlin trade theory*, eds. H. Flam and M. Flanders, 43–69. Cambridge, MA: MIT Press.

Henderson, V. 1986. "Efficiency of resource usage and city size". *Journal of Urban Economics*, 19(1): 42–70.

Hirschmann, A., ed. 1958. *The strategy of economic development.* New Haven, CT: Yale University Press.

Krugman, P. 1991. "Increasing returns and economic geography". *Journal of Political Economy*, 99: 183–199.

Krugman, P. 1993. "First nature, second nature and metropolitan location". *Journal of Regional Science*, 33: 129–144.

Krugman, P and Venables, A. J. 1995. "Globalization and the inequality of nations". *Quarterly Journal of Economics*, 110: 857–880.

Limao, N and Venables, A. 2001. "Infrastructure, geographical disadvantage and transport costs". *World Bank Economic Review*, 15(3): 451–479.

Lopez-Bazo, E., Vaya, E., Mora, A., and Surinach, J. 1999. "Regional economic dynamics and convergence in the European Union". *Annals of Regional Science*, 33: 343–370.

Lucas, R. 1988. "On the mechanics of economic development". *Journal of Monetary Economics*, 22(1): 3–42.

Magrini, S. 1999. "The evolution of income dispersion among the regions of the European Union". *Regional Science and Urban Economics*, 29: 257–281.

Myrdal, G. 1957. *Economic theory and underdeveloped regions.* London: Duckworth.

Neven, D and Gouyette, C. 1995. "Regional convergence in the European Community". *Journal of Common Market Studies*, 33(1): 47–65.

Organization for Economic Cooperation and Development. 2005. *Building competitive regions: Strategies and governance.* Paris: OECD.

Ohlin, B., ed. 1933. *Interregional and international trade.* Cambridge, MA: Harvard University Press.

Puga, D. 2002. "European regional policy in the light of recent location theories". *Journal of Economic Geography*, 2(4): 373–406.

Romer, P. 1986. "Increasing returns and long-run growth". *Journal of Political Economy*, 94(5): 1002–1037.

Ruffin, R. 1999. "The nature and significance of intra-industry trade". *Economic and Financial Review*, 4: 1–8.

Samuelson, P. 1949. "International factor-price equalization once again". *Economic Journal*, 9: 181–197.

Solow, R. 1956. "A contribution to the theory of economic growth". *Quarterly Journal of Economics*, 70: 65–94.

Swan, T. 1956. "Economic growth and capital accumulation". *Economic Record*, 32: 334–361.

Terrasi, M. 1999. "Convergence and divergence across Italian regions". *Annals of Regional Science*, 33: 491–510.

Williamson, J. 1965. "Regional inequality and the process of national development: A description of the patterns". *Economic Development and Cultural Change*, 13(4): 3–45.

## FURTHER READING

Chapman, S., Cosci, S., and L. Mirra. 2012. "Income Dynamics in an enlarged Europe: The role of capital regions". *The Annals of Regional Science*, 45: 663–93.

Charron, N., Lapuente, V., and Dijkstra, L. 2012. *Regional governance matters: A study on regional variation in quality of government within the EU*. Brussels: European Commission Directorate-General for Regional Policy.

Davies, S and Hallet, M. 2002. *Interactions between National and Regional Development* HWWA Discussion paper no 207. Hamburg: Hamburg Institute of International Economics.

European Commission. 2010. *Investing in Europe: Fifth cohesion report on economic, social and territorial cohesion*. Brussels: European Commission Directorate-General for Regional Policy.

Fischer, M and Stirbock. C. 2006. "Pan-European regional income growth and club convergence: Insights from a spatial econometric perspective". *Annals of Regional Science*, 40: 693–721.

Kuznets, S. 1955. "Economic growth and income inequality". *American Economic Review*, 45: 1–28.

Niebuhr, A. 2006. "Market access and regional disparities: New economic geography in Europe". *Annals of Regional Science*, 40: 313–334.

OECD. 2011. *Regional Outlook 2011: Building resilient regions for stronger economies*. Paris: Organization for Economic Cooperation and Development.

## FURTHER QUESTIONS

1. What results does cohesion policy produce for regional disparities?
2. Which are the fundamental obstacles in EU regional policy implementation?
3. What is the principle of concentration?
4. What is the principle of additionality?
5. Should regional policy be interventionist or should it concentrate on creating a free common market removing internal barriers to trade and movement of people?
6. Which are the similarities and the differences between 2009- and 2013 and 2014 and 2020 regional policy periods in the EU?
7. How are cohesion funds distributed between countries and regions?
8. How does cohesion policy produce regional disparities in EU?

# *Chapter 11*

# The European External Trade Policy

Analyzing EU common commercial policy is crucial to any student of the world trade since EU accounts for almost one-fifth of the global trade flows. Despite the emergence of new trading powers, the repercussions of the financial and sovereign debt crisis in euro area, and persistent low economic growth rates, EU continues to hold economic supremacy in global trade.

Understanding the essence of EU policymaking in trade issues is also necessary since EU has been accused in the past for protectionism. The pursuit of the latter with its discriminatory policies against third states leads to the notion of a "fortress Europe" which may be at the expense of the stability of the global trading system. How EU trade policy evolved from 1960s onward?

The CU came into being in 1968 among the six original EU states and a CET was applied vis-à-vis non-member states. In the next 50 years, EU commercial policy developed further not only in membership (28 states) but also in content and scope (it includes measures affecting trade in services and many trade-related regulatory policies, such as intellectual property and technical standards).

Researchers analyzed several aspects of EU trade policy trying to uncover its basic traits and patterns (Gavin, 2001; Meunier, 2005). Which are the main traits of present EU external trade policy?

First, as in the single market analysis, negative integration (reduction of tariff and nontariff trade barriers) and positive integration (implementation of domestic policies and relevant institutions in order to overcome differences in regulation, technical standards, and taxes) are vital concepts. The former was realized through elimination of tariffs (according to the CET in EU more than 10,000 products are categorized at the eight-digit level of the combined nomenclature which sets the rates applicable to each product) and other border measures in intra-EU trade and thus the interest in the last decades was oriented toward intellectual property rights, technical standards, competition issues, labor standards, and environmental regulations. Thus, much effort is currently undertaken concerning positive integration policies.

Second, EU implements a highly complex and differentiated commercial policy vis-à-vis third states mainly through the granting of trade preferences. The system is realized despite diversified trade, strategic and foreign policy targets, as well as conflicting interests of EU member states.

Third, EU trade policy exerts a strong impact on the global trade flows through application of nontariff barriers. Until the 1990s the EU has made use of various NTBs especially import quotas and voluntary export restraints (other NTBs include quantitative restrictions, price controls and discretionary licensing). Further, EU applied in targeted sectors technical barriers obliging producers from non-EU states to change their products so as to comply with EU rules based on environmental, health, safety, or consumer protection reasons (i.e., noise and emission limits for cars, labeling requirements on tobacco products, specific energy consumption levels of household appliances).

Fourth, despite many peculiarities and exemptions, EU commercial policy balances its expanding commercial policy agenda and targets with its obligations under the WTO (which came into existence in 1995).

Currently, EC (2015) supports that EU trade policy should be based on three pillars namely effectiveness (EU trade policy should be results-oriented), transparency (CCP should enforce the legitimacy of the EU policy-making), and export of EU values to the world.

This chapter investigates all aforementioned themes in separate sections. Initially, the main tenets of regional economic integration are presented and soon after a thorough analysis of the content of EU external trade policy is undertaken. The concluding section considers the future development and challenges of the CCP.

## THE THEORY OF REGIONAL TRADE INTEGRATION

Regional economic integration is the main issue in international economics in the last 60 years (Balassa, 1962; Pelkmans, 2006; Baldwin, 2008; Ornelas, 2005a; Ornelas, 2005b). There seems to be a consensus that the priority of regional economic agreements irrespective of their content and form is to create favorable terms for the trade and flows of factors of production among the states involved (Kemp-Wan, 1976; Corden, 1976; Michalopolous and Tarr, 1997; Panagariya and Findlay, 1996; Panagariya, 2000).

More specifically, usual motives for the establishment of regional economic agreements are establishment of new markets for goods and services, enforcement of investment flows, improvement of the protection of investments, elimination of trade barriers, enforcement of procedures for faster and cheaper trade, economies of scale and scope (Krugman, 1995), improvements in transborder synergies in all value added stages and efficiency in use of production factors.

The main types of regional integration agreements are the following:

a. Preferential trade agreements—when tariffs between the participating states of the agreement are reduced for specific goods or services, sometimes unilaterally but there is no general reduction of tariff barriers and no application of a CET.
b. Free trade areas—when participating states of the agreement reduce internal tariffs among them without the application of a CET regime.
c. Custom unions—when states not only abolish tariffs on trade among them but apply a CET relative to non-participating states of the agreement.
d. Common markets—when states apply in addition to a CET regime, the free movement of factors of production.
e. Economic and monetary/political union—in the former type, additionally to the common market provisions, integration includes the adoption of a common currency and common rules on monetary issues for the participating states (monetary union). In the latter there is a federal budget and a federal-supranational decision-making mechanism on economic issues which applies binding decisions for all participating states.

Traditional economic theory underlines two fundamental questions relating to a free trade area or a CU. The first concerns the welfare impact on each participating state and the area as a whole and the second is related to trade diversion at the detriment of non-union states.

Viner (1950), Meade (1955), Balassa (1967), and Lipsey (1957) have studied the results of joining regional trade agreements at both issues underlining the difference between the free trade area and a CU, while important theoretical and empirical contributions have also been made by Mundell (1964) and Corden (1976).

Robson (1987) underlines the benefits to resource use derived by the movement of goods and factors of production and the elimination of discrimination among participating states in an economic integration agreement, while Molle (1990) focuses on the successive stages of economic integration projects which lead to the coordination of national policies in all economic sectors of the participating countries.

El-Agraa (1994) refers to economic integration as the discriminatory removal of all trade obstacles between states and the establishment of certain elements of cooperation and coordination between them considering the following key motivations for economic integration:

a. Enhanced production efficiency made possible by increased specialization.
b. Increased production levels due to better exploitation of economies of scale and scope realized through the increased size of the market.
c. An improved international bargaining position because of the larger size, leading to better terms of trade.
d. Enforced efficiency brought about by intensified competition between companies.
e. Changes and technological advances affecting the amount and quality of the factors of production.

At the institutional level, WTO framework gives green light to regional agreements under the condition (article XXIV of WTO) that trade obstacles do not raise after integration against third states, tariffs and nontariff obstacles are limited in all trade conducted within the regional agreement area, and of course that the regional agreement effort is notified and approved by the WTO.

In this way, free trade agreements provide privileged market access to the involved states in a regional agreement despite the clauses of MFN (according to MFN principle all WTO countries should receive from any WTO member the same trade preferences accorded to the partner state that receives the best most-favored treatment) and national treatment of WTO.

However, MFN exceptions also hold in other cases as when states increase tariffs temporarily because of injury to an import-competing industry (GATT, article XIX) or when tariffs are implemented to offset import prices that are considered too low (GATT, article VI on antidumping). Indeed, dumping practices discriminate prices and lead to different prices in separate geographical markets so as to allow companies to export at very low prices, to earn market shares abroad, and to minimize competition.

When dumping is taking place antidumping measures are applied within the framework of WTO, especially if dumping "causes or threatens material injury to an established industry . . . or materially retards the establishment of a domestic industry." Additionally, export subsidies, are often applied in agricultural products trade (i.e., dairy products, sugar) and in the same manner WTO allows countervailing action against exports which (based on subsidies) cause or threaten to cause material injury to a domestic industry.

## WHEN REGIONAL INTEGRATION OCCURS, WHICH ARE THE KEY RESULTS FOR CONSUMERS, PRODUCERS, AND GOVERNMENTS?

Jacob Viner (1950) analyzed the static effects of CU creation (trade creation and trade diversion effect) highlighting that regional trade agreements do not necessarily result in benefits to participating states (i.e., if consumer prices and consumer surplus are too small to counterbalance the inefficiency costs) and thus under specific terms trade blocs might create losses in welfare.

In trade creation, domestic production is replaced by lower cost imports from a partner state. In trade diversion lower cost imports from the non-partner states are replaced by more expensive imports from a partner country.

In any case, one should have in mind that long-term trade diversion leads to national vested interests and opposition to trade liberalization. Inefficient companies favor preferential tariffs to the detriment of consumer welfare, avoid competition from the global market, and thus have negative effects for global trade (Grossman and Helpman, 1995; Limao, 2007). If trade diversion leads to imports into the domestic market that limits market distortions and increases consumers' options and welfare, if economies of scale lead to lower cost production (Corden, 1972) and if new competition limits the dominant position of domestic monopolies, there are positive trade results (Meade, 1955).

Balassa also (1962) analyzed thoroughly the dynamic effects of CU creation. Usually, an enlarged market increases competition pressure and companies fight fiercely to be efficient so as to gain a new market share. This presupposes realization of economies of scale and thus investment in specialized equipment. Investment inflows are facilitated from global investors in the most productive activities and technological innovations through R&D activity are realized.

Kemp and Wan (1976) further argued that if external tariffs are adjusted so that the establishment of a CU does not influence trade flows and patterns with non-custom union states, the CU is welfare-improving.

Which are the welfare effects of trade diversion when joining, for example, a CU? They are presented in figure 11.1. In the point E there is an equilibrium level (autarky) of domestic supply S and demand D for a good/service.

Before a state joining a CU it applied a common tariff on all imports of a product/service and bought from a low cost state at price P2, tariff included. After participation in a CU the state takes advantage from tariff-free imports from other states of the CU at price P1. Thus, it gains consumer surplus of (a+b+c+d) but its producers lose the producer surplus of a. The loss of governmental tariff revenue from non-CU low cost states is (c+e).

There will be a net loss from trade diversion in joining the CU if (b+d) which is the net benefit in consumer surplus is less than e (the loss of tariff revenue from non-CU low cost state). The positive welfare effect of CU accession for a state which is equal to the areas b and d is called trade creation effect (or Harberger triangle, see Harberger, 1954). A net benefit from trade diversion would be realized if (b+d) is greater than e. Conclusively, if the trade creation effect is larger than trade diversion effect the state should join the CU.

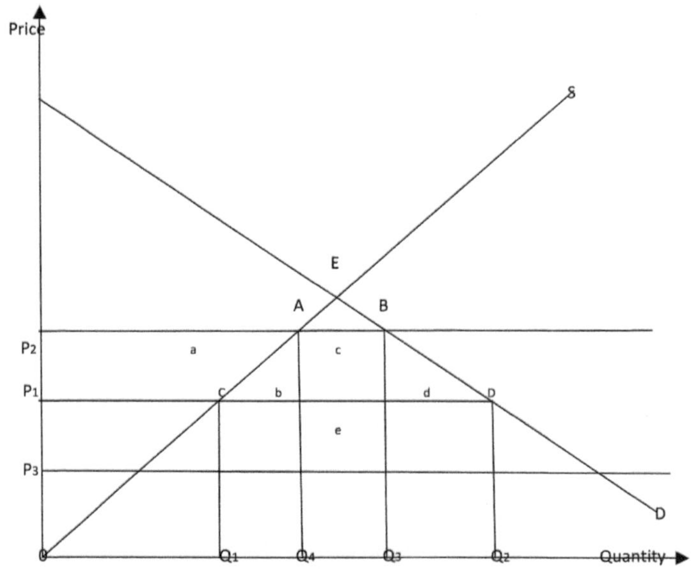


**Figure 11.1 The effects of joining a customs union.**

In any case, one should always have in mind that regional integration reshuffles wage differentials across industries and sectors and if not faced by proper income mechanisms it could raise regional inequalities between regions of the states participating in regional agreements.

## THE EU DECISION-MAKING RULES ON EXTERNAL TRADE POLICY

The Lisbon Treaty sets the common trade policy in the framework of the EU's external action (article 207 TFEU) as following, "The common commercial policy shall be based on uniform principles, particularly with regard to changes in tariff rates, the conclusion of tariff and trade agreements relating to trade in goods and services, and the commercial aspects of intellectual property, foreign direct investment, the achievement of uniformity in measures of liberalization, export policy and measures to protect trade such as those to be taken in the event of dumping or subsidies. The common commercial policy shall be conducted in the context of the principles and objectives of the Union's external action."

Trade policy is one of the exclusive powers of the EU and thus the EC negotiates with non-EU states and organizations on behalf of the whole EU closely cooperated with the European Council and European parliament who approve the agreements. The target of each agreement varies according to the participating states (i.e., reciprocal market opening in free trade agreements and development priorities in EPAs with ACP). Which is the process for the conclusion of international trade agreements in EU?

Initially, the Commission undertakes a public consultation on the provisions and options for a free trade agreement and performs an assessment of the impact of any agreement on the EU as a whole and on member states (article 294 TFEU). This early phase activity includes an informal dialogue with the state concerned on the main pillars and topics of a future negotiation (the so-called scoping exercise).

The economic analysis that is realized by the chief economist team in DG Trade and independent advisors (financed from the EC) leads to specific reports and studies on the provisions of the agreement. The assessment takes the form of an impact assessment study at the initial design stage, a sustainability impact assessment study during the trade negotiations, and an ex-post evaluation after application.

Then, the Commission needs a formal authorization (negotiating directives) from the Council to start negotiations. The Council also designates a special committee in consultation with which the negotiations must be conducted. Soon after the adoption of the negotiating directives, the Commission is given permission to start the negotiations (article 218 TFEU).

After intense and lengthy negotiations, the Commission delivers its final proposal and the Council decides on the conclusion of the agreement. This final stage presupposes an exhaustive screening of the legal texts. The EU presidency designates a person to sign on behalf of the EU. If the agreement includes provisions that fall under EU countries responsibility (mixed agreements), EU states also have to ratify the agreement according to their national rules. Following signature, the agreement is delivered to EP for consent. The committee for international trade examines the agreement and the parliament votes in a plenary session.

According to the provisions of article 291 (TFEU), "Member states shall adopt all measures of national law necessary to implement legally binding Union acts." Following consent of the EP and ratification by EU countries, the Council adopts the final decision to conclude the agreement and the latter is published in the official journal of EU.

The Lisbon Treaty improved EU's power significantly, since trade in cultural/audiovisual, educational, and social/health services, as well as foreign direct investment, are considered EU issues. Although qualified majority voting is the general rule in Council for trade policy, unanimity is required when provisions of an agreement on cultural/audiovisual services risk prejudicing EU's cultural and linguistic diversity or when provisions of an agreement on social, educational, or health services risk disturbing the national organization of these services and rendering difficult the ability of states to deliver them.

Conclusively, the Lisbon Treaty enforced the responsibilities of EP as co-legislator with the Council on trade matters and strengthened its powers since the main issues of EU trade legislation (antidumping, trade preferences) must follow the ordinary legislative procedure before being adopted by the Council. Moreover, the Commission is obliged to transmit relevant documents and report on this to the EP.

## THE INTERNATIONAL TRADE POSITION OF EU

The EU-28 accounts for around 15.1% of the world's trade in goods and for 22.6% of the world trade in services (European Commission, Trade statistical guide, June 2017). The shares for the other two significant trade powers are 14.4% (share in goods) and 17% (share in services) for USA and 14.8% (share in goods) but only 9% (share in services) for China. The value of international trade in goods (imports plus exports) significantly exceeds that of services (by about 3.5 times), reflecting the nature of some services which makes them harder to trade across borders.

Analyzing the trade positions of the dominant economic partners it becomes evident that the EU-28, China, and the USA have been the three largest global players for international trade since 2004 when China surpassed Japan (in 2016 the shares in world trade of both goods and services were 16.8% for EU, 15% for USA and 13.4% for China). More specifically, EU-28 international trade in goods with the rest of the world (the sum of extra-EU exports and imports) was 3453.5 billion euros in 2016 and the EU-28's trade surplus increased to 36.9 billion euros in 2016 (European Commission, Trade statistical guide, June 2017).

Germany was by far the largest member country in relation to extra-EU-28 trade in 2016 (the largest extra-EU-28 trade surplus in goods was also achieved by Germany) followed by significant export economies namely the UK, France, and Italy. The UK, the Netherlands, France, and Italy also accounted for a great share of imports of goods from non-member states in 2016.

Trade in goods between EU member states (intra-EU trade) is also enforced which demonstrates the impact of European integration forces on the productive/commercial networks of EU member states, although the share of total trade in goods that was accounted for by intra-EU and extra-EU flows is highly differentiated across the EU countries, mirroring historical ties and geographical location (intra-EU-28 trade increased by 4.7% across the EU-28 between 2014 and 2015 and the highest shares of intra-EU trade were achieved in Luxembourg, Estonia, Hungary, the Czech Republic, and Slovakia).

Between 2005 and 2015, the development of EU-28's exports of goods by major trading partner varied considerably. Among the main trading partners, the highest growth rate was recorded for exports to China which more than tripled, while exports to South Korea and Brazil more than doubled. Exports to Japan and Russian Federation grew more slowly and were approximately 30% higher in 2015 than they had been in 2005.

The USA is the key destination for goods exported from the EU-28 (2016), although the share of EU-28 exports to USA was reduced from 28.0% in 2002 to 20.8% by 2016. China is the second important market for EU-28 exports in 2016 (9.7% of the EU-28 total) and Switzerland the third one (8.2%) followed by Russian Federation (4.1%), Japan (3.3%), and Norway (2.8%). The same aforementioned states account for 56.4% of total imports to EU-28 (China alone for 20.2%) in 2016.

A brief sectoral analysis demonstrates that between 2010 and 2016, the highest growth rate for exports in EU was reported for food, beverages, and tobacco. The imports of these products also increased strongly but this growth was surpassed by chemicals and related products as well as machinery and transport equipment. The largest trade deficit in 2016 was recorded for mineral fuels and lubricant and related products (European Commission, Trade statistical guide, June 2017).

Concerning services the strongest growth in EU exports is recorded in transport, travel, financial services, telecommunication, computer and information services, charges for the use of intellectual property rights and other business services and the same holds true for the strongest growth in imports in services (2016). Overall, it becomes evident that EU trade policy should enforce its export shares in medium and high value added activities and it should enforce its position in international production/commercial networks.

## THE EU NETWORK OF TRADE AGREEMENTS

The EU is negotiating trade agreements with many states and regional organizations both bilaterally and multilaterally. It should be noted that evolving issues in trade (i.e., in the sector of services) make too often the negotiation process very complex and highly diversified. As a result, the EU's trade agreements are heterogeneous, mirroring the peculiarities of trading partners' economies. The main issues that are regulated through EU trade agreements are access to EU market, development assistance (EEC's association policy in part IV of the initial 1957 Treaty of Rome), and development cooperation according to "aid for trade" principles (Hynes and Holden, 2016).

Taking into account the new issue areas (i.e., intellectual property rights and FDI linkages with commercial issues, TBTs, public procurement) the Lisbon Treaty enhanced EU competences keeping national ratification as obligatory in the case that a trade agreement has a strong influence on issue areas which are exclusive competences of EU states.

The key categories of EU trade agreements are the following:

a. FTAs which put in place a free trade area in goods and services between EU and other states implementing low or no tariffs (i.e., with South Korea).
b. DCFTAs agreements which include many provisions and technical annexes on trade issues permitting access to the EU's market and vice versa (i.e., with Canada), reduce obstacles to trade in services, ameliorate access for firms, and are often part of an Association Agreement (i.e., Stabilization and Association agreements with Serbia and Albania). The DCFTAs are comprehensive (usually they cover all EU policies and competences), include most issues of the four EU freedoms (goods, services, and capital but often not persons) and provide detailed institutional provisions.
c. EPAs concern the free trade area framework between the EU and ACP and focus on market access to EU and on regional integration. The EU has also developed a complex framework of preferential trade agreements including members of the Cotonou (formerly the Lomé) agreement, the middle income and poor countries that take advantage of the GSP, and countries which are members of the WTO and receive the MFN treatment.
d. BITs or IAs which set out the terms for investments by physical and legal persons between the EU and third states.
e. CUs agreements which put in place a CET for non-CU states and remove trade obstacles between union countries (i.e., with San Marino and Andorra or the CU with Turkey).

## THE EU TRADE RELATIONS WITH DEVELOPING COUNTRIES

EU development policy faced successfully from the 1960s the challenge to provide the newly independent African states with stable trade links to EU. The Yaoundé Convention (1963) provided all associated countries with specific rights as far as it concerned national infant industries, trade relations with EEC, and local production financing (Frisch, 2016).

Soon after the UK's accession to the EEC (1973) it became necessary for EEC to follow similar regulatory patterns with the Commonwealth countries which forwarded Lomé I Convention between the EEC and the 46 ACP Group of countries putting in place internal price support mechanisms for many products (i.e., bananas, beef, rum, and sugar), important unilateral trade preferences, and development finance (Hurt, 2009).

The dynamics of trade relations with third world countries led, 30 years later, to the reformation of the Lomé agreements (Cotonou Agreement in 2000) taking into account 3 key development principles, namely, sustainability of economic and social development policies, integration of developing countries into the world economic network, and reduction of poverty. Finally, since 2007 European Partnership Agreements (EPAs) are in place (Burtels, 2007; Hulse, 2016).

The current EU GSP grants to developing countries access to EU market is governed by regulation (EU) no. 978/2012 of the European Parliament and the Council of October 25, 2012 (GSP regulation which entered into force on January 1, 2014) and is compatible with W law and the "enabling clause" (it permits an exception to the WTO's MFN principle).

The system concentrates preferences on poor developing countries and excludes states that are beneficiaries of another preferential access to the EU (i.e., a free trade agreement or a special trade regime), developing states which are considered as a high or upper-middle income per capita economies during three consecutive years (World Bank classification), and overseas countries and territories which are beneficiaries of an EU market access arrangement or are associated to another developed state.

Among the advantages of GSP system is the linkage between the trade incentives and full respect of human and labor rights, environmental protection and good governance standards, the better implementation of the trade concessions for LDC through the "Everything But Arms" terms, the effectiveness of resources allocation to fewer beneficiaries (from 177 states to 88 states), the increased transparency and stability of the GSP provisions through clearer and better-defined objective criteria, and the extended expiration date (from 3 to 10 years). Further, the system promotes sensitive and non-sensitive product distinction in the method for calculating tariff rates.

Currently (2017), three arrangements of the GSP framework are in place:

a. The standard/general GSP arrangement which provides tariff reductions to poorer developing states (which do not benefit from other preferential trade access to the EU market) through partial or entire removal of tariffs on two-thirds of all product categories (30 standard beneficiaries).
b. The special incentive arrangement for sustainable development and good governance (GSP+) which grants preferences (no tariffs) to 8 countries with low economic and trade diversification, providing that those countries

implement 27 international conventions and the derived reporting and monitoring provisions (annex VIII of the GSP Regulation) in the areas of good governance, environment, human, and labor rights (the EU monitoring process led by the EC will last until December 31, 2023).

c. The EBA arrangement for LDC (classification according to the United Nations) which grants duty-free quota-free access to all products, except for arms and ammunitions (49 states).

Although the GSP does not give a solution to long-term macroeconomic and trade problems of developing countries it provides a framework for better access of their products in EU. Indeed, according to 2014 data, imports of 50.83 billion euros have been treated under the GSP framework namely 27.3 billion euros of imports from states under the Standard GSP, around 6.5 billion euros of imports from GSP+ states, and almost 17 billion euros of imports from EBA beneficiaries.

## The European Neighborhood Policy

ENP governs, since 2003, EU's relations with 16 of the EU's neighbors, namely, Algeria, Egypt, Israel, Jordan, Lebanon, Libya, Morocco, Palestine, Syria, Tunisia, Armenia, Azerbaijan, Belarus, Georgia, Moldova, and Ukraine. Russian Federation is not a part of the ENP but participates actively in cross-border cooperation activities within ENP framework.

The targets of ENP are enhancement of prosperity, stability, and security of all participants taking into account the values of democracy, rule of law, and respect of human rights. The ENP was reviewed initially in 2011 and a further review took place following the Joint Communication of partner states published on November 18, 2015.

The reformed ENP underlines the need for application of a differentiated approach to EU neighbors taking into consideration their priorities and interests and the need for increased ownership by partner states. In addition to the aforementioned targets of the initial ENP, it prioritizes cooperation on economic development for stabilization, on the security, on migration and on mobility issues. Further, the ENP enforces civil society organizations engagement in reforms and it raises domestic ownership of the ENP programmes.

The new ENI (15.4 billion euros for the years 2014–2020) is the financial tool of ENP and thus the main source of funding to the 16 ENP partner states. The bilateral ENP action plans (priorities for cooperation) mutually agreed between the EU and each partner state. In addition to bilateral cooperation, ENI funding also provides resources for regional and cross-border cooperation programmes.

## The Southern Neighborhood Policy

The Southern Neighborhood (SN) concerns EU cooperation with Algeria, Egypt, Israel, Jordan, Lebanon, Libya, Morocco, Palestine, Syria, and Tunisia within ENP. Especially important for the SN is the cross-border cooperation which aims at economic and social development in border regions, accommodation of key common issues (environment, public health, safety, and security) and better mobility for goods, people, and capital. Considerable funding is realized for these countries through the ENI (7.5 to 9.2 billion euros for the years 2014–2020).

## The Eastern Partnership

The Eastern Partnership was launched in May 2009 (Prague Summit) acting as the Eastern dimension of the ENP. The main targets are the deepening and strengthening of links between the EU and Armenia, Azerbaijan, Belarus, Georgia, Moldova, Ukraine, based on liberty, democracy, respect for human rights, and the rule of law. The bilateral dimension of eastern partnership favors political and socioeconomic reforms in partner states so as to achieve more economic integration with the EU, to enhance sector cooperation and to ameliorate mobility of citizens.

For each partnership state there is a multi-annual programming document, complementary support for the application of accords with the EU, and additional assistance as an incentive for significant progress in building deep and sustainable democracy (the "umbrella" programme).

The multilateral dimension of the programme includes thematic platforms to exchange best practices on areas of common interest such as good governance, development and economic integration, energy, security and transport, environment, border management. Regional cooperation programmes provide crucial aid for the application of the Eastern Partnership multilateral dimension and are analyzed in the regional east programming document.

The eastern partnership states are also beneficiaries of programmes open to all neighbor states (i.e., Erasmus+, SIGMA, and the Neighborhood Investment Facility), and to cross-border cooperation programmes. As in ENP, the ENI is the main source of funding EU for cooperation with the Eastern Partnership states from the years 2014 to 2020.

## The Comprehensive Economic and Trade Agreement (CETA)

Total trade in goods between Canada and the EU was 64 billion euros in 2015, (Canada was the EU's 11th most important trade partner and the EU is Canada's 2nd most important trade partner). Trade in services (i.e., transport, insurance, and communication services) between the two regions reached 27.9 billion euros in 2014 and FDI flows followed an upward trend (EU foreign investment in Canada reached 274.7 euros and Canada was the third largest investor in the EU). Thus, there is a strong potential in bilateral economic relations which fuels the necessity for further bilateral integration.

EU-Canada negotiations for a CETA were launched in May 2009, were concluded at the EU-Canada Summit on September 26, 2014, and finally led to signature of the agreement on October 30, 2016.

The CETA is comprised of 30 chapters (1598 pages) followed by detailed annexes (the number of the annex points the chapter it refers to). Additionally, there are three protocols (rules of origin, mutual acceptance of conformity assessments, and mutual recognition of compliance for good manufacturing practices for pharmaceuticals) and three annexes on reservations (annex I has the reservations for existing measures and liberalization commitments, annex II contains the reservations for future measures, and annex III refers to issues in financial services).

Reservations in annex 1 are liable to standstill (no restrictions other than those included in the reservation can be implemented in the future) and ratchet effects (future liberalization measures cannot be taken back). The transparency-related provisions of CETA demand advance publication and notice for all unilateral proposed measures. However, many of the transparency provisions within CETA are to be operationalized by specialized committees.

The CETA intends to abolish customs duties (98.6% of goods will be tariff-free in bilateral trade within three, five, or seven years although restrictions remain on the trade of certain agricultural products such as poultry and eggs), to abolish restrictions on access to public contracts (EU and Canadian firms have the right to bid for public procurement contracts not only at federal but also at provincial governments), to limit obstacles to services market (almost half of the EU's economic benefits from CETA is expected to derive from trade in services in areas like specialized maritime services, environmental services, telecoms and finance), to promote protection of specific traditional food and drink products (known as geographical indications) from being copied, and to ameliorate investment terms in both regions (investors are treated in a nondiscriminatory manner).

Equally important, CETA enforces copyright protection by bringing Canada's rules in line with EU legislation for new technologies and digital rights, it ameliorates protection of patents for EU pharmaceutical products and it enforces border measures against counterfeit trademark and geographical indication goods as well as pirated copyright goods (in intellectual property the agreement enhances protection and extends market exclusivity for pharmaceuticals).

CETA also puts in place a dispute settlement mechanism (the three-person tribunal empowered to resolve disputes concerning investments can be subjected to review by an appellate body).

Thus, an innovation of the treaty is the operation of the ICS—a public court system with professional and independent judges appointed by the EU and Canada which works in a transparent way for the protection of investments. However, critics argue that investment provisions would allow firms to sue governments in special tribunals outside the domestic legal system, if they considered negatively affected by public policy actions. A voluntary regulatory cooperation forum will also operate within the CETA, facilitating exchange of information and best practice between the regulators.

CETA targets the services sector and intends to put in place a more open trade by lowering NTBs. EU has agreed to open up its services markets using a "negative list" meaning liberalization of all service markets except those explicitly excluded. The negative list approach means that if there is no reservation from the involved states, trade and investment are liberalized, and market access, national treatment, and MFN status are given to enterprises and investors of EU and Canada.

CETA also introduces changes in rules governing intellectual property, particularly in pharmaceuticals concerning patent restoration (the period of market exclusivity granted to new drugs), and patent appeal (the process for allowing generic drugs to enter the market) prolonging the period of protection granted to a patent holder. Exclusions include audiovisual and other cultural services as well as services supplied in the exercise of governmental authority, dairy and beef industries, health care, public education, purification, and distribution of water and other social services.

The national treatment clause of the agreement (each party shall accord to service suppliers and services of the other party treatment no less favorable than that it accords, in like situations, to its own service suppliers and services) focuses on better terms for trade without distortions and governmental interventions.

Further, CETA permits the mutual recognition of some qualifications and supports labor and environmental principles. Thus, under specific terms, it will become easier for EU professionals to temporarily provide legal, accounting, and architectural services.

The agreement is expected to make competition more effective since it puts an end to expensive and time consuming double testing is some areas, it facilitates exchange of specialized personnel for after-sales and related services support for equipment, machinery, and software between the two regions, and of course companies obtain the ability to bid for the provision of goods and services at federal, provincial, and municipal level.

In the agricultural sector exports are expected to rise for EU in wines and spirits, fruit, and vegetables and processed products and fishing. However, Canada agreed to protect 143 geographical indications (distinctive food and drink products from specific towns or regions in the EU like Roquefort and Dutch Gouda cheese). Additionally, limited quotas will apply for sensitive products such as beef, pork, and sweet corn for the EU and dairy products for Canada.

According to CETA provisions, conformity assessment certificates will be harmonized concerning testing products as far as it concerns electrical goods, electronic and radio equipment, toys, machinery, and measuring equipment.

Lastly, chapters 22, 23, and 24 of CETA include provisions on trade and sustainable development, trade and labor, and trade and environment. Indeed, CETA recognizes multilateral labor agreements (i.e., the 1998 International Labor Organization declaration on fundamental principles and rights at work) and thus it gives particular attention to the freedom of association, the right to collective bargaining, the elimination of forced or compulsory labor, the abolition of child labor, and the elimination of discrimination in employment and occupation.

Research on CETA impact predicts small, but positive, results. Tariff reductions could increase merchandize exports for Canada by about 1.4 billion US dollars by 2022 (Chu and Goldfarb, 2015). Cameron and Loukine (2001), suggested that merchandize exports could increase by 11% but GDP will rise by only 0.04% for Canada while a research of the Government of Canada and the EC predicted a rise in GDP of 0.8% for Canada.

An updated study of the Canadian parliamentary budget office (2017) titled "The Canada - EU comprehensive and trade agreement: a prospective analysis" projects an overall effect of about 0.4% of GDP on Canada's economy (the combined effect on Canada's GDP will be about 7.9 billion US dollars rather small for a 2 trillion US dollars economy) and investment. For the EU, the greatest benefits will occur in exports of textiles and apparel (in textiles, apparel, and footwear the estimated increase is for Canadian exports 84.9% and for the EU exports 98.6%), transport equipment (automobiles), and food and beverages. CETA's provisions on the extension of patent protection on pharmaceuticals will add small but positive income from royalty and dividend payments.

On the other hand, analysts argue that trade diversion will occur and thus Canada's exports to the USA will fall by 1.4 billion dollars (relative to 2015), to Mexico by about 0.7% (30 million dollars in 2015) and fall in Canadian exports to the rest of the world will be almost 0.7% (310 million dollars in 2015).

## The Transatlantic Trade and Investment Partnership

TTIP is not just an agreement on the elimination of tariff and NTBs in bilateral trade between USA and EU but it is an agreement which focuses on regulations and standards in trade and thus will influence heavily the pattern and content of bilateral trade in the long term. Moreover, due to the size of the involved parties it will have an impact not just on trade creation and trade diversion on the third states but also on WTO negotiations on trade liberalization (if USA and EU adopt measures in specific sectors no third country can ignore them) and of course on other mega trade bloc initiatives in the Asia-Pacific and in Latin America regions. TTIP will also be a dynamic and not static agreement since it will have specific institutional mechanisms to supervise the provisions of the agreement and to maximize negotiations potential.

TTIP region provides almost half of world GDP and thus it cannot be ignored either as supply or as a demand engine. The two regions (EU and USA) are highly integrated in terms of trade and investment through multiple trade and production networks and through significant and long-term FDI flows. Intra-company transfers within the Euro-Atlantic area are continuously intensified.

The 1990 Transatlantic Declaration (1990) and the New Transatlantic Agenda (1995) paved the way for negotiations almost two decades prior to the official launching. The TTIP between the EU and the USA is under negotiation since July 2013 when the USA and the EU started official negotiations with the conviction that an agreement will reap significant benefits for both of them. A report of the high-level working group on jobs and growth was published in February 2013 and in March 2013 and the EC defined the guidelines for the negotiation to the EU countries and published the impact assessment of an agreement between EU and USA as well as the results of a thorough study on the results of the agreement in several economic issue areas. Several rounds of negotiations took place after the 2013 (the 1st round in Washington, on July 7–12, 2013 and the 15th round in New York on October 3–7, 2016).

Until October 2017 the final agreement was predicted to include 24 chapters and was categorized in 4 parts, namely, market access, regulatory cooperation, rules, and institutional issues. The two parties (USA and EU) continuously update their positions in the negotiations and provide from time to time textual proposals for legal topics and position papers with information on the main goals of both EU and USA.

As far as it concerns the first category of issues in negotiations (market access) one observes that the two parties face significant obstacles in reaching a compromise and thus an agreement. Although average tariffs between the EU and the USA are under 2% in most products, one should have in mind that there are certain categories of products where the tariff percentages remain high (i.e., clothes and shoes, tobacco, peanuts, train carriages). Thus, there is still room for further elimination and reduction in levels of tariffs as well as for elimination of lengthy administrative checks.

Liberalization will also occur in public contracts under specific terms which are expected to constrain government spending and to provide transparent and nondiscriminatory rules permitting EU and US companies to take part in public tenders at central/sub-central, federal, or sub-federal level as in CETA.

Negotiations in the first part (market access) also include the services sector and diverse issues such as a fair and common playing level field, ownership percentages in firms by US and EU citizens, better access in protected activities (i.e., telecommunications), mobility of labor force (i.e., architects, engineers), mutual recognition of professional qualifications, licensing and approvals to offer services (auditing), liberalization in postal and courier services, maritime transport. On the other hand, protection will remain in selected activities such as TV, radio and films, public health, and water distribution.

Taking also into consideration that the EU and USA are the biggest financial markets, that financial services include multiple activities (i.e., insurance and banking) and that there is a strong potential for further integration in the field, it is predicted that TTIP will have a major impact on bilateral flows of the involved parties.

The rules of origin are crucial in regional trade agreements since they determine when a product can be produced in the states which are parties to an agreement and thus that only products associated to those states can take advantage of not paying customs duties. There is a volition of US and EU negotiators to determine common rules on what is needed to prove a product's origin meaning simpler rules of origin that can be easily followed by EU and US producers, rules that limit fraud, and rules that face time consuming border obstacles.

As already mentioned, differences in regulatory frameworks and the technical standards approaches do have major impact on health, food safety and quality, consumer safety, production standards, labor standards, investor state dispute settlement procedures, and on firms costs (i.e., the need for inspection of inputs, tests over processes). Regulatory arbitrage leads firms to prefer locations with a lower level of regulation (Roubini and Mihm, 2011).

TTIP pursues compatibility of regulatory frameworks through harmonization of the tests and standards for products, through recognition of equivalence, or through mutual recognition. Generally, taking into account that EU-US trade tariffs are very low (on average less than 3% for manufactures), nontariff obstacles and regulatory issues become crucial when assessing TTIP impact. Thus, enforcing the compatibility of regulatory regimes between the EU and the USA proves vital for legitimizing TTIP.

The second part of a potential agreement includes general and sectoral issues. Among them, TBTs exert a strong impact on most products/services and usually take the form of technical requirements and voluntary standards that set specific features of a product (i.e., safety of products, energy efficiency of domestic appliances, labeling, marking and packaging of a product, product testing).

Technical barriers further include price control mechanisms, licenses, distribution restrictions, various types of indirect subsidies to targeted value added stages in production, antidumping and countervailing duties, border measures, sanitary and phyto-sanitary measures, and restrictions on foreign ownership linked with market access.

In the case that a product does not comply with the standards it cannot be exported as it is considered unsafe for human health and safety, animal and plant life, or the environment. Concerning technical standards, "In the US system, in the event that a relevant standard is not available, no transparent process is foreseen to connect the development of future standards and the regulatory work . . . Even more critically . . . EU legislation refers to international standards, such as ISO and IEC, and corresponding US legislation refers instead to domestically developed standards by standard developing organizations claiming to be international" (Alemanno, 2014). TTIP targets the elimination of duplicative or burdensome processes for checking products, improvement of cooperation between EU and US standardization bodies on new standards, and transparency in the system on standards.

Especially for sanitary and phyto-sanitary issues, the negotiations focus on the elimination of duplication of checks on products, on the establishment of common procedures and decisions on regulations, on a single approval process for exports from all EU states, and on the application of more transparent processes.

Turning to the specific sectors, agro-food activities (primary agricultural sector and the processed food sector) is important both in EU (in 2013 it had a turnover over which exceeded one trillion euros) and in USA. Equally important, a key percentage of EU's production is exported to USA (i.e., spirits, wine, and beer) while EU imports oilseed and soybeans, nuts, and spirits from USA. Average EU tariffs are high on imported goods in the sector and range from 2.8 to 66.4%. However, the main trade problem continues to be the NTBs (i.e., the USA applies barriers on EU milk products and US approval process for plants, fruit and vegetables from the EU are time consuming).

The chemicals sector (it includes petrochemicals, polymers, basic inorganic chemicals, specialty chemicals, and consumer chemicals) is a very significant activity both in USA and EU (more than 25% of EU production is exported) but it is restricted by nontariff barrier measures (i.e., differences in clinical trials and labeling requirements) applied by USA and EU. Thus, if the agreement succeeds to eliminate these obstacles more time and resources will be available on safety and research-development benefiting the consumers in both regions.

The mechanical engineering products are also a major exporting activity for EU economy. However, EU companies have to address not only US tariffs up to 8% but also NTBs in standards and tests and in public procurement. The same holds true for the electrical and electronic goods sector where EU companies face obstacles due to product standards, strict testing rules on import products.

The motor vehicle sector (motor vehicles, including parts and components) holds a significant part of the transatlantic trade and will benefit from elimination of NTBs (i.e., differences in safety, emission and fuel efficiency regulations, differences in safety regulation). Concerning transport sector major benefits will derive not only from better terms on freight transport and the transportation of passengers but also indirectly due to increased trade in other sectors.

Engineering goods (i.e., plugs, mobile phones, and tractors) are a key category for US-EU trade and provide work for many employees in both regions. As in other categories of consumer products there is a need for conformity in technical regulations, standards and procedures, on safety standards.

Rigid rules in medical devices mean high costs for the companies although the problem is too often the duplication of tests which delays production and trade. There is a pressure on negotiators to agree that national systems for identifying and tracing medical devices follow the international unique device identification system and to harmonize forms for new medical devices approved.

The negotiations on pesticides take into consideration the volition of EU to keep the existing regulatory standards and the provisions of the plant protections products regulation (1107/2009) while negotiations on pharmaceuticals include inspections (how to check the way firms produce medicines), clinical trials processes, approval procedures and innovation (share of expertise and findings), staff qualifications, and intellectual property issues.

Taking into account the fierce competition from East Asian countries, TTIP seeks to enforce the sector of textiles in EU and USA focusing on rules of origin and customs duties. Among the issues negotiated are mutual recognition of care instruction symbols, product safety and consumer protection, standards, and testing methods.

As far as it concerns cosmetics the focus is on how to achieve cooperation on scientific safety assessments and animal testing and how to ameliorate technical cooperation.

The third category of TTIP negotiations includes nine subsections. Raw material trade is a priority for liberalization especially for EU which seeks sustainable access to energy resources. Such an effort includes stable and transparent investment rules to make easier the access to energy and to diversify suppliers and better terms of competition on resource exploitation and infrastructure.

Customs procedures are also a crucial area in transborder trade and demand simplification and harmonization so as to facilitate exports between the EU and the USA. The negotiations include issues such as simple and effective rules that are easy to follow by producers and exporters, harmonization of export documents and customs rules.

Especially for SMEs which are vital for EU economy the negotiations target the establishment of an online helpdesk where companies can trace all the information for export procedures customs duties, taxes and market opportunities. Small and medium-sized companies have a high percentage (88%) in the total number of EU exporting companies and represent a high value of EU exports to the USA (28%).

A key issue which diversifies TTIP from other regional agreements is the intention to set up a new ICS so as to secure the rights of investors and to avoid lengthy disputes derived from governmental intervention. An investor will have the right to bring a claim to the investment court and all disputes will be solved in a fair way especially in cases of discrimination, expropriation, nationalization, and transfer of profits.

The 15 judges of the court will be appointed by the EU and USA and there will be also an appeals tribunal with six judges. All hearings will be open to the citizens. There is also prediction for a mediation mechanism to help solve disputes amicably within specific deadlines. Further, there is volition to set up a GGDS in TTIP which will enable the involved parties to enforce the TTIP rules and to facilitate the interpretation and application of its provisions.

A very important issue for the smooth function of the US-EU economic area is that of subsidies to SOCs. Although both parties have rules for overseeing and controlling the subsidies there is a need for harmonization so as to avoid SOCs monopoly discrimination against private or foreign firms.

Intellectual property rights (patents, trademarks and designs, copyright, geographical indications) facilitate the international trade of goods/services as companies who invent or create new products or services are protected against illegal trade. Protection of products includes an agreed list of geographical indication products with regulations to stop other producers misusing them.

However, genetically modified organisms remain a controversial issue in TTIP negotiations and the EU made clear that it will keep restrictions on hormones and animal welfare but wants a common ground for the standards of use in the field chemicals. The target of the TTIP is to make regulations in many issue areas of both parties similar limiting the cost of firms to comply with different rules and principles when conducting business. The legal and institutional framework to achieve this target is far more precise than in other agreements.

Finally, concerning the institutional framework of the agreement there is a provision for a joint committee with representatives of both parties which will meet no later than one year after entry into force of the agreement and at least once a year thereafter. The Joint Committee shall be co-chaired by the US trade representative and the member of the EC responsible for trade relations, it shall review the overall progress achieved and shall suggest improvements, where appropriate. The results of that review shall be presented to the EU/US summit.

Moreover, there will be a transatlantic regulators' forum which shall meet at least once a year composed of senior officials of both parties responsible for crosscutting issues of regulatory policy and good regulatory practices. The forum shall discuss regulatory cooperation activities predicted by specific or sectoral articles in the agreement, it will prepare a joint overview of EU/US regulatory cooperation, and it will organize public sessions involving EU and US stakeholders. The negotiations also favor the establishment of a market access committee and many committees in issues like government procurement, energy and raw materials, intellectual property rights, agriculture, geographical indications, services and investment, mutual recognition of qualifications, TBTs, sanitary and phyto-sanitary obstacles, and customs cooperation.

**Table11.1 Issues Covered in TTIP Negotiations, 2017**

| Market access | Regulatory cooperation | Rules-based framework |
|---|---|---|
| Trade in goods and custom duties | Regulatory coherence | Sustainable development |
| Public procurement | Technical barriers to trade (TBTs) | energy and raw materials |
| Services | Food safety and animal and plant health (SPS) | small and medium-sized enterprises |
| Rules of origin | Sectoral annexes: chemicals, cosmetics, engineering, medical devices, pesticides, information and communication technology, pharmaceuticals, textiles, vehicles | Customs and trade facilitation |
| | | Intellectual property (IP) and Geographical indications (GIs) |
| | | Competition |
| | | Government subsidies |
| | | Government dispute settlement (GGDS) |
| | | Investment |

## Which are the Expected Benefits and Costs of TTIP?

Although regulations in the USA and EU are undergoing a thorough cost benefit analysis, there are problems to quantify all advantages disadvantages and resources linked to the provisions of international agreements (Ackerman and Heinzerling, 2004; Ackerman, 2009; Rose-Ackerman, 2013).

Many studies (Felbermayr et al. 2013a; Felbermayr et al. 2013b; Felbermayr et al. 2013c) tried to estimate the macroeconomic-sectoral benefits and costs of a TTIP (Francois, 2014; Krebs et al. 2015; Pelkmans et al. 2014). Their common ground irrespective of their methodological, econometric, and sectoral framework is that benefits are more than costs and that NTBs reduction/elimination will be the main instrument to maximize impact of the agreement on the content and quantity of bilateral transatlantic investment and trade flows.

A number of questions are raised (Hazakis, 2017). Will GDP increases derive from interindustry efficiency or from increased intra-industry trade? Will wages increase at the same rate as productivity in the two regions? How will job displacement evolve within economic and between economic sectors? Will job displacement be considerable taking into account that EU unemployment exceeds 25 million people?

The first study to answer the aforementioned issues was realized by the London-based research network CEPR (Francois et al. 2013) and estimated in its ambitious scenario (all tariffs are phased out, 25% of nontariff barriers are vanished, and 50% of NTBs in public procurement are eliminated) that there will be a positive impact on EU GDP (0.48% after 10 years) and on US GDP (0.40% after 10 years).

A less ambitious scenario (98% of tariffs are phased out, 10% of NTBs are vanished, and 25% of NTBs in public procurement are eliminated) predicted a positive impact of 0.27% and of 0.21% in GDP for EU and USA after 10 years. CEPR also predicted that the main impact of TTIP rules on EU economy will derive from regulatory cooperation. As far as it concerns job displacement, the CEPR study argues that a minimal 0.65% of employees would be displaced (Francois et al. 2013, 78). On the other hand, USA affiliates in Europe, and European affiliates in the USA will increase substantially their employees.

Egger et al. (2015) used the same model as CEPR (2013) and had an overlapping team of authors, but they found an average effect for the EU that was almost five times as big. Thus, the impact is directly linked to the extent and content of liberalization agreed upon by the parties involved in the agreement.

In an updated impact assessment EC (2017) predicted that TTIP will increase EU's GDP by 0.5% every year after 2030, national income by 0.3%, wages by 0.5% (for an older assessment of the European commission, see

Ecorys, 2009), EU exports to the USA by 27%, and US exports to the EU by 35.7%. The analysis also underlines the great differences between economic sectors with the most significant benefits traced to the motor vehicles (1.5%), leather/textiles and clothing (1.8–2.7%), and beverages and tobacco (1.1%) and most important decreases in electrical machinery (−7.9%), non-ferrous metals (−1.1%), and iron and steel (−2.5%).

The research findings (European commission, 2017) also note that EU average GDP increase will be most significant in Ireland (1.4%), Belgium (1.2%), and Lithuania (1.1%) and less significant in the Czech Republic (0.2%), Poland (0.1%), and Malta (0.1%). Finally, the research points that TTIP is expected to provoke a 0.2% rise in energy demand and CO2 emissions due to higher output the two regions.

The Ifo-Bertelsmann study (2013) predicts a much higher impact on GDP of both regions. Concerning the growth of incomes/GDP it estimates that the USA would benefit from a rise of 13.4% (average real income increase) from the TTIP, and EU would benefit from a rise of 5.2%. Ifo study predicts that there will be an increase in employment due to the agreement (124,000 employees in the EU and 69,000 employees in the USA) and job reductions outside the TTIP area (165,000).

Moreover, analyzing the trade costs and flows of products between the states that will participate in TTIP and those states that will be influenced by forms of trade diversion, the study argues that trade between EU member states and the USA will rise by an average of 76%.

Felbermayr et al. (2015) updated the earlier Ifo-Bertelsmann model, using more recent data and a larger country sample and found an average effect on GDP of 3.9% while Aichele et al. (2016) found a GDP effect of 2.1%. The study with the smallest reported GDP effect was the one conducted by the Paris think tank CEPII which found a GDP gain of 0.3%.

How are third countries affected by TTIP? Which will be the impact of TTIP on welfare and on consumers in third countries? Which will be the impact of the alignment between EU and US standards and regulation on producers in third states? How market access and the Generalized System of Preferences in EU will be influenced?

Regional trade agreements have a discriminatory nature since they grant preferences to specific participating states concerning tariffs and rules of origin leading too often to trade diversion. Thus, cost benefit analysis should not omit to analyze the impact of TTIP on third states and the world trade system (Brakman et al. 2015; Freytag et al. 2014).

Francois et al. in the CEPR study (2013) estimated that the activities in third states that will suffer losses are primary agriculture, motor vehicles, chemicals and pharmaceuticals, and processed foods. In an updated impact assessment EC (Ecorys, 2017) underlines that TTIP's influence on most developing states will be minimal (i.e., low-income states) but it will have an impact on ASEAN states and countries in Latin America (i.e., fruit juice sector in Brazil) and Africa because of their engagement in supply chains. Ifo (2013) also underlined that countries such as Brazil may suffer from trade diversion. Thus, trade diversion will also occur in third states with close trade links to the US market (Brazil, Mexico).

Aichele et al. (2014) and Egger et al. (2015) argue that TTIP will have different effects depending on the type of trade with third states (i.e., east Asia firms will face problems while states trading inputs for the EU or USA like Morocco and Turkey will take advantage of new trade opportunities). Highly important is also how third countries will react through their mega regional agreements (i.e., the regional comprehensive economic partnership agreement which links ASEAN state with key emerging economies like China and India).

Which are the prerequisites for TTIP success? Four conditions seem essential among many others and are the following:

a. TTIP will be considered a success under the condition that it reduces permanently the transaction costs in major issue areas of US-EU trade and that it constrains regulatory uncertainty linked with export activities and investment. This presupposes an efficient institutional mechanism to supervise the implementation of TTIP provisions but also to forward new initiatives for further integration of the two regions.

   What makes TTIP special is not only that TTIP regulatory cooperation council will be a permanent body but also that the proposed regulatory cooperation and the regulatory processes will be given legal force of an international treaty which means priority over domestic legislation.
b. TTIP will also deliver positive spillovers if it maximizes the competitive advantages of both regions due to better functional and operational synergies of the transatlantic productive and commercial networks delivering not only economies of scale and scope but also innovation in medium and high value added activities.
c. TTIP should address promptly and effectively all negative repercussions of integration on labor force, environment, and social conditions. This presupposes specific mechanisms for training of unemployed and specific mechanisms to forbid any kind of competitive advantage constructed not on better trade conditions and more productivity but on social dumping and environmental degradation. Legitimacy and efficiency of TTIP also presuppose high standards in all issue areas under negotiation and more specifically consumer protection, food safety, and product safety.
d. Finally, TTIP should be a holistic agreement as most advantages could accrue from interdependencies and synergies among sectors. If most

services sectors are not included in the agreement, if most NTBs are exempted, and if controversial issues such as public procurement are not included in the provisions of the agreement, then the impact will be minimal and the effects disputable.

## CONCLUSIONS AND POLICY IMPLICATIONS

Which are the main challenges of EU trade policy? First, the increasing heterogeneity among EU states makes more difficult the operation of decision-making on trade policy issues. In agreements such as the TTIP and CETA, criticism has many common traits focusing on the dispute settlement provisions and on the influence of the agreements on the regulation of public services.

The agreements also demonstrate that there are conflicts and different interests in key sectors among EU states and policy/issue areas in which EU countries struggle to hold competences. Can these problems be faced by a future abolition of mixed agreements and the concentration of all responsibilities in EU institutional edifice? Will such an option facilitate European integration or it will create another source of confrontation and Euroskepticism within EU? The jury remains out but the Brexit and the emerging Euroskepticism makes difficult any initiative in favor of deepening European integration.

Second, irrespective of the assessment reports projections EU should face all negative spillovers derived from international agreements on specific sectors and regions and this presupposes front-loaded activity of EU institutions and also permanent cooperation between regional development policy, cohesion funds, and international trade policy at EU level. If this does not take place unemployment and anemic economic growth in many EU regions will enforce populist and protectionist arguments against liberalization efforts. Public opinion and EU voters understand specific results and not good intentions for fighting unemployment and social inequality especially in sectors with low-skilled jobs.

Third, any trade regime toward third countries should face the fear of job losses in EU industry due to cheaper imports. This means that EU institutions should better communicate EU trade policy's targets and results especially their impact on consumers, workers, and national income distribution (trade distributional effects). Increased transparency and more participation of EP in all stages of trade negotiations will help efforts to contain Euroskeptic arguments in favor of a fortress Europe. Moreover, this means reforms and heavy investment in education/training of labor force and competition policies so as to make EU production networks more flexible and more adaptive to global economic pressures.

Fourth, trade regimes should enforce worker, health, and environment standards and should not compromise them under the logic of short-term benefits in other issue areas (i.e., investment access). EU trade policy should favor a rule-based multilateral trading system and not bilateral accords at the detriment of WTO effectiveness. CETA and TTIP should not enforce bilateralism but should be vehicles to enforce multilateral regulations on key issue areas such as intellectual property rights, investment disputes, and agricultural subsidies. Thus, all mega regional trade accords should be subordinate to the WTO rationale and not vice versa so as to maximize simplification coordination and harmonization of international trade principles. A turn to beggar-thy-neighbor policies will trigger trade confrontation with emerging economic powers. Moreover, political economists should focus not only on the sectoral and macroeconomic benefits of the agreements but also on the distribution of benefits and the influence of regulatory changes.

Finally, EU should face the challenges and complex institutional issues of Brexit within the next five years. European disintegration is "ante portas" if EU does not face properly and instantly the challenges from nationalist and populist parties based on Euroskeptic arguments of trade and income losses from EU trade policy. Brexit will have a major impact on EU trade mainly in the services sector (UK accounts for over 20% of total EU trade in services with non-EU states) and on EU's negotiating position in the global economic arena.

## BIBLIOGRAPHY


Ackerman, F. 2009. "Much less wrong: The Stern Review versus its critics". In *Can we afford the future? The economics of a warming world,* ed. F. Ackerman. London: ZedBooks.

Ackerman, F and Heinzerling, L. 2004. *Priceless: On knowing the price of everything and the value of nothing*. New York: New Press.

Aichele, Rahel., Felbermayr, Gabriel., and Inga, Heiland. 2016. *Going Deep: The trade and welfare effects of TTIP revised,* Ifo-Working Paper 219. Munich: Ifo.

Alemanno, A. 2014. *The Transatlantic Trade and Investment Partnership and the parliamentary regulatory cooperation.* Report to European Parliament. Accessed http://www.europarl.europa.eu/committees/en/studies.html

Balassa, B. 1962. *The theory of economic integration.* London: George Allen and Unwin.

Balassa, B. 1967. "Trade creation and trade diversion in the European common market". *The Economic Journal*, 77(305): 1–21.

Baldwin, R. E. 2008. "Sequencing and depth of regional economic integration: Lessons from the Americas from Europe". *The World Economy,* 31(1): 1–29.

Bartels, L. 2007. "The WTO legality of the EUs GSP + arrangement". *Journal of International Economic Law*, 10(4): 869–886.

Brakman, S., Kohl, T., and van Marrewijk, C. 2015. *The impact of the Transatlantic Trade and Investment Partnership (TTIP) on low income countries.* Directorate for trade policy and International economic governance. The Netherlands: Ministry of Foreign Affairs.

Cameron, R and Loukine K. 2001. *"Canada-European Union trade and investment relations, The effects of tariff elimination"* Trade and Economic Analysis division, Ottawa: Department of Foreign Affairs and International Trade.

Canadian office of the parliamentary budget officer. 2017. "The Canada–EU comprehensive and trade agreement: a prospective analysis" 2 may. Ottawa.

CEPII. 2013. *Transatlantic trade: Whither partnership, which economic consequences?* CEPII policy brief 2013-01, accessed www.cepii.fr/CEPII/fr/publications/pb/abstract.asp?NoDoc=6113

Corden, W. M. 1971. *The theory of protection.* Oxford: Clarendon press.

Corden, W. M. 1972. "Economies of scale and customs union theory". *Journal of Political Economy,* 80(3): 465–475.

Corden, W. M. 1976. "Customs unions theory and the non-uniformity of tariffs". *Journal of International Economics*, 6: 99–106.

Ecorys. 2009. "Non-Tariff Measures in EU-US trade and investment – An economic analysis, report". eds. K. Berden, J. F. Francois, S. Tamminen, M. Thelle, and P. Wymenga. OJ 2007/S180-219493. Brussels: European Commission.

Ecorys. 2017. "SIA in support of the negotiations on a transatlantic trade and investment partnership" final Report. March. Brussels: European Commission.

Egger, Peter., Francois, Joseph., Manchin, Miriam., and Nelson, Doug. 2015. "Non-Tariff barriers, integration, and the transatlantic economy". *Economic Policy,* 30(83): 539–584.

El-Agraa, A. M. 1994. *The European Union: Economies and politics*, fourth edition. London: Harvester Wheatsheaf.

European Commission Communication. 2015. *Trade for All: Towards a more responsible trade and investment policy.* Brussels: European Commission.

European Commission. 2017. DG Trade statistical guide, June, European Commission, Brussels.

Felbermayr, G., Heid, B., and Lehwald, S. 2013a. *Transatlantic trade and investment partnership (TTIP): Who benefits from a free trade deal? Part 1: macroeconomic effects.* Gótersloh: Bertelsmann Stiftung.

Felbermayr, G and Larch, M. 2013b. "The Transatlantic trade and investment partnership (TTIP): Potential, problems and perspectives". *CES Ifo Forum 2/2013:* 49–60.

Felbermayr, G., Lehwald, S., Schoof, U., and Ronge, M. 2013c. *States, branches of industry, and education levels: Who will benefit in Germany from a Transatlantic Trade and Investment Partnership (TTIP)? Part 2: microeconomic effects in Germany.* Gótersloh: Bertelsmann Stiftung.

Felbermayr, G., Heid, B., Larch, M., and Yalcin, E. 2014. "Macroeconomic potentials of transatlantic free trade: A high resolution perspective for Europe and the world" *CES ifo working paper 5019*. Center for Economic Studies Munich: Ifo Institute.

Felbermayr, Gabriel., Benedikt, Heid., Larch, Mario, and Yalcin, Erdal. 2015. "Macroeconomic potentials of transatlantic free trade: A high resolution perspective for Europe and the world". *Economic Policy*, 30(83): 491–537.

Fontagné, Lionel., Gourdon, Julien., and Sébastien, Jean. 2013. "Transatlantic trade: Whither partnership, which economic consequences?" *CEPII Policy Brief*. Paris: CEPII.

Francois, Joseph., Miriam, Manchin., Hanna, Norberg., Olga, Pindyuk., and Patrick, Tomberger. 2013. *Reducing transatlantic barriers to trade and investment: An economic assessment,* Report trade 10/A2/A16 for the European Commission, IIDE and CEPR. Brussels: European Commission.

Francois, J and Manchin, M. 2014. *Quantifying the impact of a transatlantic trade and investment partnership (TTIP) agreement on Portugal.* London: Centre for Economic Policy Research.

Freytag, A., Draper, P., and Fricke, S. 2014. *The impact of TTIP: Economic effects on the transatlantic partners, third countries and the global trade order. Volume 1*. Berlin: Konrad Adenauer Stiftung.

Frisch, D. 2016. *The future of ACP-EU relations beyond 2020: An update of my personal reflections.* Discussion paper 172. Maastricht: European Centre for development policy management.

Gavin, B., 2001. *The European Union and globalization: Towards global democratic governance?* Cheltenham: Edward Elgar.

Government of Canada and the European Commission. 2008. *Assessing the costs and benefits of a closer EU-Canada economic partnership: A joint study by the European Commission and the Government of Canada.* Canada–Brussels: Government of Canada and the European Commission.

Grossman, G and Helpman, E. 1995. "The politics of free-trade agreements". *American Economic Review*, 85: 667–690.

Hazakis, Konstantinos. 2017. "The transatlantic trade and investment partnership: A critical assessment". In *European integration*, eds. A. Kontis and S. Verny, 659–685. Athens: Papazisis Publications.

Harberger, A. C. 1954. "Monopoly and resource allocation". *American Economic Review*, May 44(2): 77–87.

Hynes, W and Holden, P. 2016. "What future for the global aid for trade initiative? Towards an assessment of its achievements and limitations". *International Development Policy Review*, 34(4): 563–619.

Hulse, M. 2016. "Economic partnership agreements: Implications for regional governance and EU-ACP development cooperation". *Briefing Paper 12/2016*. Bonn: German Development Institute.

Hurt, S. R. 2009. "Understanding EU development policy: History, global context and self-interest?" *Third World Quarterly*, 31(1): 159–168.

Ifo-Bertelsmann. 2013. *Transatlantic Trade and Investment Partnership: Who benefits from a free trade deal?* Germany: Ifo-Bertelsmann. Accessed www.bfna.org/sites/default/files/TTIP-GED%20study%2017June%202013.pdf

Ifo. 2015. *Potential impacts of TTIP on developing and emerging economies*. English Summary. Germany: Ifo-Bertelsmann. Accessed http://www.cesifogroup.de/ifo-Home/research/Projects/Archive/Projects_AH/2014/proj_AH_ttip-entwicklungslaender.html

Krebs, O and Pflüger, M. 2015. *How deep is your love? A quantitative spatial analysis of the transatlantic trade partnership*. IZA-Discussion Paper 9021. Bohn: Institute for the Study of Labor.

Kemp, M. C and Wan, H. Y. Jr. 1976. "An elementary proposition concerning the formation of customs unions". *Journal of International Economics*, 6(1) February: 95–98.

Krugman, P. R. 1995. "Increasing returns, imperfect competition and the positive theory of international trade". In *Handbook of international economics: Volume III*, eds. G. M. Grossman and K. Rogoff, 1244–1276. Amsterdam: Elsevier-North-Holland.

Limao, N. 2007. "Are preferential trade agreements with non-trade objectives a stumbling block for multilateral liberalization?" *The Review for Economic Studies*, 74(3): 821–855.

Lipsey, R. 1957. "The theory of customs unions: Trade diversion and welfare". *Economica,* 24: 40–46.

Meade, J. 1955. *The theory of customs unions*. Amsterdam: North-Holland.

Meunier, S. 2005. *Trading voices: The European Union in international commercial negotiations*. Princeton, NJ: Princeton University Press.

Michalopolous, C and Tarr, D. 1997. *The Economics of customs unions in the Commonwealth of independent states*. Policy research working papers. Washington D.C.: World Bank.

Molle, W. 1990. *The economics of European integration.* Aldershot: Dartmouth.

Mundell, R. 1964. "Tariff preferences and the terms of trade". *Manchester School of Economic and Social Studies*, 32(1): 1–13.

Ohlin, B. 1933. *Interregional and international trade*. Cambridge, MA: Harvard University Press.

Ornelas, E. 2005a. "Trade creating free trade areas and the undermining of multilateralism". *European Economic Review*, 49: 1717–1735.

Ornelas, E. 2005b. "Endogenous free trade agreements and the multilateral trading system". *Journal of International Economics*, 67: 471–497.

Panagariya, A. 1999. "The regionalism debate: An overview". *The World Economy*, 22: 477–511.

Panagariya, A., and Findlay, R. 1996. "A political-economy analysis of free-trade areas and customs unions". In *The Political Economy of Trade Reform: Essays in Honor of J. Bhagwati*, eds. R. Feenstra, G. Grossman and D. Irwin. 265–287. Cambridge, MA: MIT Press.

Panagariya, A. 2000. "Preferential trade liberalization: The traditional theory and new developments". *Journal of Economic Literature*, 38(2): 287–331.

Pelkmans, J. 2006. *European integration: Methods and economic analysis*, 3rd ed. London: Prentice Hall.
Pelkmans, J., Lejour, A., et al. 2014. *The Impact of TTIP: The underlying economic model and comparisons.* CEPS Special Report No. 93 and EU Parliament Research Service. London and Strasbourg: CEPS and EU Parliament Research Service. Accessed www.europarl.europa.eu/RegData/etudes/etudes/join/2014/528798/IPOLJOIN_ET%282014%29528798_EN.pdf
Robson, P. 1987. *The economics of international integration*, third edition. London: George Allen and Unwin.
Romer, P. M. 1994. "New goods, old theory and the welfare costs of trade restrictions". *Journal of Development Economics*, 43: 5–38.
Rose-Ackerman, S. 2013. "Precaution, proportionality, and cost/benefit analysis: False analogies". *European Journal of Risk Regulation*, 4(2): 281–286.
Roubini, N and S. Mihm. 2011. *Crisis economics*. London: Penguin Books.
Venables, A. 1987. "Custom union and tariff reform under imperfect competition". *European Economic Review*, 31: 103–110.
Viner, J. 1950. *The custom union issue*. London: Stevens and Sons for the Carnegie Endowment for International Peace.

## FURTHER READING

Baier, Scott and Jeffrey, Bergstrand. 2007. "Do free trade agreements actually increase members' trade?" *Journal of International Economics*, 71(1): 72–95.
Eichengreen, B and A. Irwin. 2010. "The slide to protectionism in the great depression: Who succumbed and why?" *The Journal of Economic History*, 70(4): 871–897.
EU. 2014. *Consolidated version of the Cotonou partnership agreement.* Accessed http://www.europarl.europa.eu/intcoop/acp/03_01/pdf/mn3012634_en.pdf
EU. 2015. *Towards a new partnership between the European Union and the African, Caribbean and Pacific countries after 2020: Joint consultation paper.* Brussels: European Union. Accessed https://ec.europa.eu/europeaid/sites/devco/files/joint-consultation-paper-post cotonou_en_0.pdf
EU. 2016a. *Joint Communication on a renewed partnership with the countries of Africa, the Caribbean and the Pacific.* Brussels: European Union. Accessed https://ec.europa.eu/europeaid/sites/devco/files/jointcommunication-renewed partnership-acp-20161122_en.pdf
Falkner, G. 2016. "The EU's current crisis and its policy effects: Research design and comparative findings". *Journal of European Integration*, 38(3): 219–235. doi:10.1080/07036337.2016.1140154.
Noland, Marcus., Hufbauer, Gary., Robinson, Sherman., and Moran, Tyler. 2016. *Assessing trade agendas in the US presidential campaign.* Washington: Peterson Institute for International Economics.

## FURTHER QUESTIONS

1. Has EU external trade policy become more protectionist toward WTO trading partners since the application of the SMP?
2. Which type of agreement do you consider as more appropriate to further facilitate EU trade and investment with developing countries and to face regulatory and market access barriers?
3. How is CETA expected to influence European producers, consumers, and employees?
4. How can the EU best strengthen the linkages between trade and development in its trade policy?
5. How can the EU external trade policy best safeguard EU companies against major trading partners who follow an asymmetric level of openness and apply sectoral protectionist measures? Are the existing EU tools sufficient to face such practices?
6. Which will be the impact of TTIP on welfare and on consumers in third countries? Which will be the impact of the alignment between EU and US standards and regulation on producers in third states? How market access and the Generalized System of Preferences in EU will be influenced?
7. To what extent is the current GSP framework suitable to the developmental targets of the countries involved?
8. What is the impact of EBA on poverty reduction?
9. Compare the main traits and benefits of CETA and TTIP to the countries involved.
10. What is the impact of ENP on competitiveness of beneficiary's countries' industries?
11. Is the monitoring framework of GSP+ suitable for attaining economic and social targets of GSP?

# *Chapter 12*

# The Brexit Question

Exit from a commercial or monetary interstate partnership is not an unusual phenomenon. However, UK's decision to exit EU is considered a sui generis case since EU is a unique economic integration scheme between countries which have reorganized their statehood together and since it covers many issue areas of EU-UK economic and public policy. The complex EU institutional structure and the already achieved EU commitments known as acquis communautaire should face the unknown challenge of European disintegration (Owen et al. 2017).

Disintegration means negative results not only for the UK which leaves but also for the 27 EU states. Indeed, disintegration process may trigger further contestation of the EU integration effort by the people of the remaining EU states. Moreover, the choice to leave a union disrupts long-established cross-border productive and commercial networks and abolishes policy and institutional cooperation between the EU and the UK in many issue areas of the economy. Thus, not only in political but also in economic terms Brexit includes real economic costs in all the EU states.

The long-term impact of the UK's exit cannot be fully assessed. As the UK is the first ever state to withdraw from the EU, nobody can foresee the range and content of repercussions on EU integration project (Dhingra, 2016). Although a more subjective assessment will be possible after many years the chapter underlines the key challenges of the Brexit and the repercussions on public policy issue areas in the UK.

## HOW UK REACHED BREXIT DECISION

UK's accession in EEC was not an easy case since France's president Charles de Gaulle opposed it during the 1960s. However, in 1973, the UK, Ireland, and Denmark, joined the EEC, and on June 5, 1975, UK voters supported in a critical referendum of UK membership in the EEC by a great majority (67.2%). More specifically, the percentages in favor of EEC were in England 69%, in Wales 65%, in Scotland 58%, and in Northern Ireland 52%.

In the 1980s UK prime minister Margaret Thatcher put into question many of the initiatives of EEC and demanded a rebate on UK contributions to the EEC arguing parallelly in favor of more liberalization and less regulation and protection in key public policy issue areas.

In 1990s the UK questioned the Schengen Area, doubted the euro, and chose an opt out of the social chapter provisions of the Maastricht Treaty. Rising euroskepticism and the negative impact of the 2008 financial crisis reopened the issue of UK participation in EU in 2015. The key arguments of euroskeptics in favor of Brexit included EU overregulation and bureaucracy, questioning of the EU ability to handle the financial and migration crises and the fear of loss of national identity.

The need to put an end in Euroskeptism debate led UK prime minister David Cameron to propose a referendum on the membership issue. The referendum held on June 23, of 2016 marked the end of a turbulent membership in EU and led UK to withdraw from EU. On the main question of the referendum, "Should the United Kingdom remain a member of the European Union or leave the European Union?" 51.9% voted to leave the EU and 48.1% voted to "Remain" (England voted to "Leave" by 53.4% and Wales 52. 5%, Scotland and Northern Ireland voted to stay by 62% and 55.8%, respectively). It is also important to note that very English region voted to leave except London.

Five days after the referendum, the EP adopted a resolution (June 28, 2016) calling for the activation of article 50 of the TEU as soon as possible. The European Council also underlined on June 29, 2016 the "need to organise the withdrawal of the UK from the EU in an orderly fashion" and argued that "it is up to the British government to notify the European Council of the UK's intention to withdraw from the Union," as well as that "this should be done as quickly as possible." Equally important, the European Council stressed that "any agreement which will be concluded with the UK as a third country will have to be based on a balance of rights and obligations" and that "access to the Single Market requires acceptance of all four freedoms."

Following the UK referendum, the UK High Court (November 3, 2016) declared that article 50 should be triggered only after a decision of UK Parliament and that the instrument giving effect to the UK's accession was the European Communities Act of 1972 that gave effect to the EU law in the UK and created rights and obligations for the UK as a member of the EU.

**Table 12.1 Breakdown of Referendum Result by Constituent Parts of the UK**

| | Electorate | Voter Turnout (%) | Votes for Remain | Votes for Leave | Vote for Remain (%) | Vote for Leave (%) |
|---|---|---|---|---|---|---|
| England, including Gibraltar | 38,981,662 | 73.0 | 13,266,996 | 15,188,406 | 46.7 | 53.3 |
| Scotland | 3,987,112 | 67.2 | 1,661,191 | 1,018,322 | 62.0 | 38.0 |
| Wales | 2,270,272 | 71.7 | 772,347 | 854,572 | 47.5 | 52.5 |
| Northern Ireland | 1,260,955 | 62.7 | 440,707 | 349,442 | 55.8 | 44.2 |
| UK | 46,500,001 | 72.2 | 16,141,241 | 17,410,742 | 48.1 | 51.9 |

*Source*: The Electoral Commission. EU referendum results, 2017: https://www.electoralcommission.org.uk/find-information-by-subject/elections-and-referendums/past-elections-and-referendums/eu-referendum/electorate-and-count-information.

Ultimately, on March 29, 2017, the European Council received the notification by the UK of its intention to withdraw from the EU and EURATOM. This also means that the two-year period set out in article 50 TEU ends on March 29, 2019. If the two-year period for the UK and the EU to reach an agreement on the UK's withdrawal is not met, the EU treaties will cease to apply to the UK from March 30, 2019, unless the European Council decides unanimously, and in agreement with the UK, to prolong the two-year period.

## HOW BREXIT IS REALIZED

Until the Lisbon Treaty member states did not have a legally defined way to leave EU in an orderly way. The legal gap is addressed by article 50 of TEU and defines the requirements for the process of withdrawal. A member state submits a formal notification deciding to withdraw "in accordance with its own constitutional requirements." Thus, the withdrawing country does not need to justify or declare the motives for its departure. Apparently, article 50 does not settle all the details for withdrawal and as Christophe Hillion (2015, 135) specified, article 50 is criticized as incomplete, unclear, and even cryptic. Moreover, article 50 refers to the process for attaining a withdrawal agreement, not what should be included in any agreement creating enough policy uncertainty (House of Commons 2016; United Kingdom Government 2016).

When European Council receives the notification letter from a government there is a two-year deadline to conclude the withdrawal agreement. Moreover, the European Council issues guidelines on the basis of which the Council will negotiate the withdrawal agreement with the country. Equally important, article 218 (3) TFEU sets the competences of the EC (it submits recommendations with regard to the negotiations), and of the Council, (it authorizes negotiations and nominates a negotiator).

It should be mentioned that EU legal framework demands the conclusion of two agreements between the UK and the EU—the one of which refers to the exit and the other to the provisions of the new relationship between the EU and the UK. The former can be based on a qualified majority of EU countries but the latter demands the agreement of all EU member countries, and consequently all national parliaments.

As article 50 does not specify the details of a leaving state relationship with EU, there is a need for an international agreement (articles 207 and 218 TFEU) between the EU and a third country, and in the case of UK there is a need to reach such an agreement by March 2019 as by that date all agreements based on the EU treaties will expire. Thus, the new agreement requires the unanimous decision of the 27 countries in Council.

To sum up, the EC is negotiating on behalf of the EU, on the basis of the European Council's guidelines and the subsequent mandate from the Council while the EP puts the principles and terms for its approval of UK withdrawal agreement. After the conclusion of the negotiations, EP must provide its consent and UK must ratify the agreements (following national legal procedure).

Based on the principle of sincere cooperation, negotiations on the arrangements for the UK's withdrawal from the EU started on June 19, 2017. The heads of state and government of the member states have approved the nomination of former Commissioner Michel Barnier as Chief Negotiator and underlined that the process has to be finalized before the 2019 EP elections.

More specifically, taking into account, the resolution of the EP of April 5, 2017, the European Council issued in April 27, 2017 guidelines following the UK's notification under article 50 TEU. According to them the EU target in these negotiations will be to preserve its interests, those of its citizens, its businesses, and its member countries. The EU Council further underlined the need for a phased approach giving priority to an orderly withdrawal so as to reduce policy uncertainty and to minimize disruption caused by the Brexit.

Accordingly, the first phase of negotiations aims to provide as much clarity and legal certainty as possible to citizens, businesses, stakeholders, and international partners on the immediate effects of the UK's withdrawal from the EU, and intends to settle the disentanglement of the UK from the EU and from all the rights and obligations the UK. As it is clearly noted, the European Council monitors progress and determines when sufficient progress has been achieved to allow negotiations to proceed to the next phase.

In the second phase, preliminary discussions will take place concerning the future EU-UK relationship, as well as the possible transitional arrangements. The European Council principles are set out in the statement of Heads of

State or Government and of the Presidents of the European Council. Moreover, the EC on June 29, 2016 expressed its wish to have the UK as a close partner in the future. Which are the principles of EU negotiation approach?

First, any agreement with the UK will have to be based on a balance of rights and obligations and will ensure a level playing field. Second, preserving the integrity of the single market excludes participation based on a sector-by-sector approach, meaning that the four freedoms of the single market are indivisible (no "cherry picking"). Thus, negotiations are conducted in transparency and as a single package (nothing is agreed until everything is agreed). Third, the aforementioned principles are equally applied to the negotiations of an orderly withdrawal, to any preliminary and preparatory discussions on the framework for a future UK-EU relationship, and to any form of transitional arrangements after UK withdrawal.

Three issues are of key importance in the first phase of the negotiations namely citizens' rights, settlement of the UK's financial obligations, and the Northern Ireland peace process.

On the issue of citizens' rights the central argument is that legal status and rights of EU-27 citizens living or having lived in the UK, and of UK citizens living or having lived in the EU-27 are subject to the principle of reciprocity, equity, symmetry, and nondiscrimination, while protecting the integrity of EU law. Evidently, the right of every EU citizen, and of his or her family members, to live, to work, or to study in any EU country is a fundamental aspect of the EU. Reciprocal guarantees to safeguard the status and rights derived from EU law at the date of withdrawal of EU and UK citizens are crucial and must be effective, enforceable, nondiscriminatory, and comprehensive, including the right to acquire permanent residence after a continuous period of five years of legal residence.

Concerning the financial settlement, EU favors a single financial settlement—including issues resulting from the MFF as well as those related to the EIB, the EDF, and theECB. Equally important, any agreement should ensure that both the EU and the UK respect the obligations resulting from the whole period of the UK membership in the EU. The settlement should cover all commitments as well as all liabilities.

Last, supporting peace and reconciliation of the Good Friday Agreement (1998) in Ireland is crucial for the success of UK withdrawal framework. Continuity and stability of the Northern Ireland peace process are priority and avoidance of a "hard" border between Ireland and Northern Ireland is a necessity.

The EU-UK agreement should also address issues stemming from EU's businesses trading with and operating in the UK and its businesses trading with and operating in the EU in order to avoid disruptions in contracts and business arrangements as well as disruptions in EU-funded programmes.

Other issues of EU-UK agreement include arrangements regarding the sovereign base areas of the UK in Cyprus (safeguarding the rights and interests of those EU citizens resident or working in the base areas) as well issues arising from the withdrawal of EU in other public policy issue areas such as policy cooperation, judicial cooperation, law enforcement, and security.

Concerning the second phase of the negotiations the European Council desires a close partnership between the EU and the UK after its departure based on the volition of UK to pursue a free trade agreement with the EU. However, the free trade agreement should be balanced and wide-ranging ensuring a level playing field, in terms of competition and state aid, and thus any agreement should achieve the avoidance of unfair competitive advantages through tax, social, environmental, and regulatory measures and practices.

## WHICH IS THE PROPER MODEL FOR UK-EU RELATIONSHIP?

Brexit decision opened the debate on the content and type of future UK-EU relation. Several studies (i.e., House of Commons Foreign Affairs Committee, 2013; Booth et al. 2015; Busch and Matthes, 2016) provide different types of UK-EU future relationship ranging from free trade agreement with the EU involving the four freedoms of the EU internal market (Norwegian type) to the adoption of WTO rules (WTO type) or mixed type cooperations (Switzerland option).

Further, the analysts coined the terms “Hard” and “Soft” Brexit to describe UK’s preferred status within the EU single market. In soft Brexit, the UK-EU relation is realized through a free trade area which means that nontariff obstacles such as differences in product market regulations remain.

In hard Brexit, all trade flows are realized according to the provisions of WTO meaning the existence of tariffs and NTBs as well as no special relationship with the EU single market. An intermediate solution could be a CU with the EU in specified categories of products meaning the implementation of a CET in these goods/services.

The question is whether the model of UK-EU will be a revised and extended form of UK’s opt out, or a transition model to keep UK linked to the closer outer circle of EU integration project and thus when conditions allow realizing again accession in EU.

Another model for association of the EU and the UK was proposed by the Bruegel institute in August 2016 (Pisanny–Ferry et al. 2016). The model includes participation in the single market process, involvement in a specific form of intergovernmental decision-making, contribution to the EU budget, and cooperation on security and defense excluding unconditional free movement of workers.

Dhingra and Sampson (2016) mention three potential types of relationship between EU and UK, namely, adoption of the Single Market (i.e., the case of Norway), bilateral trade agreements with the EU (i.e., the case of Switzerland), and trade within the framework of WTO.

In a Norway type model there will free movement of goods, services, people, and capital but there will also be an obligation to follow single market rules especially in complex and highly contested issue areas such as environment, consumer protection, and competition. UK should contribute to the EU's regional development funds (House of Commons, 2013) and will also have unrestrained access to the single market, including the passport for financial services.

Such a free trade agreement involves much less obligations contrary to the CU model. However, it is rather difficult for UK to accept in the same time what was the basis of Brexit thinking namely avoidance of EU regulation activity and control of illegal migration. In economic terms, the option will also favor the financial sector in the city which however will have to comply with EU financial regulation.

The Swiss model of relations with EU involves lengthy and thorough negotiations in each economic sector but is highly flexible concerning the EU policies to be adopted. It also involves lengthy processes of transposition of EU policies in national law and has a specific cost of contribution to certain common sectoral programs.

The Swiss type of relationship with EU also exempts free trade in services and automatic access of UK-domiciled banks to EU market. Thus, if UK adopts the Swiss model of EU-UK integration, a set of bilateral sectoral agreements will regulate specific issue areas of the economy. The UK will have the ability to join ad hoc EU programmes under certain terms and it will be free to forward new trade agreements. Further, it will not contribute to the EU budget and will not have access to EU structural funds.

The Turkish model of relations with EU (which is based on a CU) focuses on manufactured products and includes obligations to adopt the content of EU policies in specific issue areas such as competition and IP law leaving unregulated other sectors (i.e., the agricultural sector). If the UK adopts this model, UK products will avoid lengthy custom controls and if the UK also achieves an integrated agreement on services, FDI flows in the UK closely linked to EU market will not be disrupted.

However, UK Euroskeptics raise concerns over the compliance of UK to most trade regulations of EU which deprive degrees of trade independence from UK international economic policy. Further, a number of issues will have to be regulated between UK and EU including the highly controversial issue of free movement of persons.

Finally, if no agreement has been reached on the future model of EU-UK relations, WTO provisions will apply. Within WTO the countries adopt the (MFN) clause meaning no discrimination against other states and probably higher cost of exporting to the EU for UK firms due to increased nontariff obstacles. A strong benefit is that WTO does not impose any rule on the free movement of labor. However, WTO option will create obstacles to UK access in EU services market and will make necessary a renegotiation of preferential agreements between the UK and third states. The UK will be treated by EU as all EU states without a preferential market access.

## THE IMPACT OF BREXIT ON THE UK AND THE EU

It seems that exit from European Community is not an easy strategy. UK's importance on EU GDP (16% of EU) and EU population (12%) implies that EU loses a significant member. Additionally, UK exerts a crucial geopolitical role (permanent member of the United Nations Security Council and a state with nuclear capabilities). Moreover, the Brexit will undermine the provision of cross-border externalities in EU such as cross-border interconnection of trans-European transport networks and energy.

Quantifying the effects of Brexit on UK economy is difficult since it involves a diversified group of variables that should be evaluated at their combination. Studies on the impact of Brexit differ in methodology and possible scenarios. The quantitative models estimate the Brexit impact taking into consideration different hypotheses on internal market issues and different options concerning UK withdrawal from EU.

In any case, a sudden break in the UK-EU long lasting and complex relation is extremely difficult to be quantified (Hendry and Mizon, 2000; Bloomberg, 2016; JP Morgan, 2016). Brexit involves parallel policy changes on several issue areas such as trade, migration, macroeconomic policy, financial services, state aid, competition, agriculture, and energy security, which will influence UK and EU decision-making and policy for decades.

Most analyses underline that the impact of Brexit on UK economy and policy will be negative (Dhingra et al. 2017; Dhingra et al. 2016; Ebell and Warren, 2016; HM Treasury, 2016; OECD, 2016; Oxford Economics, 2016; Van Reenen, 2016; Kierzenkowski et al. 2016; IMF, 2016; Booth et al. 2015; Ottaviano et al. 2014; Aichele and Felbermayr, 2015).

Kohl, Brakman, and Garretsen (2017) argue that UK GDP reduction will range between 1% and 6% while Dhingra et al. (2016) estimate annual costs of 850 euro per household in the soft Brexit and 1,700 euro per household in the hard Brexit option. Dhingra et al. (2017) predict a UK welfare loss of 1.3% under soft Brexit option and 2.7% under hard Brexit.

OECD (2016) estimates a reduction ranging between 2.7% and 7.7%, while the UK Treasury (2016) suggests that Brexit would lead to a fall of 7.5% in GDP under the WTO option and 3.8% under the Norway option.

Ebell and Warren (2016) argue that in GDP terms the fall will be between 1.5% and 3.7%, in wages between 2.2% and 6.3%, and in consumption between 2.4% to 5.4%. Other studies suggest that the cost of Brexit might be modest. Booth et al. (2015) suggest that application of MFN tariffs and nontariff obstacles and economization of UK resources from EU budget contribution will result in a reduction of 2.2% in UK GDP but if UK achieves beneficial FTAs with the EU and third countries, the GDP will rise by 1.6%. Ottaviano et al. (2014) argue that the reduction in UK GDP will be small (−1.1%) while Boulanger and Philippidis (2015) argue that Brexit could increase per capita GDP in the UK by 0.6%.

Aichele and Felbermayr (2015) found that a UK's soft withdrawal will lower GDP by only 0.6% in 2030; however, in a hard Brexit scenario, GDP will be reduced between 1.5% and 2.8%. Similarly, Oxford Economics (2016) argue that real GDP will be reduced by only 0.1% in 2030 in the best scenario but in the worst scenario (no trade agreement with the EU, and implementation of immigration controls with the EU) GDP will fall by 3.9% in 2030. Finally, Portes and Forte (2017), argue that if EU net immigration to the UK is reduced by 91,000 a year, GDP will fall by 0.6 and 2.7% in 2020 and 2030, respectively.

Concerning the impact of Brexit in territorial terms, Los et al. (2017) underline that the impact will be less in London and the South East than in the rest of the UK. In a CEPR study titled "Brexit, trade and the economic impacts on UK cities," Clayton and Overman (2017) suggest that every local authority will face a reduction in GVA as a result of Brexit.

Cities will come up with greater losses in GVA than nonurban areas on average in all the scenarios of the study. More specifically, the average decrease in GVA in a soft Brexit scenario will be 1.2% in cities and 1.1% in nonurban local authorities. Equally important, cities with significant number of employees in private sector knowledge intensive services will face significant problems (i.e., in Reading, London and Edinburgh the reduction reaches 2.7% of GVA). The study suggests that in a hard Brexit scenario, 12 out of the 20 most affected cities are in the South, whereas just four out of the 20 least affected cities are in the South UK.

However, impact assessments of the UK withdrawal do not analyze simultaneously all four freedoms linked to EU single market, and often undermine sectoral trade specializations and their linkages.

Although it is highly risky and difficult to reach conclusions on Brexit impact, it is interesting to spot light on some potential repercussions of Brexit on key issue areas of UK economic and foreign policy.

## The Impact on Good Friday Agreement in Ireland

The Good Friday Agreement (also known as the Belfast Agreement) of April 10, 1998 made an important contribution to peace in Northern Ireland and has the form of an international agreement between UK and Irish governments (it was endorsed through two referendums held in Northern Ireland and Ireland on May 22, 1998). The agreement includes provisions on the political arrangements within Northern Ireland, on the relationship between Northern Ireland and Ireland, and on the relationship between Ireland and the UK.

The agreement put in place a consociational model of governance and gave birth to the Northern Ireland Assembly, the North-South Ministerial Council, and the British Irish Council. Among the key provisions of the agreement is the principle of consent, which confirms Northern Ireland's position in the UK, guarantees dual nationality, and provides power sharing in key institutions.

EU interest in the issue is political and economic. As far as it concerns the latter, EU financed the peace process since 1989 (total EU funding reached 1.3 billion euros in the EU peace programs from 1995 to 2013), through both EU regional policy, and EU contributions to the International Fund for Ireland. The EU's Chief Negotiator, Michel Barnier, noted eloquently in EP (April 5, 2017) that, in relation to border issues particularly in Ireland, the EU will work toward arrangements that do not call into question the existing peace process and dialogue, particularly the Good Friday Agreement arguing against a hard border policy after Brexit (see also European Council guidelines, April 29, 2017). On May 22, the Council of the EU also underlined that nothing in the UK withdrawal agreement could undermine the objectives and commitments in the Good Friday Agreement.

Thus, UK withdrawal means that issues of significant importance including border controls, the common travel area, the development of the border regions, and the island's energy market should be settled properly so as not to undermine the rationale and the content of the Good Friday Agreement.

## The Impact on Citizens Rights

As aforementioned, Brexit influences the rights of UK nationals leaving and working in other EU states as well as the rights of EU citizens and students (over three million) living in the UK. One should also mention that around

1.2 million UK nationals live in another EU country (Center for economic performance, 2016).

EU treaties provide specific rights to EU citizens. For example, article 18 of TFEU contains a right to nondiscrimination for EU citizens article 45 TFEU imposes a special nondiscrimination right for workers, and article 49 of TFEU guarantees nondiscrimination regarding the right to establishment. Losing EU citizenship means also that UK citizens will lose the right to submit petitions to the EP (article 227 TFEU) and the right to appeal to the European Ombudsman (article 228 TFEU) and other EU agencies.

The EP resolution of April 5, 2017 and the European Council guidelines for the Brexit negotiations (adopted on April 29, 2017), support the right for every EU citizen, (and of his or her family members), to live, to work, or to study in any EU country and favor the protection of this right according to principles of reciprocity, fairness, and nondiscrimination.

The Council negotiating directives of May 22, 2017 for the article 50 negotiations, state that the (withdrawal) agreement should safeguard the status and rights derived from EU law at the withdrawal date, including those the enjoyment of which will intervene at a later date (i.e., rights related to old age pensions) as well as rights which are in the process of being obtained, including the possibility to acquire them under current conditions after the withdrawal date (i.e., the right of permanent residence after a period of five years of legal residence which started before the withdrawal date).

Evidently, reciprocal guarantees to safeguard the status and rights derived from EU law at the date of withdrawal of EU and UK citizens should be effective, enforceable, nondiscriminatory, and comprehensive, especially the right to obtain permanent residence after five years of legal residence.

However, if UK and EU do not sign a post-Brexit agreement UK citizens in the EU-27 would be subject to the national and EU rules for third-state nationals meaning rigid terms for residence conditions.

## The Impact on Immigration

How the UK will draw the line between skilled and not skilled jobs in EU labor market after Brexit? Which jobs would be eligible for work permits after Brexit? In many developed states job permit systems limit eligibility by occupation favoring skilled migration which is considered to deliver more economic benefits for the national economy (Vargas-Silva, 2016; Jonathan et al. 2016; Portes, 2016). Will university degrees play a role in the process of work visas as in the USA or vocational qualifications will be the major criterion as in Australia? Is it easy to draw a line between agricultural labor, hospitality, social care activities, and financial services, for example?

How will the new UK rules act against illegal employment? Will Brexit lead to a disproportionate reduction in unskilled migration?

Euroskeptics argue that Brexit will put a brake to uncontrollable immigration from Central and Eastern Europe states ameliorating conditions and wages for low-skilled UK citizens. However, several studies put into question this argument.

UK government (Home Office and Department for Business and Skills, 2014) argued, "To date there has been little evidence in the literature of a statistically significant impact from EU migration on native employment outcomes." Nickell and Salaheen (2015) further noted that a 10% point rise in the immigrant share means a 1.5% reduction in wages for native workers in the semi/unskilled service sector.

Boubtane et al. (2015) found that migration ameliorates productivity in the UK, meaning that a 1% point in the migrant share of the working-age persons, leads to a rise in productivity from 0.4 to 0.5%. This is taking place because migrants in the UK are (relatively to other developed states) more skilled. Jaumotte et al. (2016) also noted that a 1% increase in the migrant share of the adult population results in an increase in GDP per capita and productivity of approximately 2%.

Thus, first, it seems that legal immigrants add revenue to the economy since they pay taxes and insurances and they consume products/services. Second, legal immigration counterbalances negative results on GDP, retirement funds, and public finances derived from an ageing population. Last, are legal immigrants competing with UK citizens or are they performing complementary jobs? Apparently, if legal immigrants perform the jobs without adequate supply from UK citizens (low-skilled, low-paid works) then the argument of Euroskeptics is significantly weakened. Finally, one should have in mind that Euroskeptics in other EU states can also support the same argument against immigration of 1.8 million UK citizens who contribute to EU national economies and live outside the UK.

## The Impact on Cohesion: Regional Policy

The financial repercussion of Brexit seems quite complex. EU regional policy is vital to address territorial variations in income, wealth, and productivity. As a proportion of GDP, expenditure by the UK government on regional policy followed a downward trend from 0.4% in the early 1980s to 0.1% in the 1990s (Taylor and Wren, 1997). The proportion of households in the South East UK in the wealthiest 10% is 11 times greater than that in the North East UK.

There are also significant divergences in regional gross value added per capita across the UK. Output per person in London is more than double that in Wales. If the post-Brexit agreement does not include single market access, then the UK will be freer to provide regional aid. The UK government tended to oppose increased spending on agriculture, the largest component of the EU budget and it favored the structural funds where it was one of the main beneficiaries. Evidently, regional policy is vital to address developmental asymmetries in UK.

More specifically, regional and cohesion policies account for about one-third of the EU budget (Bachtler et al. 2016). UK was initially projected to absorb, about 10.8 billion euros of EU regional policy budget (5.8 billion euros from the ERDF and 4.9 billion euros from the ESF) in 2014–2020. Equally important, structural funds expenditure in the UK is relatively small in relation to overall public expenditure, but highly concentrated in areas such as Wales and Cornwall.

Which will be the formula for UK participation in the MFF until its expiry in 2020? How the UK will accommodate the impact of quitting CAP on food prices and on subsidies for the UK farmers and fishermen? How, to what extent, and until when UK will contribute to the EU budget?

The impact of Brexit also depends on whether UK withdrawal will be realized during the budgetary planning period (2014–2020) or thereafter defining the adjustment process and the transitional period. Moreover, the impact depends on how the reduction of EU funds will be replaced by the UK resources and on which criteria the new financing will be based. Evidently, the UK will continue to take part in cross-border cooperation because there would be shared borders with the EU-27 at NUTS 2 level regions (the UK has 40 NUTS 2 regions, of which only two are currently classified as less developed namely West Wales and The Valleys and Cornwall and Isles of Scilly, they receive 2.6 billion euros in the years 2014–2020). This would involve a switch from a uniform, transparent regime, where funding is distributed centrally based on observable criteria, to one which is largely responsive to requests for greater local autonomy.

The common agriculture policy and the fisheries policy will also be influenced by the UK's withdrawal. Concerning agricultural policy it is evident that the dependence on the SFP Scheme and other payments is significant as the SFP Scheme accounts for 56% of total income and agri-environment and other payments for 15%. Is a continuation of Basic Payments (formerly SFP) feasible with limited national resources? Is it compatible with a new trade policy of the UK? Will be there a more flexible relocation of funding in disadvantaged regions?

The policy instruments in agricultural policy will not change dramatically in the short term and thus the rationale of instruments for direct payments is expected to remain due to higher cost of alternative policy options. Accordingly, it depends on the UK how it will handle pillar one and pillar two targets and financing of CAP, how it will rearrange priorities between the two pillars of CAP, and how it will define actions in the transitional period after Brexit.

Taking into consideration the already mentioned priority of the guidelines issued on April 29, 2017 by the European Council on UK withdrawal from the EU it is expected that orderly withdrawal of the UK favors the single financial settlement, according to which UK and EU meet the obligations resulting from the entire period of the UK's EU membership. The financial settlement includes all relevant commitments and liabilities relating to MFFs, the EU budget, the EIB, the EDF, and the ECB.

On the other side, as the UK is a net contributor, the influence on EU budget will be significant. However, the UK should also pay the costs related to the relocation of EU agencies or bodies from the UK to new seats. Equally important, UK would take advantage of all the EU programmes until their closure if it abides to relevant EU rules. Thus, UK should honor all the obligations undertaken during its membership of the EU.

Does UK have the necessary resources for a substitute regional and sectoral development program? The sources of the ESI funds will also have to be redistributed with crucial impact on investment and structural policies in the UK. The same problem arises in common EU projects in industry, research and energy, education.

## The Impact on Competition

Will regulatory burden be decreased after Brexit? If one takes into consideration that UK has one of the OECD's least regulated product and labor markets than probably only in specific sectors (i.e., system of carbon pricing) such a position holds true.

According to the OECD's index, the UK's markets for services and goods are less regulated than many other developed states (i.e., Australia, Canada, Ireland, New Zealand, and USA). Moreover, according to the OECD, the largest of these constraints are due to UK domestic policies (i.e., restrictions on land usage within repercussions on housing construction, on rents and on expansion of transport infrastructure). Thus, the argument for the economic effectiveness due to diminished regulatory burden is not valid unless there are sectors where regulatory costs are high.

In any case, even non-EU countries with specific agreements with EU (Norway and Switzerland) are obliged in many sectors to make their regulations compatible with EU ones.

Although it seems easy to restore the status quo ante on institutional terms (i.e., competition policy, company law, banking regulations), there are interests and economic networks that have been created during the decades on the EU edifice and thus it will take decades to redefine their targets.

Four key areas of competition law and policy are crucial in the negotiation process, namely, antitrust, merger control, state aid, and public procurement. Antitrust (article 101 TFEU) and abuse of dominance (article 102 TFEU) are issue areas where significant changes can occur. Apparently, after Brexit, articles 101 and 102 will not have implementation in UK territory and the EC will lose its enforcement jurisdiction over the UK's Competition and Markets Authority.

On the critical issue of state aid which is embedded in the competition policy framework, it is expected that post-Brexit era will permit greater flexibility to provide financial support to companies currently limited by the EU state aid rules. However, it is expected that the definition of state aid after UK withdrawal and the resources available for its implementation will not mark an interventionist policy but rather an enforcement of competitive productive practices of UK industry. Concerning public procurement, Brexit will change fundamentally the procedures according to the demands of a new UK industrial and competition policy.

## The Impact on UK Trade and Finance

When UK became a member of EEC in 1973, one-third of its trade was with the EEC. The percentage rose significantly over the years in trade of services (94 billion euros of exports from EU-27 to the UK, and 122 billion euros in imports) as well as in trade of goods (a total of 490 billion euros).

UK has a surplus with EU-27 on account of services (28 billion euros) but a deficit on account of goods (122 billion euros). The share of UK goods exports sent to the EU-27 rose from over 60% in 1999 to 47% in 2015 while exports to non-EU countries have risen about 30%. In 2014, the trade with the other EU states accounted for 45% of the UK's exports and 53% of imports (ONS, 2015).

The post-Brexit challenge in the field is triple, namely, negotiating a new trading relationship with the EU, designing the new pattern of trade relations with countries covered by the EU's generalized system of preferences, and designing trade deals with all other states outside Commonwealth. A Brexit means surely higher NTBs to trade (i.e., due to different regulations) and perhaps a marginal rise in tariffs on imports.

What will be the new trade integration pattern of UK? UK and China, for example, have complementary trade interests since the UK has a strong revealed comparative advantage in services and high-tech industry while China can realize huge investments in key industries of the manufacturing in the UK.

Equally important, the links of UK with the Commonwealth states are based on long-term historical, language, and institutional reasons. The 52

Commonwealth countries are highly diversified in terms of economic, institutional, and political structure but this is exactly where their interest as a potential trade group lies. It is estimated that intra-Commonwealth trade reached 592 billion US dollars in 2013 and under certain conditions it could reach 1 trillion dollars by 2020 (Australia, Canada, India, Malaysia, Singapore and UK accounted for 84% of Commonwealth trade). Moreover, the population of the group surpasses 2 billion people and according to UN an increase of Commonwealth population by 29.4% is expected until 2020.

Would the UK achieve better trade agreements with non-EU states? Undeniably, it will not have the same negotiating power in the international trade scene and any agreement will also (although not to same extent) take into consideration the new agreement with EU. Moreover, EU's common commercial policy is far stronger to address antidumping duties relative to other strong commercial powers than UK alone. It seems that specific sectors highly integrated in EU supply chains as manufacturing and food industry will suffer significant losses.

Taking into consideration that EU is the UK's largest trade partner it goes without saying that UK firms should quickly find new destinations for their products addressing the trade diversion effects from exit. Higher tariff and nontariff obstacles to trade will lower trade flows and will raise many prices on food products. In any case, Brexit demands reorientation of UK trade flows and reconsideration of the bilateral trade/investment treaties with non-EU states.

In finance, UK's financial sector took advantage of the European financial integration because of the removal of financial barriers, passporting rights and the EU harmonization of financial regulation since the late 1980s. The City of London became a beneficiary of the free movement of capital and labor within the EU and as a result the EU was the key market for UK exports of financial services, reaching a trade surplus of 15 billion UK sterlings in 2012, a third of the UK' s total trade surplus in financial services, which totaled 46 billion sterlings.

Indeed, data on the financial services activity clearly demonstrate the importance of the activities in UK and EU economy (financial services account for 11.8% of the UK's overall economic output and UK accounts for 78% of foreign exchange turnover and for 85% of hedge fund assets in EU, while it has 30% of equity market capitalization and 26% of bank lending in the EU, August 2016). Although there is a variance of specific sector services contribution in UK trade, many activities dominate in total EU financial services market (i.e., asset management, risk management, and wholesale markets).

How will foreign companies activated in the UK react in the long term after the realization of Brexit? Will they choose to divest? Which forms of investment would be most vulnerable? The UK is a preferred location for investment from the other markets and EU has been enforced (Pain and Young,

2004) as an FDI source in the last decades (in 1997 EU states accounted for 30% of the accumulated FDI stock and in 2012 they reached 50%).

Although UK is an open economy with strong capital markets and a significant number of publicly listed firms' inward investment, one cannot ignore the market size and economies of scale and scope in production and thus the loss of EU single market initiative will exert negative influence not only on manufacturing but also on financial services.

The deprivation of UK financial firms' ability to operate cross-border with an EU passport will be disrupted after Brexit or will be seriously downgraded due to financial regulations diversification. If UK implements a regulatory competition with EU's major financial centers it risks its financial stability.

On the other hand, from an EU point of view, the current framework on financial services activities in EU has not reached the status of a mature and highly efficient regime (i.e., in banking and in asset management) and thus Brexit is expected to raise fragmentation.

## CONCLUSIONS AND POLICY IMPLICATIONS

Brexit negotiations are taking place within a fragile and vulnerable, in political and economic terms, European environment where the Eurozone and refugee crises remain unresolved, international terrorism is rising, and euroarea macroeconomic imbalances are strong.

Will UK reinforce its global position outside EU? Will EU after Brexit become more integrated and able to "lay the foundations of an ever closer union among the peoples of Europe" (preamble of the EU treaty)? Will Brexit open the Pandora box and lead other states with a strong Euroskeptic rationale to leave EU or to push for a loose variable geometry with opt out in many policies? Will the other EU countries demand trade-offs in order to sign the new agreement between UK and EU and which will be the repercussions of this trade-offs on the European integration project?

Brexit is the most demanding political and legal exercise in peacetime which challenges European integration institutional framework and UK decision-making and economic policy. Summarizing Brexit impact is a risky and complex exercise but some general conclusions are evident on the issue.

First, predictability over the content and the impact of Brexit is low. The negotiations with the EU involve high politics and thus technical details on specific issue areas should also be compatible with political concerns in both EU and UK. Second, Brexit reshuffles the EU balance of power and the integration dynamics within EU. Will large member countries such as Germany and France become more powerful as the counterweight of the UK is gone and will new political blocs and voting patterns emerge?

Third, Brexit involves not only economic and political but also security issues. Thus, Brexit also implies less involvement of UK military and defense forces in EU operations (France will be the only country with nuclear weapons), less UK police involvement in Europol and in Frontex, and new agreements concerning frontier control in Northern Ireland and Gibraltar.

Four, although it seems easier to disentangle from conventions and agreements of EU multiple issues appeared in the case of international conventions that have been signed by both the EU and the UK.

Fifth, all analyses cannot predict the exact impact of Brexit on public finances of UK. VAT, for example, is critical for UK public revenues (147.6 billion UK sterlings of receipts anticipated by 2021–2022). Finally, how Brexit will influence intra-industry EU trade and how UK will replace long-term productive and commercial networks between and within multinational corporations in EU effectively?

On the other hand, it is also important not to focus only on the UK weaknesses which lead to Brexit but also on EU weaknesses that paved the way for Euroskepticism. Immigration policy, employment issues, EU neighborhood challenges, economic instability, social security, terrorism are not effectively faced by EU.

Although the Bratislava Declaration (adopted in the Council of Ministers meeting on September 16, 2016) reaffirms the EU as the best instrument "for addressing the new challenges we are facing," and underlined priorities on migration, external borders, internal security, defense, and economic and social issues, it remains to be seen how EU institutions will handle the critical issues. Issues like completion of EMU (establishment of a fiscal union and a banking union), more democratic accountability, strengthening of European defense within NATO are vital and demand strong political initiatives at EU level.

Historically, in the long term, the EU has always been reinforced by crises it has faced. One cannot also exclude a new referendum on the conditions of UK's withdrawal from EU within 2019. The jury remains out and as past experience teaches us, nobody can control for sure and forever all variables that shape the economic and political history in Europe.

## BIBLIOGRAPHY

Aichele, R and Felbermayr, G. 2015. Costs and benefits of a United Kingdom exit from the European Union, *Guetersloh: Bertelsmann Stiftung*. Accessed November 2 2017, available at: https://www.bertelsmannstiftung.de/fileadmin/files/BSt/Publikationen/GrauePublikationen/NW_BREXIT_EN.pdf

Bachtler, John and Carlos, Mendez. 2016. Brexit, EU Cohesion Policy and Regional Development in the UK. *European Policies Research Centre*. University of

Strathclyde. Accessed November 2 2017, available at Glasgow, http://www.eprc.strath.ac.uk/news/20160620_Brexit_blog_post.pdf

Bloomberg, 2016. Brexit Special: Modeling a surprise exit, *Bloomberg Brief* February 8. Accessed November 2 2017, available at https://www.bloomberg.com/professional/blog/brexit-special-modeling-a-surprise-exit/

Boubtane, E., Dumont, J. C., and Rault, C. 2015. Immigration and economic growth in the OECD Countries 1986-2006. *Ces Ifo Working Paper 5392.* Accessed 2 November 2017, available at http://papers.ssrn.com/sol3/Delivery.cfm/SSRN_ID2622005_code459177.pdf?abstractid=2622005&mirid=3

Boulanger, P and Philippidis, G. 2015. "The end of a romance? A note on the quantitative impacts of a Brexit from the EU". *Journal of Agricultural Economics,* 66(3): 832–842.

Booth, S., Howarth, C., Persson, M., Ruparel R., and Swidlick, P. 2015. What if . . . ? The consequences, challenges and opportunities facing Britain outside the EU. *Open Europe Report* no. 3, London. Accessed December 3 2017, available at https://openeurope.org.uk/intelligence/britain-and-the-eu/what-if-there-were-a-brexit/

Busch, B and Matthes, J. 2016. Brexit–The Economic Impact, A Meta-Analysis, *IW-Report,* nr. 10, 2016. Köln. Accessed December 20 2017, available at: www.cesifo-group.info/DocDL/forum-2016-2-busch-matthes-brexit-june.pdf

Centre for Economic Performance. 2016. Brexit 2016: Policy analysis, *Centre for Economic Performance.* Accessed December 3 2017, available at http://cep.lse.ac.uk/pubs/download/brexit08_book.pdf

Dhingra, S and Sampson T. 2016. Life after Brexit: What are the UK's options outside the European Union? *CEP,* Brexit analysis 01. February. Accessed December 3 2017, http://cep.lse.ac.uk/pubs/download/brexit01.pdf

Dhingra, S., Huang, H., Ottaviano, G., Pessoa, J., Sampson, T., and Van Reenen, J. 2016. The costs and benefits of leaving the EU. *Centre for Economic Performance.* Technical report. Available at http://cep.lse.ac.uk/pubs/download/brexit02_technical_paper.pdf

Dhingra, S., Ottaviano, G., and Sampson, T. 2017. "A Hitch-hiker's Guide to Post-Brexit Trade Negotiations: Options and Principles". *Oxford Review of Economic Policy,* 33 (Suppl.): S22–S30.

Ebell, M and Warren, J. 2016. "The long-term economic impact of leaving the EU". *National Institute Economic Review,* 236: 121–138.

Hendry, D. F and Mizon, G. E. 2000. "Reformulating empirical macroeconomic modelling". *Oxford Review of Economic Policy,* 16(4): 138–159.

Hillion, C. 2015. "Accession and withdrawal in the law of the European Union". *In The Oxford Handbook of European Union Law,* eds. A. Arnull and D. Chalmers, Oxford: Oxford University Press.

HM Treasury. 2016. *Analysis of the Long Term Economic Impact of EU Membership and Its Alternatives CM 9250.* Accessed December 3 2017, available at https://www.gov.uk/government/publications/hm-treasury-analysis-the-long-term economic-impact-of-eu-membership-and-the-alternatives

Home Office and Department for Business and Skills. 2014. *The Impacts of Migration on UK Native Employment: An Analytical Review of the Evidence,* accessed

December 3 2017, available at https://www.gov.uk/government/publications/impacts-of-migration-on-uk-native-employment-an-analytical-review-of-the-evidence

House of Commons Foreign Affairs Committee. 2013. *The future of the European Union: UK Government policy*. Accessed December 20 2017, available at: http://www.publications.parliament.uk/pa/cm201314/cmselect/cmfaff/87/87.pdf

House of Commons. 2013. *Leaving the EU*, research paper 13/42. 1st July http://researchbriefings.parliament.uk/ResearchBriefing/Summary/RP13-42

House of Commons. 2016. *Brexit, How does the Article 50 process work*? London: House of Commons available at http://researchbriefings.parliament.uk/ResearchBriefing/Summary/CBP-7551

House of Lords. 2017. *European Union Committee, Brexit and the EU budget* HL paper 125, 4 March. Accessed December 20 2017, available at https://publications.parliament.uk/pa/ld201617/ldselect/ldeucom/125/12502.htm

IMF. 2016. *World Economic Outlook (WEO) Update: Uncertainty in the aftermath of the UK referendum*. Washington, D.C.: International Monetary Fund July. Accessed December 10, 2017 available at http://www.imf.org/external/pubs/ft/weo/2016/update/02/

Jaumotte, F., Koloskova, K., and Saxena, S. C. 2016. *Impact of migration on income levels in advanced economies, Spillover task force* Washington, D.C. available at https://www.imf.org/en/Publications/Spillover-Notes/Issues/2016/12/31/Impact-of-Migration-on-Income-Levels-in-Advanced-Economies-44343

Jonathan, P and Forte, G. 2016. "The Economic Impact of Brexit-induced reductions in migration" *National Institute of Economic and Social Research paper* December. Accessed December 20 2017, available at http://www.niesr.ac.uk/publications/economic-impact-brexit-induced-reductions-migration#.WFkAD_nhBaT

Kierzenkowski, R., Pain, N., Rusticelli, E., and Zwart, S. 2016. "The Economic consequences of Brexit, a taxing decision" *OECD economic policy papers* 16:1-36. April. Accessed December 20, 2017, available at http://www.oecd-ilibrary.org/economics/the-economic-consequences-of-brexit_5jm0lsvdkf6k-en

Kohl, T., Brakman, S., and Garretsen, J. 2017. "Consequences of Brexit and options for global Britain". *CES ifo working paper* 6648, available at https://www.econstor.eu/handle/10419/161887

Los, Bart., McCann, Phillip., Spingford, John., and Thissen, Mark. 2017. "The mismatch between local voting and the local economic consequences of Brexit". *Regional Studies* 51(5): 786–799.

Morgan, JP. 2016. "Brexit: What investors should consider" *Market insights: Market bulletin* 2 June. Accessed November 12 2017, available at https://am.jpmorgan.com/blobcontent/1383308535890/83456/JPM31432%20MI%20-%20Brexit%20%20How%20investors%20should%20approach%20the%20UK%20referendum.pdf

Nickell, Stephen and Saleheen, Jumana. 2015. *The impact of immigration on occupational wages: evidence from Britain* Staff working paper 574 Bank of England. 18 December London, available at http://www.bankofengland.co.uk/research/Pages/workingpapers/2015/swp574.aspx

ONS. 2015. *How Important is the European Union to UK trade and investment?* Office for National Statistics 26 June. Accessed December 20 2017, available at http://webarchive.nationalarchives.gov.uk/20160105234136/http://www.ons.gov.uk/ons/rel/international-transactions/outward-foreign-affiliates-statistics/how-important-is-the-european-union-to-uk-trade-and-investment-/index.html

Ottaviano, Gianmarco., Pessoa, João Paulo., Sampson, Thomas., and Reenen, John van. 2014. The costs and benefits of leaving the EU. *CFS Working Paper* 472 Frankfurt available at https://papers.ssrn.com/sol3/papers.cfm?abstract_id=2506664

Overman, Henry G and Clayton Naomi. 2017. Brexit, trade and the economic impacts on UK cities. July. *CEPR* available at http://www.centreforcities.org/wpcontent/uploads/2017/07/17-07-26-Brexit-trade-and-the-economic-impacts-on-UK-cities.pdf

Owen, Erica and Walter, Stafanie. 2017. "Open economy politics and Brexit: Insights, puzzles, and ways forward". *Review of International Political Economy,* 24(2): 179–202, available at https://doi.org/10.1080/09692290.2017.130724

Oxford Economics. 2016. *Assessing the economic implications of Brexit.* March 22. Accessed November 20 2017, available at: http://www.oxfordeconomics.com/brexit/executive-summary,

Pain, N and Young G. 2004. "The macroeconomic effect of UK withdrawal from the EU". *Economic Modelling,* 21: 387–408.

Pisani-Ferry, J., Rttgen N., Sapir A., Tucker P., and Wolff, G. 2016. *Europe after Brexit, A proposal for a continental partnership.* Brussels: Bruegel Institute available at http://bruegel.org/2016/08/europe-after-brexit-a-proposal-for-a-continental-partnership/

Portes, J and Forte, G. 2017. "The Economic impact of Brexit-induced reductions in migration". *Oxford Review of Economic Policy,* 33 (suppl. 1): S31–S44.

Portes, J. 2016. "Immigration after Brexit". *National Institute Economic Review,* 238 November: R13–R21.

Taylor, J and Wren, C. 1997. "UK regional policy: An evaluation". *Regional Studies,* 31(9): 835–848.

United Kingdom Government. 2016. *Command 9216, The process of withdrawing from the European Union.* February. London: UK Government. Available at https://www.gov.uk/government/uploads/system/uploads/attachment_data/file/503908/54538_EU_Series_No2_Accessible.pdf

Van Reenen, J. 2016. "Brexit's long-run effects on the UK Economy". *Brookings Papers on Economic Activity,* 2: 367–383.

Vargas-Silva, C. 2016. *Potential implications of admission criteria for EU nationals coming to the UK* Migration Observatory Report, COMPAS University of Oxford. Available at http://www.migrationobservatory.ox.ac.uk/resources/reports/potential-implications-of-admission-criteria-for-eu-nationals-coming-to-the-uk/

## FURTHER READING

Armour, J. 2017. "Brexit and financial services". *Oxford Review of Economic Policy,* 33 (Suppl.): S54–S69.

Baier, S. L., Bergstrand, J. H., Egger P., and McLaughlin P. A. 2008. "Do economic Integration agreements actually Work? Issues in understanding the causes and consequences of the growth of regionalism". *The World Economy,* 31(4): 461–497.

Carreras, O., Ebell, M., Kirby, S., Meaning, J., Piggott, R., and Warren, J. 2016. *The long and the short of It: What price UK exit from the EU*? London: *NIESR*, available at http://www.niesr.ac.uk/blog/long-and-short-it-what-price-uk-exit-eu#.WEQ2q_mLSUl

Crafts, N. 2017. "Brexit and State Aid". *Oxford Review of Economic Policy,* 33 (Suppl.): S105–S112.

Dustmann, C and Frattini, T. 2014. "The fiscal effects of immigration to the UK". *Economic Journal,* 124(580): F593–643.

Guild, E., Peers, S., and Tomkin, J. 2014. *The EU citizenship directive, a commentary*. Oxford: Oxford University Press.

Harvey, D and Hubbard, C. 2016. *Why Brexit.* Centre for Rural Economy Discussion Paper Series 35. Accessed at 20 December 2017, available at http://www.ncl.ac.uk/cre/publish/discussionpapers/pdfs/DP35hubbard.pdf

Lisenkova, K and Sanchez-Martinez, M. 2016. The Long-term macroeconomic effects of lower migration to the UK. *NIESR Discussion paper 460*, available at http://www.niesr.ac.uk/sites/default/files/publications/dp460.pdf

Lord, C. 2015. "Utopia or Dystopia? Towards a normative analysis of differentiated integration". *Journal of European Public Policy,* 22(6): 783–798.

LSE. 2016. The costs and benefits of leaving the EU: Trade effects. London School of Economics *CEP Discussion Paper* 1478.

Miller, Vaughn. 2016. Exiting the EU: Impact in key UK policy areas. *House of Commons Library Briefing Paper 07213*. UK: House of Commons.

Minford, P. 2016. The Treasury report on Brexit: A critique. *Economists for Brexit.* https://static1.squarespace.com/static/58a0b77fe58c624794f29287/t/58a4b012ebbd1a42255bc2f6/1487187989168/Economists_for_Brexit_The_Treasury_Report_on_Brexit_A_Critique_Executive_Summary.pdf

## QUESTIONS

1. What might be the standards for justified exits from the EU?
2. Outline the major repercussions of Brexit in a specific issue area of UK economy.

# Chapter 13

# Conclusions

The EU remains vulnerable and faces significant internal problems and external challenges. The European social model has not gone too far. The CAP did not deliver the expected competitiveness results. EU regional funds did not eliminate regional inequalities and productive distortions. EU's growth is anemic and euroarea faces structural and design problems, while the tension between widening and deepening of integration is stronger than ever creating policy uncertainty and skepticism. Equally important, Brexit has been a strong hit in the heart of European integration process and it enforces Euroskepticism through Europe.

Despite the successive reforms in EU institutions and competences, many questions are still open and concern the ability of EU to address new crises/challenges effectively and timely. Can reforms be applied within the present EU's framework or there is a need for treaty changes? Are current institutional arrangements effective for EU multilevel governance? Is there a need to forward integration based on a core of EU countries? Is institutional flexibility sufficient to forward political union or is it a tool to guarantee the intergovernmental dominance in European decision-making? Is the future of Europe, one of collective European values and shared morals or one of interstate bargaining and trade-offs? One should always have in mind that any treaty reform has a strong impact on EU responsibilities to issue areas of national sovereignty (i.e., foreign policy, defense) and on the balance between the Council of Ministers, EC, and EP as well as between states and EU institutions.

Moreover, European integration resembles a pendulum shifting from the national to supranational and vice versa with no consensus on how, why, and toward which direction European integration evolves or should be evolved. Different methodological approaches lead to different explanations and research priorities. Some authors ask why a sui generis integration process is taking place in Europe while others focus on how this integration occurs through political, economic, and institutional interactions. Other scholars try to explain how European integration unfolds, how it proceeds, and which the role of involved actors is. Others analyze questions of democratic reform and legitimacy of European institutions while there are many who study the dynamics of interstate bargaining and the role of epistemic communities. Although quite a few point toward more integration, others propose the opposite and demand less integration initiatives. The jury remains out although the Brexit and the emerging Euroskepticism make difficult any initiative in favor of deepening European integration.

Evidently, there is a need to spotlight on the dynamics of the European policy process in key issue areas of the European economy and on the problems and peculiarities of the EU institutions. The complex institutional and legal framework of EU reflects the ideological/political debates and tries to accommodate the vertical relations of power between the states and the EU, the horizontal relations of power between EU institutions, and the relations between EU and its citizens.

Although the Bratislava Declaration (EU Council of Ministers meeting, September 16, 2016) reaffirmed the EU as the best instrument "for addressing the new challenges"—and underlined priorities on migration, external borders, internal security, defense, and economic and social issues—it remains to be seen how EU institutions will handle a heterogeneous and unpredictable mix of problems ranging from completion of EMU (i.e., establishment of a fiscal union and a banking union) to democratic accountability and defense/foreign policy issues.

Apparently, summarizing the European integration agenda of problems, successes, and challenges is a risky and complex exercise but some general conclusions can be reached. The book argues that there is a need to develop a new European policy framework redrawing the interconnections between EU structures, EU institutions, and EU objectives while recognizing the importance of contingent factors at the national level. A long-term and ambitious policy agenda is necessary to renovate the hierarchy and content of economic and political targets in EU integration project.

It seems that a fundamental challenge is the synthesis of existing integration theories in order to explain different perspectives of EU reality. Decades of policy formulation and policy challenges demonstrate that there is no single theoretical approach that possesses enough explanatory power to fully understand the nature, the diversity, and the complexity of the EU actors; their rationality, their intentionality, and their effectiveness; and how their preferences are formed, how their limits and opportunities are changed. But which are the key challenges for the future of EU?

At first, establishing and functioning effectively a supranational organization is not a one-off act but is a dynamic and complex one which goes through progressive phases of integration. It is also evident that internal politics of the EU countries have a major impact on European integration implementation and thus internal political variables should be seriously taken into consideration. This involves not only the issue of which social groups gain or lose from different EU polices, thus the distributional effects, but also how constellations of interest form and disintegrate, how they learn from adjustment experience, how they shape identity through learning, and of course how vested interests are translated into policy preferences and bargaining power.

Too often, national political leaders follow short-term electoral motives and adopt protectionist attitudes which are to the detriment of interstate relations and of the long-term welfare of citizens.

Equally important, effective assignment of EU targets without long-term European collective intentionality on integration seems highly fragile. This clearly presupposes proper adaptation/learning/adjustment mechanisms so as to make EU rule-following, national self-interest, and European collective intentionality mutually compatible.

Thus, the book underlines that what is often missing in European integration analysis is a holistic framework of how risks, benefits, and burdens of European integration are distributed and how they can be accommodated in European institutional/economic/cognitive structures, avoiding the ghost of multispeed or variable integration geometry. If properly addressed, European integration crises could be sources of European progress and institutional breakthroughs and not expressions of political failure.

The second main issue is the content and type of necessary reforms. A new EU framework presupposes a normative answer to the question, "What will be the ultimate purpose of a reformed EU institutional structure? (EUIS)". Thus, one needs critical and explicit reflection on the ends as well as on the means of EUIS, on the what/why as well as on the how. Apart from this, there is a need to uncover the causal linkages and asymmetries of power between EUIS structures and actors, underlining when and how national/institutional internationalities are in conflict. This clearly suggests that a relevant analysis should not focus on EU institutions per se as isolated policy units but should focus on their interactions allowing a comprehension of their dynamics and effectiveness.

Undeniably, such a reflection cannot underestimate the long-term debate around two competing logics, namely the politics of enlarged coordination among all EU states and the politics of a la carte inclusion in EU decision-making and integration mechanisms. Reconciling the abovementioned logics rests on a new social purpose of equitable European development and deeper economic integration.

No matter which policy camp one chooses, all agree on the need for reforms in EUIS. The book suggests that priorities should evolve around specific targets such as enhancement of EUIS capacity to address crises and macroeconomic shocks, real convergence of national economies, effectiveness of supranational governance, sustainable growth and employment, and containment of asymmetric threats in security and foreign policy issues.

Further, EUIS effective implementation presupposes the fulfillment of five criteria, namely, transparency, legitimacy, consistency, effectiveness, and flexibility. Legitimacy refers to the need that reforms should not only respect the existing legal framework of EU but also accommodate the ideological foundations of the EU, meaning enhancement of participation and inclusiveness in all levels of decision-making. It also means enforcement of input legitimacy (the role of the EP and European parties) and output legitimacy (linked with the effectiveness criterion) targeting sustainable welfare for European citizens. Flexibility means the possibility of granting temporary derogations for those states unable to follow all necessary reforms (i.e., for a strong fiscal union immediately).

Transparency means an enhanced role of the EP in decision-making of European integration. Finally, effectiveness and consistency mean the ability of EU to deliver sustainable growth and employment rates throughout EU regions and ability of member states to follow national structural reforms so as to achieve real economic convergence and social cohesion.

The third key issue is the role of EU institutions in the European integration project. Indeed, after more than 60 years of integration efforts it becomes apparent that the absence of efficient domestic-European economic institutions could increase asymmetric information, multiply economic uncertainty, raise transaction cost, undermine the efficiency of interstate bargaining, and disrupt linkages across policy issue areas in European integration. Although European integration is based on compromises of national interests one should not underestimate the role of European institutions in the deepening of European integration.

Indeed, in critical moments for the integration project, the EU faced its problems not only through the conviction that rules should be followed but also through the use of EU laws and institutions to enhance and deepen integration. Even when negotiations in major issue areas reach an impasse, EU institutions find regulatory solutions and common denominator issues to keep the European integration spirit alive. Of course, the special weight of each institution in each issue area of EU economy and politics varies from agenda setting to simple policy implementation.

Thus, it is apparent that EU institutions, despite shortcomings and policy imperfections, are no passive structures but co-determine expectations and norms at EU level, promote a shared belief system that enforces integration collective intentionality (the preference-convergence process), guarantee joint decision-procedures, policy implementation, and EU coordination and cooperation, and thus disseminate European integration ideas.

The fourth main challenge is how to achieve progress in critical issue areas of European integration process such as fiscal policy, single market, CAP, economic adjustment, trade and foreign/defense policy.

Concerning fiscal issues, a centrally organized fiscal policy is the next big step to achieve real economic convergence of productive/competitiveness structures of all regions of EU so as to avoid asymmetric shocks diffusion and moral hazard in sovereign debt issues. Establishing a currency or a monetary union without efficient budgetary integration and without rule-based macro-economic coordination is problematic and risky and cannot deliver long-term growth.

In euroarea there are key priorities for maximization of policy results. Completing banking union, forwarding capital market integration after Brexit, accommodating risk sharing in the banking sector of eurozone, delinking banks and sovereigns, limiting market imperfections, finding sustainable solutions to national public and private debts, creating a European Monetary Fund and a European credit assessment agency are all part and parcel of a necessary reform. This also presupposes a strong role of ECB as lender of last resort as well as efficient operation of SSM in bank surveillance.

In the single area issues, it is common truth that there is a long way to reach full potential and economic benefits. While significant progress has been made in terms of market liberalization the goal of full market integration seems to be far away reflected in the still significant price differences between EU countries.

First, implementation and effectiveness should be given an equal foot to bargaining and negotiation and thus procedures of enforcement and compliance with single market directives should be strengthened. This means that delays in the implementation of harmonized rules in EU countries' legal frameworks, as well as infringements of single market regulations, should be addressed in a systematic way.

Further, there is a need to prioritize key issue areas which lag behind in liberalization and to focus on the interconnections of different issue areas and economic sectors. For example, improving effective competition in network industries has wider benefits, as these sectors provide inputs to a large number of other economic activities. Such a policy demands more and not less federal resources and it presupposes enough funds for European infrastructure networks and innovative entrepreneurship and of course investment in skills and education of the workforce. There is also a need to promote harmonization in key issue areas like financial services, professional services security services, e-payments, and public procurements. Coordination in tax and social security issues should also be upgraded to accommodate the negative externalities of painful economic adjustment.

It is also worth noting that interregional migration of workforce in EU is at low levels due to high mobility costs, differences in professional qualifications requirements, limitations on public sector employment and cultural barriers. As a result, there is a need to enforce labor mobility, limiting the administrative burden linked with recognition of professional qualifications.

Concerning macroeconomic adjustment in euroarea states, it often proved to be ineffective because of four failures: failures of policy mix (simultaneous application of expenditure reduction and tax increases as well as implementation of wrong fiscal and investment multipliers), inadequate knowledge of national economic/structural terms (due to national economic path dependency as well as national economic priorities for development), overestimation of national administration capabilities, and overestimation of political will (and thus underestimation of vested interests).

A new type of adjustment in Eurozone is necessarily focusing more on "flexible enforcement" (incentive-driven compliance), domestic ownership of programs, accountability of surveillance mechanisms to EP (through relevant modifications in decision-making), and transparency of program policies.

The two pillars (collective intentionality of euroarea states on the targets/means plus domestic ownership of APs) create a strong cognitive framework and link in a legitimate and predictable way the ordering of adjustment norms/targets to the ordering of adjustment actions/policies. This does not mean that fiscal discipline is not important but that it must be exercised within a growth-oriented policy programme taking into consideration the idiosyncrasies of EU states. It also becomes evident that adjustment should equally target from the beginning structural reforms and fiscal consolidation, enforcement of local productive networks, taking into consideration the necessity to protect the most vulnerable social groups in an economy.

Another crucial concern for the next decade and especially after 2020 is the reform of the CAP so as to facilitate adjustment of agricultural producers to global changes and to achieve rationalization of EU agricultural production. Although the existing CAP offers the EU countries flexibility (the distribution of funds between the first and second pillar of the CAP), and the new Pillar II promotes knowledge transfer and innovation, many challenges lie ahead and will definitely determine the future of this EU policy.

First, CAP's ability to include specificities and priorities of EU states in a common policy framework should be enforced, taking into consideration the differences in socioeconomic conditions and the traits of national agricultural sectors.

Second, there is still the issue of how to achieve an enlarged policy agenda within an economic-financial crisis. At an analytical level there is no doubt that policy measures need to be properly targeted to well-defined objectives and that the number of policy measures applied needs to match the number of targets pursued.

Third, the decision-making system needs to reexamine farm competitiveness and full application of the green measures on farms while attaining in the same time equity and fairness within agricultural population.

Fourth, there is still room for more transparency and control of subsidies allocation safeguarding that the subsidies are allocated properly and that any irregular payments are detected and recovered.

Finally, despite CAP improvement in decision-making there are problems in the linkages of CAP policy with other crucial policies in EU such as energy, trade, health, climate action policy.

In international trade policy matters, there is always the danger of a fierce interstate competition, mercantilist policies, aggressive trade practices, and protectionism even from traditional allies of European states. This creates the necessity for intensification of EU trade and investment negotiations with major international economic players. However, the increasing heterogeneity among EU states makes more difficult the operation of decision-making on trade policy issues (as the TTIP and CETA negotiations demonstrated) where there were conflicts and different national interests in key sectors among EU states.

Obviously, EU should face all negative spillovers derived from international agreements on specific sectors and regions and this presupposes front-loaded activity of EU institutions and also a strong interaction between regional development policy, cohesion funds, and EU trade policy. If this does not take place unemployment and anemic economic growth in many EU regions will enforce populist and protectionist arguments against liberalization efforts. One should always have in mind that voters look for specific results and not good intentions in problems like unemployment and social inequality.

This further means that EU institutions should better communicate EU trade policy's targets and results especially EU trade impact on consumers, workers, and national income distribution (trade distributional effects). Increased transparency and more participation of EP in all stages of trade negotiations will help efforts to contain Euroskeptic arguments.

In any case, EU trade policy should favor a rule-based multilateral trading system and not bilateral accords to the detriment of WTO effectiveness. Agreements like CETA and TTIP should be vehicles to enforce multilateral regulations on key issue areas (i.e., IP rights, investment disputes, and agricultural subsidies) and not sources of tensions and trade confrontation with emerging economic powers.

Another key challenge to European integration that demands increased attention is how to handle efficiently the exit of a state from the EU. Brexit challenges European integration institutional framework, UK decision-making, and EU economic policy and reshuffles the EU balance of power. It further rings a bell that European disintegration is ante portas if EU does not face properly and instantly the challenges from Euroskeptic nationalist and populist parties (i.e., persistent problems in immigration policy, employment, EU neighborhood relations, social security, and terrorism).

Concluding, the last key challenge to EU project is the enforcement of European defense and foreign policies based on better organized mechanisms of cooperation and coordination of activities and more available resources. Defense collaboration includes also joint procurement initiatives and military research projects which reduce national military spending and strengthen the efficiency of EU in security issues.

To sum up, the European environment seems toxic since the Eurozone and refugee crises remain unresolved, international terrorism is rising, and growth drivers are anemic. Is there a prospect in EU after two or three decades? As long as EU inertia persists, the veil of uncertainty over the future of European economic and political integration will hold.

Of course, it is too early to reach a jury on whether European economic and political integration is enduring or it will fall over due to interstate rivalries, political populism, and unexpected international and regional economic problems. Even if the latter comes true, nothing can reduce the impact of European integration process in the last seven decades and nothing can limit the value of European institutions.

Having in mind all aforementioned challenges, I sincerely hope that the book provoked more questions rather than ready-made answers to European integration issues and I cordially hope that irrespective of electoral and economic cycles, all political, economic, and intellectual leaders of Europe realize that unity, cooperation, and peace are at all times better than conflict and disarray.

# Index

Page references for figures are italicized

# About the Author

**Dr. Konstantinos J. Hazakis** is associate professor at the Department of Economics in Democritus University of Thrace and a research fellow at the Institute of International Economic Relations in Athens. He holds a BSc from Panteion University of Athens, an MSc from London School of Economics, and a PhD from Panteion University of Athens. He has published three books in Greek and he is the author of several articles of economic policy in academic journals. His research interests include European union political economy, economic development, institutional economics, international economic policy coordination, and Group-7 economic summits.

# About the Author

www.ingramcontent.com/pod-product-compliance
Ingram Content Group UK Ltd.
Pitfield, Milton Keynes, MK11 3LW, UK
UKHW012035150926
475560UK00001B/17

9 781498 560054